THE HARPERCOLLINS DICTIONARY OF ECONOMICS

THE HARPERCOLLINS DICTIONARY OF

ECONOMICS

Christopher Pass, Bryan Lowes,
Leslie Davis, Sidney J. Kronish

Series Editor, Eugene Ehrlich

HarperPerennial
A Division of HarperCollins*Publishers*

Library of Congress Cataloging-in-Publication Data

Pass, Christopher, 1942–
    [Collins dictionary of economics]
    Harper dictionary of economics / Christopher Pass, Bryan Lowes,
    Leslie Davies. — 1st U.S. ed., 1st HarperPerennial ed.
        p. cm.
    "Originally published 1988 in Great Britain by William Collins
    Sons & Co. under the title: Collins dictionary of economics"—T.p.
    verso.
    ISBN 0-06-271504-6—0-06-461017-9 (pbk.)
    1. Economics—Dictionaries. I. Lowes, Bryan. II. Davies,
    Leslie, 1951– .III. Kronish, Sidney J. IV. Title.
    HB61.P39 1991
    330'.03—dc20   90–55512

91 92 93 94 95 CC/MK 10 9 8 7 6 5 4 3 2 1

ACKNOWLEDGMENT

In preparing the *HarperCollins Dictionary of Economics*, we were privileged to have the assistance of the distinguished American economist Anna J. Schwart, Research Associate at the National Bureau of Economic Research, in New York City. A prolific writer in her own right, Dr. Schwartz is also widely known for her collaboration with economist Milton Friedman on such landmark works as *A Monetary History of the United States, 1867–1960* (1962) and *Monetary Trends in the United States and the United Kingdom: Their Relation to Income, Prices, and Interest Rates, 1867–1975* (1982).

Dr. Schwartz provided careful review of the original text of our dictionary and made many suggestions for new entries, deletion of inappropriate entries, and ways of achieving better balance of competing economic points of view. We hope that she will approve of the final form of the dictionary.

EUGENE EHRLICH
Series Editor

THE HARPERCOLLINS
DICTIONARY OF ECONOMICS

A

ability-to-pay principle of taxation the principle that TAXA-
TION should be based on the financial standing of the individual.
Thus, persons with high income are better able to pay, and should
pay, larger amounts of tax than people on low incomes. In practice, the ability-to-pay approach has been adopted by most countries as the basis of their taxation systems (see PROGRESSIVE TAXA-
TION). Unlike the BENEFITS-RECEIVED PRINCIPLE OF TAXATION,
the ability-to-pay approach is compatible with the idea that such
a system is just. However, a progressive tax, one based on ability
to pay, may undermine incentive to work and invest. See REDIS-
TRIBUTION-OF-INCOME PRINCIPLE OF TAXATION.

above-normal profit or **excess profit** a PROFIT greater than
that which is just sufficient to ensure that a business will continue
to supply its existing product or service (see NORMAL PROFIT).
Short-term, that is, temporary above-normal profits resulting from
an imbalance of market supply and demand promote an efficient
allocation of resources if they encourage new companies to enter
the market and increase market supply. By contrast, long-term,
that is, persistent above-normal profits (MONOPOLY or *supernor-
mal profits*) distort the RESOURCE ALLOCATION process because
they reflect the overpricing of a product by monopoly suppliers
protected by BARRIERS TO ENTRY. See PERFECT COMPETITION.

above the line promotional expenses associated with advertising.

absolute advantage an advantage possessed by a country when,
using a given resource input, it is able to produce more output
than other countries possessing the same resource input. This is
illustrated in Fig. 1 with respect to two countries, A and B, and two
goods, X and Y. Country A's resource input enables it to produce
either 100X or 100Y; the same resource input in country B enables
it to produce either 180X or 120Y. It can be seen that country B

is absolutely more efficient than country A since it can produce more of both goods. Superficially this suggests there is no basis for trade between the two countries. However, it is COMPARATIVE ADVANTAGE not absolute advantage, that determines whether INTERNATIONAL TRADE is beneficial, because even if country B is more efficient at producing both goods, it may pay country B to specialize (see SPECIALIZATION) in producing good X, at which it has the greater advantage.

Physical output of X and Y
from a given factor input

Country	Good	
	X	Y
A	100	100
B	180	120

FIG. 1. **Absolute advantage.** The relationship between resource input and output.

absolute concentration measure see CONCENTRATION MEASURES.

absolute value a mathematical term for the magnitude of a number, ignoring its sign. The absolute value of a positive number is the number itself; the absolute value of a negative number is the number without its minus sign.

In estimating PRICE ELASTICITY OF DEMAND for example, our interest is in the degree of responsiveness of quantity demanded to changes in price, and the fact that a price *increase* causes a *decrease* in quantity demanded and vice versa, giving a negative elasticity number, is of little interest. Here, taking the absolute value of the elasticity number is more appropriate.

accelerator the relationship between the amount of net or INDUCED INVESTMENT (gross investment less REPLACEMENT INVESTMENT) and the *rate of change* of NATIONAL INCOME. A rise in income and consumption spending will put pressure on existing capacity and encourage businesses to invest not only to replace existing capital goods as they wear out but also to invest in *new* plant and equipment to meet the increase in demand.

By way of simple illustration, let us suppose a business meets existing demand for its product by utilizing 10 machines, one of which is replaced each year. If demand increases by 20%, the business must invest in two new machines to accommodate that demand, in addition to the one replacement machine.

Investment may be thought of, in part, as a function of changes in the level of income: $I = f(\Delta Y)$. A rise in induced investment, in turn, serves to reinforce the MULTIPLIER effect in increasing national income. A change in investment will induce a change in income and consumption and, therefore, a multiplied change in national income:

$$\uparrow\Delta I \rightarrow \uparrow\Delta Y \rightarrow \uparrow\Delta C \rightarrow \uparrow\Delta Y$$

The combined effect of accelerator and multiplier forces working through an *investment cycle* has been offered as an explanation for changes in level of economic activity associated with the BUSINESS CYCLE. Because the *level* of investment depends on the *rate of change* of GNP, when GNP is rising rapidly, investment will be at a high level as producers seek to add to their capacity (time t in Fig. 2). This high level of investment will add to AGGRE-GATE DEMAND and help maintain a high level of GNP. However, as the rate of growth of GNP slows down from time t onward, businesses will no longer need to add as rapidly to capacity, and investment will decline toward replacement investment levels. This lower level of investment will reduce aggregate demand and contribute to an eventual fall in GNP. Once GNP has persisted at a low level for some time, machines will gradually wear out and businesses will need to replace some of the machines in order to maintain sufficient production capacity to meet even the lower level of aggregate demand experienced. This increase in level of investment at time t_1 will increase aggregate demand and stimulate growth of GNP. See MULTIPLIER.

acceptance a bill of exchange that has been accepted by a bank or other financial institution on behalf of a client who may then use it to extend credit or to be extended credit.

accepting house a COMMERCIAL BANK or similar organization that underwrites (guarantees to honor) a commercial BILL OF EX-CHANGE in return for a fee. See DISCOUNT, FACTORING.

accounting period the time period over which a business pre-

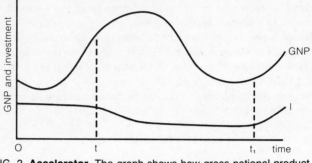

FIG. 2. **Accelerator.** The graph shows how gross national product and the level of investment vary over time. See entry.

pares its financial statement and at the end of which it draws up its balance sheet. Corporations are required by law to prepare ANNUAL REPORTS, and most other companies do so as well. Many now prepare quarterly, monthly, or even weekly reports to give prompt information about performance.

accounts the financial statements of an individual or organization prepared from a system of recorded financial transactions. Public corporations are required to publish their year-end or period-end financial statements, which must comprise at least a financial statement and balance sheet, to enable shareholders to assess their company's financial performance during the period under review. AUDITORS also require a set of year-end or period-end accounts to enable them to undertake appropriate tests so as to form and submit their opinion on them to the company's stockholders. Nonincorporated bodies, such as sole proprietors and partnerships, are not subject to such rigorous internal constraints but must prepare appropriate financial statements to submit to the INTERNAL REVENUE SERVICE as a basis for tax assessments. See LEDGER.

accounts payable the money owed to individuals or companies because they have sold goods, services, or raw material for which they have not yet been paid or because they have made loans.

accounts receivable the money owed by individuals or companies because they have bought goods, services, or raw materials for which they have not yet paid or because they have borrowed money.

accruals principle of accounting the principle that all of a company's costs and revenues should be counted in its accounts from the date when the expenses are legally incurred and when the revenues are receivable, not when the expenses are actually paid or the cash is received.

actuary a statistician who calculates insurance risks and premiums. See RISK AND UNCERTAINTY, INSURANCE COMPANY.

adaptive expectations hypothesis (of inflation) the hypothesis that EXPECTATIONS of the future rate of INFLATION are based on the inflationary experience of the recent past. As a result, once under way, inflation is thought to feed on itself. For example, labor unions may demand an increase in wages during contract negotiations that takes into account the expected future rate of inflation. Such increases are thought, in turn, to lead to further price rises. See EXPECTATIONS-ADJUSTED/AUGMENTED PHILLIPS CURVE, INFLATIONARY SPIRAL.

adjustable peg system a form of FIXED EXCHANGE-RATE SYSTEM originally operated by the INTERNATIONAL MONETARY FUND, in which the EXCHANGE RATES between currencies are fixed (pegged) at particular values (for example, at the hypothetical rate $3 = £1), but which can be changed to new fixed values should circumstances require it. For example, $2 = £1, the repegging of the dollar at a higher value in terms of the pound (REVALUATION); or $4 = £1, the repegging of the dollar at a lower value in terms of the pound (DEVALUATION).

adjustment mechanism a means of correcting imbalances in foreign payments. There are three main ways of removing payments, deficits, or surpluses: (a) external price adjustments, (b) internal price and income adjustments, and (c) trade and foreign-exchange restrictions. See BALANCE-OF-PAYMENTS EQUILIBRIUM.

administered price 1. a price for a PRODUCT that is set by an individual producer or group of producers. In PERFECT COMPETITION characterized by many producers, the price charged is determined by interaction of market demand and market supply, and the individual producer or buyer has no control over this price. By contrast, in an OLIGOPOLY and a MONOPOLY, the few producers have considerable discretion over the prices they charge and can, for example, use some administrative formula such as FULL-COST PRICING to determine the price charged. A number of producers may combine to administer the price of a product by operating a CARTEL or price-fixing agreement.

2. a price for a product or CURRENCY, etc. that is set by the government or an international organization. For example, an individual government or INTERNATIONAL COMMODITY AGREE-MENT may fix the prices of agricultural produce or commodities, such as coal, to support producers' incomes. Under an internationally managed FIXED EXCHANGE-RATE SYSTEM, member countries establish fixed values for the exchange rates of their currencies.

See PRICE SUPPORT, PRICE CONTROLS.

administrative costs the COSTS of maintaining an organization within which goods or services can be produced. They include salaries of managers, accounting, personnel, and secretarial staff; rent, heat, and light of the offices they occupy; and stationery, postage, and office equipment and furniture costs. See OVERHEAD.

administrative lag in setting monetary policy, the time between recognition that an action is needed and the taking of the action. The presence of lags makes the timing of monetary policy a hazardous process.

ad valorem tax a TAX levied as a percentage of price of a unit of output at the manufacturing, wholesale, or retail levels. The retail sales tax and value-added taxes common in Europe are ad valorem taxes.

advances see LOANS.

advertising a means of stimulating demand for a product and establishing BRAND LOYALTY. Advertising is one of the main forms of PRODUCT DIFFERENTIATION competition and is used both to inform prospective buyers of a brand's particular attributes and to persuade them that the brand is superior to competitors' offerings.

There are two contrasting views of the effect of advertising on MARKET PERFORMANCE.

Traditional, static market theory emphasizes the misallocative effects of advertising. Advertising is depicted as being solely concerned with brand-switching between competitors within a static overall market demand and serving to increase total supply costs and the price paid by the consumer. This is depicted in Fig. 3a. (See PROFIT MAXIMIZATION).

The alternative view of advertising emphasizes its role as one of expanding market demand and ensuring that a company's demands are maintained at levels enabling it to achieve economies of large-scale production (see ECONOMIES OF SCALE). Thus, advertising may be associated with a higher market output and lower prices than allowed for in the static model. This is illustrated in Fig. 3b.

affirmative action employment rules set up or administered by local, state, and national governments that are intended to eliminate discrimination in labor markets and to offset the effects of previous, long-standing discrimination.

age-earnings profile the relationship between age and earnings. Typically, on leaving school, people will see their earnings increase rapidly, but the rate of increase diminishes as wage earners approach 40, from then on declining faster and faster. This profile reflects the accumulation of capital to provide for old age until, as old age approaches, wage earners save less and less and, at retirement, begin to use up accumulated savings.

agent an individual or business that acts on behalf of a client, for example, by buying or selling products or assets, or by representing a client's interests in a negotiation in return for a COMMISSION.

aggregate concentration see CONCENTRATION MEASURES.

aggregate demand or **aggregate expenditure** the total amount of expenditure (in nominal terms) on goods and services. In the CIRCULAR FLOW OF NATIONAL INCOME MODEL, aggregate demand is made up of CONSUMPTION expenditure (C) [see CONSUMPTION(1)], investment expenditure (I), GOVERNMENT EXPENDITURE (G), and net EXPORTS (exports less imports) (E):

$$\text{aggregate demand} = C + I + G + E$$

Some of the components of aggregate demand are relatively stable and change only slowly over time, for example, consumption expenditure. Others are much more volatile and change rap-

AGGREGATE DEMAND

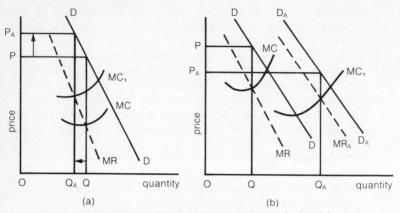

(a)   (b)

FIG. 3. **Advertising.** (a) The static market effects of advertising on demand (D). The profit maximizing (see PROFIT MAXIMIZATION) price-output combination (PQ) without advertising is shown by the inter-section of the marginal revenue curve (MR) and the marginal cost curve (MC). By contrast, the addition of advertising costs serves to shift the marginal cost curve to MC_1, so that the PQ combination (shown by the intersection of MR and MC_1) now results in higher price (P_A) and lower quantity supplied (Q_A). (b) The initial profit maximizing price-output combination (PQ) without advertising is shown by the intersection of the marginal revenue curve (MR) and the marginal cost curve (MC). The effect of advertising is to expand total market demand from DD to $D_A D_A$ with a new marginal revenue curve (MR_A). This expansion of market demand enables the industry to achieve economies of scale in production, more than offsetting the additional advertising cost. Hence, the marginal cost curve in the expanded market (MC_1) is lower than the original marginal cost curve. The new profit maximizing price-output combination, deter-mined by the intersection at MR_A and MC_1, results in a lower price (P_A) than before and a larger quantity supplied (Q_A). See BARRIERS TO ENTRY, MONOPOLISTIC COMPETITION, OLIGOPOLY, DISTRIBUTIVE EFFI-CIENCY.

idly, causing fluctuations in the level of economic activity, for example, investment expenditure.

Aggregate demand interacts with AGGREGATE SUPPLY to determine the EQUILIBRIUM LEVEL OF NATIONAL INCOME. Governments may seek to regulate the level of aggregate demand, and monetary authorities apply monetary policy, in order to maintain FULL EMPLOYMENT, avoid INFLATION, promote ECONOMIC GROWTH, and secure BALANCE-OF-PAYMENTS EQUILIBRIUM through use of FISCAL POLICY and MONETARY POLICY.

See AGGREGATE DEMAND SCHEDULE, DEFLATIONARY GAP, INFLATIONARY GAP, BUSINESS CYCLE, STABILIZATION POLICY.

aggregate demand/aggregate supply approach to national income determination see EQUILIBRIUM LEVEL OF NATIONAL INCOME.

aggregate demand schedule a schedule depicting total spending on goods and services at various levels of NATIONAL INCOME. It is constructed by adding together the CONSUMPTION, INVESTMENT, GOVERNMENT EXPENDITURE, and EXPORTS schedules, as indicated in Fig. 4a.

A given aggregate demand schedule is drawn up on the usual CETERIS PARIBUS conditions. It will shift upward or downward if some determining factor changes. See Fig. 4b.

aggregate expenditure see AGGREGATE DEMAND.

aggregate supply the total amount of domestic goods and services supplied by businesses and government, including consumer products and capital goods. Aggregate supply interacts with AGGREGATE DEMAND to determine the EQUILIBRIUM LEVEL OF NATIONAL INCOME (see AGGREGATE SUPPLY SCHEDULE).

In the short term, aggregate supply will tend to vary with the level of demand for goods and services, although the two need not correspond exactly. For example, businesses could supply more product than demanded in the short term, the difference showing up as a buildup of unsold STOCKS (unintended INVENTORY INVESTMENT). On the other hand, businesses could supply less product than demanded in the short term, the difference being met by running down stocks. However, discrepancies between aggregate supply and aggregate demand cannot be very large or persist for long, and businesses generally will only offer to supply output if they expect spending to be sufficient to sell all that output.

AGGREGATE SUPPLY

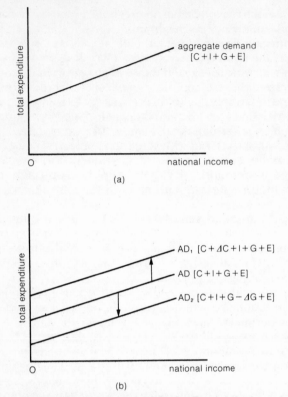

(a)

(b)

FIG. 4. **Aggregate demand schedule.** (a) The graph shows how
AGGREGATE DEMAND varies with the level of NATIONAL INCOME. (b)
Shifts in the schedule due to changes in determining factors. For
example, if there is an increase in the PROPENSITY TO CONSUME, the
consumption schedule will shift upward, serving to shift the aggregate demand schedule upward from AD to AD_1. A reduction in government spending, some economists believe, will shift the schedule
downward from AD to AD_2.

In the long run, aggregate supply can increase as a result of increases in the size and quality of the labor force, increases in the quantity and quality of capital stock, and improvements in labor productivity.

See POTENTIAL GROSS NATIONAL PRODUCT, ECONOMIC GROWTH.

aggregate supply schedule a schedule depicting the total amount of domestic goods and services supplied by businesses at various levels of total expenditure. The AGGREGATE SUPPLY schedule is generally drawn as a 45° line, because businesses will offer any given level of national output only if they expect total spending (AGGREGATE DEMAND) to be just sufficient to sell all that output. Thus, in Fig. 5 $100 million of expenditure calls forth $100 million of aggregate supply, $200 million of expenditure calls forth $200 million of aggregate supply, and so on. This process cannot continue indefinitely, however, for once an economy's resources are fully employed in supplying products, additional expenditure cannot be met from additional domestic resources because the potential output ceiling of the economy has been reached. Consequently, beyond the full employment level of national product, Y_f, the aggregate supply schedule becomes vertical. See POTENTIAL GROSS NATIONAL PRODUCT.

Aggregate supply interacts with aggregate demand to determine the EQUILIBRIUM LEVEL OF NATIONAL INCOME.

aggregation problem the problem of deriving predictable macroeconomic behavior from the behavior of the underlying microeconomic units. In short, can all firms be lumped together as if, in their investment decisions, they were concerned with a single good called capital? Analytic use of such aggregates as capital, labor, and investment as though the production side of the economy could be treated as a single firm is a problematic procedure. Notwithstanding, macroeconomists continue to use such aggregates.

agricultural policy a policy concerned both with protecting the economic interests of the agricultural community by subsidizing farm prices and incomes, and with promoting greater efficiency by encouraging farm consolidation and mechanization. See Fig. 6.

The rationale for supporting agriculture partly reflects the spe-

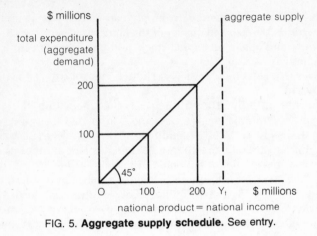

FIG. 5. **Aggregate supply schedule.** See entry.

cial nature of the industry itself: agriculture, unlike manufacturing, is assumed to be especially vulnerable to events outside its immediate control. Supply tends to fluctuate erratically from year to year, depending on such vagaries as weather, attack by insects, and disease (S_1, S_2, and S_3 in Fig. 6a), causing wide changes in farm prices and farm incomes. Over the long term, while the demand for many basic foods and animal produce has grown only slowly (from DD to D_1D_1 in Fig. 6b), significant PRODUCTIVITY improvements associated with farm mechanization, chemical fertilizers, pesticides, etc. have tended to increase supply at a faster rate than demand (from SS to S_1S_1 in Fig. 6b), causing farm prices and incomes to fall.

Farming can thus be a hit-and-miss affair, and governments concerned with the impact of changes in food supplies and prices (on, for example, the level of farm incomes, the balance of payments, and inflation rates) may well feel the need to regulate the situation. But there are also social and political factors at work, for example, the desire to preserve rural communities and the fact that even in some advanced industrial countries, for example, the European Community and the United States (since all 50 states have two senators each), the agricultural sector often commands

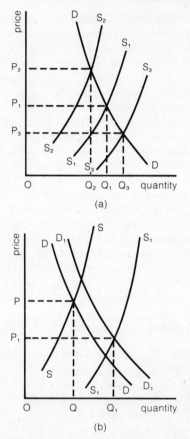

FIG. 6. **Agricultural policy.** (a) The short-term shifts in supply (S) and their effects on price (P) and quantity (Q). (b) Long-term shifts caused by the influence of productivity improvement on supply.

a political vote out of all proportion to its economic weight. Governments cannot be indifferent to the possibility of an inadequate domestic food suppply. For this reason, subsidies to food producers and food retailers are common. See ENGEL'S LAW, COBWEB THEOREM, PRICE SUPPORT, INCOME SUPPORT.

ALLOCATION

allocation the breakdown of COSTS and REVENUES between different products, functions, or company departments in which it is possible to attribute costs and revenues directly to the departments where they arise. For example, in analyzing costs, the depreciation OVERHEAD of factories can be allocated precisely between the production departments where the specific fixed assets are located. See BUDGETING, APPORTIONMENT.

allocative efficiency an aspect of MARKET PERFORMANCE that denotes optimum allocation of scarce resources between end uses, in order to produce the combination of goods and services that best accords with the pattern of consumer demand. This is achieved when all market prices and profit levels are consistent with the real resource costs of supplying products. Specifically, consumer welfare is optimized when for each product the price is equal to the lowest real resource cost of supplying that product, including a NORMAL PROFIT reward to suppliers. Figure 7a depicts a normal profit equilibrium under conditions of PERFECT COMPETITION, with price being determined by intersection of market supply and demand curves, and with MARKET ENTRY/MARKET EXIT serving to ensure that price (P) is equal to minimum supply cost in the long run (AC).

By contrast, where some markets are characterized by monopoly elements, in those markets output will tend to be restricted so that fewer resources are devoted to producing those products than the pattern of consumer demand warrants. In such markets, prices and profit levels are not consistent with the real resource costs of supplying the products. Specifically, in MONOPOLY markets the consumer is exploited by having to pay a price for a product that exceeds the real resource cost of supplying it, this excess showing up as an ABOVE-NORMAL PROFIT for the monopolist.

Figure 7b depicts the profit maximizing price-output combination for a monopolist, determined by equating marginal cost and marginal revenue. This involves a smaller output and a higher price than would be the case under perfect competition, with BARRIERS TO ENTRY serving to ensure that the output restriction and excess prices persist over the long run. See PARETO OPTIMALITY, PROFIT MAXIMIZATION.

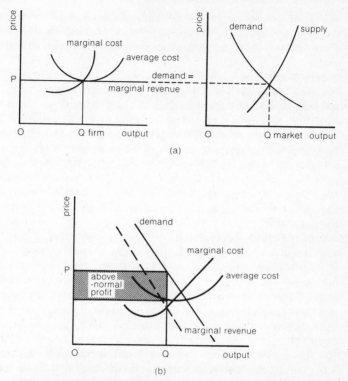

FIG. 7. **Allocative efficiency.** (a) A normal profit equilibrium under conditions of perfect competition. (b) The profit maximizing price-output combination for a monopolist.

amalgamation see MERGER.

American Federation of Labor and Congress of Industrial Organizations (AFL-CIO) the peak labor organization. Its membership consists of independent national and international unions, trade departments, state and local bodies, and directly affiliated local unions. It is the AFL-CIO affiliates that engage in collective bargaining.

The principal functions of the AFL-CIO have been to serve as the voice of the labor movement, prevent jurisdictional strife among unions, lobby government officials on issues of importance to organized labor, mobilize support for political candidates in elections, and represent American unions at international conferences.

amortization repayment of the principal of a loan in installments over the life of the loan. Also see DEPRECIATION(2).

analysis of variance a statistical method of breaking down the total variation in a dependent variable into the proportion accounted for by variation in individual or groups of explanatory variables and the unexplained or residual variation. Such methods test the null hypothesis (see HYPOTHESIS TESTING) that samples have been drawn from the same POPULATION or from identical populations. The tests will vary according to whether the samples drawn are related in some way or unrelated. See STATISTICAL INFERENCE.

annual meeting the yearly meeting of shareholders of corporations required by law to convene in order to enable shareholders to discuss their company's ANNUAL REPORT, elect directors, and approve the DIVIDEND payouts suggested by directors. In practice, general meetings usually are poorly attended, and only rarely do directors fail to be reelected on the strength of PROXY votes cast in their favor.

annual report a yearly report by the directors of a corporation to the shareholders. It includes a copy of the company's BALANCE SHEET and a summary financial statement, along with other information that directors are required by law to disclose to shareholders. A copy of the annual report is sent to every shareholder prior to the company's ANNUAL MEETING.

annuity a series of equal payments at fixed intervals from an original lump-sum INVESTMENT. Where an annuity has a fixed time span it is termed a *fixed annuity* and the periodic receipts comprise both a phased repayment of principal (the original lump-sum payment) and interest, such that at the end of the fixed term there is a zero balance in the account. A *perpetual annuity* also called a *perpetuity* and an *annuity bond*, does not have a fixed time span but continues indefinitely and receipts can therefore only come from interest earned.

antipoverty programs measures to reduce or eliminate POV-

ERTY. These are generally organized as income maintenance or manpower development projects.

antitrust policy a policy concerned with promoting efficient use of economic resources and protecting interests of consumers. The objective is to secure optimal market performance: specifically, least-cost supply, fair prices and profit levels, technological advance, and product improvement. Antitrust policy covers a number of areas, including monopolization of a market by a single supplier, creation of monopoly positions through mergers and takeovers, collusion between sellers, and anticompetitive practices.

Antitrust policy is implemented mainly through control of market structure and market conduct but also, albeit rarely, through direct control of market performance itself by, for example, stipulating maximum levels of profit.

There are two basic approaches to control of market structure and conduct: the nondiscretionary approach and the discretionary approach. The nondiscretionary approach lays down acceptable standards of structure and conduct and prohibits any transgression of these standards. Typical ingredients of this approach include:

(a) stipulation of maximum permitted market share limits, for example, no more than 20% of the market, in order to limit seller concentration and prevent emergence of a monopoly supplier. Thus, for example, under this ruling any proposed merger or takeover that would take the combined group's market share above the allowed limit would automatically be prohibited.

(b) outright prohibition of all forms of shared monopoly involving price fixing, market sharing, or the like.

(c) outright prohibition of specific practices designed to reduce or eliminate competition, for example, exclusive dealing and refusal to supply.

Thus, the nondiscretionary approach attempts to preserve conditions of workable competition by direct attack on the possession and exercise of monopoly power as such.

By contrast, the discretionary approach takes a more pragmatic line, recognizing that high levels of seller concentration and certain agreements between companies may serve to improve economic efficiency rather than impair it. In the discretionary approach, each situation is judged on its own merits rather than condemned automatically. Thus, mergers, restrictive agreements, and practices of the kind noted above are evaluated in terms of their possible benefits and detriments. If they appear on balance to be detrimental, then and only then are they prohibited.

The United States and the European Community by and large take the nondiscretionary approach, whereas the United Kingdom has a history of preferring the discretionary approach. State and federal laws to reduce the consequences of trusts have been available since the final years of the nineteenth century. The principal federal laws are: Sherman Act (1890); Clayton Act (1914); Robinson Patman Act (1936); and Celler-Kefauver Act (1956). The rigor with which the laws have been enforced has depended on the philosophical positions—pro- or anti-business—of the administration in office and the Supreme Court. In recent years, except for a few extraordinary cases, such as the ATT case, there has been little antitrust court action.

applied economics the application of economic analysis to real economic situations. Applied economics seeks to employ the predictions emanating from ECONOMIC THEORY in offering advice on formulation of ECONOMIC POLICY. See ECONOMIC MODELS, HYPOTHESIS, HYPOTHESIS TESTING.

apportionment the breakdown of COSTS and REVENUES between different products, functions, or company departments where it is not possible to attribute costs and revenues directly to the departments in which the cost or revenue concerned arises. For example, it is generally impossible to allocate rent and taxes precisely between departments in a factory, so they can only be apportioned on some equitable basis, such as the respective floor areas of departments. See BUDGETING, ALLOCATION.

appreciation 1. an increase in the value of a CURRENCY against other currencies under a FLOATING EXCHANGE-RATE SYSTEM. An appreciation in value of a currency makes IMPORTS cheaper and EXPORTS more expensive, thereby encouraging additional imports and curbing exports and so assisting in the removal of a BALANCE OF PAYMENTS surplus and the excessive accumulation of INTERNATIONAL RESERVES.

How successful an appreciation is in removing a payments surplus depends on the reactions of export and import volumes to the change in relative prices, that is, the PRICE ELASTICITY OF DE-MAND for exports and imports. If these values are low, that is, demand is inelastic, trade volume will not change very much and the appreciation may in fact make the surplus larger. On the other hand, if export and import demands are elastic, the change in trade volumes will operate to remove the surplus. BALANCE-OF-PAYMENTS EQUILIBRIUM will be restored if the sum of export and import elasticities is greater than unity (the MARSHALL-LERNER CONDITION). See DEPRECIATION(1), INTERNAL-EXTERNAL BALANCE MODEL.

   2. an increase in the price of an ASSET. Also called *capital appreciation*. Assets held for long periods, such as factory buildings, offices, and homes, are most likely to appreciate in value because of the effects of INFLATION and increasing site values, although the value of short-term assets, such as STOCKS, can also appreciate. Where assets appreciate, their REPLACEMENT COST will exceed their HISTORIC COST and such assets may need to be revalued periodically to keep their book values in line with their market values. See DEPRECIATION(2), REVALUATION PROVISION, INFLATION ACCOUNTING.

a priori known to be true independently of the subject under debate. Economists frequently develop their theoretical models by reasoning deductively from certain prior assumptions to general predictions.

   For example, operating on the assumption that consumers behave rationally in seeking to maximize their utility from a limited income, economists' reasoning leads to the prediction that consumers will tend to buy more of those products whose relative price has fallen. See ECONOMIC MAN, CONSUMER EQUILIBRIUM.

arbitrage the buying or selling of assets between two or more MARKETS in order to take profitable advantage of any differences in the prices quoted in these markets. By simultaneously buying in a low-price market and selling in the high-price market, an *arbitrageur* (or arbitrager) can make a profit from any disparity in prices between them, although in the process of buying and selling the arbitrageur will add to DEMAND in the low-price market and add to SUPPLY in the high-price market and so narrow or eliminate the price disparity.

   Arbitrage is practiced especially in commodity markets, currency markets, and stock futures markets, where it serves to iron out price disparities across markets. See SPOT MARKET, FUTURES MARKET.

arbitration a procedure for settling disputes, most notably LABOR DISPUTES, in which a neutral third party, or arbitrator, after hearing presentations from all sides in dispute, issues an award that may be binding on each side. Interest arbitration is sometimes used as a last resort when negotiations have failed to bring about agreement on the terms of a new contract or other issue. Grievance arbitration is commonly provided for in collective bargaining agreements and is usually made binding on all parties.

arc elasticity see ELASTICITY OF DEMAND.

arithmetic mean see MEAN.

arithmetic progression a series of discrete values showing a growth pattern of the form:

$$a + (a + r) + (a + 2r) + (a + 3r), \text{etc.}$$

where a is the original amount at the start and r is the amount added each time. Such a progression would show a linear growth trend over time. Arithmetic progressions can be used to analyze many problems in economics, such as SIMPLE INTEREST on LOANS. Compare GEOMETRIC PROGRESSION.

Arrow, Kenneth (born 1921) winner with John Hicks of the Nobel Prize in Economic Science for 1972. Arrow and Hicks were cited for "pioneering contributions to general equilibrium theory and welfare theory." Arrow sought to establish the conditions under which group decisions could be rationally and democratically derived from individual preferences. In collaboration with Gerard Debreu, winner of the Nobel Prize in 1983, he presented proof of the existence of a competitive equilibrium.

asset an item or property owned by an individual or a business that has a money value. Assets are of two main types: (a) physical assets such as plant and equipment, land, consumer durables (cars, refrigerators, etc.); (b) financial assets such as currency, bank deposits, stocks, and bonds. See INVESTMENT, LIQUIDITY, BALANCE SHEET, LIABILITY.

asset-growth maximization a company objective in the THEORY

OF THE FIRM that is used as an alternative to the traditional assumption of PROFIT MAXIMIZATION. Salaried managers of large CORPORATIONS are assumed to seek to maximize the rate of growth of net assets as a means of increasing their salaries, power, etc., subject to maintaining a minimum share value, so as to avoid having the company taken over. In Fig. 8 the rate of growth of assets is shown on the horizontal axis, and the ratio of the market value of company shares to the book value of company net assets (the share-valuation ratio) on the vertical axis. The valuation curve rises at first as increasing asset growth increases share value, but beyond growth rate (G) excessive retention of profits to finance growth will reduce dividend payments to shareholders and depress share values. Managers will tend to choose the fastest growth rate $(G\star)$ that does not depress the share valuation below the level (V^1) at which the company risks being taken over. See also MANAGERIAL THEORIES OF THE FIRM, COMPANY OBJECTIVES, DIVORCE OF OWNERSHIP FROM CONTROL.

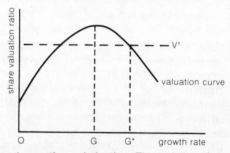

FIG. 8. **Asset-growth maximization.** The variation of share valuation ratio against the company growth rate.

asset stripper a predator company or *corporate raider* that takes control of another company (see TAKEOVER) with a view to selling off its ASSETS wholly or in part, for financial gain rather than continuing as an on-going business.

The classical recipe for asset-stripping arises when the realizable market value of the company's assets are much greater than what it would cost the predator to buy the company, that is, where there is a marked discrepancy between the asset value per share of the target company and the price per share required to take the company over. This discrepancy usually results from a combination of two factors: (a) gross undervaluation of the company's assets in the BALANCE SHEET and (b) mismanagement or bad luck resulting in low profits or losses, both of which serve to depress the company's share price.

asset structure the proportions of various types of assets held by a company as shown in the BALANCE SHEET. For example, a large manufacturing company or public utility is likely to have proportionately large FIXED ASSETS while retail companies are likely to have proportionately large CURRENT ASSETS, such as ACCOUNTS RECEIVABLE and INVENTORIES. A company's asset structure helps determine the way in which financing is arranged, in particular the balance of long-term LOANS and short-term DEBT. See CAPITAL GEARING.

asset value per share or **liquidation value** the total value of a company's tangible book ASSETS less all short- and long-term LIABILITIES as shown in the BALANCE SHEET. The net assets figure is divided by the number of shares of common stock outstanding to show approximately how much asset value supports each share. In the case of a LIQUIDATION it would be of some use to the SHAREHOLDERS in estimating how much they may reasonably expect to receive from sale of the company or of its assets. Book values of assets may be a reasonable estimate of their value to the company as a going concern but in liquidation they tend to be worth considerably less, depending on the alternative uses to which they can be put. See also ASSET STRIPPER, SHARE CAPITAL.

asset value theory (of exchange rate determination) an explanation of the volatility of EXCHANGE RATE movements under a FLOATING EXCHANGE-RATE SYSTEM. Whereas the PURCHASING-POWER PARITY THEORY suggests that SPECULATION is consistent with achievement of BALANCE-OF-PAYMENTS EQUILIBRIUM, the asset value theory emphasizes that in all likelihood it will not be. In this theory the exchange rate is an asset price, the relative price at which the money, bills, bonds, and other financial assets of a country will be willingly held by foreign and domestic asset holders. An actual alteration in the exchange rate or a change in expectations about future rates can cause asset holders to alter their portfolios. The resultant change in demand for holdings of foreign currency relative to domestic currency assets can at times produce sharp fluctuations in exchange rates. In particular, uncertainty about future market rates and the unwillingness of banks and other large financial participants in the foreign exchange markets to take substantial positions in certain currencies, especially SOFT CURRENCIES, may diminish funds for stabilizing speculation that would in turn reduce or avoid erratic exchange rate movements.

If this should prove to be the case, financial asset switching is likely to reinforce and *magnify* exchange rate movements initiated by current account transactions (that is, changes in imports and exports), and in consequence may produce exchange rates that are inconsistent with effective overall balance-of-payments equilibrium in the longer run.

asymptote a line that continually approaches a given AXIS of a GRAPH but never quite meets it. The line, in economics, is frequently a curve of the form

$$y = \frac{a}{x},$$

a RECTANGULAR HYPERBOLA where a is a constant.

asymptotic of or relating to an ASYMPTOTE.

atomistic competition a market structure comprising many small companies, so each company competes independently. Also see PERFECT COMPETITION.

auction a method of selling GOODS and SERVICES by competitive bidding. The sale is made to the highest bidder subject to a reserve price being attained.

audit the legal requirement for a CORPORATIONto have its BALANCE SHEET, FINANCIAL STATEMENT, and underlying accounting system and records examined by a qualified AUDITOR so as to enable an opinion to be formed as to whether the financial statements accurately represent the company's financial condition and whether they comply with relevant statutes.

auditor a certified public accountant appointed to check the accuracy of a company's accounts and financial statements and to present an independent report to shareholders on whether the accounts present a *true and fair view* of the company's affairs.

Austrian school a group of late nineteenth century economists at the University of Vienna who established and developed a particular line of theoretical reasoning. The tradition originated with Professor Carl Menger, who argued against the classical theories of value, which emphasized PRODUCTION and SUPPLY. The classical economists—Smith, Ricardo, and Malthus—relied on costs of production as determinants of prices. Instead, Menger initiated the subjectivist revolution, reasoning that the value of a good was not derived from its cost but from the pleasure, or UTILITY, the CONSUMER can derive from it. This type of reasoning led to the MARGINAL UTILITY theory of value, whereby successive increments of a commodity yield DIMINISHING MARGINAL UTILITY.

Friedrich von Wieser, who developed the tradition further, is credited with introducing the economic concept of OPPORTUNITY COST. Eugen von Böhm-Bawerk helped develop the theory of INTEREST and CAPITAL, arguing that the price paid for use of capital depends on consumer preference for present CONSUMPTION relative to future consumption. Ludwig von Mises and Friedrich von Hayek subsequently continued the tradition established by Carl Menger et al. See also CLASSICAL ECONOMICS.

autocorrelation or **serial correlation** an econometric problem in which there is a particular pattern in the residual or error terms after an estimate has been calculated from sample observations of INDEPENDENT VARIABLES and DEPENDENT VARIABLES. If the estimated REGRESSION coefficients are good, unbiased estimates of the true population coefficients of the independent variables, then the residual values should be randomly distributed, showing no consistent relationship with each other. If they are not, the estimated regression equation is an inaccurate fit or has missed other important independent variables that are affecting the dependent variable. Autocorrelated error terms occur when a series of error terms are related, and they are a frequent problem in TIME-SERIES ANALYSIS, in which values of the error terms in consecutive time periods may be correlated. See also DURBIN-WATSON TEST.

automatic stabilizers built-in, nondiscretionary elements in FIS-CAL POLICY that serve to automatically reduce the impact of fluctuations in economic activity. A fall in NATIONAL INCOME and output reduces government tax receipts and increases its unemployment and welfare payments. Lower tax receipts and higher payments increase the government's BUDGET DEFICIT and restore some of the lost income (see CIRCULAR FLOW OF NATIONAL INCOME MODEL). See also FISCAL DRAG.

automation the application of advanced technology to industrial processes to ensure that all or nearly all of an activity, for example, automobile assembly, is undertaken by machines and not by manual labor. See PRODUCTIVITY, TECHNOLOGICAL UNEMPLOYMENT, TECHNOLOGICAL PROGRESSIVENESS, CAPITAL-LABOR RATIO.

autonomous investment the part of INVESTMENT that is independent of the level of and changes in NATIONAL INCOME. Autonomous investment depends mainly on long-run considerations and competitive factors such as plant modernization by businesses in order to cut costs or to take advantage of a new invention. See INDUCED INVESTMENT, INVESTMENT SCHEDULE.

average see MEAN.

average cost 1. in the *long run*, static analysis, the unit cost (TOTAL COST divided by number of units produced) of producing outputs for plants of *different* sizes. The position of the SHORT RUN average total cost (ATC) curve depends on its existing size of plant. In the long run a company can alter the size of its plant. Each plant size corresponds to a different U-shaped short-run ATC curve. As the company expands its scale of operation, it moves from one curve to another. The path along which the company expands—the LONG RUN ATC curve—is thus the *envelope curve* of all the possible short-run ATC curves (see Fig. 9a).

It will be noted that the long-run ATC curve is typically assumed to be a shallow U-shape, with a least-cost point indicated by output level OX. To begin with, average cost falls, reflecting ECONOMIES OF SCALE. Eventually, however, the company may experience DISECONOMIES OF SCALE and average cost begins to rise.

Empirical studies of companies' long-run average-cost curves

AVERAGE COST

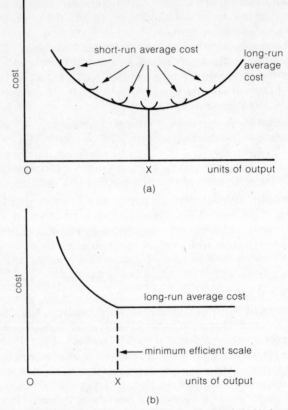

FIG. 9. **Average cost (long run).** (a) The characteristic U-shape of the long-run average-cost curve. (b) The characteristic L-shaped curve that normally results from expansion.

suggest, however, that diseconomies of scale are rarely encountered within the typical output ranges over which companies operate, so that most companies' average-cost curves are L-shaped, as in Fig. 9b. Where diseconomies of scale are encountered, the MINIMUM EFFICIENT SCALE at which a company will operate corresponds to the minimum point of the long-run average-cost curve (Fig. 9a). Where diseconomies of scale are not encountered within the typical output range, minimum efficient scale corresponds with the output at which economies of scale are exhausted and constant returns to scale begin (Fig. 9b).

2. In the *short run*, the unit cost (TOTAL COST divided by number of units produced) of producing particular volumes of output in a plant of a given (fixed) size.

Average total cost (ATC) is the sum of average FIXED COST (AFC) and average VARIABLE COST (AVC). AFC declines continuously as output rises as a given total amount of fixed cost is spread over a greater number of units. For example, with fixed costs of $1000 a year and annual output of 1000 units, fixed costs per unit would be $1, but if annual output rose to 2000 units, the fixed cost per unit would fall to 50 cents (see AFC curve in Fig. 10a).

Over the entire potential output range within which a company can produce, AVC falls at first (reflecting increasing RETURNS TO THE VARIABLE FACTOR INPUT—output increases faster than costs), but then rises (reflecting DIMINISHING RETURNS to the variable inputs—costs increase faster than output), as shown by the AVC curve in Fig. 10a. Thus, the conventional SHORT RUN ATC curve is U-shaped.

However, over the more restricted output range in which companies typically operate, constant returns to the variable input are more likely to be experienced, because as more variable inputs are added to the fixed inputs employed in production, equal increments in output result. In such circumstances AVC will remain constant over the whole output range (as in Fig. 10b) and as a consequence ATC will decline in parallel with AFC.

average-cost price a selling PRICE for a product or service that is set equal to AVERAGE COST. See FULL-COST PRICING.

average-cost pricing a pricing principle that argues for setting PRICES equal to the AVERAGE COST of production, when average costs include normal profits, so that prices cover both variable costs and FIXED OVERHEAD costs incurred through past investments. This involves the sometimes arbitrary APPORTIONMENT of fixed (overhead) costs to individual units of output, although it

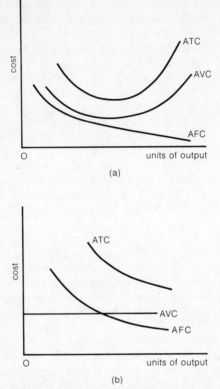

FIG. 10. **Average cost (short run).** (a) The characteristic curves of average total cost (ATC), average variable cost (AVC), and average fixed cost (AFC) over the whole output range. (b) The characteristic curves of ATC and AFC and constant line of AVC over the restricted output range.

does seek to recover in the price charged all the costs that would have been avoided by not producing the product. See also MAR-GINAL COST PRICING, FULL-COST PRICING.

average deviation a measure of variation within a group of numerical observations, that is, the average of the (absolute values of the) deviations of the observations from the group MEAN. For example, if five products have prices of $5, $4, $3, $2, and $1, the mean price is:

$$£\frac{5 + 4 + 3 + 2 + 1}{5} = £\frac{15}{5} = £3$$

and the amounts by which the various prices depart from the mean price are:

		absolute values:	
$5−3=	$2		|2|
$4−3=	$1		|1|
$3−3=	$0		|0|
$2−3=	−$1		|1|
$1−3=	−$2		|2|
	$0		$|6|

Unfortunately, the average of these deviations is always zero because in using a mean for a group of observations, the positive deviations from the mean will always exactly match the negative deviations from the mean. To get around this problem and concentrate on the magnitude of the deviations rather than their signs, the ABSOLUTE VALUES of the deviations can be considered. The sum of the absolute values of the deviations in the example above is $6 and the average of the absolute deviations is therefore $6/5 = $1.2. If the observations are grouped closely around the mean, their dispersion is small and the average of the absolute deviations will be small. If the observations are spread over a considerable distance from the mean then their dispersion is large and the average of the absolute deviations will be large. Compare STANDARD DEVIATION.

average fixed cost see AVERAGE COST.

average physical product the average OUTPUT in the SHORT RUN theory of supply produced by each extra unit of VARIABLE FACTOR INPUT (in conjunction with a given amount of FIXED FACTOR INPUT). See RETURNS TO THE VARIABLE FACTOR INPUT.

average propensity to consume (APC) the fraction of a given level of DISPOSABLE PERSONAL INCOME that is spent on CONSUMPTION:

$$APC = \frac{consumption}{income}$$

See also PROPENSITY TO CONSUME, MARGINAL PROPENSITY TO CONSUME.

average propensity to import (APM) the fraction of a given level of NATIONAL INCOME that is spent on IMPORTS:

$$APM = \frac{imports}{income}$$

See also PROPENSITY TO IMPORT, MARGINAL PROPENSITY TO IMPORT.

average propensity to save (APS) the fraction of a given level of NATIONAL INCOME that is saved (see SAVINGS):

$$APS = \frac{saving}{income}$$

See also PROPENSITY TO SAVE, MARGINAL PROPENSITY TO SAVE.

average propensity to tax (APT) the fraction of a given level of NATIONAL INCOME that is appropriated by the government in TAXATION:

$$APT = \frac{taxation}{income}$$

See also PROPENSITY TO TAX, MARGINAL PROPENSITY TO TAX, AVERAGE RATE OF TAXATION.

average rate of taxation the total tax paid by an individual divided by the total income on which the tax was based. For example, if an individual earned $50,000 in 1 year, on which that individual had to pay a tax of $5000, the average rate of taxation would be 10%. See MARGINAL RATE OF TAXATION, PROPENSITY TO TAX, PROPORTIONAL TAXATION, REGRESSIVE TAXATION, PROGRESSIVE TAXATION.

average revenue the total revenue received (price × number of units sold) divided by the number of units. Price and average revenue are in fact equal: that is, in Fig. 11, the price $10 = average revenue ($10 × 10 ÷ 10) = $10. It follows that the DEMAND CURVE is also the average revenue curve facing the company.

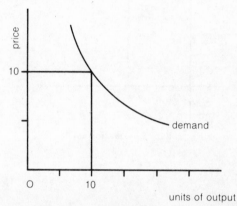

FIG. 11. **Average revenue.** The demand curve or average revenue curve.

average variable cost see AVERAGE COST.

axis a straight line that intersects with another straight line at right angles to form the reference points of a GRAPH. The axes determine the locus of any point within their bounds by reference to COORDINATES, that is, the measurements along each of the two axes. The vertical axis is referred to as the y-axis and is at right angles to the horizontal or x-axis. The axes divide the graph into four quadrants, and where the two axes meet is called the origin, denoted by O in Fig. 12. Each point in a two-dimensional plane is referred to by a coordinate (X,Y) and each coordinate represents a unique point in that plane. Positive values of a variable, such as quantity demanded, would lie above the origin on the y-axis or to the right of it on the x-axis. In Fig. 12, point A has positive coordinates OX_1, OY_1.

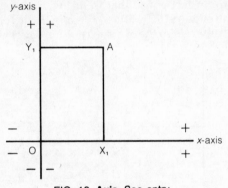

FIG. 12. **Axis.** See entry.

B

backdoor financing borrowing by US government agencies from the US Treasury to avoid going to Congress for authorization to raise money.

bad debt an accounting term for money owed to a company that is unlikely to be paid, for example, because a customer has become insolvent (see INSOLVENCY). Such bad debts are written off against the PROFITS of the company as a business cost.

balanced budget a situation in which GOVERNMENT (PUBLIC) EXPENDITURE is equal to TAXATION and other receipts. When a government spends more than it receives in taxation, a BUDGET DEFICIT is incurred. When a government spends less than it receives in taxation, a BUDGET SURPLUS ensues. See BUDGET, FISCAL POLICY.

balanced budget multiplier a change in AGGREGATE DEMAND brought about by a change in GOVERNMENT EXPENDITURE that is exactly matched by a change in revenues received from TAXATION and other sources. In the framework of the simple income-expenditure model, the change in government expenditure has an immediate effect on aggregate demand and generates income of an equivalent size. By contrast, the change in taxation does not change aggregate demand by an equivalent amount, because some of the increased or reduced DISPOSABLE PERSONAL INCOME will be offset by changes in SAVING. Consequently, an increase in government expenditure and taxation of equal amounts will have a net expansionary effect on aggregate demand and incomes, whereas a decrease in government expenditure and taxation of equal amounts will have a net contractionary effect. See BUDGET, FISCAL POLICY.

balance of payments a statement of a country's trade and financial transactions with the rest of the world over a particular period

BALANCE OF PAYMENTS

of time, usually 1 year. Figure 13 shows a standard presentation of balance of payments. The account is divided into two main parts: (a) current account and (b) investment and other capital transactions.

U.S. International Transactions, 1987, in millions of dollars

A. *Current Account*
    I. Merchandise

Exports	249,570	
Imports	409,850	
Net	−160,280	

    II. Investment income

Receipts	103,756	
Payments	83,381	
Net	20,375	

III. Net Military Transactions	2,368
IV. Net Travel and Transportation Receipts	10,281
V. Other Services, Net	12,035
VI. Balance of Goods and Services	140,519
VII. Remittances, Pensions, and Other Unilateral Transfers	13,445
VIII. Balance on Current Account	−153,964

B. *Capital Account*
    I. U.S. Assets Abroad (net decrease/capital inflow)

A. Total	75,987
B. U.S. Official Reserve Assets	9,149
C. Other U.S. Government Assets	1,162
D. U.S. Private Assets	86,297

    II. Foreign Assets in the U.S. (net increase/capital inflow)

A. Total	211,490
B. Foreign Official Assets	44,968
C. Other Foreign Assets	166,522
D. Total (sum of items with signs reversed)	18,461

FIG. 13. **Balance of payments.** The US balance of payments for 1987, −18,461 million dollars. Source: *Economic Report of the President, January 1989.*

The current account shows the country's profit or loss in day-to-day dealings. It is made up under two headings. The *visible* trade balance (BALANCE OF TRADE) indicates the difference between the value of EXPORTS and IMPORTS of goods (raw materials and fuels, food, semi-finished products, and finished manufactures).

The second group of transactions make up the *invisible* balance. These transactions include earnings from and payments for such services as banking, insurance, and tourism. It also includes interest and profits on investments and loans, government receipts, and spending on defense.

In addition to current account transactions, there are also currency flows into and out of the country related to capital items—investment money spent by companies on new plants and the purchase of assets abroad, plus US official reserves and other government assets, and foreign assets in the United States.

The statistical discrepancy between the sum of the payments flowing into the United States and payments going out is a measure of errors and omissions in the balance.

A balance-of-payments deficit or surplus can be dealt with in a number of ways, including external price adjustments, internal price and income adjustments, and trade and currency restrictions.

See BALANCE-OF-PAYMENTS EQUILIBRIUM.

balance-of-payments disequilibrium see BALANCE-OF-PAYMENTS EQUILIBRIUM.

balance-of-payments equilibrium a situation in which, over a number of years, a country spends and invests abroad no more than other countries spend and invest in it. Thus, the country neither adds to its stock of INTERNATIONAL RESERVES nor sees them reduced.

There are three main ways of restoring balance-of-payments equilibrium when an imbalance occurs:

(a) *external price adjustments.* Alterations in the EXCHANGE RATE between currencies involving (depending on the particular exchange rate system in operation) the DEVALUATION or DEPRECIATION and REVALUATION or APPRECIATION of the currencies concerned to make exports cheaper or more expensive and imports dearer or less expensive in foreign currency terms. For example, with regard to exports, in Fig. 14a if the pound-dollar exchange rate is devalued from $1.60 to $1.40, this would allow British exporters to reduce their prices by a similar amount, thus increasing their price competitiveness in the American market.

(b) *internal price and income adjustments.* The use of deflationary and reflationary (see DEFLATION) monetary and fiscal poli-

BALANCE-OF-PAYMENTS EQUILIBRIUM

UK domestic price of a product	Exchange rate	Price of the UK product exported to US
£1	£1 = $1.60	$1.60
£1	£1 = $1.40	$1.40

(a)

UK domestic price of a product	Exchange rate	Price of the UK product exported to US
£1	£1 = $1.60	$1.60
75p	£1 = $1.60	$1.20

(b)

FIG. 14. **Balance-of-payments equilibrium.** (a) Exchange rate adjustment. (b) Internal price adjustment.

tionary and reflationary (see DEFLATION) monetary and fiscal policies to alter the prices of domestically produced goods and services vis-a-vis products supplied by other countries so as to make exports relatively cheaper or dearer and imports more expensive or cheaper in foreign currency terms. For example, again with regard to exports, if it were possible to reduce the domestic price of a British product, as shown in Fig. 14b, given an unchanged exchange rate, this would allow the dollar price of the product in the American market to be reduced, thereby improving its price competitiveness vis-a-vis similar American products. The same policies are used to alter the level of domestic income and spending, including expenditure on imports.

(c) *trade and foreign exchange restrictions.* The use of TARIFFS, QUOTAS, EXCHANGE CONTROLS etc. to affect the price and availability of goods and services, and of the currencies with which to purchase these products.

Under a FIXED EXCHANGE-RATE SYSTEM, minor payments imbalances are corrected by appropriate domestic adjustments, but fundamental disequilibriums require in addition a devaluation or revaluation of the currency. It must be emphasized, however, that a number of favorable conditions must be present to ensure success of devaluations and revaluations (see, especially, DEVALUATION).

In theory, a FLOATING EXCHANGE-RATE SYSTEM provides an automatic mechanism for removing payments imbalances before they become a problem: a deficit results in an immediate exchange-rate depreciation, and a surplus results in an immediate appreciation of the exchange rate (see PURCHASING-POWER PARITY THEORY). Again, however, a number of favorable conditions must be present to ensure success of depreciations and appreciations. See also J-CURVE EFFECT, INTERNAL-EXTERNAL BALANCE MODEL, MARSHALL-LERNER CONDITION.

balance of trade a statement of a country's trade in GOODS (visibles) with the rest of the world over a particular period of time. The term "balance of trade" specifically excludes trade in services (invisibles), and concentrates on finished manufactures, intermediate products, and raw materials that can be seen and recorded as they cross national boundaries. See BALANCE OF PAYMENTS.

balance sheet an accounting statement of a company's ASSETS and LIABILITIES on the last day of an accounting period. The balance sheet lists the assets the company owns and sets against these the balancing obligations or claims of the institutions that provided the funds to acquire the assets. Assets take the form of FIXED ASSETS and CURRENT ASSETS, while obligations take the form of shareholders' capital employed, long-term loans, and CURRENT LIABILITIES. The balance sheet is compiled by summarizing information derived from accounting records.

A simple balance sheet is illustrated in Fig. 15. Assets include fixed assets (such things as equipment and buildings) and current assets (inventories, accounts receivable, and cash). Liabilities include money owed to banks and to suppliers of raw materials and components. The difference between assets and liabilities is referred to as the net worth of the company and represents funds supplied by SHAREHOLDERS (the owners of the company), together with any profits retained in the business. Thus, fixed assets + (current assets − current liabilities) = net worth.

bank traditionally defined as an authorized deposit-taking institution that receives deposits of money it must pay out when an appropriate instrument is presented. Banks are primarily traders whose stock is other people's money. Their principal source of income is the interest they charge for making money available to individuals and firms.

BANK

Assets employed

	$	$	$
Fixed assets			
Equipment	500,000		
Factory	300,000		
			800,000
Current assets			
Stock	600,000		
Debtors	175,000		
Cash	25,000		
		800,000	
Current liabilities			
Trade creditors	300,000		
Bank overdraft	200,000		
		500,000	
Net current assets			300,000
Net assets employed			1,100,000
Financed by:			
Shareholders capital			900,000
Retained profits			200,000
			1,100,000

FIG. 15. **Balance sheet.** An example of a hypothetical company's balance sheet on the last day of an accounting period.

The United States, unlike other countries, has a dual banking system: banks that are chartered by the federal government and banks that are chartered by state governments. The 12 Federal Reserve Banks constitute the nation's central bank. All nationally chartered banks must join the Federal Reserve System. Banks chartered by states are permitted to join the system.

Recent state and federal legislation that led to bank deregulation expanded interstate and foreign banking and fostered emergence of new, nonbanking financial institutions. These and other developments have blurred some of the distinctions defining different kinds of banks and some of the differences between banks and nonbanking financial institutions. There is still some usefulness in employing the traditional terms for the principal types of banks: *commercial banks, credit unions, investment banks,* and *savings and loan institutions.*

See FEDERAL RESERVE SYSTEM, CENTRAL BANK, COMMERCIAL

BANK, CREDIT UNIONS, INVESTMENT BANKS, SAVINGS AND LOAN INSTITUTION, DUAL BANKING SYSTEM.

bank deposit a sum of money held on deposit with a bank. Bank deposits are of two main types: demand deposits, which are withdrawable on demand; time deposits, which are withdrawable subject legally to some notice being given. (This notice is seldom demanded.) Demand deposits represent instant LIQUIDITY—they are used to finance day-to-day transactions and regular payments, either in the form of a CURRENCY withdrawal or a CHECK transfer. Time deposits are usually held for longer periods to meet irregular payments and as a form of savings. Bank deposits constitute an important component of the MONEY SUPPLY.

Bank for International Settlements (BIS) an international bank situated in Basel, Switzerland, and established in 1930, that originally acted as a coordinating agency for the central banks of Germany, France, Italy, Belgium, and the United Kingdom in settling BALANCE OF PAYMENTS imbalances and for other intercentral bank dealings. Now its membership comprises all West European central banks together with those of the United States, Canada, and Japan. Although the INTERNATIONAL MONETARY FUND is the main institution responsible for conducting international monetary affairs, and the EUROPEAN MONETARY SYSTEM specifically for EUROPEAN COMMUNITY members, the BIS is still influential in providing a forum for discussion and surveillance of international banking practices.

banking system a network of COMMERCIAL BANKS and other banking institutions engaged in transmitting money and providing loans and credit facilities. Deposits with the banking system are a key element in the money supply, so the banking system is regulated by the monetary and governmental authorities. See DEMAND DEPOSIT CREATION, MONEY SUPPLY, MONETARY POLICY, FEDERAL RESERVE SYSTEM.

bank loan CREDIT made available to private and business customers by banks and nonbanking financial institutions. Such loans may be for fixed periods of time at agreed rates of interest, or *overdrafts* or lines of credit by means of which customers can borrow as much as they require up to a prearranged total limit and are charged interest on outstanding balances.

bank note the paper CURRENCY formerly issued by US national banks as national bank notes forming part of the country's MONEY SUPPLY. Federal Reserve issue now constitutes the paper money used.

bank reserves see RESERVES.

bankruptcy see INSOLVENCY.

barriers to entry an element of MARKET STRUCTURE that refers to obstacles in the way of potential newcomers to a market. These obstacles operate in a number of ways to discourage entry:

(a) lower cost advantages to established firms arising from the possession of substantial market shares and the realization of ECONOMIES OF SCALE in production and distribution.

(b) strong consumer preferences for the products of established firms resulting from PRODUCT DIFFERENTIATION activities.

(c) control of essential raw materials, technology, and market outlets by established firms either through direct ownership or through PATENTS, FRANCHISES, and EXCLUSIVE DEALING contracts.

(d) large capital outlays required by entrants to set up production and to cover losses during the initial entry phase.

The economic significance of barriers to entry lies in their capacity for blocking MARKET ENTRY, thereby allowing established firms to earn ABOVE-NORMAL PROFIT and affecting the RESOURCE ALLOCATION function of markets.

See also CONDITION OF ENTRY, LIMIT PRICING, POTENTIAL ENTRANT, OLIGOPOLY, MONOPOLY.

barter the EXCHANGE of one economic good or service for another. As an exchange mechanism, barter suffers from a number of serious disadvantages, for example, deciding on an appropriate rate of exchange: how many apples = one orange? These disadvantages can largely be overcome by using MONEY. See COUNTERTRADE.

base period the initial period from which a system of INDEXATION proceeds. For example, the present US Consumer Price Index has as its base period 1982—1984 = 100. By convention, the base period always commences from the number 100. See PRICE INDEX.

batch production the manufacture of a product in small quantities, using labor-intensive methods of production (see LABOR-IN-

TENSIVE COMPANY/INDUSTRY). Batch production is typically employed in industries where the product supplied is nonstandardized, with consumers demanding a wide variety of product choice. Batch production industries are usually characterized by low levels of SELLER CONCENTRATION, easy entry conditions, and high unit costs of supply. See MASS PRODUCTION, CONDITION OF ENTRY.

bear a person who expects future prices in a STOCK EXCHANGE or COMMODITY MARKET to fall, and who seeks to make money by selling stocks or commodities or their equivalent. By contrast, a *bull* is a person who expects future market prices to rise and seeks to make money by buying stocks or commodities or their equivalent. See SPOT MARKET, FUTURES MARKET.

bearer bonds FINANCIAL SECURITIES that are not registered under the name of a holder but whose possession serves as proof of ownership. Such securities are popular in the US financial system.

beggar-my-neighbor policy a course of action entered into by a country unilaterally in pursuit of its own self-interest in INTERNATIONAL TRADE even though this might adversely affect the position of other countries. For example, country A might decide to impose TARIFFS or EXCHANGE CONTROLS on imports from other countries in order to protect certain domestic industries. One danger of such a policy is that it can be self-defeating, since other countries may retaliate by imposing tariffs, etc., of their own on country A's exports, with the result that everybody's exports suffer. To avoid confrontations of this kind, various international organizations have been established to regulate the conduct of international trade and monetary dealings.

See GENERAL AGREEMENT ON TARIFFS AND TRADE, INTERNATIONAL MONETARY FUND, EXPORT INCENTIVES, IMPORT RESTRICTIONS, DIRTY FLOAT, DUMPING.

behavioral theory of the firm an alternative to the traditional, profit-maximizing THEORY OF THE FIRM. The behavioral theory examines the inherent conflict between the goals of individuals and subgroups within the organization and suggests that organizational objectives grow out of the interaction among these individuals and subgroups.

Cyert and March, who helped develop the behavioral theory,

suggested five major goals relevant to companies' sales, output, and pricing strategies: (a) production goal; (b) inventory goal; (c) sales goal; (d) market-share goal; and (e) profit goal. Each of these will be the primary concern of certain managers in the organization, and these managers will press their particular goals. The goals become the subject of bargaining among managers, and the overall goals that emerge will be compromises, often stated as satisfactory-level targets (see SATISFICING THEORY). However, this intergroup conflict rarely threatens the organization's survival because ORGANIZATIONAL SLACK provides a pool of emergency resources that permits managers to meet their goals when the economic environment becomes hostile.

In order to make rational decisions, it would be necessary to eradicate inconsistencies between goals and resolve conflicts between objectives. Traditional economic theory suggests that rationality can be achieved, painting a picture of ECONOMIC MAN able to specify objectives and take actions consistent with their achievement. By contrast, the behavioral theory argues that goals are imperfectly rationalized so that new goals are not always consistent with existing policies; and that goals are stated in the form of aspiration-level targets rather than maximizing goals, targets being raised or lowered in the light of experience. Consequently, not all objectives will receive attention at the same time, and objectives will change with experience.

The behavioral theory also focuses attention on problems of internal communications in large organizations, pointing out that decision-making is distributed throughout the firm rather than concentrated at the apex of the organizational pyramid. This happens because lower-level managers do not merely execute the orders of those at the top; they exercise initiative (a) in detailed planning within broad limits set by top management and (b) in summarizing information to be passed upward as a basis for decisions by their superiors. These communications problems make it difficult for senior managers to impose their objectives on the organization.

Although the behavioral theory of the firm is somewhat descriptive, lacking the determinism necessary to generate testable predictions, it has offered useful insights into the objectives of large companies.

See also MANAGERIAL THEORIES OF THE FIRM, PROFIT MAXIMI-
ZATION.

below-the-line promotion expenditures for sales promotion by
businesses, for example, premium programs and free samples, as
contrasted with ABOVE THE LINE promotion.

benefits-received principle of taxation the principle that
those who benefit most from government-supplied goods and services should pay the TAXES that finance them. A criticism directed
toward this proposition, apart from the obvious difficulties of quan-
tifying the benefits received by individuals, particularly in regard
to providing such items as national defense, police protection, etc.,
is that it cannot be reconciled with the wider responsibilities accepted by government in providing social services and welfare
benefits, that is, it would make no sense to tax an unemployed
person in order to finance that person's unemployment benefits.
See ABILITY-TO-PAY PRINCIPLE OF TAXATION, REDISTRIBUTION-
OF-INCOME PRINCIPLE OF TAXATION.

best linear unbiased estimates (BLUE) a statistical property of
estimates of the regression coefficients in a REGRESSION ANALYSIS.
If the estimates of the regression coefficients meet this test, the
residual or error terms will be small and randomly distributed.

beta coefficients 1. a statistical term for the estimated coefficients of VARIABLES in a regression equation when INDEPENDENT
VARIABLES measured in different units are converted into standard units of measurement. This makes it possible to directly compare the relative importance of each independent variable in affecting the value of the DEPENDENT VARIABLE, arriving at an
estimate of the elasticity of response of the dependent variable to
changes in each of the independent variables. See REGRESSION
ANALYSIS.

   2. a measure of the responsiveness of the expected return of a
particular security relative to movements in the average expected
return of all other securities in the market. The Dow-Jones index
is usually taken as a proxy measurement for general market movements. In the CAPITAL ASSET PRICING MODEL, the beta coefficient
(β) is taken as a measure of the SYSTEMATIC RISK of a particular
security. The beta coefficient is a LINEAR RELATIONSHIP between
the return on the security and the return on the market. The slope
of the line, called the *characteristic line*, determines β. The aver-

age market risk of all securities is where $\beta = 1$, that is, a 10% increase in market return is reflected in a 10% increase in the return of, say, security A. If the return on, say, security B, is 20%, but there is only a 10% increase in market return, this security has a $\beta = 2$, which indicates a risk greater than the market. If security C has a $\beta = 0.5$, this indicates a security less risky than the market in general. Risk is attached to any security with β greater than 0. See EFFICIENT MARKET HYPOTHESIS, NONSYSTEMATIC RISK.

bid 1. an offer by a company to purchase all the STOCK of another, thua effecting a TAKEOVER by becoming the majority shareholder. **2.** an indication of willingness to buy a stock at a price named by the potential buyer. **3.** an indication of willingness to purchase an item that is for sale at the prevailing selling price. This may occur at auction when many purchasers bid for items on sale, the final sale going to the purchaser offering the highest price unless a predetermined reserve price has been set that was not reached. See AUCTION.

bilateral flows movements of money between sectors of the economy to match opposite flows of goods and services. For example, income in return for factor inputs supplied, and consumption expenditure in payment for goods and services consumed. Bilateral flows make it possible to ignore flows of goods and services in the economy and to concentrate on money movements in the CIRCULAR FLOW OF NATIONAL INCOME MODEL.

bilateral monopoly a market situation comprising one seller (such as a MONOPOLY) and one buyer (such as a MONOPSONY).

bilateral oligopoly a market situation with a significant degree of seller concentration (such as OLIGOPOLY) and a significant degree of buyer concentration (such as OLIGOPSONY). See COUNTERVAILING POWER.

bilateral trade the trade between two countries. Bilateral trade is a part of INTERNATIONAL TRADE, which is multilateral in scope. See MULTILATERAL TRADE, COUNTERTRADE.

bill of exchange a FINANCIAL SECURITY representing an amount of CREDIT extended by one business to another for a short period of time, usually 3 months. The lender draws up a bill of exchange for a specified sum of money payable at a given future date, and the borrower signifies agreement to pay the amount indicated by signing (accepting) the bill. Most bills are discounted, that is, bought by commercial banks for an amount less than the face value of the bill.

bimodal (of a set of data) exhibiting two MODES. For example, if five people had weekly incomes of $100, $100, $150, $250, and $250, there would be two modal incomes—$100 and $250.

binomial distribution a special kind of PROBABILITY DISTRIBUTION that applies to DISCRETE VARIABLES. It shows the probability of obtaining a certain number of successes in a given number of trials. Binomial distribution can be approximated by NORMAL DISTRIBUTIONS for purposes of statistical analysis.

birth rate the number of people born into a POPULATION per thousand per year. In 1987, for example, the US birth rate was 15.7 people per 1000 of the population. The difference between this rate and the DEATH RATE is used to calculate the rate of growth of the population of a country over time. The birth rate tends to decline as a country attains higher levels of economic development. See DEMOGRAPHIC TRANSITION.

black economy or **underground economy** nonmarketed economic activity that is not recorded in the NATIONAL INCOME ACCOUNTS, either because such activity does not pass through the marketplace or because it is illegal. Illegality is not the same as nonmarketed activity. Illegal economic activity may operate efficiently in the usual PRICE SYSTEM, which may be determined by SUPPLY and DEMAND. Examples may be the purchase and sale of illegal drugs on the street, or alcohol during Prohibition, or quantities of meat during World War II, when meat was rationed. Nonmarketed activity does not have a price determined by demand and supply. Certain nonmarketed activity may be undertaken for altruistic reasons, for example, the domestic services of a woman or man on behalf of their children, and the work of volunteers. Other nonmarketed activity is done on a BARTER basis, for example, when a mechanic repairs an automobile belonging to an electrician who in return installs new wiring in the mechanic's house. Money has not changed hands and the activity is not recorded. The term "black economy" usually refers to the illegal situation of people working for pay without declaring their income. See BLACK MARKET.

black knight see TAKEOVER BID.

black market an unofficial market that may arise when a government keeps the price of a product below its equilibrium rate, that is, the price at which quantity supplied equals quantity demanded, and is then forced to operate a RATIONING system to allocate the available supply among buyers. Given that some buyers are prepared to pay a higher price, some dealers will be tempted to divert supplies away from the official market by creating an under-the-counter secondary market. See BLACK ECONOMY.

board of directors the group responsible to shareholders for running a CORPORATION. The board of directors meets periodically to decide on major policy matters within the company and the appointment of key managers. Directors are elected by holders of common stock at the company's ANNUAL MEETING.

bond a FINANCIAL SECURITY issued by businesses and by the government as a means of long-term funds. Bonds are typically issued for periods of several years. They are repayable on maturity, may (in the case of bonds issued by corporations) be convertible into common or preferred stock, and bear a fixed rate of interest.

Once a bond has been issued at its nominal value, the market price at which it is subsequently sold will vary in order to keep the EFFECTIVE RATE OF INTEREST on the bond in line with current prevailing interest rates. For example, a $1000 bond with a nominal 5% interest rate, thus paying $50 a year, would have to be priced at $500 if current market interest rates were 10%, so that a buyer could earn an effective return of $50 = 10% on such an investment.

Monetary authorities may use government bonds as a means of regulating the MONEY SUPPLY. For example, if the authorities wish to reduce the money supply, they can sell bonds to the general public, thereby reducing the reserves of the banking system as customers pay for these bonds.

See also OPEN-MARKET OPERATION, DEMAND DEPOSIT CREATION, SPECULATIVE DEMAND FOR MONEY.

boom a phase of the BUSINESS CYCLE characterized by FULL EMPLOYMENT levels of output and some upward pressure on the general PRICE LEVEL. Boom conditions depend on a high level of AGGREGATE DEMAND and incentives for the private sector to invest because of expansionary FISCAL POLICY and MONETARY POL-ICY. See DEMAND MANAGEMENT, STABILIZATION POLICY.

borrower a person, company, or institution that obtains a LOAN in order to finance CONSUMPTION or INVESTMENT. Borrowers are frequently required to offer some COLLATERAL SECURITY to lenders, which lenders may retain in the event that borrowers fail to repay the loan. See DEBT, ACCOUNTS RECEIVABLE, FINANCIAL SYSTEM.

bottom line an accounting term denoting the NET PROFIT from a business operation after all costs have been paid. In accounting terms, profit is net sales revenue less all costs of production, marketing, finance, taxes, etc. Profit is generally stated before the payment of dividends or appropriation to RESERVES.

Box-Jenkins forecasting method a forecasting technique using TIME-SERIES ANALYSIS to EXTRAPOLATE past values of a variable. This method has the particular advantage of enabling the statistician to compile error terms for the data. See FORECASTING.

boycott 1. the withholding of supplies of GOODS from a distributor by a producer or producers in order to force that distributor to resell the goods only on terms specified by the producer. In the past, boycotts were often used as a means of enforcing RESALE PRICE MAINTENANCE. **2.** the prohibition of certain imports or exports, or a complete ban on INTERNATIONAL TRADE with a particular country by other countries.

brand loyalty the continuing willingness of consumers to purchase and repurchase the brand of a particular supplier in preference to competitive products. Suppliers cultivate brand loyalty by PRODUCT DIFFERENTIATION strategies aimed at emphasizing real and imaginary differences between competing brands. See ADVERTISING.

brand name the name given to a product by a supplier in order to differentiate the offering from similar products supplied by competitors. Brand names are used as a focal point of PRODUCT DIFFERENTIATION between suppliers.

In most countries brand names must be registered with a central authority to ensure that they are uniquely applied to a single, specific product. This makes it easier for consumers to identify the product when making a purchase and also protects suppliers against unscrupulous imitators. See INDUSTRIAL PROPERTY RIGHTS.

brand proliferation an increase in the number of brands of a particular product, each additional brand being very similar to those already available. Brand proliferation occurs mainly in oligopolistic markets (see OLIGOPOLY), where competitive rivalry is centered on PRODUCT DIFFERENTIATION strategies, and is especially deployed as a means of MARKET SEGMENTATION. In the THEORY OF MARKETS, excessive brand proliferation is generally considered to be against consumers' interests because it tends to result in higher prices by increasing total ADVERTISING and sales promotional expenses. See OLIGOPOLY.

break-even the short-term rate of output and sales at which a supplier generates just enough revenue to cover fixed and variable costs, earning neither a PROFIT nor a LOSS. If the selling price of a product exceeds its unit VARIABLE COST, each unit of product sold will earn a CONTRIBUTION toward FIXED COSTS and profits. Once sufficient units are being sold so that their total contributions cover the supplier's fixed costs, the company breaks even. If less than the break-even sales volume is achieved, total contributions will not meet fixed costs and the supplier will have a loss. If the sales volume achieved exceeds the break-even volume, total contributions will cover the fixed costs and leave a surplus, which constitutes profit. See Fig. 16.

break-up value see ASSET VALUE PER SHARE.

Bretton Woods System see INTERNATIONAL MONETARY FUND.

Buchanan, James M. (born 1919) awarded Nobel Memorial Prize in Economic Sciences in 1986 for his work in public choice theory. While a graduate student at the University of Chicago, he became a zealous advocate of the market order. Professor Buchanan has been recognized as an outstanding authority on public choice theory, which applies methods of economics to subjects that traditionally have fallen within the scope of political science.

Public choice theory seeks to predict how the behavior of individuals in their political roles, whether as voters, taxpayers, lobbyists, candidates for political office, elected representatives, members of political parties, bureaucrats, or judges, can affect the entire community.

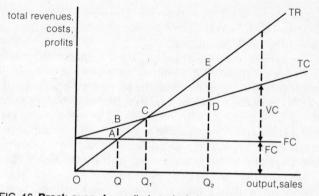

FIG. 16. **Break-even.** A supplier's typical short-term costs and revenues. Fixed costs do not vary with output and so are shown as the horizontal line FC. Total cost comprises both fixed costs and total variable costs and is shown by line TC. Total revenue rises as output and sales are expanded and is depicted by line TR. At low levels of output, such as Q, total costs exceed total revenues, and the supplier makes a loss equal to AB. At high levels of output such as Q_2, revenues exceed costs and the supplier makes a profit equal to DE. At output Q_1 total revenues exactly match total costs (at C) and the supplier breaks even.

budget (firm) a company's predetermined plan, expressed in quantitative or financial terms, for a given future period. The sales budget is generally compiled with the aid of sales forecasts and may show quantities and values of planned sales broken down by product group, area, and type of customer. The linked selling costs budget shows planned selling and advertising costs, and the distribution costs budget shows planned distribution activity measured in packages handled, tonnage, etc., and associated warehousing and transport costs. Once the sales budget is complete, the consequences of planned sales can be spelled out in the production budget, after making allowance for any planned changes in finished goods inventory. The production budget specifies the quantities of various goods to be produced and the planned direct materials, direct labor, and factory OVERHEAD associated with these production plans, with a purchasing budget showing

49

planned purchases of raw materials. The administrative costs budget shows the planned cost of personnel, accounting, and similar administrative departments.

The capital expenditure budget is concerned with planned expenditure on FIXED ASSETS, itemizing what new or replacement assets are to be required during the forthcoming period and making the necessary financing available. The cash budget shows the overall cash position, with cash inflows resulting from planned sales and cash outflows resulting from planned expenditure on raw materials, wages, capital expenditure, etc. so that any anticipated cash surpluses or deficits show up in time to deal with them. Finally, the master budget combines all the former budgets to produce an operating budget showing profit that will be earned and the anticipated year-end position, provided that operations go according to plan. See BUDGETING, BUDGETARY CONTROL.

budget (government) a financial statement of a government's planned revenues and expenditures for a fiscal year. The main sources of current revenues for the Federal Government, as shown in Fig. 17, are TAXATION, principally income and expenditure taxes, and SOCIAL SECURITY TAX payments. The main current GOVERNMENT (PUBLIC) EXPENDITURES are for national defense, nondefense discretionary spending, entitlement programs, other mandatory spending, and net interest owed.

budgetary control a system for controlling costs and revenues by comparing actual results with BUDGET estimates and then taking corrective action where necessary.

budget deficit the excess of GOVERNMENT (PUBLIC) EXPENDITURE over government receipts in any one fiscal year. Government receipts are primarily in the form of TAXATION of individuals and institutions but there are other miscellaneous receipts.

budgeting the process of preparing BUDGETS and exercising BUDGETARY CONTROL. Budgeting encourages managers to think ahead, helps coordinate different functions and departments in a company, defines the responsibilities of individual managers, provides a framework for delegating responsibility, and provides incentives by setting standards of achievement. Budgeting also provides an instrument for control and a basis for modifying plans, where necessary.

Federal Government Receipts and Expenditures [Billions of dollars]

	1987	1988	Seasonally Adjusted at Annual Rates					
			1987	1988				1989
			IV	I	II	III	IV	Iʳ
Receipts	916.5	975.2	944.4	951.0	983.0	975.5	991.5	1,024.0
Personal tax and nontax receipts	405.6	413.4	422.3	404.6	425.0	408.3	415.8	431.6
Income taxes	396.8	404.0	414.1	395.9	415.1	398.6	406.4	422.1
Estate and gift taxes	7.4	7.9	6.7	7.1	8.2	8.3	7.9	7.9
Nontaxes	1.4	1.6	1.6	1.5	1.7	1.4	1.5	1.5
Corporate profits tax accruals	105.8	111.4	107.7	107.2	111.7	113.1	113.8	116.0
Federal Reserve banks	17.7	18.6	17.9	18.4	18.3	19.1	18.5	19.7
Other	88.1	92.9	89.8	88.8	93.4	94.0	95.3	96.4
Indirect business tax and nontax accruals	54.0	56.7	55.0	55.9	55.9	57.1	57.9	58.3
Excise taxes	31.8	33.1	32.2	32.4	33.0	33.2	33.9	33.7
Customs duties	15.4	16.4	15.8	16.5	15.9	16.3	16.8	17.3
Nontaxes	6.8	7.2	7.0	7.0	7.0	7.5	7.2	7.2
Contributions for social insurance	351.0	393.7	359.4	383.4	390.3	397.0	404.0	418.2
Expenditures	1,074.2	1,117.6	1,104.9	1,106.1	1,116.3	1,099.0	1,149.0	1,182.5
Purchases of goods and services	382.0	381.0	391.4	377.7	382.2	367.7	396.3	397.8
National defense	295.3	298.4	299.2	298.4	298.8	294.3	301.9	299.8
Nondefense	86.7	82.6	92.2	79.3	83.4	73.4	94.3	98.1
Transfer payments	414.2	440.1	422.5	434.4	437.6	440.7	447.5	460.5
To persons	402.0	427.2	406.1	422.9	426.5	428.3	430.9	448.8
To foreigners	12.2	12.9	16.4	11.5	11.0	12.5	16.6	11.7

FIG. 17. **Budget (government).** The US budget for 1986—1987.
Source: *Economic Report of the President January 1989.*

Federal Government Receipts and Expenditures [Billions of dollars] (Continued)

	1987	1988	1987 IV	Seasonally Adjusted at Annual Rates 1988 I	II	III	IV	1989 I^p
Grants-in-aid to State and local governments	102.7	111.5	101.4	111.1	110.4	111.5	113.0	118.9
Net interest paid	143.0	153.9	149.5	149.9	152.1	154.9	158.9	168.9
Interest paid	162.5	174.4	168.4	172.5	171.8	174.3	179.1	188.4
To persons and business	138.4	146.7	143.8	146.0	145.0	146.5	149.5	157.0
To foreigners	24.1	27.7	24.6	26.6	26.8	27.8	29.6	31.4
Less: Interest received by government	19.4	20.5	18.9	22.6	19.8	19.4	20.2	19.5
Subsidies less current surplus of government enterprises	32.4	31.1	39.7	33.0	34.0	24.1	33.3	36.3
Subsidies	30.8	28.6	37.6	29.6	32.5	16.8	35.4	34.6
Less: Current surplus of government enterprises	−1.6	−2.5	−2.1	−3.3	−1.5	−7.3	2.1	−1.8
Less: Wage accruals less disbursements	0	0	−.2	0	0	0	0	0
Surplus or deficit (−), national income and product accounts	−157.8	−142.3	−160.4	−155.1	−133.3	−123.5	−157.5	−158.5
Social insurance funds	27.5	53.2	34.9	44.8	49.8	56.0	62.1	61.3
Other	−185.3	−195.5	−195.3	−199.8	−183.1	−179.5	−219.6	−219.7

budget line a line showing the alternative combinations of goods that can be purchased by a consumer with a given income facing given prices. See Fig. 18. See also CONSUMER EQUILIBRIUM, REVEALED PREFERENCE THEORY, PRICE EFFECT.

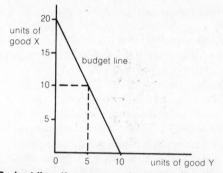

FIG. 18. **Budget line.** If a consumer has an income of $10 and the price of good X is 50 cents and the price of good Y is $1, the consumer can buy 20 units of X or 10 units of Y, or some combination of both, for example, 10 units of X and 5 units of Y. The slope of the budget line measures the relative prices of the two goods.

budget surplus a surplus of tax receipts over GOVERNMENT EXPENDITURE. Budget surpluses may be used as instruments of FISCAL POLICY to reduce the level of AGGREGATE DEMAND by retiring debt in the economy. See BUDGET DEFICIT.

buffer stock a stock of a COMMODITY (copper, sugar, etc.) held by a business oganization or government as a means of regulating the price of that commodity. An official price for the commodity is established and if the open-market price falls below this because there is excess supply at the fixed price, the authorities will buy the surplus and add it to the buffer stock in order to force the price back up. By contrast, if the open-market price rises above the fixed price because there is excess demand at the fixed price, the authorities will sell some of their buffer stock in order to bring the price down. Through this mechanism the price of the commodity can be stabilized over time, avoiding erratic, short-term fluctuations in price. However, if the official price is set at too high a level, this will encourage oversupply in the long run and result in expenses of stockpiling; if the official price is set at too low a level, this will discourage supply in the long run and lead to shortages. See also INTERNATIONAL COMMODITY AGREEMENT, PRICE SUPPORT.

built-in stabilizers see AUTOMATIC STABILIZERS.

bull see BEAR.

bullion silver and gold coins and bars. Bullion serves as a STORE OF VALUE, and government holdings of bullion form part of the country's INTERNATIONAL RESERVES.

Bundesbank the CENTRAL BANK of Germany.

burden of debt interest charges on DEBT that arise as a result of borrowing by individuals, companies, and governments.

In the case of governments, interest charges on the NATIONAL DEBT are paid for out of TAXATION and other receipts. The term "burden of debt" seems to imply that government borrowing is bad insofar as it passes on financial obligations from present, overspending generations to future generations. However, the fundamental point is that the interest paid on the national debt is a TRANSFER PAYMENT and so, according to many economists, *does not* represent a net reduction in the capacity of the economy to provide goods and services, as long as most of the debt is owed to domestic citizens. When interest payments on the debt rise faster than national output, however, government borrowing and taxation may lead to inflation, transfer of resources from the private to the public sector, and damping of incentives to work, save, and invest. Finally, the overhang of a large debt constrains rational decision-making. This is because politicians are opposed to budget deficits, but are never inclined to discuss tax increases openly. See NATIONAL DEBT.

business a supplier of goods and services. The term can also denote a company. In economic theory, businesses play two roles. On the one hand they enter the marketplace as producers of goods and services bought by HOUSEHOLDS; on the other hand they buy factor inputs from households in order to produce those goods and services. The term "businesses" is used primarily in macro (national income) analysis, whereas the term "firms" or "companies" is used primarily in micro (supply and demand) analysis. See also CIRCULAR FLOW OF NATIONAL INCOME MODEL.

business cycle fluctuations in the level of economic activity, alternating between periods of depression and boom conditions.

The business cycle is characterized by four phases (see Fig. 19): (a) DEPRESSION a period of rapidly falling AGGREGATE DEMAND accompanied by very low levels of output and heavy unemployment; (b) RECOVERY an upturn in aggregate demand accompanied by rising output and a reduction in unemployment; (c) BOOM aggregate demand reaches and then exceeds sustainable output levels. Full employment is reached, and the emergence of excess demand causes the general price level to increase; and (d) RECESSION the boom comes to an end and is followed by recession. Aggregate demand falls, initially bringing with it modest falls in output and employment, but as demand continues to contract, the onset of depression.

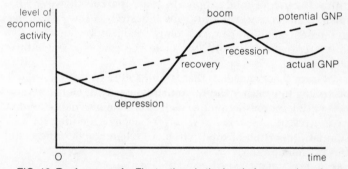

FIG. 19. **Business cycle.** Fluctuations in the level of economic activity.

What causes the economy to fluctuate in this way? There are many complex causes. A succinct Keynesian explanation follows:

One prominent factor is the volatility of FIXED INVESTMENT and INVENTORY INVESTMENT expenditures (the investment cycle). At the top of the cycle, income begins to level off, and investment in new supply capacity finally catches up with demand (see ACCELERATOR). This causes a reduction in INDUCED INVESTMENT and, via contracting MULTIPLIER effects, leads to a fall in national income that reduces investment even further. At the bottom of the depression, investment may rise exogenously (due, for example, to the introduction of new technologies) or through

55

the revival of REPLACEMENT INVESTMENT. In this case, the increase in investment spending will lead, via expansionary multiplier effects, to an increase in national income and a greater volume of induced investment.

Monetarist economists have insisted that change in the money supply is the principal cause of fluctuation. They have recommended that the money supply changes should regularly be the same—an amount equal to the average rate of increase of the gross national product. This is the so-called Friedman Rule.

See also DEMAND MANAGEMENT, STABILIZATION POLICY.

buyer see CONSUMER.

buyer concentration an element of MARKET STRUCTURE that refers to the number and size distribution of buyers in a market. In most markets, buyers are numerous, with each purchasing only a tiny fraction of total supply. In some markets, however, most notably in INTERMEDIATE GOODS industries, a few large buyers purchase a significant proportion of total supply. Such situations are described as OLIGOPSONY, or in the case of a single buyer, MONOPSONY.

Market theory predicts that MARKET PERFORMANCE will differ according to whether there are many buyers in the market, each accounting for only a minute fraction of total purchases (PERFECT COMPETITION), or only a few buyers, each accounting for a substantial proportion of total purchases (oligopsony), or as a single buyer (monopsony).

See COUNTERVAILING POWER.

buyer's market a SHORT TERM market situation in which there is EXCESS SUPPLY of goods or services at current prices, which forces prices down to the advantage of the buyer. Compare SELLER'S MARKET.

by-product a product secondary to the main product emerging from a production process. For example, the refining of crude oil to produce petroleum generates a range of by-products, such as bitumen, naphtha, and creosote.

C

calculus see DIFFERENTIAL CALCULUS.

call money interest-bearing loans, often made to brokerage firms, on which repayment may be demanded at any time.

Cambridge equation see QUANTITY THEORY OF MONEY.

capacity 1. the maximum amount of output a company or industry is physically capable of producing, given the fullest and most efficient use of its existing plant. In microeconomic theory, the concept of *full capacity* is specifically related to the cost structures of companies and industries. Industry output is maximized, that is, full capacity is attained, when all companies produce at the minimum point on their long-term average total cost curves (see PERFECT COMPETITION). If they fail to produce at this point, the result is EXCESS CAPACITY.

 2. in macroeconomics, capacity refers to POTENTIAL GROSS NATIONAL PRODUCT. The percentage relationship of actual output in the economy to capacity, that is, potential national income, shows capacity utilization. See also MONOPOLISTIC COMPETITION.

capital the contribution to productive activity made by investment in *physical capital* (for example, factories, offices, machinery, tools) and in HUMAN CAPITAL (for example, general education, vocational training). Capital is one of the three main FACTORS OF PRODUCTION, the other two being LABOR and NATURAL RESOURCES. Physical and human capital makes a significant contribution toward ECONOMIC GROWTH.

 See CAPITAL ACCUMULATION, CAPITAL STOCK, CAPITAL WIDENING, CAPITAL DEEPENING.

capital account 1. the section of the NATIONAL INCOME ACCOUNTS that records INVESTMENT expenditure by government on infrastructure, such as roads, hospitals, and schools; and investment expenditure by the private sector on plant and machinery.

CAPITAL ACCUMULATION

2. the section of the BALANCE OF PAYMENTS accounts that records movements of funds associated with purchase or sale of long-term assets and borrowing or lending by the private sector.

capital accumulation or **capital formation** 1. the process of adding to the net physical CAPITAL STOCK of an economy in an attempt to achieve greater total output. Capital accumulation has been a weighty concern for economists throughout modern history. In general, economists have regarded capital formation in two ways: (1) expansion of the productive potential of society or (2) a process that transforms the technical and productive organization of the economy.

A great deal of economic theory has been devoted to examination of the social, political, and economic conditions necessary to launch sustained economic growth.

A branch of economics called DEVELOPMENT ECONOMICS devotes much of its analysis to determining appropriate rates of capital accumulation, type of capital required, and types of investment projects to maximize development in underdeveloped countries (see DEVELOPING COUNTRY). In developed countries, the RATE OF INTEREST influences SAVINGS and INVESTMENT (capital accumulation) decisions to a greater or lesser degree in the private sector (see KEYNESIAN ECONOMICS) and can therefore be indirectly influenced by government. Government itself invests in the economy's INFRASTRUCTURE. The nature of capital accumulation, whether CAPITAL WIDENING or CAPITAL DEEPENING, is also of considerable importance. See also CAPITAL CONSUMPTION, INVENTION, INNOVATION, CAPITAL-OUTPUT RATIO.

2. the process of increasing the internally available CAPITAL of a particular company by retaining earnings to add to RESERVES.

capital allowances standard allowances for TAXATION purposes against expenditure on FIXED ASSETS by a company in lieu of DEPRECIATION. A business may choose its own rates of depreciation for fixed assets, which may differ from the statutory capital allowances. Capital allowances may also be varied by the government as a tool of FISCAL POLICY to encourage or discourage capital INVESTMENT. See CAPITAL GOODS, DEPRECIATION(2).

capital appreciation see APPRECIATION(2).

capital asset pricing model a method of computing the cost of a FINANCIAL SECURITY that specifically identifies and measures the single-period risk factor within a PORTFOLIO holding. In this respect the capital asset pricing model may be viewed as a share price valuation model in which the major factors of short-term share price determination are explained. The expected RATE OF RETURN on a particular investment has two constituent components. The first is the risk-free percentage return that could be obtained from, say, TREASURY BILLS. The second component is the risk return associated with an investment. Risk itself can be split into SYSTEMATIC RISK and NONSYSTEMATIC RISK. This relationship between risk and return is shown in Fig. 20.

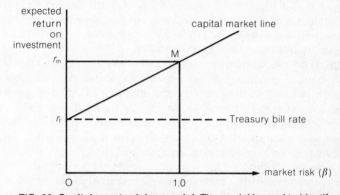

FIG. 20. **Capital asset pricing model.** The model is used to identify the market risk factor for the expected rate of investment. See entry.

The total expected return on an investment is Or_m, but risk only attaches to other than gilt-edged securities, which is why the capital market line intercepts the vertical axis at r_f. The capital market line shows how, in a competitive market, the additional risk premium varies in direct proportion to β, known as the BETA COEFFICIENT. At point M in the figure there is perfect correlation between movements in the market generally, as detailed by a broad market index, and a particular investment. Therefore, $\beta = 1$ at point M. Where there is no risk, as in Treasury bills, $\beta = 0$. β is a measure of systematic, or market, risk because investors have it within their power to diversify away nonsystematic, or specific, risk to almost zero because of the random nature of such events. Specific risk is sometimes referred to as *diversifiable risk* and market risk as *nondiversifiable risk.* It is possible to estimate the beta coefficient of a security from published information.

See also EFFICIENT MARKET HYPOTHESIS, RANDOM WALK.

capital budgeting the planning and control of CAPITAL expenditure within a company. Capital budgeting involves a search for suitable investment opportunities, evaluating particular investment projects, raising LONG-TERM CAPITAL to finance investments; assessing the COST OF CAPITAL, dealing with CAPITAL RATIONING problems, applying suitable expenditure controls to ensure that investment outlays conform with the expenditures authorized, and ensuring that adequate funds are available when required for investments. See PAYBACK PERIOD, INVESTMENT, MARGINAL EFFICIENCY OF CAPITAL.

capital consumption the reduction in a country's CAPITAL STOCK incurred in producing a year's GROSS NATIONAL PRODUCT (GNP). In order to maintain or increase the next year's GNP, a proportion of new INVESTMENT must be devoted to replacing worn-out and obsolete capital stock. Effectively, capital consumption represents the aggregate of DEPRECIATION charges of all businesses for a year, plus damage to capital equipment.

capital deepening an increase in the CAPITAL input in the economy (see ECONOMIC GROWTH) at a *faster* rate than the increase in the LABOR input so that proportionally more capital to labor is used to produce national output. See CAPITAL WIDENING, CAPITAL-LABOR RATIO, PRODUCTIVITY.

capital employed see LONG-TERM CAPITAL EMPLOYED.

capital expenditure see INVESTMENT.

capital formation see CAPITAL ACCUMULATION.

capital gain the surplus realized when an ASSET (home, common stock, etc.) is sold at a higher price than was originally paid for it. Because of INFLATION it is important to distinguish between NOMINAL VALUES and REAL VALUES. After allowing for the effects of inflation, what appears to be a large nominal gain may turn out to be a very small real gain. Furthermore, in an ongoing business, provision has to be made for the REPLACEMENT COST of assets, which can be much higher than the HISTORIC COST of the assets being sold. See CAPITAL GAINS TAX, CAPITAL LOSS, REVALUATION PROVISION, APPRECIATION(2).

capital gains tax a TAX on the surplus obtained from the sale of an ASSET for more than was originally paid for it. Because a capital gains tax is generally levied on the nominal CAPITAL GAIN in a period of sustained INFLATION, it can seriously overtax companies whose real gains, after allowing for the high REPLACEMENT COST of assets, are considerably smaller than their nominal gains.

capital gearing or **leverage** the proportion of fixed-interest DEBT CAPITAL to equity capital employed in financing a company. When a company raises most of the funds it requires by issuing stock and uses few fixed-interest loans, it has low leverage. When a company raises most of the funds it needs from fixed-interest loans and few funds from shareholders, it is highly leveraged.

Leveraging is important to company shareholders because fixed-interest charges on loans have the effect of gearing up or down the eventual residual return to shareholders from trading profits. When the trading return on total funds invested exceeds the interest rate on loans, any residual surplus accrues to shareholders and enhances their return. On the other hand, when the average return on total funds invested is less than interest rates, interest still has to be paid and this has the effect of reducing the residual return to shareholders. Compare two companies, one financed solely from equity capital (*unleveraged*) and another that raises half its capital from fixed-interest loans on which it must pay 10% interest (*highly leveraged*). Figure 21 shows how returns to shareholders vary more violently when a company is highly leveraged.

The extent to which a company can employ fixed-interest capital as a source of long-term funds depends to a large extent on the stability of its profits over time. For example, large retailing companies whose profits tend to vary little from year to year tend to be more highly leveraged than, say, mining companies whose profit record is more volatile. See JUNK BOND.

capital goods the long-lasting *durable goods*, such as machine tools and furnaces, that are used as FACTOR INPUTS in the production of other products, as opposed to being used directly by consumers. See CAPITAL, CONSUMER GOODS, PRODUCER GOODS.

CAPITAL INFLOW

	Firm A: unleveraged	Firm B: highly leveraged
Common Shares	$1,000	500
Fixed interest loans	—	500
Total capital employed	1,000	1,000

Year 1 trading profit = 15% on total capital employed

Trading profit	150	150
Less loan interest (at 10%)	—	50
Net profit	150	100
Return to shareholders:	$\frac{150}{1,000} = 15\%$	$\frac{100}{500} = 20\%$

Year 2 trading profit = 7% on total capital employed

Trading profit	70	70
Less loan interest (at 10%)	—	50
Net profit	70	20
Return to shareholders:	$\frac{70}{1,000} = 7\%$	$\frac{20}{500} = 4\%$

FIG. 21. **Capital gearing** or **leverage.** Returns to company A from ungeared long-term capital, and to company B from high-geared capital.

capital inflow a movement of funds into the domestic economy from abroad, representing either the purchase of domestic FINANCIAL SECURITIES and physical ASSETS by foreigners, or the borrowing of foreign funds by domestic residents.

Capital inflows involve receipt of money by one country, the host, from one or more foreign countries, the source countries. There are many reasons for the transfer of funds between nations:

(a) foreign direct INVESTMENT by MULTINATIONAL FIRMS in physical assets, such as establishment of local manufacturing plant.

(b) the purchase of financial securities in the host country that are considered to be attractive PORTFOLIO investments.

(c) host-government borrowing from other governments or international banks to alleviate short-term BALANCE OF PAYMENTS deficits.

(d) SPECULATION about the future RATE OF EXCHANGE of the host country currency and interest rates, expectation of an appreciation of the currency leading to a capital inflow as speculators hope to make a capital gain after the APPRECIATION of the currency.

By contrast, a CAPITAL OUTFLOW is the payment of money from one country to another for the kinds of reasons already mentioned. See also FOREIGN INVESTMENT, HOT MONEY.

capital-intensive company/industry a company or industry that produces its output of goods or services using proportionately large inputs of CAPITAL equipment and relatively small amounts of LABOR. The proportions of capital and labor a company uses in production depends mainly on the relative prices of labor and capital inputs and their relative productivities. This in turn depends on the degree of standardization of the product. Where standardized products are sold in large quantities, it is possible to employ large-scale capital-intensive production methods that facilitate ECONOMIES OF SCALE. Aluminum smelting, oil refining, and steel production are examples of capital-intensive industries. See MASS PRODUCTION, CAPITAL-LABOR RATIO.

capitalism see PRIVATE ENTERPRISE ECONOMY.

capital-labor ratio the proportion of CAPITAL to LABOR inputs in an economy. If capital inputs in the economy increase over time at the same rate as the labor input, the capital-labor ratio remains unchanged (see CAPITAL WIDENING). If capital inputs increase at a faster rate than the labor input, CAPITAL DEEPENING takes place. The capital-labor ratio is one element in the process of ECONOMIC GROWTH. See AUTOMATION.

capital loss the deficit realized when an ASSET (home, common stock, and the like) is sold at a lower price than was originally paid for it. Compare CAPITAL GAIN.

capital market the market for long-term company bonds and stocks and government bonds. The capital market together with the MONEY MARKET, which provides short-term funds, are the main sources of external finance for business and government. The financial institutions involved in the capital market may include COMMERCIAL BANKS, savings banks, INSURANCE COMPANIES, PENSION FUNDS, UNIT TRUSTS, and INVESTMENT BANKS.

New equity capital is most frequently raised through issuing houses or investment banking companies, which arrange for the sale of shares on behalf of client companies. Shares can be issued in a variety of ways, including: directly to the general public at an arranged fixed price; a TENDER, in which the issue price is determined by averaging out the bid prices offered by prospective purchasers of the stock subject to a minimum price bid; a RIGHTS ISSUE of shares to existing shareholders at a fixed price; placement of the shares at an arranged price with selected investors, often institutional investors. See STOCK EXCHANGE.

capital movements the flows of FOREIGN EXCHANGE between countries representing both short-term and long-term INVESTMENT in physical ASSETS and FINANCIAL SECURITIES and borrowing.

capital outflow a movement of domestic funds abroad representing either the purchase of foreign FINANCIAL SECURITIES and physical ASSETS by domestic residents, or the borrowing of domestic funds by foreigners. See CAPITAL INFLOW, BALANCE OF PAYMENTS, FOREIGN INVESTMENT, HOT MONEY.

capital-output ratio a measure of how much additional CAPITAL is required to produce each extra unit of OUTPUT or, put the other way around, the amount of extra output produced by each unit of added capital. The capital-output ratio indicates how efficient new INVESTMENT is in contributing to ECONOMIC GROWTH. Assuming, for example, a 4:1 capital-output ratio, four units of extra investment enable national output to grow by one unit. If the capital-output ratio is 2:1, each two units of extra investment expand national income by one unit. See CAPITAL ACCUMULATION, PRODUCTIVITY.

capital rationing a situation in which a company selects an annual capital budget that is less than the amount required to undertake all INVESTMENTS promising a rate of return above the cost of capital. For example, if a firm requires a minimum of 20% return on any investment, then *all* the appropriate investment opportunities available to the firm that promise a return of 20% or more may involve a total expenditure of, say, $10 million. However, if the company decides it is willing to spend only $6 million, then it must rank investment opportunities in descending order of rate of return, undertaking those with the highest promised return and rejecting others even though the latter opportunities promise a return greater than the 20% cost of capital. The company is said to be in a situation of capital rationing because it is investing less than the amount dictated by usual PROFIT MAXIMIZING criteria. See MARGINAL EFFICIENCY OF CAPITAL/INVESTMENT.

capital stock the net accumulation of a physical STOCK of CAPITAL GOODS (buildings, plant, machinery, etc.) by a company, industry, or economy at any single point in time (see POTENTIAL GROSS NATIONAL PRODUCT). The transformation of physical quantities—machines, machine tools, etc.—to money sums is a perilous process. The measurements most frequently used for the value of a country's capital stock are from the NATIONAL INCOME and expenditure statistics. These statistics take private and public expenditure on capital goods and deduct CAPITAL CONSUMPTION [see DEPRECIATION(2)] to arrive at net accumulation, which may be positive or negative. The more relevant value of capital stock, from the economist's point of view, is the present value of the stream of income such stock can generate. More broadly, the size of a country's capital stock has an important influence on its rate of ECONOMIC GROWTH. See PRODUCTIVITY, CAPITAL-OUTPUT RATIO.

capital structure the composition of a corporation's long-term capital that reflects the sources of the capital, for example, equity capital and debt capital. See CAPITAL GEARING.

capital widening an increase in the CAPITAL input in the economy (see ECONOMIC GROWTH) at the same rate as the increase in the LABOR input so that the proportion in which capital and labor are combined to produce national output remains unchanged. See CAPITAL DEEPENING, CAPITAL-LABOR RATIO, PRODUCTIVITY.

cardinal utility the measurement of (subjective) UTILITY on an absolute scale. Early economists coined the term UTIL to refer to the satisfaction derived from consuming a unit of a product. because it proved impossible to construct an accurate measure of cardinal utility, HOWEVER, ORDINAL UTILITY measures based on a preference scale replaced the idea of cardinal utility in the theory of CONSUMER EQUILIBRIUM. See DIMINISHING MARGINAL UTILITY.

cartel an extreme form of COLLUSION, particularly associated with the desire of profit-maximizing oligopolistic suppliers to secure JOINT PROFIT MAXIMIZATION. Under a full cartel arrangement, a central administration agency could determine the price and output of the industry, and the output quotas of each of the separate member companies in such a way as to restrict total industry output and maximize the joint profits of the group. Price and output will thus tend to approximate those of a profit-maximizing monopolist. See Fig. 22.

cash see CURRENCY.

cash discount see DISCOUNT.

cash flow the money coming into a business from sales and other receipts and going out of the business in the form of cash payments to suppliers, employees, etc.

caveat emptor a Latin phrase meaning "let the buyer beware." Put simply, this means the supplier has no legal obligation to inform buyers about any defects in goods or services sold. The burden is on the buyer to determine whether the goods or services are satisfactory.

caveat venditor a Latin phrase meaning "let the seller beware." This means the supplier may be legally obliged to inform buyers of any defects in goods or services sold.

central bank a banking system—in the United States, the Federal Reserve System—that is designed to provide money and credit, stable prices, and economic growth. See DEMAND DEPOSIT CREATION, COMMERCIAL BANK, FEDERAL RESERVE SYSTEM, OPEN-MARKET OPERATION.

centrally planned economy or **state economy** or **collectivism** a method of organizing the economy to produce goods and services. Under this ECONOMIC SYSTEM economic decisions are centralized in the hands of the state with collective ownership of the means of production, except labor. The state decides what goods and services are to be produced in accordance with its centralized national plan. Resources are allocated between producing units, and final outputs between customers by the use of physical quotas or money values. See PRIVATE ENTERPRISE ECONOMY, MIXED ECONOMY, NATIONALIZATION, COMMUNISM.

certainty equivalent see DECISION TREE.

ceteris paribus a Latin term meaning "other things being equal." It is widely used in economic analysis as an expository technique. It allows us to isolate the relationship between two variables. For

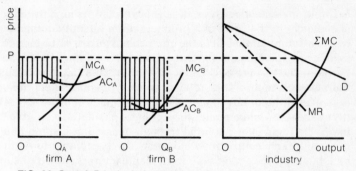

FIG. 22. **Cartel.** D is the industry demand curve, showing the aggregate quantity the combined group may sell over a range of possible prices, and MR is the industry marginal revenue curve. The industry marginal cost curve ΣMC is constructed from the marginal cost curves of the individual companies making up the cartel. For any given level of industry output, the cartel is required to calculate the allocation of the output among member companies on the basis of their individual marginal costs to obtain the lowest possible aggregate cost of producing their output.

To maximize industry profit, the cartel will set price OP and produce output OQ. Quotas of Q_A and Q_B are given to companies A and B respectively where a horizontal line drawn from the intersection of MR and ΣMC (the line of aggregate marginal costs) intersects MC_A and MC_B.

Profit contributed by each company is computed by multiplying the number of units produced by the difference between industry price and the company's average cost at that level of output.

The aggregate profit is then divided among the member companies in some agreed manner but not necessarily, it is to be noted, in the same proportion as actually contributed by each of the individual companies. Disputes over the sharing of aggregate profit frequently lead to breakup of cartels.

Looser forms of cartels like the ORGANIZATION OF PETROLEUM EXPORTING COUNTRIES (OPEC) try to assign output quotas, but they are breached by the members.

example, in demand analysis, the DEMAND CURVE shows the effect of a change in the price of a product on the quantity demanded on the assumption that all of the other things (incomes, tastes, etc.) influencing the demand for that product remain unchanged. See PARTIAL CORRELATION COEFFICIENT, DIFFERENTIAL CALCULUS.

chain store a multibranch retail firm. All types of retailers can be organized to take advantage of the economies of HORIZONTAL INTEGRATION. Unlike single-store retailers, chain stores are able to maximize their sales potential through geographical spread and maximize their competitive advantage by being able to secure bulk-buying price concessions from manufacturers and other suppliers.

Chamberlin, Edward (1899—1967) American economist who, independently and simultaneously with Joan Robinson, developed the theory of MONOPOLISTIC COMPETITION in his book *The Theory of Monopolistic Competition* (1933). Prior to Chamberlin's work, economists classified markets into two groups: (a) perfect competition, in which a company's products are perfect substitutes; and (b) monopoly, in which a company's products have no substitutes. Chamberlin argued that in real markets, goods are often partial substitutes for other goods, so that even in markets with many sellers the individual company's demand curve might be downward sloping. He then proceeded to analyze the company's price and output decisions under such conditions and derive the implications for market supply and price. See also ROBINSON.

cheap money In the late twentieth century, money has not often been cheap, so cheap or cheaper money now usually refers to a fall in real interest rates.

Cheap money policy, when supplemented by government investment, is essentially the Keynesian TRANSMISSION MECHANISM for increasing AGGREGATE DEMAND. See MONEY SUPPLY/SPENDING LINKAGES, TIGHT MONEY.

check a BILL OF EXCHANGE drawn on a bank by the holder of an account with that bank, and payable on demand.

Chicago school a prominent group of economists at the University of Chicago, among the most notable being Milton FRIEDMAN, who have adopted and refined the QUANTITY THEORY OF MONEY, arguing that the money supply should be stabilized. Within the broad limits set by stable money growth, the Chicago school stresses the importance of the market system as an allocative mechanism, leaving firms and consumers free to make economic decisions with minimal government interference. See MONETA-RISM.

chi-square distribution a special kind of PROBABILITY DISTRIBU-TION used in formulating tests of significance for HYPOTHESIS TESTING when we wish to decide whether observed *proportions* in SAMPLES may reasonably be attributed to chance. Areas under the chi-square distribution curve indicate the criterion probabilities concerned. When the observed frequencies in different samples diverge greatly from the frequencies we could have expected—embodied in a null hypothesis—we can conclude that the null hypothesis must be false.

The chi-square criterion may be used to test whether it is justifiable to approximate an observed distribution with a normal curve.

choice because of scarcity of resources relative to wants, the necessity for CENTRALLY PLANNED ECONOMIES and PRIVATE ENTER-PRISE ECONOMIES to choose which goods and services to produce and in what quantities, which resources to be used, and who gets what.

C.I.F. *abbreviation for* cost-insurance-freight, that is, charges incurred in transporting imports and exports of goods from one country to another. In BALANCE OF PAYMENTS terms, such charges are added to the basic prices of imports and exports of goods in order to compute the total foreign currency flows involved. See F.O.B.

circular flow of national income model a simplified exposition of money and physical or real flows through an economy that serves as the basis for macroeconomic analysis. In Fig. 23a, the solid lines show how, in monetary terms, HOUSEHOLDS purchase goods and services from BUSINESSES using income received from supplying factor inputs to businesses. In physical terms, shown by the broken lines in the figure, businesses produce goods and services using factor inputs supplied to them by households.

The basic model can be developed to incorporate a number of INJECTIONS to, and WITHDRAWALS from, the income flow. In

CIRCULAR FLOW OF NATIONAL INCOME MODEL

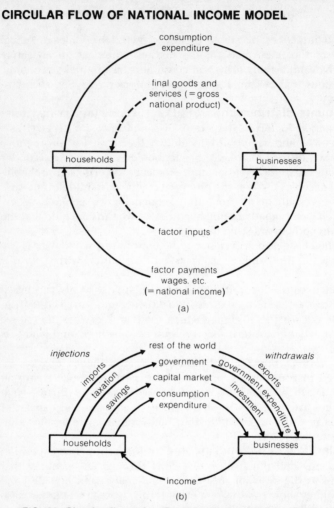

FIG. 23. **Circular flow of national income model.** (a) The basic model of the relationship between money flows and physical flows. (b) A more complex model, incorporating injections to and withdrawals from the income flow.

Fig. 23b, not all the income received by households is spent—some is saved. SAVINGS is a withdrawal from the income flow. INVESTMENT expenditure injects funds into the income flow. Part of the income accruing to households is taxed by the government and serves to reduce disposable income available for consumption expenditure. TAXATION is a withdrawal from the income flow. GOVERNMENT (PUBLIC) EXPENDITURE on products and factor inputs injects funds into the income flow. Households spend some of their income on imported goods and services. IMPORTS are a withdrawal from the income flow. On the other hand, some output is sold to overseas customers. EXPORTS represent a demand for domestically produced goods and services and hence constitute an injection into the income flow. See also AGGREGATE DEMAND, EQUILIBRIUM LEVEL OF NATIONAL INCOME.

City (of London) the center of the United Kingdom's financial system. The City is also a major international financial center and earns Britain substantial amounts of foreign exchange on exports of financial services.

classical economics a school of thought or a set of economic ideas based on the writings of SMITH, RICARDO, MALTHUS, MILL, et al. that dominated economic thinking until about 1870, when the marginalist revolution occurred.

Classical economists were concerned with economic programs and economic justice. They inquired into the causes of increase in national wealth and the conditions that determiuned how income was divided among claimants. They wanted to show how the interplay of separate decisions by workers and capitalists could be harmonized through the market system to generate economic wealth. Their belief in the power of market forces led them to support LAISSEZ FAIRE and they also supported the idea of FREE TRADE among nations. After about 1870 classical economic ideas were augmented as the emphasis shifted to what has become known as NEOCLASSICAL ECONOMICS embodying marginalist concepts.

Classical economists, with the possible exception of Malthus, denied any possibility of UNEMPLOYMENT caused by deficient AGGREGATE DEMAND, arguing that market forces would operate to keep aggregate demand and POTENTIAL GROSS NATIONAL PRODUCT in balance (SAY'S LAW). They argued that business recessions would cause interest rates to fall under the pressure of accumulating savings, thus encouraging businesses to borrow and invest more, and would cause wage rates to fall under the pressure of rising unemployment, thus encouraging businesses to employ more workers.

See LABOR THEORY OF VALUE, KEYNES, PRIVATE ENTERPRISE ECONOMY.

clearinghouse system a centralized mechanism for settling indebtedness between COMMERCIAL BANKS. For example, when a customer of bank A draws a check in favor of a customer of bank B, and the second customer deposits the check in bank B, then bank A is indebted to bank B for the amount of that check. There will be many millions of similar transactions going on day-by-day, creating indebtedness between all banks. The role of the clearing system is to bring together all of these checks, cross cancel them, and determine at the end of each day any net indebtedness between the banks. This net indebtedness is then settled by transferring balances held by the commercial banks at the CENTRAL BANK.

closed economy an economy that is not influenced by any form of INTERNATIONAL TRADE, that is, there are no EXPORTS or IMPORTS of any kind. By concentrating on a closed economy, it is possible to simplify the CIRCULAR FLOW OF NATIONAL INCOME MODEL and focus on income and expenditure within an economy.

In terms of the circular flow, AGGREGATE DEMAND in a closed economy is represented by:

$$Y = C + I + G$$

where Y = national income
C = consumption expenditure
I = investment expenditure
G = government expenditure

By contrast, the OPEN ECONOMY allows for the influence of imports and exports, and here aggregate demand is represented in the circular flow as:

$$Y = C + I + G + (X - M)$$

where X = exports
M = imports

Cobb-Douglas production function a physical relationship between OUTPUT of products and FACTOR INPUTS (LABOR and CAPITAL) used to produce these outputs. This particular form of the PRODUCTION FUNCTION suggests that where there is effective competition in factor markets, the ELASTICITY OF TECHNICAL SUBSTITUTION between labor and capital will be equal to one; that is, labor can be substituted for capital in any given proportions and vice versa without affecting output.

The Cobb-Douglas production function suggests that the share of labor input and the share of capital input are relative constants in an economy, so that although labor and capital inputs may change in absolute terms, the *relative* share between the two inputs remains constant.

See PRODUCTION POSSIBILITY BOUNDARY, CAPITAL-LABOR RATIO, PRODUCTION FUNCTION, CAPITAL-INTENSIVE COMPANY/INDUSTRY, LABOR-INTENSIVE FIRM/INDUSTRY, ISOQUANT CURVE, ISOQUANT MAP.

cobweb theorem a theory designed to explain the path followed in moving toward an equilibrium situation when there are lags in the adjustment of either SUPPLY or DEMAND to changes in prices. COMPARATIVE STATIC EQUILIBRIUM ANALYSIS predicts the effect of demand or supply changes by comparing the original equilibrium price and quantity with the new equilibrium that results. The cobweb theorem focuses on the dynamic process of adjustment in markets by tracing the path of adjustment of prices and output in moving from one equilibrium situation toward another (see DYNAMIC ANALYSIS). See AGRICULTURAL POLICY.

coefficient see PARAMETER.

coefficient of determination a statistical term, usually denoted r^2, that measures the proportion of the variance of a DEPENDENT VARIABLE, such as consumption expenditure, explained by the linear influence of an INDEPENDENT VARIABLE, such as disposable income. If two variables are strongly related with a CORRELATION COEFFICIENT (r) of, say, 0.9 then the coefficient of determination is 0.81. The values of r^2 lie between 0 and 1. It is frequently used in economics to assess the estimated relationship between variables, such as disposable income and consumption expenditure (see Fig. 24).

coefficient of variation a measure of relative variation that ex-

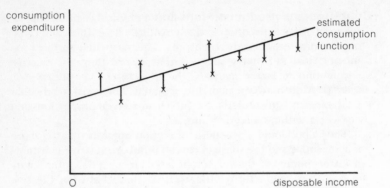

consumption expenditure

estimated consumption function

O   disposable income

FIG. 24. **Coefficient of determination.** The scatter diagram displays the line of estimated consumption function. This is the line that best fits the consumption/income observations recorded. When all the observations lie exactly on the line, r^2 *is equal to 1.*

presses the magnitude of the variation within a group of numerical observations in relation to the group mean, specifically, the STANDARD DEVIATION expressed as a percentage of the MEAN. For example, if five products had prices of $5, $4, $3, $2, and $1, so that their mean price was $3 and their standard deviation was $1.41, then the coefficient of variation would be:

$$\frac{1.41}{3.00} \times 100 = 47\%$$

By using the coefficient of variation, it is possible to compare the variability of several groups of observations, each of which is measured in different units (dollars, yen, etc.), since all the group dispersion measures will be expressed in common percentage terms.

coinage the metallic CURRENCY issued by the mint of the United States Treasury. Coins have become a relatively unimportant part of the MONEY SUPPLY. In our earlier history, gold and silver (bimetallism) were coined and circulated. In the present century, the United States has been on a gold-coin, gold-bullion, and now paper standard with a remote connection to gold.

Gold and silver have been replaced by other metals as the coin material of choice. The federal government has a coinage monopoly, for obvious reasons. Since no coin in circulation is worth as much metal as its face value, the government makes a profit (seigniorage) on coinage.

coincident indicators economic data that tend to move with the business cycle, advancing when business moves, falling back when business moves down.

collateral security the ASSETS pledged by a BORROWER as security for a LOAN, for example, the deed to a house. In the event the borrower defaults on the loan, the LENDER can claim these assets in lieu of the sum owed. See DEBT.

collective bargaining the negotiation of WAGE RATES, conditions of employment, etc. by representatives of the labor force (usually labor union officials) and management. Collective bargaining agreements are negotiated at a number of different levels ranging from local unions and a single factory, hospital, etc. to international unions and an entire industry or trade group. Most commonly, agreements are between a single employer and a single union local. See LABOR UNION, INDUSTRIAL RELATIONS.

collective products also known as collective goods, any goods or services that cannot be provided other than on a group basis because the quantity supplied to any one individual cannot be independently varied. It is virtually impossible to get consumers to reveal their preferences regarding collective goods because rational consumers will attempt to become FREE RIDERS, all understating their demands in the hope of avoiding their share of the cost without affecting the amount they obtain. Consequently, such products cannot be marketed in the conventional way and we cannot use market prices to value them. Many goods and services supplied by government are of a collective nature, for example, national defense and police protection, and here government decides on the amounts of such products to provide and compels individuals to pay for them through taxation. See SOCIAL PRODUCTS.

collectivism see CENTRALLY PLANNED ECONOMY.

collusion an agreement between companies covering their market actions. Successful collusion requires acceptance of a common objective for all companies, for example, JOINT-PROFIT MAXIMIZATION, and the suppression of behavior inconsistent with achievement of this goal, for example, price competition. Collusion may be overt or tacit. Overt collusion may take the form of a written agreement or an oral agreement arrived at through direct consultation between the firms concerned. Alternatively, collusion may take the form of an unspoken understanding arrived at through companies' repeated experiences with each other's behavior over time. See CARTEL, RESTRICTIVE TRADE AGREEMENT.

collusive duopoly see DUOPOLY.

commercial bank a nondefinitive term for a general, all-purpose bank. Such a bank accepts deposits, maintains savings departments, issues mortgages, makes business loans, etc. Some commercial banks now provide stock brokerage services. Commercial banks are the banks most widely used by businesses and the general public. See DEMAND DEPOSIT CREATION, MONETARY POLICY, CLEARINGHOUSE SYSTEM.

commercial paper negotiable notes, bills, etc. drawn to finance trade or other production or commercial activities.

commission payments to AGENTS for performing services on behalf of a seller or buyer. Commissions are usually based on the value of the product being sold or bought. Examples of commissions include salespersons' commissions, real estate agents' fees, and insurance brokers' commissions.

commodity 1. see GOODS. **2.** raw materials rather than goods in general, for example, tea, coffee, iron ore, and aluminum.

commodity broker a dealer in raw materials. See COMMODITY MARKET.

commodity market a market for the buying and selling of raw materials, such as tea, coffee, iron ore, and aluminum. See SPOT MARKET, FUTURES MARKET.

common external tariff see CUSTOMS UNION, COMMON MARKET.

common law the body of law built up over many generations as a result of custom and court decisions interpreting legislation. The legal precedents thus established are followed consistently in subsequent court cases.

common market a form of TRADE INTEGRATION between a number of countries in which members eliminate all trade barriers

(TARIFFS etc.) among themselves on goods and services and may establish a uniform set of barriers against trade with the rest of the world, in particular, a common external tariff (see CUSTOMS UNION). In addition, a common market provides for free movement of labor and capital across national boundaries. The aim of a common market is to secure the benefits of international SPECIALIZATION, thereby improving members' real living standards.

The short-term and medium-term impacts of the formation of a common market are mainly felt through an increase in trade between member countries. TRADE CREATION is typically associated with a reallocation of resources within the market favoring least-cost supply locations and a reduction in prices resulting from elimination of tariffs and lower production costs. (See GAINS FROM TRADE.)

In addition, a common market can be expected to promote longer-term (dynamic) changes conducive to economic efficiency through:

(a) COMPETITION. The removal of tariffs etc. can be expected to widen the area of effective competition; high-cost producers are eliminated, whereas efficient and progressive suppliers are able to exploit new market opportunities.

(b) ECONOMIES OF SCALE. A larger domestic market enables companies to take advantage of economies of large-scale production and distribution, thereby lowering supply costs and enhancing COMPARATIVE ADVANTAGE.

(c) TECHNOLOGICAL PROGRESSIVENESS. Wider market opportunities and exposure to greater competition can be expected to encourage companies to invest and innovate new techniques and products.

(d) INVESTMENT and ECONOMIC GROWTH. Finally, rising income per person, growing trade, increased productive efficiency, and investment may be expected to combine to produce higher growth rates and real standards of living.

The EUROPEAN COMMUNITY is one example of a common market.

common stock shares of ownership, generally with voting rights, in a corporation. Shareholders may receive dividends and distribution of company assets after claims of preferred shareholders and others are satisfied. Generally, holders of common stock elect the corporation's board of directors.

communism the term used to describe a totalitarian society in which the government has a monopoly on political power and, through economic planning, determines the allocation of scarce resources, as found in some of the COMECON countries and China.

In the utopian scheme of economic evolution of Karl Marx, communism was to be the ultimate stage in the development of governments. After successful socialism had overcome the scarcity of resources problem, governments would wither and die, and communism would be at hand.

Recent events in Eastern Europe appear to indicate that people there have a terrible distaste for communism Russian style. What will be next?

company see FIRM.

company location the area in which a company chooses to locate its business. In principle a profit-maximizing company will locate where its production and distribution costs are minimized relative to revenues earned. Often companies are faced with competing pulls of nearness to their market (to reduce product distribution costs), and nearness to their raw material supplies (to reduce materials transport costs), and must try to balance these costs. Some companies have little choice in this regard, service companies being forced to locate near customers, and mineral extraction companies having to locate near material sources. Many companies are relatively footloose and are free to locate anywhere, influenced by the general attractiveness of an area; the quality of its transport, communications, and education infrastructure; skills and reputation of its work force, etc. See REGIONAL POLICY.

company objectives an element of MARKET CONDUCT that denotes the goals of a company in supplying GOODS and SERVICES. In the traditional THEORY OF THE FIRM and the THEORY OF MARKETS, in order to facilitate intermarket comparisons of performance, *all* companies, whether operating under conditions of PERFECT COMPETITION, MONOPOLISTIC COMPETITION, OLIGOPOLY, or MONOPOLY, are assumed to be seeking PROFIT MAXIMIZATION. More recent contributions to this body of theory have postulated

a number of alternative firm objectives, including SALES-REVENUE
MAXIMIZATION and ASSET-GROWTH MAXIMIZATION. In these for-
mulations profits are seen as contributing to attainment of some
other objective rather than as an end in themselves. See MANAGE-
RIAL THEORIES OF THE FIRM, DIVORCE OF OWNERSHIP FROM CON-
TROL, BEHAVIORAL THEORY OF THE FIRM, SATISFICING THEORY,
MANAGEMENT-UTILITY MAXIMIZATION.

comparative advantage the advantage possessed by a country
engaged in INTERNATIONAL TRADE if it can produce a certain
good at a lower resource input cost than other countries. Also
called *comparative cost principle.* This proposition is illustrated in
Fig. 25 with respect to two countries (A and B) and two GOODS (X
and Y).

Country	Output of good		Opportunity cost ratio		
	X	Y	X		Y
A	100	100	1	:	1
B	180	120	1	:	$\frac{2}{3}$ (or $1\frac{1}{2}$:1)

FIG. 25. **Comparative advantage.** The physical output of X and Y
from a given factor input, and the opportunity cost of X in terms of
Y. The opportunity cost of producing one more unit of X is 1Y in
country A, and ⅔Y in country B. The opportunity cost of producing
one more unit of Y is 1X in country A, and 1½X in country B.

The same given resource input in both countries enables them
to produce either the quantity of good X or the quantity of good
Y indicated in the figure. It can be seen that country B is absolutely
more efficient than country A, since it can produce more of both
goods. However, it is comparative advantage, not ABSOLUTE AD-
VANTAGE, that determines whether trade is beneficial or not.
Comparative advantage arises because the marginal OPPORTU-
NITY COSTS of one good in terms of the other good differ as be-
tween countries (see HECKSCHER-OHLIN FACTOR PROPORTIONS
THEORY).

It can be seen that country B has a comparative advantage in
the production of good X, for it is able to produce it at a lower
factor cost than country A; the resource or opportunity cost of
producing an additional unit of X is only ⅔Y in country B,
whereas in country A it is 1Y.

COMPARATIVE COST PRINCIPLE

Country A has a comparative advantage in the production of good Y, for it is able to produce it at lower factor cost than country B. The resource or opportunity cost of producing an additional unit of Y is only 1X, whereas in country B it is 1½X.

Both countries, therefore, stand to increase their economic welfare if they specialize (see SPECIALIZATION) in production of the good in which they have a comparative advantage. (See GAINS FROM TRADE entry for an illustration of this important proposition.) The extent to which each will benefit from trade will depend on the real terms of trade at which they agree to exchange X and Y.

comparative cost principle see COMPARATIVE ADVANTAGE.

comparative static equilibrium analysis a method of economic analysis that compares the differences between two or more equilibrium states that result from changes in EXOGENOUS VARIABLES. Consider, for example, the effect of a change in export demand on the EQUILIBRIUM LEVEL OF NATIONAL INCOME as shown in Fig. 26. Assume that foreigners demand more of the country's products. Exports rise and the aggregate demand schedule shifts upward to a new level (AD_2), resulting in establishment of a new equilibrium level of national income Y_2 (at point H). The effect of the increase in exports can then be measured by comparing the original level of national income with that of the new level of national income. See DYNAMIC ANALYSIS, EQUILIBRIUM MARKET PRICE (CHANGES IN).

compensation principle see WELFARE ECONOMICS.

competition 1. a form of MARKET STRUCTURE in which the number of firms supplying the market is used to indicate the type of market it is—for example, PERFECT COMPETITION (many competitors), OLIGOPOLY (few competitors). **2.** a process in which companies strive against each other to secure customers for their products, that is, the active rivalry of companies for customers using price variations, PRODUCT DIFFERENTIATION strategies, etc. See METHODS OF COMPETITION, MONOPOLISTIC COMPETITION, MONOPOLY.

competition policy a policy concerned with promoting effective competition between suppliers by regulating practices that may restrict, distort, or eliminate competition in a market.

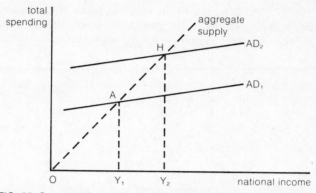

FIG. 26. **Comparative static equilibrium analysis.** The initial level of national income is Y_1 (at point A), where the AGGREGATE DEMAND SCHEDULE (AD$_1$) intersects the AGGREGATE SUPPLY SCHEDULE (AS).

complementary products GOODS or SERVICES whose demands are interrelated (a *joint demand*), so that an increase in the price of one of the goods results in a fall in demand for the other. For example, if the price of tennis rackets goes up, this may result not only in a decrease in the demand for rackets but, because less tennis is now played, a fall also in the demand for tennis balls. See SUBSTITUTE PRODUCTS, CROSS ELASTICITY OF DEMAND.

compound interest INTEREST on a LOAN based not only on the original amount of the loan but the amount of the loan plus previous accumulated interest. This means that over time interest charges grow exponentially, for example, a $100 loan earning compound interest at 10% a year would accumulate to $110 at the end of the first year and $121 at the end of the second year, etc., based on the formula:

$$\text{compound sum} = \text{principal} \; (1 + \text{interest rate})^{\text{number of periods}}$$

concave (of a line on a GRAPH) bulging away from the origin, as in Fig. 27. Concavity is encountered in various areas of economic analysis, most notably in OPPORTUNITY COST analysis (PRODUCTION POSSIBILITY BOUNDARY). Compare CONVEX.

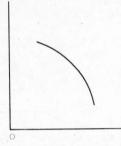

FIG. 27. **Concave.** The characteristic shape of a concave line.

concealed unemployment see DISGUISED UNEMPLOYMENT.

concentration measures the measures of the size distribution of firms engaged in economic activities. The broadest concentration measure is the *aggregate concentration* measure, which considers the share of total activity in an economy accounted for by the larger firms, for example, the proportion of total industrial output accounted for by the largest 200 firms; or the share of total manufacturing output produced by the 100 largest companies. Various size criteria may be used for this measure, in particular, sales, output, numbers employed, and capital employed, each of which can give slightly different results because of differences in capital intensity. Such measures serve to give an overall national view of concentration and how it is changing over time.

Although aggregate concentration measures are useful, they are generally too broad for purposes of economic analysis in which interest focuses on markets and performance in these markets. Consequently, economists have developed several measures of MARKET concentration that seek to measure SELLER CONCENTRATION or BUYER CONCENTRATION. The most common of these measures is the CONCENTRATION RATIO, which records the percentage of a market's sales accounted for by a given number of the largest companies in that market. In the United States it has been customary to estimate the concentration ratio for the four largest companies.

However, the concentration ratio only records seller concentration at one point along the cumulative concentration curve, as Fig. 28a indicates. This makes it difficult to compare concentration curves for two different markets, such as A and B in the figure, where their concentration curves intersect. For example, using a three-company concentration ratio, market A is more concentrated, but using a five-company ratio shows market B to be more concentrated. An alternative concentration index called the HERFINDAHL INDEX gets around this problem by taking into account the number and market shares of all companies in the market. The Herfindahl index is calculated by summing the squared market shares of all companies. The index can vary between a value of zero (where there are a large number of companies of equal size) and one (where there is just one company).

Concentration measures like the concentration ratio and the Herfindahl index are known as *absolute concentration* measures, since they are concerned with the market shares of a given (absolute) number of companies. By contrast, *relative concentration measures* are concerned with inequalities in the share of total companies producing for the market. Such irregularities can be recorded in the form of a Lorenz curve, as in Fig. 28b. The diagonal straight line shows what a distribution of complete equality in company shares would look like, so the extent to which the Lorenz curve deviates from this line gives an indication of relative seller concentration. For example, the diagonal line shows how we might expect 50% of market sales to be accounted for by 50% of the total companies, whereas in fact 50% of market sales are accounted for by the largest 25% of total companies, as the Lorenz curve indicates. The *Gini coefficient* provides a summary measure of the extent to which the Lorenz curve for a particular market deviates from the linear diagonal. It indicates the extent of the bow-shaped area in the figure by dividing the area above the Lorenz curve by the area above the line of equality. The value of the Gini coefficient ranges from 0 (complete equality) to 1 (complete inequality).

In practice, most market-concentration studies use concentra-

CONCENTRATION MEASURES

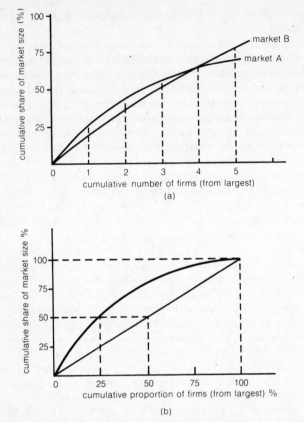

(a)

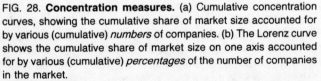

(b)

FIG. 28. **Concentration measures.** (a) Cumulative concentration curves, showing the cumulative share of market size accounted for by various (cumulative) *numbers* of companies. (b) The Lorenz curve shows the cumulative share of market size on one axis accounted for by various (cumulative) *percentages* of the number of companies in the market.

tion ratios calculated from data derived from the census of production.

concentration ratio a measure of the degree of SELLER CONCENTRATION in a MARKET. The concentration ratio shows the percentage of market sales accounted for by, for example, the largest four or largest eight companies. The concentration ratio is derived from the market concentration curve, which can be plotted on a graph with the horizontal scale showing the number of companies cumulated from the largest size, and the vertical scale showing the cumulative percentage of market sales accounted for by particular numbers of companies. See Fig. 29. See CONCENTRATION MEASURES, MARKET STRUCTURE.

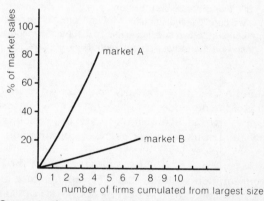

FIG. 29. **Concentration ratio.** Market A is here highly concentrated, with the four largest companies accounting for 80% of market sales, whereas market B has a relatively low level of concentration.

conciliation a procedure for settling disputes, most notably labor disputes, in which a neutral third party meets with the disputants and tries to help them resolve their differences and reach agreement through continued negotiation. See MEDIATION, ARBITRATION, INDUSTRIAL RELATIONS, COLLECTIVE BARGAINING.

conditional distribution a special kind of PROBABILITY DISTRIBUTION showing likely values of the DEPENDENT VARIABLE predicted by a regression equation for a given fixed value of the INDEPENDENT VARIABLE. See Fig. 30.

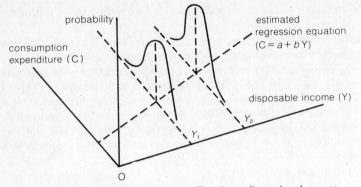

FIG. 30. **Conditional distribution.** The three-dimensional curves show two conditional distributions for consumption expenditure (C), corresponding to two specific levels of disposable income, Y_1 and Y_2, based on the regression equation: $C = a + bY$.

Conditional distributions arise because we cannot expect predictions of the dependent variable based on a regression equation to always give an identical, accurate prediction, since we are merely predicting what, *on average*, consumption expenditure will be for a given level of disposable income. Consequently, it is useful to construct a CONFIDENCE INTERVAL for the true underlying consumption spending that corresponds to a given level of disposable income, such as Y_1. The STANDARD DEVIATION of these conditional distributions forms the basis for calculating the STANDARD ERROR of the estimates, which establishes a confidence interval (see REGRESSION ANALYSIS).

condition of entry an element of MARKET STRUCTURE that refers to the ease or difficulty new suppliers face in entering a market. Market theory indicates that at one extreme, entry may be entirely free with, as in PERFECT COMPETITION, new suppliers being able to enter the market and compete immediately on equal terms with established firms. At the other extreme, in OLIGOPOLY and MONOPOLY markets, BARRIERS TO ENTRY operate that severely limit the opportunity for new entry. The significance of barriers to entry in market theory is that they allow established firms to secure a long-term profit return in excess of the NORMAL PROFIT equilibrium attained under fully competitive (free entry) conditions. See MARKET ENTRY, POTENTIAL ENTRANT, LIMIT PRICING.

confidence interval the range of values or interval within which we can assert (with a suitable probability) that the true POPULATION mean will lie. For example, with a 95% confidence interval, there is a 0.95 probability that this interval contains the true MEAN of the population. The limits of the numerical interval within which we would be 95% confident of finding the population mean can be calculated by means of a formula linking the mean of a random sample, the sample STANDARD DEVIATION, and sample size. If we increase the degree of certainty required from 95% to 99%, the numerical limits arising from the formula become wider. On the other hand, if we decrease the degree of certainty required and calculate 90% confidence intervals, the limits will be narrower.

Confidence intervals like these are generally applicable only to large samples; for small samples, confidence intervals are established by means of the T DISTRIBUTION.

consols United Kingdom government BONDS that have an indefinite life rather than a specific maturity date. People acquire consols (Consolidated Stocks) in order to buy a future nominal annual income without any expectation of repayment of the issue, although they can be bought and sold on the STOCK EXCHANGE. Because they are never redeemed by the government, the market value of consols can vary greatly in order to bring their EFFECTIVE RATE OF INTEREST in line with their NOMINAL RATE OF INTEREST. For example, a £100 consol with a nominal rate of interest of 5% would yield a return of £5 per year. If current market interest rates were 10%, then the market price of the consol would need to fall to £50 so that a buyer would earn an effective return on it of £5/£50 = 10%. The term *consol* today denotes an 1888 bond issue bearing 2.5% interest.

consortium a temporary grouping of independent companies, organizations, and governments brought together to pool their resources and skills in order to undertake a large project, such as a major construction program, the building of new aircraft or a new generation of computer technology, or to combine their buying power in bulk buying.

conspicuous consumption the CONSUMPTION of goods and services not for the UTILITY derived from their use but for the utility derived from the ostentatious exhibition of such goods and services.

A person may buy and operate a Rolls Royce automobile not just as a vehicle for transportation but because it suggests to the outside world something about the owner. That person may wish to be seen as affluent or as a person of taste. This phenomenon, known also as the VEBLEN EFFECT, can be viewed as an alternative to the more usual consumption theories in which the quantity of a particular good varies inversely with its price, a downward-sloping DEMAND CURVE. Conspicuous consumption goods may well have an UPWARD-SLOPING DEMAND CURVE so that the quantity demanded increases with its price. See VEBLEN.

constant a term that takes only a single numerical value, as opposed to a VARIABLE, which can take a range of numerical values. Variables and constants are used in constructing ECONOMIC MODELS. See ECONOMETRICS, HYPOTHESIS TESTING.

constant returns 1. (in the short run) constant returns to the VARIABLE FACTOR INPUT that occur when additional units of variable input added to a given quantity of FIXED FACTOR INPUT generate equal increments in output. With an unchanged price for variable factor inputs, constant returns will cause the short-run unit variable cost of output to stay the same over an output range. See RETURNS TO THE VARIABLE FACTOR INPUT. **2.** (in the long run) constant returns that occur when successive increases in all factor inputs generate equal increments in output. In cost terms this means the long-run unit cost of output remains constant so long as factor input prices stay the same. See MINIMUM EFFICIENT SCALE, ECONOMIES OF SCALE.

consumer or **buyer** the basic consuming/demanding unit of economic theory. In economic theory, a consuming unit can be an individual purchaser of goods or services, a HOUSEHOLD (a group of individuals who make joint purchasing decisions), or a government.

consumer credit loans made available to buyers of products to assist them in financing purchases. Consumer credit facilities include installment credit, BANK LOANS, and CREDIT CARDS.

consumer durables, CONSUMER GOODS, such as houses, cars, and televisions, which are consumed over relatively long periods of time rather than immediately. Compare CONSUMER NONDURABLES.

consumer equilibrium the point at which the consumer maximizes his or her TOTAL UTILITY or satisfaction from the spending of a limited (fixed) income. The economic problem of consumers is that they have only a limited amount of income to spend and therefore cannot buy all the goods and services they would like to have. Faced with this constraint, demand theory assumes that the goal of the consumers is to select the combination of goods in line with their preferences that will maximize total utility or satisfaction. Total utility is maximized when the MARGINAL UTILITY of a dollar's worth of good X is exactly equal to the marginal utility of a dollar's worth of each of the other goods purchased, or, restated, when the prices of goods are different, the marginal utilities are proportional to their respective prices. For two goods X and Y, total utility is maximized when:

$$\frac{\text{marginal utility of X}}{\text{price of X}} = \frac{\text{marginal utility of Y}}{\text{price of Y}}$$

Consumer equilibrium can also be depicted graphically using INDIFFERENCE CURVE analysis. See Fig. 31. See also REVEALED PREFERENCE THEORY, PRICE EFFECT, INCOME EFFECT, SUBSTITUTION EFFECT, ECONOMIC MAN, CONSUMER RATIONALITY.

consumer goods goods purchased to satisfy wants, as opposed to capital goods, which are used to create other goods. Compare CAPITAL GOODS, PRODUCER GOODS.

consumerism an organized movement to protect the economic interests of CONSUMERS. The movement developed in response to the growing market power of large companies and the increasing technical complexity of products. For these reasons, *Consumer*

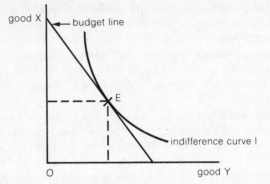

FIG. 31. **Consumer equilibrium.** The optimal combination of good X and good Y is at point E when the BUDGET LINE is tangential to indifference curve I. At this point the slope of the budget line (the ratio of prices) is equal to the slope of the indifference curve (the ratio of marginal utilities), so the goods' marginal utilities are proportional to their prices.

Reports, a monthly magazine, has flourished for many years, and Ralph Nader has become nationally known for his consumer advocacy.

consumer nondurables consumer goods that yield up all their UTILITY at the point of consumption. They include such items as beer, steak, and cigarettes. Compare CONSUMER DURABLES.

consumer price index an index of changes in the prices of goods and services to typical consumers, based on the cost of the same goods in a base period. See PRICE INDEX.

consumer rationality or **economic rationality** the assumption in demand theory that CONSUMERS try to obtain the greatest possible satisfaction from the money resources they have available when making purchases. Because economic theory tends to sum household demands in constructing market DEMAND CURVES, it is not important if a few households do not conform to rational behavior as long as the majority of consumers or households act rationally. See ECONOMIC MAN.

consumer sovereignty the power of CONSUMERS to determine what is produced, since they are the ultimate purchasers of goods and services. In general terms, if consumers demand more of certain goods, then more of those goods will be supplied. This implies that PRODUCERS are passive agents in the PRICE SYSTEM, simply responding to what consumers want. However, in certain kinds of markets, notably OLIGOPOLY and MONOPOLY, producers are so powerful vis-a-vis consumers that it is they who effectively determine the range of choice open to the consumer. See REVISED SEQUENCE.

consumers' surplus the extra satisfaction or UTILITY gained by consumers from paying actual prices for goods that are *lower* than the consumers would have been prepared to pay. See Fig. 32a. The consumers' surplus is maximized only in PERFECT COMPETITION, where price is determined by the free play of market demand and supply forces. Where market price is not determined by demand and supply forces in competitive market conditions, but is instead determined administratively by a profit-maximizing MONOPOLIST, then the resulting restriction in market output and the increase in market price cause a loss of consumer surplus, indicated by the shaded area PP_mXE in Fig. 32b. See ADMINISTERED PRICES, DIMINISHING MARGINAL UTILITY.

consumption 1. the satisfaction obtained by CONSUMERS from the use of goods and services. Certain CONSUMER DURABLE products, for example, washing machines, are consumed over long periods of time, whereas products such as cakes are consumed immediately after purchase. The DEMAND CURVE for a particular product reflects consumers' satisfactions from consuming it. See WANTS, DEMAND.

2. the proportion of NATIONAL INCOME spent by HOUSEHOLDS on final goods and services. Personal consumption expenditures are the largest component of AGGREGATE DEMAND and spending in the CIRCULAR FLOW OF NATIONAL INCOME MODEL. It is one of the most stable components of aggregate demand, showing little fluctuation from period to period. See CONSUMPTION SCHEDULE, GROSS NATIONAL PRODUCT.

consumption function a statement of the general relationship between the dependent variable CONSUMPTION expenditure and the various independent variables that determine consumption, such as current DISPOSABLE PERSONAL INCOME and income from

CONSUMPTION FUNCTION

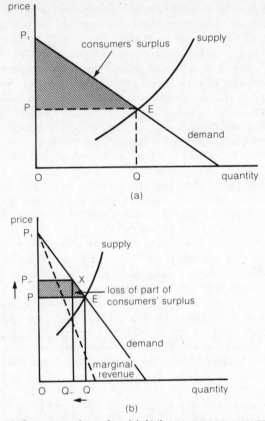

(a)

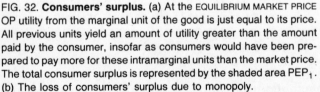

(b)

FIG. 32. **Consumers' surplus.** (a) At the EQUILIBRIUM MARKET PRICE OP utility from the marginal unit of the good is just equal to its price. All previous units yield an amount of utility greater than the amount paid by the consumer, insofar as consumers would have been prepared to pay more for these intramarginal units than the market price. The total consumer surplus is represented by the shaded area PEP_1. (b) The loss of consumers' surplus due to monopoly.

previous periods. See CONSUMPTION SCHEDULE, LIFE-CYCLE HYPOTHESIS, PERMANENT INCOME HYPOTHESIS.

consumption schedule a schedule depicting the relationship between CONSUMPTION and the level of INCOME. Also called *consumption function*. At low levels of DISPOSABLE PERSONAL INCOME, households consume more than their current income (see DISSAVINGS), drawing on past savings, borrowing, or selling assets in order to maintain consumption. At higher levels of disposable income they consume only a part of their current income and save the rest (see SAVINGS). See Fig. 33.

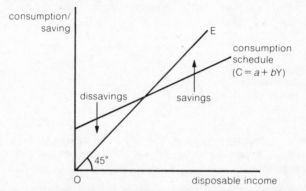

FIG. 33. **Consumption schedule.** A simple consumption schedule that takes the linear form C = *a* + *b*Y, where C is consumption, *a* is the minimum level of consumption expenditure at zero disposable income, and *b* is the proportion of each extra $ (dollar) of disposable income spent. The 45° line OE shows what consumption expenditure would have been had it exactly matched disposable income. The difference between OE and the consumption schedule indicates the extent of dissavings or savings at various income levels. The slope of the consumption schedule is equal to the MARGINAL PROPENSITY TO CONSUME.

contestable market a MARKET in which there is freedom of entry, and exit is costless. Companies are able to recoup their capital costs, less depreciation. Consequently, it is not possible for established firms to earn ABOVE-NORMAL PROFIT, as this will be eroded by the entry of new companies or, alternatively, the mere

threat of such new entry may be sufficient to ensure that estab-
lished firms set prices yielding only a NORMAL PROFIT return. See
WORKABLE COMPETITION, CONDITION OF ENTRY, BARRIERS TO
ENTRY.

contingency table a table that sets out in matrix form the relations between two quantitative or qualitative VARIABLES. This
matrix can then be used to test the strength of any relationship
that exists between the variables. For example, if we wished to
determine whether there is any relationship between a family's
disposable income and the family's means of transport, we would
choose appropriate classifications for income and means of transport, and set up a contingency table like that of Fig. 34.

		Car	Bus	
Disposable income	High	70 (50)	30 (50)	100
	Low	30 (50)	70 (50)	100
		100	100	grand total = 200

FIG. 34. **Contingency table.** The cells of the table report the distribution of results from a random sample of 200 families' choice of
transport.

If we formulate the null hypothesis that there is no relationship
between family income and means of transport, then we would
expect the proportions of families using automobiles and buses to
be the same for each income group. These expected cell frequencies can be calculated by multiplying each cell's row total by its
column total and then dividing by the grand total, which generates the numbers enclosed in parentheses in the table. These expected cell frequencies can be compared with the observed sample cell frequencies and a HYPOTHESIS TEST can be carried out,
using the CHI-SQUARE DISTRIBUTION. If the test value for chi-
square is sufficiently large, the null hypothesis is rejected and we
can conclude that there is a significant correlation between the
two variables. The strength of this relationship can be assessed by
a measure called the *contingency coefficient*.

In this particular case the figures suggest that there is a valid relationship between income and transport mode, with high-income consumers favoring automobile transport and low-income consumers favoring buses.

continuous distribution a graphical presentation of a FREQUENCY DISTRIBUTION in which the frequency or probability of each category or numerical value is portrayed by means of the height of a smooth curve. For example, in the continuous distribution graph in Fig. 35, the variable "weekly income" is depicted on the horizontal axis, and frequencies or probabilities on the vertical axis. As with HISTOGRAMS, the frequencies or probabilities associated with particular categories or numerical values are represented by the corresponding area under the curve.

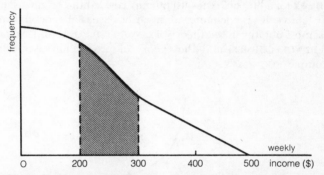

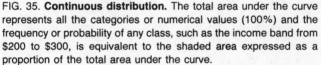

FIG. 35. **Continuous distribution.** The total area under the curve represents all the categories or numerical values (100%) and the frequency or probability of any class, such as the income band from $200 to $300, is equivalent to the shaded area expressed as a proportion of the total area under the curve.

continuous variable a VARIABLE that can take an infinite variety of values, increasing or decreasing in tiny increments along a continuous scale. Compare DISCRETE VARIABLE.

contract a legally enforceable agreement between two or more parties. A contract involves obligations on the part of the contractors that may be spoken or written. For example, a company may enter into an agreement to supply a product to another company at a given future date and on specified terms. Both parties would then be legally bound to honor their agreement to sell and to buy the product.

contract curve see EDGEWORTH BOX.

convertibility the extent to which one foreign currency or INTERNATIONAL RESERVEasset can be exchanged for another foreign currency or international reserve asset.

International trade and investment opportunities are maximized when the currencies used to finance them are fully convertible, that is, free of EXCHANGE CONTROL restrictions.

convertible bonds or **convertible debentures** bonds issued by a corporation that may be converted at the option of the lender into COMMON STOCK at a predetermined share price.

convex (of a line on a GRAPH) bulging toward the origin, as in Fig. 36. Convexity is encountered in various areas of economic analysis, most notably in the theory of CONSUMER EQUILIBRIUM (INDIFFERENCE CURVES) and the theory of production (ISOQUANTS). Compare CONCAVE.

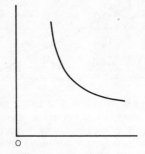

FIG. 36. **Convex.** The characteristic shape of a convex line.

cooperative a form of business owned and run by a group of individuals for their mutual benefit. Examples of cooperatives include:

(a) *worker* or *producer cooperatives*—businesses owned and managed by their employees, who share in the net profit of the business.

(b) *retail cooperatives*—businesses whose membership comprises a multitude of small independent retailers. The prime objective of such a group is to use its combined buying power to obtain discounts and concessions from manufacturers similar to those achieved by large chains.

(c) *consumer cooperatives*—businesses run in the interest of customers holding membership rights entitling them, for instance, to receive an annual dividend or refund in proportion to their spending at the cooperative's stores.

See RETAILING, CHAIN STORE.

coordinates the specific magnitudes used to locate the position of a point or plane within a GRAPH defined by the axes, as in Fig. 37. The vertical AXIS, axis y, for example, we may call price (P). The horizontal axis, axis x (at right angles to the vertical axis), we may call quantity. The point O, where the axes intersect, is called the origin. Point A in Fig. 37 has the coordinates OP_1 and OQ_1.

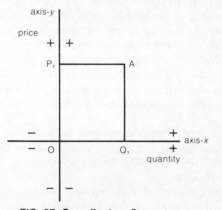

FIG. 37. **Coordinates.** See entry.

Coordinates may have negative magnitudes, as well as positive ones. Negative values of a variable, such as quantity demanded, would lie below the origin on the y-axis or to the left of the origin on the x-axis. Positive values would lie above the origin on the y-axis or to the right of it on the x-axis, as shown by the minus and plus signs in Fig. 37.

copyright the ownership of the rights to publication of a book, magazine, newspaper, etc., giving legal entitlement and powers of redress against theft and unauthorized publication or copying. See INDUSTRIAL PROPERTY RIGHTS.

corner to buy or attempt to buy up all of the supplies of a particular product on the MARKET, thereby creating a temporary MONOPOLY situation with the aim of exploiting the market.

corporate sector the part of an ECONOMY concerned with the transactions of BUSINESSES. Businesses receive income from supplying goods and services and influence the workings of the economy through their use of, and payment for, factor inputs and INVESTMENT decisions. The corporate sector, together with the PERSONAL SECTOR and FINANCIAL SECTOR, constitute the PRIVATE SECTOR. The private sector, PUBLIC (GOVERNMENT) SECTOR, and FOREIGN SECTOR make up the national economy. See CIRCULAR FLOW OF NATIONAL INCOME MODEL.

corporation a form of company in which a number of people and institutions may contribute funds in return for shares of stock in the company. Corporations are able to raise funds by issuing stock to large numbers of shareholders and thus are able to raise more capital to finance their operations than can a sole proprietor or a partnership. Once a corporation is formed, it becomes a separate legal entity apart from its shareholders, and able to enter into contracts with suppliers and customers. Corporations are managed by a board of directors elected by shareholders. The directors must report on the progress of the company to the shareholders at an *annual meeting*, at which shareholders in principle can vote to remove existing directors if they are dissatisfied with their performance.

The development of corporations was given a considerable boost by introduction of the principle of LIMITED LIABILITY, which put a cap on the maximum loss a shareholder was liable for in the event of company failure. This protection for shareholders encouraged many more of them to invest in companies.

Most big firms are corporations, since this is the only practical way of obtaining access to large amounts of capital. Although the shareholders are the owners of a public company, very often it is the company management that effectively controls its affairs.

corporation tax an income tax levied by a government on the taxable income accruing to corporations. The federal income tax on corporations is criticized for establishing rates that are high enough to discourage investment, and because the income of corporations is subject to so-called double taxation of dividends—once at the corporate level and again as personal income. See TAXATION, FISCAL POLICY.

correlation a statistical term that describes the degree of association between two VARIABLES. Two variables that tend to change together are said to be correlated, and the extent to which they are correlated is measured by means of the CORRELATION COEFFICIENT.

correlation coefficient a statistical term (usually denoted by r) that measures the strength of the association between two VARIABLES. Where two variables are completely uncorrelated, their correlation coefficient is 0. Where two variables are perfectly correlated, their correlation is 1. A high correlation coefficient between two variables merely indicates that the two generally vary together—it does not imply causality in the sense of changes in one variable causing changes in the other.

Where high values of one variable are associated with high values of the other, and vice versa, they are said to be *positively correlated*. Where high values of one variable are associated with low values of the other, and vice versa, they are said to be *negatively correlated*. Thus, correlation coefficients can range from $+1$ for perfect positive association to -1 for perfect negative association, with 0 representing the case in which there is no association between the two.

The correlation coefficient also serves to measure the *goodness of fit* of a regression line (see REGRESSION ANALYSIS) that has been fitted to a set of sample observations by the technique of ordinary least squares. A large positive correlation coefficient will be found when the regression line slopes upward from left to right and fits closely with the observations. A large negative correlation coefficient will be found when the regression line slopes downward from left to right and closely matches the observations. Where the regression equation contains two or more independent variables, a multiple correlation coefficient can be used to measure how closely the three-dimensional plane, representing the multiple regression equation, fits the set of data points.

cost-benefit analysis a technique for enumerating and evaluating the total SOCIAL COSTS and total social benefits associated with an economic project. Cost-benefit analysis is generally used by public agencies when evaluating large-scale public INVESTMENT projects, such as major new highways or airports, in order to assess the welfare or net social benefits that will accrue to the state or nation from these projects. This generally means the sponsoring bodies must take a broader and longer-term view of a project than would a commercial organization concentrating on project profitability alone.

The main principles of cost-benefit are encompassed within four key questions:

(a) Which costs and which benefits are to be included? All costs and benefits should be enumerated and ranked according to their remoteness from the main purpose of the project so that more remote costs and benefits are excluded. This requires careful definition of the project and estimation of project life, and consideration of EXTERNALITIES and secondary benefits.

(b) How are these costs and benefits to be valued? The values placed on costs and benefits should take into account likely changes in relative prices but not the general price level, since the general price level prevailing in the initial year should be taken as the base level. Although market prices are normally used to value costs and benefits, difficulties arise when investment projects are so large that they significantly affect prices; where monopoly elements distort relative prices; where taxes artificially inflate the resource costs of inputs; and where significant unemployment of labor or other resources means that labor or other resource prices overstate the social costs of using inputs that are in excess supply. In such cases SHADOW PRICES may be needed for costs and benefits. In addition, there are particular problems of establishing prices for INTANGIBLE PRODUCTS and COLLECTIVE PRODUCTS.

(c) At what interest rate will costs and benefits be discounted? This requires consideration of the extent to which social time preference will dictate a lower DISCOUNT RATE than private time preference because social time preference discounts the future less heavily; and OPPORTUNITY COST considerations that militate against using a lower discount rate for public projects for fear that mediocre public projects may displace good private sector projects if the former have an easier criterion to meet.

(d) What are the relevant constraints? This group includes legal, administrative, and budgetary constraints, and constraints on the redistribution of income. Essentially, cost-benefit analysis concentrates on the economic efficiency benefits from a project and, provided that the benefits exceed the costs, recommends acceptance of the project, regardless of who benefits and who bears the costs. However, where decision-makers feel that the redistribution of income associated with a project is unacceptable, they may reject that project despite its net benefits.

There is always uncertainty surrounding the estimates of future costs and benefits associated with a public investment project, and cost-benefit analysis needs to allow for this uncertainty by testing the sensitivity of the net benefits to changes in such factors as project life and interest rates.

See WELFARE ECONOMICS, COST EFFECTIVENESS.

cost center a group of machines or a factory department or the like under the control of a manager, for which costs can be ascertained and used for purposes of cost control. See also PROFIT CENTER.

cost effectiveness the achievement of maximum provision of goods or services from *given* quantities of resource inputs. Cost effectiveness is often established as an objective when organizations have a rather fixed level of expenditure available to them and are seeking to provide the maximum amount of service in such situations where service outputs cannot be valued in money terms, for example, the operation of a community hospital. When it is possible to estimate the money value of outputs as well as the money value of inputs, COST-BENEFIT ANALYSIS can be applied.

cost function a function that depicts the general relationship between costs of FACTOR INPUTS and cost of OUTPUT in a company. To determine the cost of achieving a particular output, it is necessary to know not only the required quantities of the various inputs but also their prices. The cost function can be derived from the PRODUCTION FUNCTION by adding the information about factor prices. It would take the general form:

COST MINIMIZATION

$$Qc = f(p1\ I1,\ p2\ I2 - pn\ In)$$

where Qc is the cost of producing a particular output Q, and $p1$, $p2$, etc. are the prices of the various factors used, while $I1, I2$, etc. are the quantities of factors 1, 2, etc. required. The factor prices $p1$, $p2$, etc. that a company must pay in order to attract units of these factors will depend on interaction of the forces of demand and supply in factor markets. See EFFICIENCY.

cost minimization production of a given OUTPUT at minimum cost by combining FACTOR INPUTS with due regard to their relative prices. See COST FUNCTION, ISOQUANT CURVE.

cost of capital the payments made by a company for the use of long-term capital employed in its business. The average cost of capital to a company that uses several sources of long-term funds to finance its investments will depend on the individual cost of each separate source of capital, for example, INTEREST on loans, weighted in accordance with the proportions of each source used. See CAPITAL GEARING, DISCOUNT RATE.

cost of goods sold or **cost of sales** the relevant cost that is compared with sales revenue in order to determine GROSS PROFIT. When a company has unsold inventory of finished goods, the cost of goods sold is not the same as purchases of finished goods. Rather, purchases of goods must be added to inventory at the start of the business period to determine the goods available for sale. Then the inventory left at the end of the business period must be deducted from this to determine the cost of the goods sold during the period. See INVENTORY COST.

cost of living the general level of prices of goods and services measured in terms of a PRICE INDEX. To protect peoples' living standards from being eroded by price increases (INFLATION), labor contracts, old age pensions, etc. sometimes contain cost-of-living adjustment provisions that operate automatically to increase wages, pensions, etc. in proportion to price increases. *Cost-of-living a*djustments are known as COLAs. See INDEXATION.

cost-plus pricing a method of arriving at a selling price for a product by taking the actual COSTS incurred in producing and distributing it and adding to them a PROFIT MARGIN. The profit margin is frequently calculated by taking a percentage of actual cost so that the selling price becomes actual cost plus percentage added, or the agreement between purchaser and seller may state that selling price is actual costs plus an agreed fixed amount of profit per unit. Such pricing methods may be found in large capital projects, or in defense contracts in which the length of time of construction or changing technical specifications lead to a high degree of uncertainty in the costing procedure. Cost-plus pricing is frequently criticized for failing to give the supplier an incentive to keep costs down and sometimes an incentive to raise them. See also COST PRICE, FULL-COST PRICING.

cost price a PRICE for a product that just covers its production and distribution COSTS with no PROFIT MARGIN added.

cost-push inflation a general increase in PRICES caused by increases in FACTOR INPUT costs. Factor input costs may rise because WAGE RATES in the economy increase at a faster rate than output per employee (PRODUCTIVITY), or because raw materials and energy costs increase due to world-wide shortages or the operation of CARTELS, for example, oil. Faced with increased input costs, producers try to pass on increased costs by charging higher prices. In order to maintain profit margins, producers would need to pass on the full increased costs in the form of higher prices leading to inflation. Whether producers are able to pass on costs depends on PRICE ELASTICITY OF DEMAND for their products. See INFLATION.

costs the payments (both EXPLICIT COSTS and IMPLICIT COSTS) incurred by a company in producing its output. See TOTAL COST, AVERAGE COST, MARGINAL COST, PRODUCTION COSTS.

countertrade a form of INTERNATIONAL TRADE based on the physical exchange of one product or commodity for some other product or commodity (BARTER) as opposed to the use of currencies.

Companies and dealers resort to countertrade when particular foreign currencies are in short supply or when, because of balance of payments difficulties, countries apply EXCHANGE CONTROLS.

countervailing duty a TAX levied on an imported product (see IMPORTS) that raises its price in the domestic market as a means of counteracting trading practices of other countries. Countervailing duties are frequently employed against imported products that are dumped (see DUMPING) or subsidized by EXPORT INCENTIVES. See TARIFF, IMPORT DUTY, BEGGAR-MY-NEIGHBOR POLICY.

countervailing power the ability of large buyers to offset the market power of large suppliers as in BILATERAL OLIGOPOLY. Large buyers usually have the upper hand in a vertical market chain, for example, multiple retailers buying from food manufacturers, because unless suppliers collude (see COLLUSION), a large buyer is able to play one supplier off against another and obtain favorable discounts on bulk purchases. Provided that competition is strong in final selling markets, countervailing power can play an important role in checking monopolistic abuse.

GALBRAITH uses the phrase "countervailing power" in a slightly different way to refer also to the growth of labor unions and consumer groups in response to the growth of oligopolies. Frequently, with the help of government, weak institutions organize countervailing power to offset the original market power of oligopolists or monopolists. Galbraith cites agricultural policies as an example of government-sponsored countervailing power.

coupon 1. a document that shows proof of legal ownership of a FINANCIAL SECURITY and entitlement to payments thereon. For example, a BEARER BOND certificate. **2.** a means of promoting the sale of a product by offering coupons to buyers of the product that can be redeemed for cash, gifts, or other goods.

coupon rate of interest see NOMINAL (COUPON) RATE OF INTEREST.

Cournot, Augustin (1801—1877) French economist who explored the problems of price in conditions of competition and monopoly in his book *The Mathematical Principles of the Theory of Wealth* (1838).

Cournot concentrated attention on the exchange values of products rather than their utilities and used mathematics to explore the relationship between the sale price of products and their costs, developing the idea of a MONOPOLY price. Cournot is also known for his work on DUOPOLY his analysis showing that two firms would react to one another's output changes until they eventually reached a stable output position from which neither would wish to depart.

Cournot duopoly see DUOPOLY.

covenant a specific condition in a legal agreement or CONTRACT. For instance, a formal agreement between a COMMERCIAL BANK and a CORPORATION to which it is lending money might contain a covenant stipulating a limit on dividend distributions from profits.

crawling-peg exchange-rate system a form of FIXED EXCHANGE-RATE SYSTEM in which the EXCHANGE RATES between currencies are fixed (pegged) at particular values (for example, $1 = £.62), but which are changed frequently (weekly or monthly) by small amounts to new fixed values to reflect underlying changes in the FOREIGN EXCHANGE MARKETS. For example, $1 = £.55, the repegging of the dollar at a lower pound value (DEVALUATION), or $1 = £.70, the repegging of the dollar at a higher pound value (REVALUATION).

credit LOANS and other deferred payment methods made available to consumers and companies to enable them to purchase goods and services, raw materials, and components. See BANK LOANS, CREDIT CARD, CREDIT CONTROLS, TRADE CREDIT.

credit card a plastic card used to finance the purchase of products by gaining point-of-sale CREDIT. Credit cards are issued by commercial banks, hotel chains, large retailers, and others.

credit controls 1. the regulation of borrowing from the FINANCIAL SYSTEM as part of MONETARY POLICY. OPEN-MARKET OPERATIONS are one general means of limiting the expansion of credit. A more selective form of control is consumer installment credit regulation. Under this arrangement the purchase of certain goods is regulated by the authorities, stipulating a minimum down payment and a maximum period of repayment.

2. the control a company exercises over those who owe it money in order to ensure that customers pay their DEBTS promptly and to minimize the risk of bad debts. Credit control involves: (a) assessing the creditworthiness of new and established customers; (b) persuading tardy customers to pay quickly through cash discounts for prompt payment, reminder letters, etc.; and (c) seeking to recover bad debts. The purpose of credit control is to minimize the funds a company has to tie up in debtors, thus improving profitability and LIQUIDITY.

See FACTORING, WORKING CAPITAL, WORKING CAPITAL RATIO.

credit creation see DEMAND DEPOSIT CREATION.

CREDITOR NATION

creditor nation a nation that has been a net lender to or investor in other countries and has accumulated a large volume of claims on those countries. In recent years, the United States has moved from being a major creditor nation toward becoming a major debtor nation.

credit squeeze any action taken by the monetary authorities to reduce the amount of CREDIT granted by COMMERCIAL BANKS and others. Such action forms part of a government's MONETARY POLICY directed toward reducing AGGREGATE DEMAND by making less credit available and forcing up RATES OF INTEREST.

credit unions traditionally, nonprofit associations organized, often, by employees of a single organization to collect savings and put the savings to work by making consumer loans to their members.

creeping inflation the small and continuing increases in the general level of prices in an economy. See INFLATION, HYPERINFLATION.

critical path analysis or **network analysis** a framework for establishing the shortest time in which a project can be completed. At each stage of PRODUCTION of a commodity, for example, whether it be it a bicycle or a nuclear power station, certain activities have to be performed before the next stage of production can be launched. By making a schematic diagram of these operations, it is possible to plan production so that the time taken is reduced to an absolute minimum.

The whole diagram is referred to as a *network* and the *sequential path* that takes least time to achieve the goal is called the *critical path*. Such analysis can help identify problem areas where bottlenecks may occur and action can be taken to remove them before and while the operation is underway.

cross elasticity of demand a measure of the degree of responsiveness of the DEMAND for one good to a given change in the PRICE of some other good.

$$\text{cross elasticity of demand} = \frac{\%\text{ change in quantity demanded of good A}}{\%\text{ change in price of good B}}$$

If a given change in the price of good B, for example, tea, results in some change in the quantity demanded of good A, for example, coffee, then the two goods are SUBSTITUTE PRODUCTS. The degree of suitability is reflected in the cross elasticity measure. If a small change in the price of good B results in a large change in the quantity of good A (highly cross elastic), then goods A and B are close substitutes.

Cross elasticities provide a useful indication of the substitutability of products and so help to indicate the boundaries between markets. A group of products with high cross elasticities of demand constitutes a distinct market whether or not they share technical characteristics. For example, mechanical and electronic watches are regarded by consumers as close substitutes.

Cross elasticities are also helpful in analyzing relationships between COMPLEMENTARY PRODUCTS where interdependence means that a rise in the price of good B will tend to reduce the quantity of good A demanded.

cross-sectional of or referring to SAMPLE observations collected at a particular time. For example, we could collect data on company size and the remuneration of chief executives in the current year (the *cross section*), embracing a wide range of different sized firms, as a basis for investigating the relationship between executive remuneration and company size. Compare LONGITUDINAL.

crowding-out effect an increase in GOVERNMENT (PUBLIC) EXPENDITURE that has the effect of reducing the level of private sector spending. Financial crowding-out of the type described in the caption to Fig. 38 would only occur to the extent that the MONEY SUPPLY is fixed, so that additional loanable funds are not forthcoming to finance the government's additional expenditure. If money supply is fixed, increases in government expenditure requiring additional borrowing will tend to increase interest rates. As the government borrows more, the higher interest rates serve to discourage private sector investment. On the other hand, if additional loanable funds are obtainable from abroad, then additional government borrowing can be financed with little increase in interest rates or effect on private investment.

The term "crowding out" is also used in a broader sense to denote the effect of larger government expenditure in preempting national resources, leaving less for private consumption spend-

CROWDING-OUT EFFECT

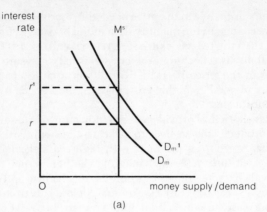

(a)

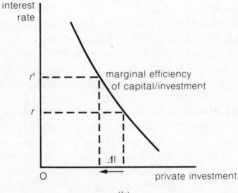

(b)

FIG. 38. **Crowding-out effect.** (a) An increase in government expenditure raises real NATIONAL INCOME and output, which in turn increases the demand for money from D_m to $D_m{}^1$, with which to purchase the greater volume of goods and services being produced. (b) This causes the equilibrium RATE OF INTEREST to rise (from r to r^1), which then reduces—crowds out—an amount of private INVESTMENT ($\Delta 1$).

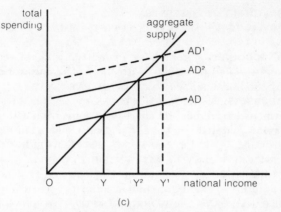

FIG. 38. (continued)**Crowding-out effect** (c) An increase in government expenditure by itself would increase AGGREGATE DEMAND from AD to AD^1, but allowing for the fall in private investment, the net result is to increase aggregate demand to only AD^2.

ing, private sector investment, and exports. Such real crowding out would only occur to the extent that total national resources were fixed and fully employed so that expansion in public sector claims on resources causes the amount left for the private sector to contract. Where unemployed resources can be brought into use, additional claims by the public and private sectors can be met. See MONEY SUPPLY/SPENDING LINKAGES, MARGINAL EFFICIENCY OF CAPITAL/INVESTMENT.

cum dividend (of a particular stock) including the right to receive the DIVIDEND attached to it. If shares are purchased on the stock exchange "cum div.," the purchaser is entitled to the dividend accruing to that stock when the dividend is next paid. Compare EX DIVIDEND.

currency the money issued by the monetary authorities that forms part of an economy's MONEY SUPPLY. The term *currency* is often used interchangeably with the term *cash* in economic analysis and monetary policy.

currency appreciation see APPRECIATION(1).

currency depreciation see DEPRECIATION(1).

currency drain see RESERVES.

currency ratio see MONETARY POLICY, DEMAND DEPOSIT CREATION.

current account a statement of a country's trade in goods (visibles) and services (invisibles) with the rest of the world over a given period of time. See BALANCE OF PAYMENTS.

current assets ASSETS, such as STOCKS, money owed by debtors, and cash, which are held for short-term conversion within a company as raw materials are bought, made up, sold as finished goods, and eventually paid for. See FIXED ASSETS, WORKING CAPITAL, WORKING CAPITAL RATIO, ACCOUNTS RECEIVABLE.

current liabilities all obligations to pay out cash at some date in the near future, including amounts a company owes to its creditors and its BANK LOANS. See WORKING CAPITAL, WORKING CAPITAL RATIO, ACCOUNTS PAYABLE.

current ratio or **acid-test ratio** an accounting measure of a company's ability to pay its short-term liabilities out of its quickly realizable CURRENT ASSETS, which expresses the company's liquid current assets (ACCOUNTS RECEIVABLE plus cash) as a ratio of CURRENT LIABILITIES. See WORKING CAPITAL RATIO.

current-weighted index or **Paasche index** a weighted index number that uses current-year weights. For example, in calculating a PRICE INDEX, the respective quantities of various products bought in the base year would be noted and the prices of products combined to form a single price index number. At some later time the new prices of these products would be combined to form a new price index number, making allowance for changes in the relative quantities of the products bought over time as their prices change.

customs duty a tax levied on imported products (see IMPORTS). Unlike tariffs, customs duties are intended primarily as a means of raising revenue for the government rather than as a means of protecting domestic producers from foreign competition. See TAXATION.

customs union a form of TRADE INTEGRATION between a number of countries, in which members eliminate all trade barriers (TARIFFS etc.) among themselves on goods and services, and establish a uniform set of barriers against trade with the rest of the world, in particular a *common external tariff.* The aim of a customs union is to secure the benefits of international SPECIALIZATION, thereby improving members' real living standards. See GAINS FROM TRADE, TRADE CREATION, EUROPEAN COMMUNITY.

cyclical fluctuation the short-term movements, both upward and downward in some economic variable about a long-term SECULAR TREND line. See Fig. 39. See STABILIZATION POLICY, DEMAND MANAGEMENT.

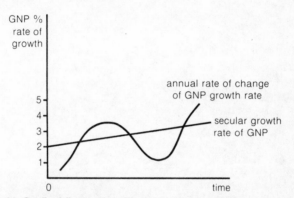

FIG. 39. **Cyclical fluctuation.** The pronounced short-term swings in output growth rates over the course of the BUSINESS CYCLE, about a rising long-term trend growth line for the country's GROSS NATIONAL PRODUCT.

cyclical unemployment the UNEMPLOYMENT that occurs as a result of a fall in the level of business activity during the RECESSION and DEPRESSION phases of the BUSINESS CYCLE.

cyclical variation see TIME-SERIES ANALYSIS.

D

dawn raid a situation in which a potential TAKEOVER bidder for a company buys a substantial share of the target company at current market prices, often through intermediaries, to disguise the identity of the bidder. This position can then be used as a platform for a full takeover bid for all the shares at a stated offering price. See TAKEOVER BID.

dear money see TIGHT MONEY.

death rate the number of people in a POPULATION who die per thousand per year. In 1987, that is, the US death rate was 8.7 people per 1000 of the population. The difference between this rate and the BIRTH RATE is used to calculate the rate of growth of the population of a country over time. The death rate tends to decline as a country attains higher levels of economic development. See DEMOGRAPHIC TRANSITION.

debentures a means of financing companies through fixed-interest LOANS secured against company ASSETS.

In some cases the company may offer a specific asset, such as a particular machine as security for the loan. In other cases lenders are offered security in the form of a general claim against all company assets in the event of default.

Debreu, Gerard (born 1921) winner of Nobel Memorial Prize in Economic Sciences in 1983 for contributing to understanding of general equilibrium theory in an abstract economy.

Debreu has been concerned with the central issue in economic theory: attainment of general equilibrium. In France he worked with Maurice Allais, winner of the Nobel Memorial Prize in Economic Sciences in 1988. In the United States Debreu has collaborated with Kenneth ARROWon study of the existence of an equilibrium for a competitive economy. Debreu has made contributions to economic theory in other areas as well: welfare theory, utility theory, and derivation of demand functions. These contributions have been largely abstract and mathematical in nature.

debt an amount of money owed by one person, company, etc. to another. Debts result from borrowing money to purchase a product, service, or financial asset. Debt contracts provide for eventual repayment of the sum borrowed and include INTEREST charges for the duration of the LOAN. See BORROWER.

debt capital the money employed in a company that has been borrowed from external sources for fixed periods of time by the issue of debentures etc.

debt servicing the cost of meeting INTEREST payments and regular contractual repayments of principal on a LOAN along with any administrative charges borne by the BORROWER.

deciles the numerical values that divide a group of numerical observations into 10 parts, each containing an equal number of observations. Deciles are frequently applied to data arranged in decreasing numerical order. Consequently, one tenth of the observations will exceed the first decile, two tenths will exceed the second decile, etc. Compare QUARTILES, PERCENTILES.

decision tree an aid in making decisions in uncertain conditions that sets out alternative courses of action and the economic consequences of each alternative, and assigns subjective statistical probabilities to the likelihood of future events occurring. For example, a retailer thinking of opening a store whose success will depend on consumer spending (and thus the state of the economy) would have a decision tree like that of Fig. 40.

In order to make a decision, the retailer needs a decision criterion to enable choice of the best of the eligible acts, and since these choices involve an element of risk, we need to know something about the retailer's attitudes toward risk. If the retailer were neutral in attitude toward risk, we could calculate the *certainty equivalent* of the "open store" act using the expected money value criterion, which takes the financial consequence of each outcome and weights it by the probability of its occurrence, thus:

$$0.5 \times + \$40,000 = + \$20,000$$
$$0.5 \times - \$30,000 = - \$15,000$$
$$+ \$5,000$$

which being greater than the $0 for certain of not opening the store, appears to justify going ahead with the project.

However, if the retailer were averse to risk, the expected money value criterion might not be regarded as appropriate, for the retailer might require a risk premium as an inducement to take the risk. Application of a more cautious certainty equivalent criterion would reduce the certainty equivalent of the "open store" branch and might even tip the decision against going ahead.

decreasing returns see DIMINISHING RETURNS.

deficiency payment see INCOME SUPPORT.

deficit financing the financing required of a government when expenditures deliberately exceed income. Also used to refer to the financing of a planned deficit.

deflation a reduction in the level of NATIONAL INCOME and output, usually accompanied by a fall in the general price level (DISINFLATION).

Deflation is often deliberately brought about by the authorities in order to reduce INFLATION and to improve the BALANCE OF PAYMENTS by reducing import demand. Instruments of deflationary policy include fiscal measures, for example, tax increases, and monetary measures, for example, high interest rates. See MONETARY POLICY, FISCAL POLICY.

deflationary gap the shortfall in total spending (AGGREGATE DEMAND) at the FULL EMPLOYMENT level of national income (POTENTIAL GROSS NATIONAL PRODUCT) in KEYNESIAN ECONOMICS. Because of a deficiency in spending, some of the economy's resources lie idle and GNP is below potential GNP. To counteract this deficiency in spending, the authorities may choose to use FISCAL and MONETARY POLICY to expand aggregate demand. See Fig. 41. See also DEFLATION, INFLATIONARY GAP.

degrees of freedom the quantity $n - 1$, when using a SAMPLE of size n to estimate the MEAN and STANDARD DEVIATION of a population. The sum of the deviations from the mean is always equal to zero, because positive deviations from the mean always exactly offset negative deviations from the mean (see AVERAGE DEVIATION). Consequently, if we already know $n - 1$ deviations from the mean, the nth is automatically determined. For example, if five

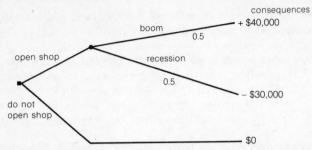

FIG. 40. **Decision tree.** The retailer has two options, *open store* and *do not open store*, and has to consider two states of nature or events that can occur, economic boom or recession. The retailer must assess the likelihood of each of these events occurring and, in this case, based on knowledge and experience, estimates that there is a one-in-two chance of a boom and a 0.5 PROBABILITY of a recession. Finally, the retailer estimates the financial consequences as a $40,-000 profit for the store if there is a boom, and a $30,000 loss if there is a recession.

products have prices of $5, $4, $3, $2, and $1, the mean price is:

$$\$\frac{5 + 4 + 3 + 2 + 1}{5} = \$3$$

and the deviations of these prices from the mean price are $2, $1, $0, −$1, and −$2, respectively. If we knew any four of these deviations from the mean, then the 5th deviation from the mean would be determined. In the above example, if the first four deviations were known, then by summing the first four we can determine what the offsetting final deviation must be:

$$(\$2 + \$1 + \$0 - \$1) - \$2 = \$0$$

Since $n - 1$ of the deviations determine the nth, then effectively the standard deviation is based on $n - 1$ independent quantities, denoted by the term $n - 1$ degrees of freedom.

deindustrialization a sustained fall in the proportion of national output accounted for by the industrial and manufacturing sectors

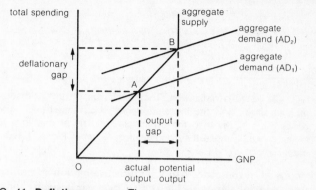

FIG. 41. **Deflationary gap.** The AGGREGATE SUPPLY SCHEDULE is drawn as a 45° line because businesses will offer any particular level of national output only if they expect total spending (*aggregate demand*) to be sufficient to sell all of that output. Once the economy reaches the full employment level of GNP, however, actual output cannot expand further and at this level of output the aggregate supply schedule becomes vertical.

If aggregate demand is at a low level (AD_1), actual output will be determined by the intersection of AD_1 and the aggregate supply schedule at point A. This output is less than potential output, leaving an output gap. An output gap can be removed by the authorities by expanding aggregate demand to the full employment level of aggregate demand (AD_2), where actual output (determined by the intersection of AD_2 and the aggregate supply schedule at point B) corresponds to potential GNP.

of the economy, a process often accompanied by a decline in the number of people employed in industry (compare INDUSTRIAL-IZATION).

There is a well-established trend in advanced economies for the industrial sector to grow more slowly than the service sector, as shown in Fig. 42. For the United States, the share of industry in GDP (gross domestic product) fell from 38% in 1960 to 32% in 1984, whereas the share of services increased from 58% to 66%.

Changes in sector shares may reflect changes in the pattern of final demand for goods and services over time, and as such may be considered a natural development associated with a maturing

DELIVERED PRICING

	Agriculture		Industry		Manufacturing		Services	
	1960	1984	1960	1984	1960	1984	1960	1984
UK	3	2	43	32	32	18	54	66
US	4	2	38	32	29	21	58	66
Japan	13	4	45	42	34	30	42	54
W. Germany	6	2	53	46	40	35	41	52

FIG. 42. **Deindustrialization.** The distribution of gross domestic product shows how the industrial sector in advanced economies grows more slowly than the service sector. The percentages for industry include those for manufacturing. Source: *World Development Report,* World Bank, 1984.

economy. On the other hand, deindustrialization stemming from supply-side deficiencies—high costs, an overvalued exchange rate, lack of investment and innovation—which put a country at a competitive disadvantage in international trade (see IMPORT PENETRATION) is a more serious matter. Deindustrialization in this case often brings with it a fall in national output, rising unemployment, and difficulties in maintaining a desirable balance of payments.

The extent of deindustrialization in the United States was even more marked in the early 1980s because of an artificially high exchange rate, which caused the nation's businesses to lose overseas markets. See STRUCTURE OF INDUSTRY, STRUCTURAL UNEMPLOYMENT.

delivered pricing the charging of a PRICE for a product that includes the cost of transporting the product from the manufacturer to the customer. The delivered prices quoted by a manufacturer might accurately reflect the actual costs of transportation to different areas, or alternatively, discriminatory prices might be used to cross-subsidize areas in order to maximize sales across the country.

demand or **effective demand** the WANT, need, or desire for a product backed by the money to purchase it. In economic analysis, demand is always based on willingness and ability to pay for a product, not merely on a desire for the product. Total consumer demand for a product is reflected in the DEMAND CURVE. Compare SUPPLY.

demand curve a line showing the relationship between the PRICE of a PRODUCT and the quantity DEMANDED per time period, as in Fig. 43.

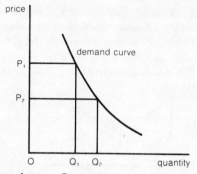

FIG. 43. **Demand curve.** Demand is the total quantity of a good or service that buyers are prepared to purchase at a given price. Demand is always taken to be *effective demand*, backed by the ability to pay, not just based on want or need. The typical market demand curve slopes downward from left to right, indicating that more is demanded as the price falls. Thus, if it falls from OP_1 to OP_2, the quantity demanded will increase from OQ_1 to OQ_2.

Most demand curves slope downward because (a) as the price of the product falls, consumers will tend to substitute this (now relatively cheaper) product for others in their purchases; (b) as the price of the product falls, this serves to increase consumers' real income, enabling them to buy more products (see PRICE EFFECT, INCOME EFFECT, SUBSTITUTION EFFECT). In a small number of cases, products can have an UPWARD-SLOPING DEMAND CURVE.

The slope of the demand curve reflects the degree of responsiveness of quantity demanded to changes in the prices of products. For example, if a large reduction in price results in only a small increase in quantity demanded, as would be the case where the demand curve has a steep slope, demand is said to be *price-inelastic* (see PRICE ELASTICITY OF DEMAND).

The demand curve interacts with the SUPPLY CURVE to determine the EQUILIBRIUM MARKET PRICE. See DEMAND FUNCTION, DEMAND CURVE (SHIFT IN), DIMINISHING MARGINAL UTILITY.

demand curve (shift in) a movement of the DEMAND CURVE from one position to another, either left or right, as a result of some economic change other than price. A given demand curve is always drawn on the CETERIS PARIBUS assumption that all the other

DEMAND DEPOSIT CREATION

factors affecting demand (income, tastes, etc.) are held constant. If any of these factors change, there will be a shift in the demand curve. For example, if income increases, the demand curve will shift to the right, so that more is now demanded at each price than formerly. See Fig. 44. See also DEMAND FUNCTION, INCOME ELASTICITY OF DEMAND.

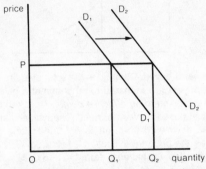

FIG. 44. **Demand curve (shift in).** An increase in income shifts the demand curve D,D, to D_2D_2, increasing the quantity demanded from OQ_1 to OQ_2. The magnitude of this shift depends on the INCOME ELASTICITY OF DEMAND for the product.

demand deposit creation a process by which commercial banks can add to or subtract from the money supply. Because of the fractional reserve system of banking, banks need only keep a portion of their deposits and lend or invest the rest. Assume that the required reserve is 20%. A simplified chart is provided showing the maximum additional money the banking system can create:

Multiplying Capacity of Reserve Money Through Bank Transactions[1] (In dollars)

	Transactions	Deposited in Checking Accounts	Lent	Set Aside As Reserves
Bank	1	100.00	80.00	20.00
	2	80.00	64.00	16.00
	3	64.00	51.20	12.80
	4	51.20	40.96	16.24

5	40.96	32.77	8.19
6	32.77	26.22	6.55
7	26.22	20.98	5.24
8	20.98	16.78	4.20
9	16.78	13.42	3.36
10	13.42	10.74	2.68
Total for 10 banks	446.33	357.07	89.26
Additional banks	53.67	[2] 42.93	[2] 10.74
Grand total, all banks	500.00	400.00	100.00

[1] Assuming an average member bank reserve requirement of 20 per cent of demand deposits.

[2] Adjusted to offset rounding in proceeding figures.

From *The Federal Reserve System: Purposes and Function*, 1963.

This idea can be expressed as a simple formula. An increase of 100% in the system's reserves led to an increase in totaling $500. Let D be the change in demand deposits, E the excess reserves, and R the required reserve ratio. Then

$$D = E \times \frac{1}{R}$$
$$= 80 \times \frac{1}{\frac{1}{5}}$$
$$= 80 \times 5 = 400$$

The demand deposit expansion multiple is the inverse of the required reserve ratio, for example,

$$= \frac{1}{\frac{1}{5}} \frac{1}{R} \ 5$$

This increase in money supply by the banks is the maximum possible. Less money will be created for a variety of reasons. The banks may maintain, for reasons of caution, excess reserves, called leakage into bank vaults. The public may keep more than is customary outside the banking system, called leakage into hand-to-hand circulation. Banks, for whatever reason, perhaps in a business recession or depression, may find themselves unable to lend or invest their excess reserves even when they wish to do so.

See FEDERAL RESERVE SYSTEM.

demand elasticity see ELASTICITY OF DEMAND.

demand function a form of notation linking the DEPENDENT VARIABLE quantity demanded (Qd) with various INDEPENDENT VARIABLES that determine quantity demanded, such as product price (P), income (Y), prices of substitute products (Ps), and advertising (A):

$$Qd = f(P,Y,Ps,A, \text{ etc})$$

Changes in any of these independent variables will affect quantity demanded, and if we wish to investigate the effect of any one of these variables on quantity demanded, we can hypothetically hold the influence of the other independent variables constant (CETERIS PARIBUS), while we focus on the effects of that independent variable. See DEMAND CURVE, DEMAND CURVE (SHIFT IN).

demand management the control of the level of AGGREGATE DEMAND in an economy, using FISCAL POLICY and MONETARY POLICY to moderate or eliminate fluctuations in the level of economic activity (see BUSINESS CYCLE). The general objective of demand management is to ensure that aggregate demand is neither deficient relative to POTENTIAL GROSS NATIONAL PRODUCT, thereby avoiding a loss of output, nor overfull, thereby avoiding INFLATION). See Fig. 45.

demand-pull inflation a general increase in prices caused by a level of AGGREGATE DEMAND in excess of the supply potential of the economy. At full employment levels of output (POTENTIAL GROSS NATIONAL PRODUCT), excess demand bids up the price of a fixed real output (see INFLATIONARY GAP). According to MONETARISM, excess demand results from an increase in the MONEY SUPPLY beyond the rate of increase of the gross national product. See INFLATION, QUANTITY THEORY OF MONEY, COST-PUSH INFLATION.

demand schedule a table listing various prices of a product and

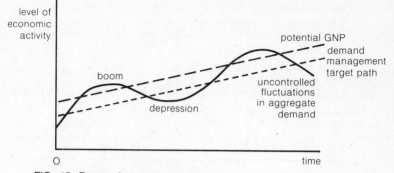

FIG. 45. **Demand management.** The management of aggregate demand in an economy.

the specific quantities demanded at each of these prices. The information provided by a demand schedule can be used to construct a DEMAND CURVE showing the price-quantity demanded relationship in graphical form.

demand theory see THEORY OF DEMAND.

demographic transition a POPULATION cycle associated with the ECONOMIC DEVELOPMENT of a country. In underdeveloped countries, BIRTH RATES and DEATH RATES are both high, so there is little change in the overall size of the population. With economic development (INDUSTRIALIZATION), INCOME PER CAPITA begins to rise and there is a fall in the death rate (through better nutrition, sanitation, medical care, etc.), which brings about a period of rapid population growth. Provided that ECONOMIC GROWTH is consistently greater than increase in population, income per capita continues to expand and eventually serves to reduce the birth rate. (Small families appear to become the norm in society as people seek to preserve their growing affluence.) At this point population growth slows down and may eventually level off. See Fig. 46. See POPULATION TRAP, DEVELOPING COUNTRY.

Most advanced industrial countries have gone through a demographic transition of the kind described above and are today characterized by both low birth and death rates and slowly growing populations.

DEMOGRAPHY

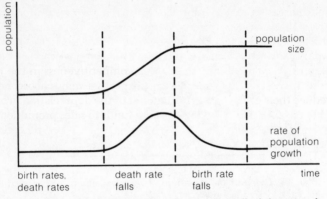

FIG. 46. **Demographic transition.** The leveling-off of the rate of population growth during a country's economic development.

demography the study of human POPULATIONS, including total size; population changes over time as determined by changes in BIRTH RATES, DEATH RATES, and MIGRATION; age and sex distribution of populations; and geographical and occupational distributions. Statistical data on populations are compiled from census data, and records of births, deaths, etc. See DEMOGRAPHIC TRANSITION.

dependent variable a VARIABLE affected by some other variable in a model. For example, the demand for a product will be influenced by its price. It is conventional to place the dependent variable on the left-hand side of an EQUATION and to show it on the vertical axis of a GRAPH. If, therefore, demand is a function of price of a good, P (the INDEPENDENT VARIABLE), demand D is dependent on P. Notationally, this is written:

$$D = f(P)$$

See FUNCTIONAL NOTATION.

depreciation 1. a fall in the value of a CURRENCY against other currencies under a FLOATING EXCHANGE-RATE SYSTEM, as shown in Fig. 47a. A depreciation of a currency's value makes IMPORTS more expensive and EXPORTS cheaper, thereby reducing imports and increasing exports, and so assisting in the removal of a BAL-ANCE OF PAYMENTS deficit. For example, as shown in Fig. 47b, if the yen-dollar exchange rate depreciates from ¥142 to ¥130, this would allow American exporters to reduce their prices by a similar amount, thus increasing their price competitiveness in the Japanese market, although American exporters may choose not to reduce their prices by the full amount of the depreciation in order to boost profitability or devote more funds to sales promotion etc. By the same token, the depreciation serves to raise the price of products imported into the United States, thereby making them less price-competitive than US products in the home market.

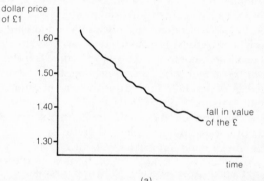

(a)

Exchange rate	UK domestic price of a product	Price of the UK product exported to US	US domestic price of a product	Price of the US product imported into UK
£1 = $1.60	£1	$1.60	$1	62p
£1 = $1.40	£1	$1.40	$1	71p

(b)

FIG. 47. **Depreciation (1).** (a) A depreciation of the pound against the dollar. (b) The effect of depreciation on export and import prices.

In order for a currency depreciation to work, three basic conditions must be satisfied:

DEPRECIATION

(a) how successful the depreciation is depends on the reactions of export and import volumes to the change in relative prices, that is, the PRICE ELASTICITY OF DEMAND for exports and imports. If these volumes are low, that is, demand is inelastic, trade volumes will not change much and the depreciation may in fact worsen the situation. On the other hand, if export and import demand are elastic, the change in trade volume will improve the payments position. Balance-of-payments equilibrium will be restored if the sum of export and import elasticities is greater than unity (the MARSHALL-LERNER CONDITION).

(b) on the supply side, resources must be available and sufficiently mobile to be switched from other sectors of the economy into industries producing exports and products that will substitute for imports. If the economy is fully employed already, domestic demand will have to be reduced and/or switched by deflationary policies to accommodate the required resource transference.

(c) over the longer term, offsetting domestic price rises must be contained. A depreciation increases the cost of essential imports of raw materials and foods, which can push up domestic manufacturing costs and the cost of living. This in turn can serve to increase domestic prices and money wages, thereby necessitating further depreciations to maintain price competitiveness.

See BALANCE-OF-PAYMENTS EQUILIBRIUM, INTERNAL-EXTERNAL BALANCE MODEL, PRICE ELASTICITY OF SUPPLY, APPRECIATION(1).

2. the fall in the value of an ASSET during the course of its working life, also called *amortization*. The condition of the plant and equipment used in production deteriorates over time, and these items will eventually have to be replaced. Accordingly, a company is required to make financial provision for depreciation of its assets.

Depreciation is an accounting means of dividing up the historic cost of a FIXED ASSET over a number of accounting periods that correspond with the asset's estimated life. The depreciation charged against the revenue of successive time periods serves to spread the original cost of a fixed asset that yields benefits to the company over several trading periods. In the period-end BAL-

DEPRECIATION

ANCE SHEET, such an asset would be included at its cost less depreciation deducted to date. This depreciation charge does not attempt to calculate the reducing market value of fixed assets, so balance sheets do not show realization values.

Different formulas (LAST-IN FIRST-OUT and FIRST-IN FIRST-OUT) used to calculate depreciation can lead to variations in the balance sheet value of a fixed asset and in the charge against GROSS PROFIT for depreciation. The formula in Fig. 48 gives a large depreciation charge in the early periods of the fixed asset's life and a small charge in the later years. In the interests of consistency, and to conform to tax laws, companies generally do not change the depreciation formula used for their fixed assets but stick to the same formula.

Straight-line method

	Opening book value	Depreciation ($21,000÷ 3)	closing book value
Year 1	$24,000	$7,000	$17,000
Year 2	17,000	7,000	10,000
Year 3	10,000	7,000	3,000

(a)

Reducing-balance method

	Opening book value	Depreciation (50%)	Closing book value
Year 1	$24,000	$12,000	$12,000
Year 2	12,000	6,000	6,000
Year 3	6,000	3,000	3,000

(b)

FIG. 48. **Depreciation (2).** (a) In this example, the *straight-line method* divides the original cost of a fixed asset ($24,000) by its estimated life (3 years), giving equal depreciation charges in each business period. (b) The *reducing-balance method* writes off in each period a fixed percentage of the net book value of the fixed asset at the beginning of the period.

All these depreciation formulas base the depreciation charge of the HISTORIC COST of fixed assets. However, during a period of

INFLATION it is likely that the REPLACEMENT COST of an asset is likely to be higher than its original cost. Thus, prudent companies need to make PROVISION for higher replacement costs in the form of a revaluation reserve.

depressed area a region of an economy characterized by significantly higher rates of UNEMPLOYMENT and lower levels of INCOME PER CAPITA compared with the national average. See REGIONAL POLICY.

depression a phase of the BUSINESS CYCLE characterized by a severe decline (*slump*) in the level of economic activity. Real output and INVESTMENT are at low levels and there is a high rate of UNEMPLOYMENT. A depression caused mainly by a fall in AGGREGATE DEMAND can be fought by adopting expansionary FISCAL POLICY and MONETARY POLICY. See DEFLATIONARY GAP, DEMAND MANAGEMENT, STABILIZATION POLICY.

derivative see DIFFERENTIAL CALCULUS.

derived demand the DEMAND for a particular FACTOR INPUT or PRODUCT that is dependent on there being a demand for some other product. For example, the demand for labor to produce automobiles is dependent on there being a demand for the product in the first place; the demand for coffee mugs is dependent on there being a demand for coffee. See MARGINAL REVENUE PRODUCT, FACTOR MARKETS, COMPLEMENTARY PRODUCTS.

deseasonalized data see TIME-SERIES ANALYSIS.

devaluation an administered reduction in the value of a CURRENCY against other currencies under a FIXED EXCHANGE RATE SYSTEM, as shown in Fig. 49. The purpose of a devaluation is to assist in removing a deficit in a country's BALANCE OF PAYMENTS. See DEPRECIATION(1) and Fig. 47b.

developed country an economically advanced country whose economy is characterized by large industrial and service sectors and high levels of INCOME PER CAPITA. See STRUCTURE OF INDUSTRY, DEVELOPING COUNTRY, ECONOMIC DEVELOPMENT.

developing country or **underdeveloped country** or **Third World country** a country in which the level of GROSS DOMESTIC PRODUCT and INCOME PER CAPITA is presently inadequate to generate the SAVINGS necessary to embark on substantial agricultural and industrial investment programs. Such countries are typically

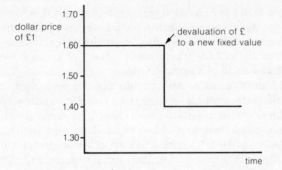

FIG. 49. **Devaluation.** A devaluation of the pound against the dollar.

characterized by a large PRIMARY SECTOR, usually agriculture, in which the majority of the POPULATION exists at or near subsistence levels, producing barely enough for immediate needs and thus being unable to release the amounts of food required to support a large urbanized industrial population. To facilitate an increase in urban population necessary for INDUSTRIALIZATION, a nation may either IMPORT the necessary commodities from abroad with the FOREIGN EXCHANGE earned from the EXPORT of predominantly primary goods, or it can attempt to improve its own agriculture. Originally, it was believed that industrialization would provide the impetus needed to achieve a breakthrough into sustained ECONOMIC GROWTH. The present emphasis has shifted to increasing PRODUCTIVITY from an indigenous agricultural sector, thereby releasing both LABOR and goods to assist the INDUSTRIAL SECTOR. With appropriate ECONOMIC AID from industrialized countries and the ability and willingness on the part of a developing country, the transition could be made into a NEWLY INDUSTRIALIZED COUNTRY.

However, certain problems do exist. For instance, achieved increases in real income must be maintained, which means keeping the population growth in check. Illiteracy and a perceived need for large families tend to work against governmental efforts to increase the STANDARD OF LIVING of its citizens. Also, most of the foreign exchange earned by such countries is through exporting, mainly COMMODITIES but increasingly augmented by manufactures as industrialization progresses. In both these areas, however, the developing countries have been up against adverse developments in the world economy, particularly since the oil price increases of 1973 and the ensuing advent of recessionary conditions and spread of PROTECTIONISM.

development area or **enterprise zone** a severely DEPRESSED AREA that is formally recognized by a country's REGIONAL POLICY as in need of industrial regeneration. The usual practice is to encourage establishment of new companies, expansion of existing companies, and establishment of new industries by offering a variety of investment incentives: investment grants and allowances, tax write-offs, rent- and tax-free factories, etc.

development economics the branch of economics seeking to explain how a DEVELOPING COUNTRY increases in productive capacity, both agricultural and industrial, in order to achieve sustained ECONOMIC GROWTH. Economic growth is frequently measured in terms of INCOME PER CAPITA, which raises problems associated with measuring economic welfare in terms of GROSS NATIONAL PRODUCT, and creates difficulties in making international comparisons of GNP figures.

Much work in development economics has focused on the way in which growth can be achieved, and how to arrive at the optimal balance of contributing factors. For instance, there is the question of whether agriculture ought to be developed in tandem with industry, or whether leading industries should be allowed to move forward independently, thus encouraging all other sectors of society. Another controversial question is whether less developed countries are using the most appropriate technology. Many economists argue for intermediate technology as most appropriate rather than very modern plants initially requiring Western technologists and managers to run them. Sociocultural factors are also influential in attempting to achieve takeoff into sustained economic growth.

differential calculus a set of mathematical techniques that focus on the slope of a line, investigating how a DEPENDENT VARIABLE changes when there is an infinitesimal change in an INDEPENDENT VARIABLE. For example, if we wish to know how consumption expenditure (C) changes when disposable income (Y) changes, we use the symbol Δ to indicate a change in a variable, and can express the relationship in the ratio $\Delta C/\Delta Y$, which tells us how C changes as Y changes. For a LINEAR EQUATION (of the form C = $a + b$ Y), this ratio will always be constant and equal to b (the slope of the line).

However, for nonlinear equations containing squares or cubes of the variables, such as:

$$C = a + bY - cY^2$$

the slope of the line will not remain constant, so it becomes important to state the income range over which we are measuring the slope of the equation. Figure 50 shows a typical nonlinear relationship based on the above equation. The slope of this line varies considerably, being very steep for the low income range (OY_1) and less steep for higher income ranges $(Y_1 Y_2)$, until at income Y_2 the line reaches a maximum where its slope is zero. The fact that the line has a zero slope tells us it has reached a maximum (or minimum).

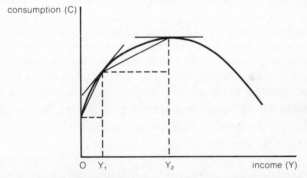

FIG. 50. **Differential calculus.** The characteristic slope of a nonlinear equation. See entry.

If we wanted to measure the sensitivity of consumption to small changes in income at a particular level of income, such as OY_1, we could reduce the income range over which we measure $\Delta C/\Delta Y$ in the vicinity of income level OY_1, until ΔY is a minute change.

DIFFERENTIATED PRODUCT

Then the ratio $\Delta C/\Delta Y$ would effectively measure the slope of the tangent to the curve at this income level OY_1. This measure is called the first *derivative* of consumption with respect to income, labeled dC/dY (technically dC/dY is the limiting value of $\Delta C/\Delta Y$ as ΔY approaches zero). Derivatives are used in many areas of economics where we are concerned with the slopes of functions. For example, MARGINAL REVENUE is the first derivative of TOTAL REVENUE (with respect to quantity). MARGINAL COST is the first derivative of TOTAL COST (with respect to quantity). Derivatives are used to measure ELASTICITY OF DEMAND/SUPPLY.

Where a dependent variable is influenced by two or more independent variables, the relationship can only be visualized as a curved surface on a multidimensional graph. However, even here techniques of differentiation can be used to measure the slope of the surface of the plane at a particular point, by calculating a *partial derivative*. For example, if consumption expenditure (C) is affected by both disposable income (Y) and consumer credit terms (I), it is possible to calculate the partial derivative of consumption with respect to income: dC/dY, which shows how consumption changes as income varies, holding constant the influence of consumer credit terms on consumption. Thus, partial derivatives serve to hold other things equal (CETERIS PARIBUS), enabling examination of the influence of just one independent variable on the dependent variable. See PARTIAL CORRELATION COEFFICIENT, BETA COEFFICIENTS.

differentiated product see PRODUCT DIFFERENTIATION.

diminishing average returns see DIMINISHING RETURNS.

diminishing marginal returns see DIMINISHING RETURNS.

diminishing marginal utility a concept suggesting that as a person consumes a greater quantity of a good or service, the extra satisfaction obtained from each additional unit will progressively fall. See Fig. 51.

This concept together with that of CONSUMER EQUILIBRIUM can be used to explain why DEMAND CURVES slope downward. For two goods, X and Y, the condition for consumer equilibrium is:

$$\frac{\text{marginal utility of X}}{\text{price of X}} = \frac{\text{marginal utility of Y}}{\text{price of Y}}$$

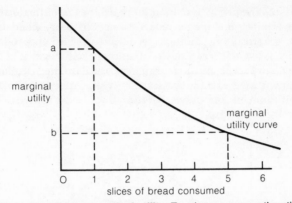

FIG. 51. **Diminishing marginal utility.** To a hungry person the utility of the first slice of bread consumed will be high (O_a), but as his or her appetite becomes satiated, successive slices of bread yield smaller and smaller amounts of satisfaction. For example, the fifth slice of bread yields only O_b of additional utility.

Assume now that this situation is disturbed, as a result of a fall in the price of X. To restore equilibrium, that is, make the two ratios equal again, the marginal utility of X has to fall, and that of Y to increase. According to diminishing marginal utility theory, this will occur if the consumer purchases more of X and less of Y. Hence, a fall in the price of a good induces an increase in the quantity demanded.

However, analysis can only be undertaken in this form if CARDINAL UTILITY measurement is possible, that is, measurement of an individual's subjective UTILITY FUNCTION to quantify the distances O_a and O_b in Fig. 51. In practice, it is not possible to measure utility with this degree of precision and so cardinal utility analysis was superseded by the concept of ORDINAL UTILITY.

Demand curves are now generally constructed from INDIFFERENCE CURVES, which are based on ordinal utility and sometimes on the similar concept of the REVEALED PREFERENCE THEORY. See TOTAL UTILITY, UTIL.

diminishing returns the law in the short run theory of supply of diminishing marginal returns or *variable factor proportions* stating that as equal quantities of one VARIABLE FACTOR INPUT are added into the production function, with the quantities of all other factor inputs remaining fixed, a point will be reached beyond which the resulting addition to output (that is, the MARGINAL PHYSICAL PRODUCT of the variable input) will begin to decrease as shown in Fig. 52. As the marginal physical product declines, this will eventually cause the AVERAGE PHYSICAL PRODUCT to decline as well (*diminishing average returns*).

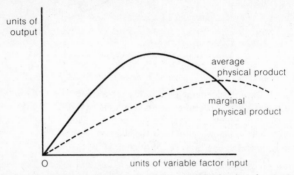

FIG. 52. **Diminishing returns.** The rise and fall of units of output as units of variable factor input are added to the production function.

The marginal physical product changes because additional units of the variable factor input do not add equally readily to units of the fixed factor input. At low levels of output, marginal physical product rises with the addition of more variable inputs to the (underworked) fixed input, the extra variable inputs bringing about a more intensive use of the fixed input. Eventually, as output is increased, an optimal factor combination is attained at which the variable and fixed inputs are mixed in the most appropriate proportions to maximize marginal physical product. Thereafter, additions of variable inputs to the (now overworked) fixed input leads to a less than proportionate increase in output so that marginal physical product declines. See RETURNS TO THE VARIABLE FACTOR INPUT.

direct advertising expenditures and **above-the-line promotion** the promotion of goods and services through ADVERTISING in the press and on television and radio, as distinct from *below-the-*

line promotion, such as direct mailing and in-store exhibitions and displays. See SALES PROMOTION AND MERCHANDISING .

direct cost see PRIME COST.

direct investment any expenditure on physical ASSETS, such as plant, machinery, and inventory. See INVESTMENT.

direct tax a tax levied by a government on the income and wealth received by households and businesses in order to raise revenue. Traditionally, the distinction between direct and indirect taxes was based on the question of whether the impact and incidence of the tax coincided, that is, who paid and who bore the burden of the tax. Examples of direct taxes are INCOME TAX, CORPORA-TION TAX, and INHERITANCE TAX. Direct taxes are progressive insofar as the amount paid varies according to the income and wealth of the taxpayer. By contrast, INDIRECT TAX is regressive insofar as the same amount is paid by each tax-paying consumer regardless of income. See TAXATION, PROGRESSIVE TAXATION, RE-GRESSIVE TAXATION.

dirty float the manipulation by the monetary authorities of a country's EXCHANGE RATE under a FLOATING EXCHANGE-RATE SYS-TEM primarily in order to gain an advantage over trading partners. Thus, the authorities could intervene in the FOREIGN EXCHANGE MARKET to stop the exchange rate from otherwise appreciating [see APPRECIATION(1)] in the face of market forces, or they could deliberately engineer a DEPRECIATION of the exchange rate. See BEGGAR-MY-NEIGHBOR POLICY.

discount 1. a deduction from the published LIST PRICE of a good or service allowed by a supplier to a customer. The discount may be offered for prompt payment in cash (*cash discount*) or for bulk purchases (*trade discount*).

2. the purchase of a company's issued stock or bonds at a price below the average market price of those of other companies oper-ating in the same field. The price is lower because investors feel less optimistic about that company's prospects.

3. a fall in the prices of all stocks and bonds in anticipation of a downturn in the economy.

4. the purchase of a BILL OF EXCHANGE or BOND for less than its nominal value. Bills and bonds are redeemable at a specific future date for a specified sum of money. The original purchaser

will buy the bill or bond for less than its nominal value (at a discount). The discount between the price paid and the nominal value of the bill or bond represents interest received on the loan made against the security of the bill or bond. If the owner of the bill or bond then wishes to sell it prior to maturity (rediscount it), he or she may have to accept less than its nominal value, although more than originally paid for it. The difference between the original price paid and the price received will depend largely on the length of time before maturity. For example, if a bond with a nominal value of $10,000 redeemable in 1 year's time were bought for $9000, then the $1000 discount on redemption value represents an interest rate of $1000/9000 = 11.1% on the loan.

5. the extent to which a foreign currency's market EXCHANGE RATE falls below its official exchange rate under a FIXED EXCHANGE-RATE SYSTEM.

discounted cash flow a cash flow associated with economic projects that are adjusted to allow for the timing of the cash flow and the potential interest on the funds involved. Such an allowance for timing is important, since most INVESTMENT projects have their main costs or cash outflows in the first year or so, whereas their revenues or cash inflows are spread over many future years.

For example, with interest rates at 10% a company could invest $100 now and have it accumulate at compound interest of $110 at the end of 1 year and $121 at the end of 2 years. So $100 in the hands of the company now is worth the same as $110 in a year's time or $121 in 2 year's time. Looking at this cash flow the other way around, the company would regard $110 receivable in 1 year's time or $121 receivable in 2 years' time as having a present value of $100. Following this principle, it is possible to calculate the present value of the estimated stream of future cash outflows associated with an investment project, *and the present value* of the estimated stream of future cash inflows from the project and compare the two. If the present value of the cash inflows from the project exceeds the present value of outflows when both are discounted at, say 10%, the *net present value* is positive. This suggests that it would be worthwhile for a company to use its own money or borrow money at 10% and undertake the project, for it will earn a return in excess of its financing costs.

Alternatively, it is possible to calculate the percentage internal rate of return that will equate the present value of the stream of cash outflows associated with an investment project with the present value of the stream of cash inflows from the project, so as to give a zero net present value. This calculated internal rate of return can then be compared with a predetermined DISCOUNT RATE, which is usually based on market rates of interest. If the calculated internal rate of return, say 15%, exceeds the discount rate, say 12%, the project is worthwhile, otherwise not.

discount rate 1. the RATE OF INTEREST at which the streams of cash inflows and outflows associated with an INVESTMENT project are to be discounted. For private-sector projects the discount rate is frequently based on the weighted-average COST OF CAPITAL to the company, with the interest cost of each form of finance (long-term loans, equity, etc.) being weighted by the proportion that each form of finance contributes to total company finances. **2.** the rate of interest the Federal Reserve Banks charge banks that borrow *at the window*.

In most public investment appraisals, the discount rate applied has tended to follow current prevailing private-sector interest rates. See DISCOUNTED CASH FLOW, COST-BENEFIT ANALYSIS, TIME PREFERENCE THEORY, FEDERAL RESERVE SYSTEM.

discrete variable a VARIABLE that can take only a limited number of values, increasing or decreasing in large increments. Compare CONTINUOUS VARIABLE.

discriminating monopolist a monopolist (see MONOPOLY) who is sometimes able to increase profits by dividing a market in two and charging discriminating prices. Apart from the requirement that the two markets be in some way distinct, so that buyers in one market cannot resell to those being asked a higher price in another market, price discrimination is only worthwhile when the PRICE ELASTICITY OF DEMAND in each market is different. See Fig. 53.

discrimination a situation in which forces in a normally competitive market are not permitted to play their decisive roles. In recent decades, governments have tried to reduce the incidence of discrimination in housing, employment, education, etc.

discriminatory tariff a TARIFF applied on an imported product at different rates depending on the countries of origin of those IM-

DISECONOMIES OF SCALE

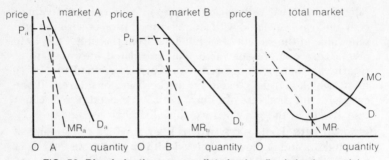

FIG. 53. **Discriminating monopolist.** A price-discriminating model involving two markets. The demand curve (D_a) facing the monopolist in market A is less elastic than (D_b) in market B. The horizontal addition of D_a and D_b gives D_t, and the horizontal addition of the MARGINAL REVENUE curves MR_a and MR_b gives MR_t. MC is the monopolist's MARGINAL COST curve. The profit-maximizing output (see PROFIT MAXIMIZATION) for the monopolist is determined by the intersection of the MC curve for total output and the aggregated MR_t curve. The broken horizontal line connects the two diagrams at the level where the MR of the monopolist in market A is equal to the MR in market B, and this aggregate MR_t is equal to the MC of the total output. It follows that the profit-maximizing output in market A is OA, and in market B it is OB. At these outputs, the discriminating monopolist will charge OP_a in market A and the lower price OP_b in market B.

PORTS. Discriminating tariffs distort the pattern of international trade and are generally prohibited by the GENERAL AGREEMENT ON TARIFFS AND TRADE (GATT) unless practiced within a CUSTOMS UNION.

diseconomies of scale the possible increase in long-run unit or AVERAGE COST that may occur as the scale of the output of a business is increased beyond some critical point.

As output is increased, long-run average costs may at first decline, reflecting the presence of ECONOMIES OF SCALE, but after a certain point long-run average costs may begin to rise. See Fig. 54.

The most frequently cited sources of such diseconomies are the managerial and administrative problems of controlling and coor-

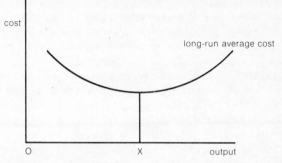

FIG. 54. **Diseconomies of scale.** In the range of output beyond point X, the company is experiencing diseconomies of scale, with costs increasing as output increases.

dinating large-scale operations and labor relations problems in large plants. See MINIMUM EFFICIENT SCALE.

disequilibrium a situation in which a state of EQUILIBRIUM has not been attained, or having been attained, ceases to be maintained. If there is a natural tendency toward equilibrium, the system is said to be *stable*. If the reverse is true, the system is said to be *unstable*. See COBWEB THEOREM, DYNAMIC ANALYSIS.

disguised (concealed) unemployment see HIDDEN UNEMPLOYMENT.

disinflation a fall in the general price level, frequently accompanied by a reduction in the level of national income (DEFLATION). A disinflation is sometimes brought about deliberately by the authorities in order to combat INFLATION and to eliminate a BALANCE OF PAYMENTS deficit. Instruments of disinflationary policy include fiscal measures, for example, tax increases; monetary measures, for example, higher interest rates; and price and income controls. See FISCAL POLICY, MONETARY POLICY, PRICES AND INCOMES POLICY, INFLATIONARY GAP, INTERNAL-EXTERNAL BALANCE MODEL.

disintermediation a situation in which a FINANCIAL INTERMEDIARY, such as a SAVINGS AND LOAN INSTITUTION, is forced to reduce its lending operations because of the withdrawal of deposits from it, and because it is unable to attract new funds. Disintermediation usually occurs, and then only temporarily, when an intermediary (see INTERMEDIATION) fails to adjust its borrowing rates on deposits promptly when interest rates rise, so that its rates are insufficiently competitive vis-a-vis other deposit-taking institutions.

disinvestment 1. a decrease in a country's CAPITAL STOCK that occurs when there is insufficient new INVESTMENT to cover CAPITAL CONSUMPTION/DEPRECIATION, capital lost due to wear and tear. **2.** also called *divestment* the sale or closure by a company of part of its business. For example, a diversified company may decide to pull out altogether from a particular activity by selling the subsidiary involved to another company or to the subsidiary's management team (see MANAGEMENT BUYOUT).

dispersion see VARIANCE(2).

disposable personal income the amount of income available to HOUSEHOLDS after payment of personal INCOME TAXES and Social Security contributions. Disposable personal income is an important determinant of the level of CONSUMPTION expenditure and SAVINGS in the economy. See CONSUMPTION SCHEDULE, SAVINGS SCHEDULE.

dissavings the excess of current CONSUMPTION expenditure over current DISPOSABLE PERSONAL INCOME, the difference being met by HOUSEHOLDS by borrowing or by drawing on past SAVINGS. See SAVINGS SCHEDULE.

distribution see FREQUENCY DISTRIBUTION.

distribution of income see INCOME DISTRIBUTION.

distributive efficiency an aspect of MARKET PERFORMANCE that denotes the EFFICIENCY of a market in distributing its outputs from suppliers to consumers. The costs of distribution include transportation, storage, and handling expenses together with the distributor's profit margins. In addition, suppliers incur ADVERTISING and other PRODUCT DIFFERENTIATION expenditures in creating and sustaining demand for their products. Optimal distributive efficiency is achieved when physical distribution costs are minimized and selling costs are maintained at the minimum level needed to sustain total market demand.

disutility the dissatisfaction or pain that a person encounters in consuming a product or in working. Compare UTILITY.

diversification the process by which a region, company, or individual tries to reduce risks associated with excessive specialization. Government policies sometimes are directed toward reducing the vulnerability of an area whose economy rests, for example, on a single crop or industry. Firms sometimes try to reduce risks by operating in several, not necessarily related, markets. Individuals may try to buttress the security of stock portfolios by avoiding the hazards of *putting all their eggs in one basket*.

Diversification by firms may lead to intensification of competition. However, so-called mutual nonaggression pacts among diversified companies could lead to lessening of such competition in some markets.

divestment see DISINVESTMENT.

dividend a payment made by a CORPORATION to its shareholders for providing equity capital. Dividends are a distribution of the PROFITS of the company.

dividend cover ratio or **times covered ratio** an accounting measure of the extent to which a company's earnings cover DIVIDEND payments on common stock that expresses PROFIT after tax and interest charges as a ratio of total dividend payments.

dividend yield the DIVIDEND paid by a CORPORATION for a given ACCOUNTING PERIOD, usually 1 year, as a proportion of the current market price of its shares. For example, if company X declared a dividend of $1 per share for the 12-month accounting period ended December 31, and the current market price of a share in company X was $8, the dividend yield would be:

$$\frac{\text{Dividend per share}}{\text{Price per share}} = \frac{\$1}{\$8} = 12\tfrac{1}{2}\%$$

division of labor see SPECIALIZATION.

divorce of ownership from control a situation in which, although a company is owned by its SHAREHOLDERS, it is actually controlled by the company's management—the board of directors, elected by the shareholders at the annual general meeting to run the business on their behalf. This idea first achieved prominence through the writings of A.A. Berle and G. Means. Because the average size of individual ownership tends to be extremely small and shareholders are remote from day-to-day decisions, it is the company's management that effectively determines the policies of the company. Recognition of the control power exercised by management has led economists to develop theories of the firm that substitute managerial objective for the traditional hypothesis of PROFIT MAXIMIZATION. See MANAGERIAL THEORIES OF THE FIRM.

dollar the domestic CURRENCY of the United States. The dollar also performs various international roles, in particular as an INTERNATIONAL RESERVE asset, and as the NUMERAIRE of the international oil trade. See also EUROCURRENCY MARKET.

Domar economic growth model a theoretical construct that examines the dual role of INVESTMENT in expanding AGGREGATE DEMAND and the economy's AGGREGATE SUPPLY capacity (POTENTIAL GROSS NATIONAL PRODUCT) over time.

As one of the components of aggregate demand, investment expenditure has the effect of adding to total demand. According to the Keynesian theory of income determination, income will increase until the saving generated by the additional income offsets the higher level of investment (see EQUILIBRIUM LEVEL OF NATIONAL INCOME). Thus, if we designate the increase in investment as ΔI, income (Y) will increase by the amount:

$$\Delta Y = \frac{\Delta I}{\propto}$$

where ∞ is the MARGINAL PROPENSITY TO SAVE.

This short-term theory of income determination ignores the other effect of investment spending, that is, it adds to productive capacity. This capacity-creating effect is negligible in the short term, but ECONOMIC GROWTH has to do with the long term, and in the long term the role of investment in adding to productive capacity needs to be considered along with its demand-creating effect.

The question posed by Domar was: "If investment increases productive capacity and also creates income, at what rate should investment grow in order to make the increase in income equal to that of productive capacity?" To answer this question, Domar set up an equation, one side of which represented the rate of increase of productive capacity, the other the rate of increase of income, and the solution of which gave the required rate of growth.

Let each dollar of investment, I, add to productive capacity by the amount $\$\theta$ a year. For example, if it requires \$3000 of capital to produce \$1000 of output per year, θ will be one third or 33% per year. The symbol θ represents the CAPITAL-OUTPUT RATIO, which is the relationship between increments of investment and the resulting increments of output. The productive capacity of the economy has therefore increased by $I\theta$, which is the capacity-creating effect of investment and the supply side of our equation.

To use this additional capacity, demand must increase by an equal amount. Turning to the demand side of the equation, MULTIPLIER theory tells us that with any given marginal propensity to save, ∞, an increase in national income is a function not of I but of the increment in investment, ΔI, that is, the absolute annual increase in investment. The corresponding absolute annual increase in income is then:

$$\Delta Y = \Delta I . \frac{I}{\propto}$$

where $1/\infty$ is the multiplier. To fulfill the condition that income and capacity should increase at the same rate requires that

$$\Delta I . \frac{1}{\propto} = I\theta$$

which is the fundamental equation set up by Domar. To solve the equation, we multiply both sides by ∞ and divide by I to get

$$\frac{\Delta I}{I} = \propto \theta$$

DOMESTIC CREDIT EXPANSION (DCE)

The left-hand side expression is the annual percentage rate of growth of investment that, in order to maintain an assumed full employment with growing productive capacity, must grow at the annual percentage rate $\infty\theta$. Income must also grow at the same annual percentage rate.

See SOLOW ECONOMIC GROWTH MODEL, HARROD ECONOMIC GROWTH MODEL.

domestic credit expansion (DCE) a monetary aggregate sometimes used by the INTERNATIONAL MONETARY FUND in requiring monetary restraint on the part of a member country with a balance of payments deficit as a condition of access to the Fund's resources. The main elements of DCE are made up primarily of the annual rate of change of the domestic MONEY SUPPLY (defined in a number of possible ways) and annual rate of change of external borrowing by the private and public sectors. Under a FIXED EXCHANGE-RATE SYSTEM excessive monetary expansion either by an increase in the money supply or overseas financing can lead to domestic price levels rising at a faster rate than prices of trading partners, resulting in a balance-of-payments deficit. It follows, therefore, that monetary restraint (or, in the last resort, a currency DEVALUATION) is necessary to restore balance-of-payments equilibrium. Under a FLOATING EXCHANGE-RATE SYSTEM, tight control of monetary expansion is less urgent, it is argued, because divergences in domestic price levels between countries will be offset by exchange rate movements. See PURCHASING-POWER PARITY THEORY.

dominant company a company that accounts for a significant proportion of the supply of a particular good or service. Such a company exercises considerable power in determining the supply terms of the product (see PRICE LEADERSHIP) and may be tempted to further its own interests at the expense of consumers. A *monopoly company* is one that controls the entire supply of a particular product (*monopoly of scale*).

dominant company-price leader see PRICE LEADERSHIP.

double taxation 1. the TAXATION OF INCOMES and PROFITS both in the country where they arise, and again where these incomes and profits are remitted to the income earner's home country.

Such double taxation can be a significant deterrent to international labor and capital movements. For this reason many countries have negotiated double taxation agreements that limit taxation liability to the country in which the income is earned.

2. double taxation of dividends. See CORPORATION TAX. Compare UNITARY TAXATION.

Dow Jones Average see SHARE PRICE INDEX.

drawing right see INTERNATIONAL MONETARY FUND.

dual banking system the system in which commercial banks are chartered as national or as state banks. This is a structure not found outside the United States.

dual economy an economy in which capital-intensive and technologically advanced sectors exist side by side with labor-intensive and technologically primitive sectors. An area of study within DEVELOPMENT ECONOMICS, the problem is whether to achieve ECONOMIC GROWTH through leading technological sectors or to attempt to spread an economy's resources more thinly across all sectors to achieve balanced growth. The concept is mainly applied within the context of a DEVELOPING COUNTRY. See INDUSTRIALIZATION.

dummy variable an additional INDEPENDENT VARIABLE introduced into an estimated regression equation in a simple binary (0/1) form to test whether the presence of the variable (1) helps improve the fit of the estimated equation to the available data, compared with a situation in which the variable is absent (0). See REGRESSION ANALYSIS.

dumping the EXPORT of a good at a price below the full cost of producing it. Dumping may occur as a short-term response to a domestic recession, that is, surplus output is sold abroad at a cut price to get rid of it, or as a longer-term strategic means of penetrating export markets—once a foothold has been gained, prices are increased to generate profits. Either way, dumping is viewed as unfair trade and is outlawed by international trade pacts, such as the GENERAL AGREEMENT ON TARIFFS AND TRADE. See BEGGAR-MY-NEIGHBOR POLICY, COUNTERVAILING DUTY.

duopoly a subset of OLIGOPOLY describing a MARKET with only two suppliers. The two firms sell to a large number of consumers.

DUOPSONY

Each consumer is too small to affect the market price of the goods or commodities purchased and therefore cannot keep the market competitive. On the sellers' side, the market is a two-player variable sum game. The models of duopoly markets fall into two main categories:

(a) *nonreactive models*, which do not allow for any anticipation by a company of its competitor's reaction to either a price or quantity change. For example, in the *Bertrand duopoly* model, each supplier assumes that its rival will not change price in response to its own initial price cut, and this assumption will encourage the supplier to cut its price in order to increase sales. Since both companies reason in this way, the price will eventually be driven down to a competitive level, that is, a NORMAL PROFIT equilibrium. In the *Cournot duopoly* model, quantity not price is adjusted, with one company altering its output on the assumption that a rival's output will remain unchanged. Since both companies reason in this way, output will eventually be expanded to the point at which the companies share the market equally and both secure only normal profits.

(b) *reactive models*, explicitly assuming that the two companies recognize that their actions are interdependent and hence will attempt to avoid mutually ruinous forms of rivalry. Also called *collusive duopoly*. Specifically, companies will attempt to maximize their joint profits by establishing agreed prices above the competitive equilibrium price. This can be achieved by informal means, such as acceptance by both duopolists that one of them acts as price leader (see PRICE LEADERSHIP model) or by means of formal COLLUSION between the two duopolists (see CARTEL).

duopsony a MARKET situation in which there are only two buyers, but many sellers. Compare DUOPOLY.

durable goods see CAPITAL GOODS.

Durbin-Watson test a statistical test that checks for presence of a pattern in the residuals or error terms, after an estimated regression equation has been calculated from observations of INDEPENDENT VARIABLES and DEPENDENT VARIABLES. See AUTOCORRELATION, REGRESSION ANALYSIS.

dynamic analysis a method of economic analysis that traces out the path of adjustment from one state of EQUILIBRIUM to another. Consider, for example, the effects of a change of the export demand on the EQUILIBRIUM LEVEL OF NATIONAL INCOME. See Fig. 55. See COMPARATIVE STATIC EQUILIBRIUM ANALYSIS, DISEQUILIBRIUM.

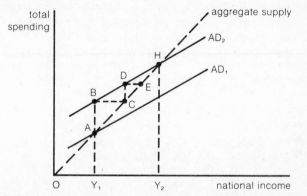

FIG. 55. **Dynamic analysis.** An increase in export demand raises AGGREGATE DEMAND from AD₁ to AD₂ and results in an increase in the equilibrium level of national income from Y_1 to Y_2. In moving from Y_1 to Y_2, a number of steps are involved. The initial increase in exports raises aggregate demand from A to B and produces an increase in real output from B to C. This extra output creates additional income via the MULTIPLIER effect and expands aggregate demand further from C to D. The extra spending in turn produces an increase in real output from D to E. These movements continue until a new equilibrium position is reached at point H.

E

earned income the return accruing to LABOR for work done. Earned income generally comprises WAGES, SALARIES, FEES, COMMISSION, and PROFITS attributable to sole proprietors and partners within partnerships. *Unearned income* is an idea introduced into economic theory by Adam Smith, embellished by David Ricardo, blown up by Marxists, undermined by Marginalists, and largely discarded by twentieth-century economists. The distinction between earned and unearned income is not a useful one in economics, as FACTORS OF PRODUCTION can be said to earn income.

earnings the returns accruing to FACTORS OF PRODUCTION, such as WAGES, SALARIES, FEES and COMMISSIONS, PROFITS, RENTS, DIVIDENDS, and INTEREST payments.

earnings drift the propensity for earnings, primarily WAGES and SALARIES, to increase at a rate faster than agreed rates per unit of labor. Many factors contribute to an earnings drift, such as OVERTIME, bonuses, special agreements, restructuring of PIECEWORK PAYMENTS agreements, and so forth. Areas in which a particular skill is in demand will pay higher rates than areas in which such shortages do not exist. The ability to negotiate terms and conditions, sometimes informally, between employer and employee, leads to significant weakening in the case for an incomes policy as a tool of economic management due to the ease by which it can be circumvented. Earnings drift tends to be associated with conditions of full employment under which employers will more readily concede wage increases to retain their labor force. See INFLATION, PRICES AND INCOMES POLICY.

earnings per share NET PROFIT after tax accruing to common stockholders in a CORPORATION, divided by the number of common stock shares.

econometrics the discipline within economics that attempts to measure and estimate statistically the relationship between economic VARIABLES. For example, economic theory suggests that consumption expenditure is a function of disposable income [C = $f(Y)$] or, more precisely, that consumption expenditure is linked to disposable income through the equation C = $(a + b)Y$. For each level of disposable income, consumption can be measured and a statistical relationship established between the two variables by making numerical estimates of the PARAMETERS, a and b in the equation. Because consumption depends on income, it is termed the DEPENDENT VARIABLE while disposable income is termed the INDEPENDENT VARIABLE. Econometric models can have many hundreds of measured variables, linked by several hundred estimated equations, not just one, as is the case when models are constructed for macroeconomic FORECASTING purposes. See REGRESSION ANALYSIS.

economic aid the provision of financial and physical forms of assistance to (mainly) the DEVELOPING COUNTRIES as a means of strengthening their economies. Economic aid is provided both on a bilateral basis by individual governments and private institutions (for example, commercial banks), and on a multilateral basis through the WORLD BANK and other international organizations, for example, the European Community's Overseas Development Fund. Such assistance augments the foreign exchange earnings and domestic savings of recipient countries, as well as providing techniques and managerial resources and skill otherwise unobtainable locally. See ECONOMIC DEVELOPMENT.

economic cost see OPPORTUNITY COST.

economic development a process of economic transition involving structural transformation of an economy through INDUSTRIALIZATION and raising gross domestic product and INCOME PER CAPITA. Generally speaking, DEVELOPING COUNTRIES are characterized by subsistence primary production, mainly agriculture, and low levels of income per capita. DEVELOPED COUNTRIES are characterized by large manufacturing and service sectors and high levels of income per capita.

Capital INVESTMENT is a significant factor in the transformation process. Investment not only enlarges an economy's capacity to produce goods and service and raise the PRODUCTIVITY of resources, but also, via multiplier effects, increases aggregate demand and national income. An increase in national income raises the level of savings, thereby providing financing for further capital accumulation. See DEMOGRAPHIC TRANSITION, STRUCTURE OF INDUSTRY.

economic efficiency an aspect of PRODUCTION seeking to identify, for a given level of OUTPUT, the combination of FACTOR INPUTS that minimizes the COST of producing the output. See EFFICIENCY, COST FUNCTION.

economic forecasts see FORECASTING.

economic goods see GOODS.

economic growth the growth of the real OUTPUT of an economy over time. The physical ability of an economy to produce more goods and services depends on:

(a) increase in the quantity and quality of its capital goods (CAPITAL ACCUMULATION).

(b) increase in the quantity and quality of its LABOR FORCE.

(c) increase in the quantity and quality of its NATURAL RESOURCES.

(d) efficient use of these factor inputs so as to maximize their contribution to the expansion of output through improved PRODUCTIVITY.

(e) development and introduction of innovative techniques and new products (TECHNOLOGICAL PROGRESSIVENESS).

Whether or not an economy realizes its growth potential depends on one further consideration:

(f) level of AGGREGATE DEMAND. The level of demand needs to be high enough to ensure full utilization of increased productive capabilities of the economy.

Achievement of a high rate of economic growth is one of the four main objectives of MACROECONOMIC POLICY. The significance of economic growth lies in its contribution to the general prosperity of the community. Growth is desirable because it enables the community to consume more private goods and services, and it contributes to the provision of a greater quantity of social goods and services (health, education, etc.), thereby improving real living standards.

Economic growth is usually measured in terms of increase in

ECONOMIC GROWTH MODELS

GROSS DOMESTIC PRODUCT (GDP) over time (see Fig. 56) or an increase in per capita GDP over time. The latter measure relates increases in total output to changes in the population. Therefore, if total output rises only a little faster than the increase in population, there will be only a small improvement in average living standards. See CAPITAL-LABOR RATIO, CAPITAL-OUTPUT RATIO, CAPITAL WIDENING, CAPITAL DEEPENING, POTENTIAL GROSS NATIONAL PRODUCT.

Average annual % increases

Japan	4.4
US	3.0
W. Germany	2.2
UK	2.5

FIG. 56. **Economic growth.** The increase in gross national product from 1974 to 1985.

economic growth models see DOMAR ECONOMIC GROWTH MODEL, HARROD ECONOMIC GROWTH MODEL, SOLOW ECONOMIC GROWTH MODEL.

economic man an assumption in economic theory that people act rationally in specifying their objectives and then make decisions consistent with those objectives. Thus, ENTREPRENEURS will set goals of PROFIT MAXIMIZATION and adjust their outputs and prices to achieve those goals. Again, CONSUMERS will seek to maximize their UTILITY or satisfaction and will make their purchases in the light of their tastes for products and the relative prices of those products. See Fig. 57 for an illustration of rational consumer choice. See CONSUMER RATIONALITY, CONSUMER EQUILIBRIUM, BEHAVIORAL THEORY OF THE FIRM.

economic model a construct or model incorporating two or more VARIABLES that (a) describes the relationship that exists between the variables, (b) depicts the economic outcome of their relationships, and (c) predicts the effects of changes in the variables on the economic outcome.

There are numerous economic models portrayed in this book, for example, EQUILIBRIUM MARKET PRICE, EQUILIBRIUM MARKET PRICE (CHANGES IN), EQUILIBRIUM LEVEL OF NATIONAL INCOME, MULTIPLIER. See also ECONOMETRICS, HYPOTHESIS TESTING.

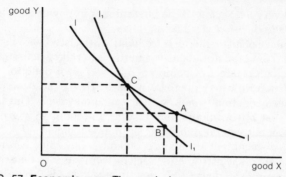

FIG. 57. **Economic man.** The graph demonstrates why, if the assumption of rational consumer behavior holds, a consumer's INDIF-
FERENCE CURVES cannot cross. Indifference curves II and $I_1 I_1$ show
a consumer's preference between two products, X and Y. Point A on
indifference curve II represents a higher level of satisfaction to the
consumer than point B on indifference curve $I_1 I_1$, because point A
represents more of both products than point B. Yet point C lies on
both curves. This suggests that the consumer, having preferred the
combination of goods indicated by point A to the combination represented by point B, now regards them as equal at point C. If the
consumer is rational, such an inconsistent set of preferences would
not arise, and indifference curves do not intersect.

economic policy a strategy established by a government to
achieve its economic objectives.

The objectives a community sets for itself in a democracy are
reflected through the ballot box in voting for candidates of a particular party with a given mandate. The goals an elected government sets itself are political and of a normative nature, since they
may involve views about the most appropriate INCOME DISTRIBU-
TION. That is, value judgments are made about the relative effects
of policies on subgroups within the community, and the desirabil-
ity of helping some groups at the expense of others.

Consequently, these objectives may be the subject of debate
between political parties. Even if political parties had the *same*
objectives, such as achieving ECONOMIC GROWTH, reducing
UNEMPLOYMENT, controlling INFLATION, and achieving BALANCE
OF PAYMENTS surplus, the *degree* of importance attached to each

would vary according to the government in power and the time when the decision was taken.

Welfare of an economy is frequently associated with consumption and use of material goods, but this is not the whole story. The psychological effect of being unemployed or of pollution from a production unit may decrease welfare. That is, an economy can produce economic *bads* as well as economic *goods*. This is something that governments may take into account to a greater or lesser extent when establishing economic policy.

The government attains its economic policy objectives through the use of policy instruments. Such instruments may take the form of increasing or decreasing the MONEY SUPPLY through OPEN-MARKET OPERATIONS (monetary instrument) or increasing or decreasing the rate of TAXATION (fiscal instrument), as well as subsidies and transfer payments.

See FISCAL POLICY, NORMATIVE ECONOMICS, MONETARY POLICY, WELFARE ECONOMICS, MACROECONOMIC POLICY.

economic rent a payment made for use of a FACTOR OF PRODUCTION, such as land, that is in fixed supply both in the short term and, generally, in the long term. Because such FACTOR INPUTS cannot be transferred to other uses, their TRANSFER EARNINGS are zero, and any payments made for them represent economic rent. The equilibrium rent is determined by demand for, and supply of, land. See Fig. 58. See also QUASI-RENT.

economics the study of the problem of using available FACTORS OF PRODUCTION as efficiently as possible so as to attain maximum fulfillment of society's unlimited demands for GOODS and SERVICES. The ultimate purpose of economic endeavor is to satisfy human wants for goods and services. The problem is that whereas wants are virtually without limit, resources—NATURAL RESOURCES, LABOR, and CAPITAL—available at any one time to produce goods and services are limited in supply. That is, resources are scarce (see SCARCITY) relative to the demands they are called on to satisfy. The fact of scarcity means we must always be making CHOICES. To take a simple example, if more resources are devoted to producing tractors, fewer resources are then available for providing hospitals and other goods. See OPPORTUNITY COSTS, PRODUCTION POSSIBILITY BOUNDARY, EFFICIENCY.

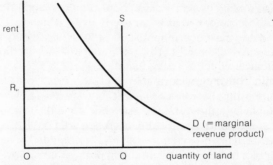

rent

S

R_e

D (= marginal
revenue product)

O   Q   quantity of land

FIG. 58. **Economic rent.** The demand curve (D) for land as a factor
input slopes downward, reflecting a fall in the marginal productivity
of land as more land is used (see MARGINAL PHYSICAL PRODUCT and
MARGINAL REVENUE PRODUCT). By definition, the supply of land is
fixed, so the supply curve is perfectly inelastic (S). The equilibrium
rate of rent is R_e, where the two curves intersect.

economic sanctions bilateral or multinational embargoes on the
EXPORT and IMPORT of goods, services, and capital to and from a
particular country. Economic sanctions are applied as an adjunct
to political pressure being brought to bear on a country by another
country or by the international community to encourage that
country to change its political/economic policies, for example,
abolition of the system of apartheid in South Africa.

economic statistics the statistics collected by government and
other bodies to show where an economy is at the time of collecting
the data and to facilitate comparisons and analyses with other data
and indices of previous time periods. Such data may be analyzed
by conventional statistical methods or by ECONOMETRICS to establish significant relationships between the indices of the variables
involved.

economic system the institutional arrangements made for at-
tacking the twin problems of SCARCITY and CHOICE. Because economic resources are limited relative to society's demand for goods
and services, some means of allocating resources between alternative ends is required. In the modern world three basic allocative
mechanisms perform this function: the market system, in which

resources are allocated through supply and demand; CENTRALLY PLANNED ECONOMY, that is, an economy in which resources are allocated by the government; and MIXED ECONOMY, in which resources are allocated both by the market and by the government.

economic theory the formulation of ECONOMIC MODELS about the relationships between economic VARIABLES in order to generate testable hypotheses from these models and the testing of these hypotheses against empirical data. When a HYPOTHESIS conflicts with actual data, the hypothesis should be amended or abandoned in favor of a better one. When the hypothesis is confirmed by the data, it can form a valuable guide in formulating ECONOMIC POLICY. See HYPOTHESIS TESTING.

economic union a form of TRADE INTEGRATION between a number of countries that provides not only the COMMON MARKET features of free trade and factor movements but also the unification of members' general economic objectives in respect to economic growth, employment, etc., and the harmonization of monetary, fiscal, and other policies.

Benelux, the alliance of Belgium, the Netherlands, and Luxembourg, formed in 1921, is one example of an economic union, although they remain politically separate sovereign states. By definition, all the regions making up the nation state constitute an economic union. Economic union is one of the long-term objectives of the EUROPEAN COMMUNITY.

economies of scale the long-term reduction in average (or unit) costs that occurs as the scale of a company's output is increased, all FACTOR INPUTS being variable. There are available in most industries economies of scale, so that producing a greater quantity of a product reduces average or unit costs. See Fig. 59.

Economies of scale may operate both at the level of the individual plant and the company, operating a number of plants, and arise due to: (a) indivisibilities in machinery and equipment, especially where a number of processes are linked together; (b) economies of increased dimensions—for many types of capital equipment (tankers, boilers), both setup and operating costs increase less rapidly than capacity; (c) economies of SPECIALIZATION—at larger outputs there is more scope for using specialist labor and

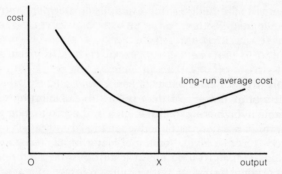

FIG. 59. **Economies of scale.** A typical U-shaped long-term average cost curve for a plant. OX is the scale of output at which average cost is minimized and economies of scale are exhausted. Thereafter, DISECONOMIES OF SCALE may set in, although this is not always the case (see MINIMUM EFFICIENT SCALE).

capital equipment; (d) superior techniques or organization of production—as scale is increased, automatic machinery may be used instead of manually operated equipment, or it may be possible to substitute continuous MASS PRODUCTION for BATCH PRODUCTION; (e) economies of bulk buying of raw materials and supplies; (f) marketing economies resulting from use of mass advertising media and greater density of deployment of sales forces; (g) financial economies, which arise from the ability of large companies to raise capital on advantageous terms; and (h) managerial economies through use of specialist management techniques, such as time-motion studies, operational research, and critical path analysis.

The potential for economies of scale can be limited for a variety of reasons. In some industries the nature of the product and the processes of manufacture or the technology may be such that DISECONOMIES OF SCALE are encountered at modest output levels. On the demand side, total market demand may be insufficient to permit companies to attain minimal efficient scale, or a company's individual market share may be too small. Where consumers demand a wide variety of products, this militates against standardization and long production runs.

Where economies of scale are substantial, SELLER CONCENTRA-

TION tends to be high, as, for example, in petrochemicals and automobile manufacture. See AVERAGE COST, EXTERNAL ECONOMIES OF SCALE, NATURAL MONOPOLY.

economize to produce: (a) a *given* OUTPUT of a product using fewer FACTOR INPUTS than previously; (b) *more* output than before from the *same* number of factor inputs; (c) a given output of a product at lower cost than before by substituting cheaper factor inputs for more expensive ones in the production process (the optimum position is attained when the largest possible output is produced from a given volume of factor inputs using available technology); (d) a given output at lowest possible factor cost.

In its original formulation, *economize* referred to management of the budget of a household or a society because of scarcity of resources relative to wants.

See PRODUCTIVITY, EFFICIENCY, PRODUCTION POSSIBILITY BOUNDARY.

economy a country defined in terms of the total and composition of its economic activities. The total value of goods and services produced in an economy in any 1 year is called its GROSS NATIONAL PRODUCT (GNP). The contribution made to GDP by the various subdivisions of the economy may be viewed in various ways, for example, by broad sectors (the PERSONAL or household SECTOR, the CORPORATE or business SECTOR, the FINANCIAL SECTOR, PUBLIC (GOVERNMENT) SECTOR, the FOREIGN SECTOR), or by individual industries.

Edgeworth box a conceptual device for analyzing possible trading relationships between two individuals or countries, using INDIFFERENCE CURVES. It is constructed by taking the *indifference map* of one individual (B) for two goods (X and Y) and inverting it to face the indifference map of individual A for the same goods, as in Fig. 60. Individual A's preferences are depicted by the three indifference curves A_1, A_2, and A_3, corresponding to higher levels of satisfaction as we move outward from origin OA. Individual B's preferences are depicted by the three indifference curves B_1, B_2, and B_3, corresponding to higher levels of satisfaction as we move outward from origin OB. Both consumers' preferences in regard to products X and Y are reflected in the slopes of their indifference curves, with the slope of a curve at any point reflecting the MARGINAL RATE OF SUBSTITUTION of X for Y.

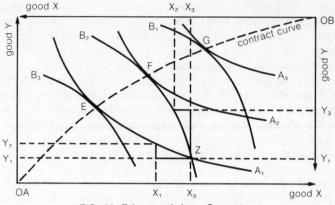

FIG. 60. **Edgeworth box.** See entry.

Only where individual A's indifference curves are tangential to individual B's indifference curves (points E, F, and G in Fig. 60) will A's marginal rate of substitution of product X for product Y be the same as B's marginal rate of substitution of X for Y, so their relative valuations of the two products are the same. Starting from any other point, say Z, the two can gain by trading with one another. At point Z, individual A has a lot of product X and little of product Y; consequently, A values product Y more highly than product X, being prepared to give up a lot of product X (X_1 X_3) to gain just a little of product Y (Y_1 Y_2). This is why A's indifference curve A_1 is relatively flat at point Z. On the other hand, at point Z individual B has a lot of product Y and little of product X; consequently, B values product X more highly than product Y, being prepared to give up a lot of product Y (Y_1 Y_3) to gain just a little of product X (X_2 X_3). This is why B's indifference curve B_2 is relatively steep at point Z.

These two sets of relative valuations of product X and product Y offer the promise of mutually beneficial exchange. If A offers some of his plentiful and low-valued product X in exchange for extra units of scarce and highly valued product Y, he can gain from trade. Similarly, if B offers some of his plentiful and low-valued product Y in exchange for extra units of scarce and highly valued product X, he can also gain from trade. The two will continue to exchange product X in return for product Y (individual A) and product Y in return for product X (individual B) until they reach a point such as E or F where the indifference curves have the same slope, with the result that their marginal rates of substitution of the two products are the same.

The *contract curve* or *offer curve* in Fig. 60 traces out the path of all the points, such as E, F, and G, where the indifference curves are tangential, and if individuals A and B start with any combination of products X and Y other than ones lying along the contract curve, they have an incentive to redistribute products X and Y between themselves through exchange. Where they come to lie along the contract curve will depend on their relative bargaining strength and skills. If individual A is stronger, they may end up at a point like G, far from A's origin OA and putting individual A on a high indifference curve A_3, whereas individual B ends up on a low indifference curve B_1 near his origin OB. On the other hand, if individual B is stronger, they may end up at a point like E, far from B's origin OB and putting individual B on a high indifference curve B_3, whereas individual A ends up on a low indifference curve A_1 near his origin OA. See also PARETO OPTIMALITY, THEORY OF CONSUMER BEHAVIOR, THEORY OF INTERNATIONAL TRADE.

EEC see EUROPEAN COMMUNITY.

effective demand see DEMAND.

effective rate of interest or **yield** the RATE OF INTEREST payable on the purchase price of a BOND. For example, a bond with a face value of $1000 and a NOMINAL (COUPON) RATE OF INTEREST of 5% generates a nominal return of $50 a year. If, however, the bond can be purchased for $500 on the open market, then the effective interest rate rises to 10%, representing a 10% return on the $500 invested. The lower the purchase price of a bond with a given nominal rate of interest, the higher its effective rate of interest will be and vice versa. There is thus an inverse relationship between the price paid for a bond and its effective rate of interest.

effective rate of protection the real amount of PROTECTION accorded to domestic suppliers of a final product when a TARIFF is applied to a competing imported final product (see IMPORTS) but either no tariff or a lower rate of tariff is applied on FACTOR INPUTS imported to produce that product. For example, assume that initially the same domestic final product and imported final product are priced at $100. Assume further that the price of the domestic product is made up of 50% value added by *domestic inputs* and 50% by *imported raw materials*. If an *ad valorem* tariff of 10% is now applied to the imported final product, its price will increase to $110. If no tariff is applied to imported raw materials, however, the import price of these materials will remain at $50. This allows domestic VALUE ADDED and prices to increase by up to $10 with the domestic final product still remaining fully competitive with the imported final product. The effective rate of protection accorded to domestic suppliers is thus 20% (that is, $10 additional value added/$50 existing value added). See NOMINAL RATE OF PROTECTION.

efficiency the relationship between scarce FACTOR INPUTS and OUTPUTS of goods and services. This relationship can be measured in physical terms (TECHNICAL EFFICIENCY) or cost terms (ECONOMIC EFFICIENCY). The concept of efficiency is used as a criterion in judging how well MARKETS have allocated resources. See MARKET PERFORMANCE, RESOURCE ALLOCATION, ECONOMIZE.

efficient market hypothesis a hypothesis suggesting that an efficient financial market exists in which all available information that may influence the price of a FINANCIAL SECURITY is reflected in that price. This implies that PERFECT COMPETITION exists within such a market, so that changes in the price of securities will be affected only by the acquisition of new information. The hypothesis suggests that due to the rapid assimilation of this new information by the market, expectations of future price changes are revised randomly about the intrinsic value of a security. Statisticians term such occurrences a *random walk*. For example, if a stock has an initial price of $10, the next change in price has an equal chance of being an increase or a decrease in value. If it goes up to, say, $11, the next change in price has an equal chance of going up or down. The implication that stock market prices follow a random walk implies that price changes are independent of one another.

Empirical tests of the efficient market hypothesis have been classified as weak-form tests, semistrong-form tests, and strong-form tests. The weak-form tests suggest that future prices cannot be predicted from past prices, and this is supported by the random walk hypothesis. The semistrong-form tests suggest that stock prices reflect all publicly available information. The strong-form tests suggest that stock prices reflect *all* information. It is unlikely that the efficient market hypothesis holds in its strong form as it is clearly difficult to be in possession of *all* necessary information.

See CAPITAL ASSET PRICING MODEL, STOCK EXCHANGE.

elastic relatively responsive to change. See PRICE ELASTICITY OF DEMAND, PRICE ELASTICITY OF SUPPLY, INCOME ELASTICITY OF DEMAND, CROSS ELASTICITY OF DEMAND.

elasticity of demand a measure of the responsiveness of DEMAND to changes in PRICE, INCOME, etc. In the case of PRICE ELASTICITY OF DEMAND, it is the ratio of the percentage change in quantity demanded (Q) to the percentage change in price (P) over a price range, such as $P_0 P_1$ in Fig. 61. Elasticity of demand is expressed notationally as:

$$e = \frac{Q_1 - Q_0}{P_1 - P_0} \times \frac{P_1 + P_0}{Q_1 + Q_0}$$

where P_0 = original price, Q_0 = original quantity, P_1 = new price, Q_1 = new quantity.

Because elasticity of demand measures *e* over a price range or arc of the demand curve, it is only an approximation of demand elasticity at a particular price (POINT ELASTICITY). Where significantly large changes in price are involved, a reformulation of the terms will yield a more precise measure:

$$e_0 = \frac{\dfrac{Q_1 - Q_0}{Q_0 + Q_1}}{\dfrac{P_1 - P_0}{P_0 + P_1}}$$

However, the arc elasticity of demand formula gives a reasonable degree of accuracy in approximating point elasticity when price and/or quantity changes are small.

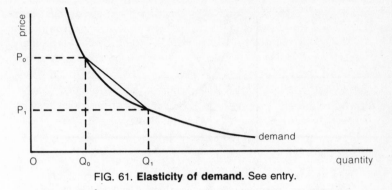

FIG. 61. **Elasticity of demand.** See entry.

See PRICE ELASTICITY OF DEMAND, INCOME ELASTICITY OF DEMAND, CROSS ELASTICITY OF DEMAND.

elasticity of supply the degree of responsiveness of quantity supplied of a particular product (see SUPPLY) to changes in the price of the product. See PRICE ELASTICITY OF SUPPLY.

elasticity of technical substitution the rate at which one FACTOR INPUT can be substituted for another with OUTPUT remaining constant. For example, the rate of substitution between CAPITAL and LABOR may be expressed as:

$$e = \frac{\text{\% change in the ratio of amounts of factors of production employed}}{\text{\% change in the ratio of their marginal physical products}}$$

The denominator in the above expression is known as the MARGINAL RATE OF TECHNICAL SUBSTITUTION. Essentially, the elasticity of substitution is the change in factor proportions used (the numerator) in relation to their substitutability (the denominator). The above expressions may be illustrated graphically using ISOQUANT CURVES (equal product curves) and PROCESS RAYS (see Fig. 62).

The elasticity of substitution between factor inputs is not infinite. Where no substitution is possible ($e = 0$) inputs must be used

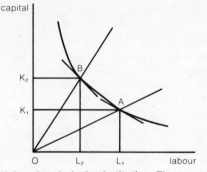

FIG. 62. **Elasticity of technical substitution.** The numerator of the expression is the percentage change in factors employed when moving from process ray OA to process ray OB. The denominator is the change in each factor's relative MARGINAL PHYSICAL PRODUCT, given by the slope of the isoquant curve at the points of tangency A and B.

in fixed proportions; where factors are perfect substitutes, $e = \infty$. The actual measure will lie somewhere between the two. Where it is one, as exhibited in the COBB-DOUGLAS PRODUCTION FUNCTION, there exist constant returns to scale, that is, labor can be substituted for capital in any given proportions and vice versa, without affecting output.

eligible paper assets that Federal Reserve Banks are willing to accept as security for loans to member banks.

embargo the prohibition of the IMPORT and EXPORT of particular types of product, for example, military equipment, or a complete ban on trade with a particular country, especially as an adjunct to the political policies pursued by the government.

empirical testing the process of testing economic theories against empirical data. See HYPOTHESIS, HYPOTHESIS TESTING.

employee a person hired by another person or company to provide LABOR services as a FACTOR INPUT in production of a good or service.

employer a person or company that hires LABOR as a FACTOR INPUT in production of a good or service.

employment the use of LABOR as a FACTOR INPUT in production of a good or service.

Employment Act of 1946 legislation establishing acceptance by the Federal Government of a degree of responsibility to work toward the goals of high employment and relatively stable prices. This act created the Council of Economic Advisers to assist the President. The 1946 act has been supplemented by such legislation as the Humphrey-Hawkins Act of 1976 and the Full Employment Act of 1978.

employment contract a contract between an employee and the company for which he or she works, specifying the terms and conditions governing that employment.

endogenous money or **inside money** the part of the MONEY SUPPLY created inside the banking sector, as opposed to being put into the system from outside by the government or by nonbanking financial institutions (EXOGENOUS MONEY). See DEMAND DEPOSIT CREATION, MONEY SUPPLY SCHEDULE.

endogenous variable a VARIABLE in an ECONOMIC MODEL that affects and is itself affected by the relationship depicted in the model. For example, in the EQUILIBRIUM LEVEL OF NATIONAL INCOME model, an increase in consumption spending increases aggregate demand and raises the level of national income. By the same token, an increase in the level of national income, which results, say, from an increase in investment, will induce an increase in consumption spending. Compare EXOGENOUS VARIABLE.

Engel's law as originally formulated by Ernst Engel in the midnineteenth century, and corroborated by later research, the relationship between income and expenditure as family income increases. The principal findings are: (1) the percentage spent on food decreases, (2) the percentage spent on housing and household operation remains about the same, and (3) the percentage spent on all other items increases. See INFERIOR PRODUCTS, INCOME ELASTICITY OF DEMAND, INCOME CONSUMPTION CURVE, AGRICULTURAL POLICY.

enterprise zone an area established by government to act as a magnet for new investment and job creation. See DEVELOPMENT AREA.

entrepôt trade a commercial warehousing operation in which goods are imported into a country and reexported without distribution within the importing country (see IMPORTS, EXPORTS). Entrepôt transactions are confined in the main to certain COMMODI-TIES, and a MIDDLEMAN located in one of the commodity centers can arrange for sale of the commodity and worldwide shipment to customer countries.

entrepreneur a person who assembles and organizes FACTORS OF PRODUCTION to undertake a venture with a view to PROFIT. The entrepreneur may supply one or more of the other factors of production (NATURAL RESOURCES, LABOR, CAPITAL) or may hire or buy any or all factors in the expectation of future profits. The entrepreneurial function is usually called a *fourth factor of production*.

The entrepreneur was seen in the nineteenth century as an individual proprietor who supplied most or all of the factors of production but especially managerial skill. The advent of the corporation led to division of management and supply of capital, so that *entrepreneur* became a more hypothetical abstract term attached to any individual or group that performs the risk-bearing and organizing functions above. The traditional THEORY OF THE FIRM suggests that entrepreneurs attempt to maximize profit, but since the 1930s there has been growing awareness that the DIVORCE OF OWNERSHIP FROM CONTROL in large companies influences behavioral attitudes of groups of individuals within organizations, which may lead to companies following objectives other than PROFIT MAXIMIZATION.

See BEHAVIORAL THEORY OF THE FIRM, MANAGERIAL THEORIES OF THE FIRM, RISK AND UNCERTAINTY.

entry see MARKET ENTRY, CONDITION OF ENTRY, BARRIERS TO ENTRY, POTENTIAL ENTRANT.

entry-forestalling price see LIMIT PRICING.

envelope curve see AVERAGE COST.

equation a means of portraying arithmetically the relationship between VARIABLES. For example, the equation $C = 1000 + 0.9Y$ suggests a relationship between consumer expenditure (C) and disposable income (Y), which would be true for certain values of C and Y (such as 10,000 and 10,000, respectively), but not true of other values of C and Y (such as 6000 and 10,000, respectively). Equations are generally written with an equals sign (=) with the value to the left of the sign being equal to the value to the right of the sign. The validity of an equation can be tested statistically by collecting paired observations of the variables involved and testing to determine whether or not the observations conform with the equation formulated. See IDENTITY, INEQUALITY.

equilibrium a state of balance with no tendency to change. See EQUILIBRIUM MARKET PRICE, EQUILIBRIUM LEVEL OF NATIONAL INCOME.

equilibrium level of national income 1. the level of NATIONAL INCOME at which the purchasing and production plans of the economy are synchronized. This occurs at the point of intersection of the AGGREGATE DEMAND SCHEDULE with the AGGREGATE SUPPLY SCHEDULE, which is point E in Fig. 63a. Equilibrium income is not necessarily the level of income at which FULL EMPLOYMENT is attained, for an equilibrium level of income can occur at any level of economic activity. Full employment equilibrium is a special case in which aggregate demand corresponds exactly with POTENTIAL GROSS NATIONAL PRODUCT, leaving no INFLATIONARY GAP or DEFLATIONARY GAP. For example, aggregate demand 2 in Fig. 63b represents a full employment equilibrium where E_2 corresponds with full employment output.

2. the level of national income at which total INJECTIONS (investment + government expenditure + exports) are exactly equal to WITHDRAWALS (saving + taxes + imports). Also called *injections-withdrawals approach to national income determination.* In the CIRCULAR FLOW OF NATIONAL INCOME MODEL, income = consumption + withdrawals, and spending = consumption + injections. See Fig. 63c, d.

equilibrium market price the PRICE at which the quantity demanded of a good is exactly equal to the quantity supplied (see DEMAND, SUPPLY). The DEMAND CURVE depicts the quantity that consumers are prepared to buy at particular prices. The SUPPLY CURVE depicts the quantity that producers are prepared to sell at particular prices. See Fig. 64. Also see KEYNESIAN ECONOMICS, NATIONAL INCOME ACCOUNTS.

equilibrium market price (changes in) an increase or decrease in PRICE resulting from a shift in the DEMAND CURVE or SUPPLY CURVE. See Fig. 65. See DEMAND CURVE (SHIFT IN), SUPPLY CURVE (SHIFT IN).

EQUILIBRIUM MARKET PRICE (CHANGES IN)

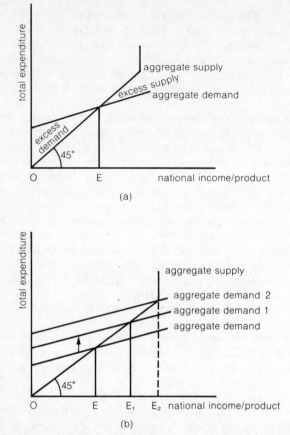

(a)

(b)

FIG. 63. (continued) **Equilibrium level of national oncome.** (c) Equilibrium is achieved when withdrawals = injections, that is, point E, which is the same as point E in the aggregate demand/aggregate supply schedules in (b). If withdrawals exceed injections, total expenditure will fall, resulting in contraction of income and output. Conversely, if injections exceed withdrawals, total expenditure will rise, resulting in an increase in income and output. Only when injections and withdrawals are equal will income and output remain unchanged. (d) The equilibrium level of national income will change if there is a shift in either the injection or withdrawal schedules. For example, an increase in investment spending will shift the injection schedule from I to I_1, resulting in an increase in the equilibrium income level from E to E_1 (see also PARADOX OF THRIFT).

EQUILIBRIUM MARKET PRICE (CHANGES IN)

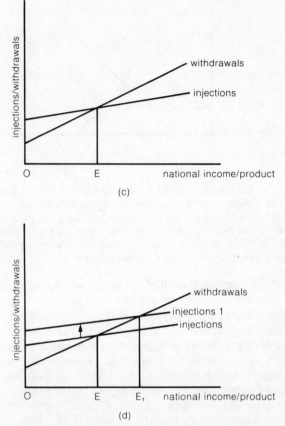

FIG. 63. (continued)**Equilibrium level of national oncome.** (c) Equilibrium is achieved when withdrawals = injections, that is, point E, which is the same as point E in the aggregate demand/aggregate supply schedules in (b). If withdrawals exceed injections, total expenditure will fall, resulting in contraction of income and output. Conversely, if injections exceed withdrawals, total expenditure will rise, resulting in an increase in income and output. Only when injections and withdrawals are equal will income and output remain unchanged. (d) The equilibrium level of national income will change if there is a shift in either the injection or withdrawal schedules. For example, an increase in investment spending will shift the injection schedule from I to I_1, resulting in an increase in the equilibrium income level from E to E_1 (see also PARADOX OF THRIFT).

EQUILIBRIUM MARKET QUANTITY

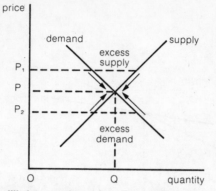

FIG. 64. **Equilibrium market price.** The equilibrium market price, OP, is generated by the intersection of the demand and supply curves. A higher initial price such as OP_1 results in EXCESS SUPPLY, which forces the price down. A lower initial price such as OP_2 results in EXCESS DEMAND, which forces the price up. Only at price OP are buying and supply intentions fully synchronized.

equilibrium market quantity see EQUILIBRIUM MARKET PRICE.

equity capital see COMMON STOCK.

error term see REGRESSION ANALYSIS.

Eurobond market see EUROCURRENCY MARKET.

Eurocurrency market or **Eurobond market** a market based primarily in Europe that is engaged in the lending and borrowing of US dollars and other major currencies outside their countries of origin to finance international trade and investment.

The main financial instrument used in the Eurocurrency market for long-term investment purposes is the Eurobond (see BOND), a form of fixed-interest security denominated in a particular currency or currencies. Depositors in the Eurocurrency market include commercial banks, industrial companies, and central banks. Borrowers for the most part are companies that have resorted to Eurofinance during times of domestic credit restrictions and/or when domestic interest rates have been high in comparison to those prevailing in the Eurocurrency market. See FOREIGN EXCHANGE MARKET.

Eurodollar see EUROCURRENCY MARKET.

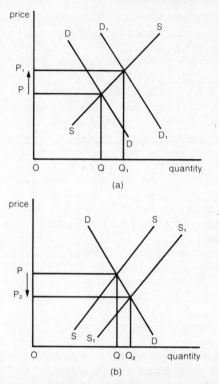

FIG. 65. **Equilibrium market price (changes in).** (a) If there is a shift in the demand curve from DD to $D_1 D_1$ with supply unchanged, the equilibrium price will rise from OP to OP_1. (b) If there is a shift in the supply curve from SS to $S_1 S_1$ with demand unchanged, the equilibrium price will fall from OP to OP_2.

European Community (EC) or (formerly) **European Economic Community (EEC)** a regional alliance established by the Treaty of Rome in 1958 with the general objective of integrating the economies of member countries. There were six founding countries of the EC: West Germany, France, Italy, The Netherlands, Belgium, and Luxembourg, which had previously cooperated (with the exception of The Netherlands) in the European

171

Coal and Steel Community. Other countries have since joined the EC: the United Kingdom, Eire, and Denmark in 1973, Greece (1981), Spain and Portugal (1986).

European Currency Unit (ECU) a monetary asset held by member countries of the EUROPEAN MONETARY SYSTEM (EMS) as part of their INTERNATIONAL RESERVES. Unlike other reserve assets, such as gold, ECUs have no tangible life of their own. They are created by the EMSs European Monetary Cooperation Fund in exchange for payment of gold and other reserve assets by members and take the form of bookkeeping entries in a special account managed by the Fund. The value at the ECU is based on a weighted basket of members' national currencies. See EUROPEAN COMMUNITY.

European Economic Community see EUROPEAN COMMUNITY.

European Monetary Cooperation Fund See EUROPEAN MONETARY SYSTEM.

European Monetary System (EMS) the monetary system established by the EUROPEAN COMMUNITY (EC) in 1979 to coordinate and stabilize EXCHANGE RATES of member countries. The EMS is based on a FIXED EXCHANGE RATE mechanism, a pool of FOREIGN EXCHANGE and gold reserves for settling payments imbalances, and the EUROPEAN CURRENCY UNIT a monetary unit used to value, on a common basis, exchange rates and reserves.

The EMS is managed by the *European Monetary Cooperation Fund.* Membership in the EMS is voluntary, and two countries, the United Kingdom and Greece, as of 1990 have decided not to participate in the exchange-rate arrangements of the EMS, although they are fully involved in operation of the reserve pool.

The exchange-rate system used by the EMS is a variant of the ADJUSTABLE PEG fixed exchange-rate system formerly used by the INTERNATIONAL MONETARY FUND. Exchange rate movements are controlled by a parity grid. Each currency is given a central par value expressed in terms of the ECU. A currency may move to a limit of 2.25% on either side of its central rate, but the Italian lira is allowed a 6% move on either side. If a currency reaches its outer limit, the country's central bank must intervene directly in the foreign exchange market and/or adjust domestic interest rates to stabilize the rate.

Should the central rate itself prove to be overvalued or undervalued against other members' currencies, then, with the approval of the European Monetary Cooperation Fund, a member may devalue or revalue its currency, repegging at a new fixed central parity rate (see DEVALUATION, REVALUATION). See EUROPEAN CURRENCY UNIT.

European Recovery Program the Marshall Plan of 1948, in which the United States helped European countries recover economically from the effects of World War II. The United States supplied about $12,000,000 in grants, a sum that approximated about 4% of those countries' national incomes. George C. Marshall, US Secretary of State, was awarded the Nobel Peace Prize in 1953 for inspiring the program. The cooperation stimulated by the Marshall Plan led to establishment of the Organization for Economic Cooperation and Development (OECD).

ex ante being applied from before an action. The concept of an ex ante approach to economics, together with that of *ex post* (from after) is widely employed in economic analysis to examine the change in some economic phenomenon as it moves from a state of DISEQUILIBRIUM to one of EQUILIBRIUM. For example, ex ante in the Keynesian model of national income determination, planned investment may be greater than planned saving so that the economic system is in a state of disequilibrium. The excess of investment, however, serves to inject additional income into the economy and, via the MULTIPLIER effect, increases both income and saving, bringing about an eventual ex post equilibrium at which realized investment equals realized savings. See EQUILIBRIUM LEVEL OF NATIONAL INCOME.

excess capacity 1. a situation in which a company or industry has more than enough plant available to supply a product than is currently being demanded. As a result a proportion of the company or industry's CAPACITY stands idle. Excess capacity can result from a temporary downturn in demand, a secular fall in demand, or overinvestment in new plant relative to long-term demand potential. In the latter two instances, excess capacity may be eliminated by an intensification of competitive pressures (see EXCESS SUPPLY) that forces inefficient suppliers to leave the industry, or by RATIONALIZATION schemes.

EXCESS DEMAND

2. in economic theory, the cost structures of companies operating in imperfect markets. Industry output is maximized, that is, full capacity is attained, when all companies produce at the minimum point on their long-term average total cost curves (see PERFECT COMPETITION). See Fig. 66 for the effect of MONOPOLISTIC COMPETITION.

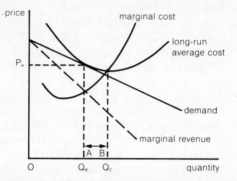

FIG. 66. **Excess capacity.** Under the imperfect market conditions of monopolistic competition, the equilibrium (PROFIT MAXIMIZING) position for a company is at a point (Q_e) to the left of the cost-minimizing point (Q_c) on the long-term average total cost curve. Industry output is less, and costs are higher than the optimum position. Thus, excess capacity is measured as the difference between actual industry output and the cost-minimizing level of industry output (distance AB).

excess demand or **shortages** a situation in which the quantity demanded of a product (OQ_2 in Fig. 67) exceeds the quantity supplied (OQ_1) at the *existing* market price (OP). In competitive markets there will be upward pressure on price, reflecting shortage of the product, but where the price is controlled the excess can persist. See EQUILIBRIUM MARKET PRICE, EXCESS SUPPLY, PRICE CONTROLS.

excess profit see ABOVE-NORMAL PROFIT.

excess supply a situation in which the quantity supplied of a product (OQ_2 in Fig. 68) exceeds the quantity demanded of the product (OQ_1) at the *existing* market price (OP). In a competitive market there will be downward pressure on price as suppliers

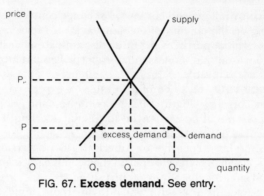
FIG. 67. **Excess demand.** See entry.

compete to dispose of surpluses, but where there is government intervention the situation can persist. See EQUILIBRIUM MARKET PRICE, EXCESS DEMAND, PRICE CONTROLS, PRICE SUPPORT.

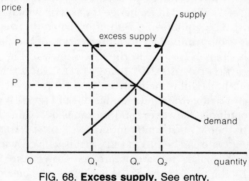
FIG. 68. **Excess supply.** See entry.

exchange 1. the buying and selling of goods and services either in the form of BARTER or through a MARKET. 2. the means of financing the purchase of goods and services in a market. See MONEY, FOREIGN EXCHANGE.

exchange controls a means of limiting the extent to which a country's CURRENCY can be exchanged freely for foreign currencies. Controls are applied to assist in removal of a BALANCE OF PAYMENTS deficit and to protect a FIXED EXCHANGE RATE against

EXCHANGE RATE

HOT MONEY inflows and outflows. Exchange control systems place a ceiling on the amount of currency available for overseas trade and investment purposes and often discriminate against particular items, for example, nonessential imports. See BALANCE-OF-PAYMENTS EQUILIBRIUM.

exchange rate the price of a CURRENCY expressed in terms of another currency. Figure 69a shows the rate, or price, at which dollars ($s) might be exchanged for pounds sterling (£s). The demand curve (D) for £s slopes downward, reflecting the fact that if £s become less expensive to Americans, British goods, services, and assets will become cheaper to them. This causes Americans to demand greater quantities of British goods, etc., and therefore greater amounts of £s with which to buy those items. The supply curve (S) of £s is upward-sloping, reflecting the fact that as the dollar price of £s rises, American goods, services, and assets become cheaper to the British. This causes the British to demand greater quantities of American goods, etc. and hence the greater the supply of £s offered in exchange for $s with which to purchase those items. The equilibrium rate of exchange between the two currencies is determined by the intersection of the demand and supply schedules ($2 = £1, in the case shown in Fig. 69a).

Under a FIXED EXCHANGE-RATE SYSTEM the exchange rate, once established, will remain unchanged for relatively long periods. If the exchange rate gets too far out of line with underlying market conditions, however, and becomes overvalued, resulting in a country being persistently in BALANCE OF PAYMENTS deficit, the exchange rate can be DEVALUED, that is, refixed at a new lower value, which makes imports more expensive and its exports cheaper. By the same token, if the exchange rate becomes undervalued, resulting in a country being persistently in balance of payments surplus, the exchange rate can be revalued, that is, refixed at a new higher value, which makes imports cheaper and its exports more expensive (see REVALUATION).

Under a FLOATING EXCHANGE-RATE SYSTEM the exchange rate is free to fluctuate day by day and will fall [see DEPRECIATION(1)] or rise [see APPRECIATION(1)] in line with changing market conditions, serving to keep a country's balance of payments more or less in equilibrium on a continuing basis.

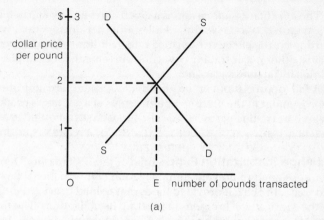

(a)

(b)

FIG. 69. **Exchange rate.** (a) The graph shows the interaction of demand (D) and supply (S) in determining the exchange rate between pounds and dollars. (b) The effective exchange rate of sterling. The graph shows the monthly average of daily rates, with 1975 = 100.

177

EXCHANGE STABILIZATION FUND

The *effective exchange rate* is a given currency's value in terms of a WEIGHTED AVERAGE of a basket of other currencies. Figure 69b depicts the effective exchange rate over time of the UK pound against other major trading countries' currencies, for example, the US dollar, Japanese yen, etc.

A fall (depreciation) in the effective exchange rate indicates an improvement in the price competitiveness of a country's products vis-a-vis its trading partners. See also PURCHASING-POWER PARITY THEORY, ASSET VALUE THEORY, BALANCE-OF-PAYMENTS EQUILIBRIUM, INTERNATIONAL FISHER EFFECT.

Exchange Stabilization Fund a fund of the US Treasury Department designed to prevent destabilization of international finance and trade. In 1982, it provided funds that helped prevent a default by the Mexican government in meeting its obligations. The funds provided, together with money and credit supplied by the International Monetary Fund and the US Federal Reserve System, were sufficient to keep the Mexican government afloat. A similar arrangement was made for Brazil in 1985.

excise duty an INDIRECT TAX levied by a government on certain goods, most notably tobacco, gasoline, and alcoholic beverages. If demand for these goods is price-inelastic (see PRICE ELASTICITY OF DEMAND), duty increases implemented as part of FISCAL POLICY will not only raise government revenue but also leave customers with less money to spend on other goods. See TAXATION.

exclusive dealing a practice whereby a supplier contracts with distributors to deal only in that supplier's products to the exclusion of competitors' products. Exclusive dealing may be beneficial in some cases by permitting distribution costs to be lowered, but if exclusive dealing is pursued by several large firms in a market, the access of smaller suppliers and potential entrants to established distributive outlets may be severely restricted.

ex dividend (of a particular security) excluding entitlement to the DIVIDEND that attaches to the stock. If shares are purchased on the stock exchange "ex div.," the purchaser is not entitled to the dividend accruing to that stock when the dividend is next paid. Compare CUM DIVIDEND.

exit see MARKET EXIT.

exogenous money the part of the MONEY SUPPLY put into the economic system from outside by the government and by non-banking financial institutions, as opposed to being created inside the system by the banking sector (ENDOGENOUS MONEY).

exogenous variable a VARIABLE that affects the operation of an ECONOMIC MODEL but is not itself affected by any of the relationships depicted in the model. For example, in the EQUILIBRIUM LEVEL OF NATIONAL INCOME model, an increase in exports will increase AGGREGATE DEMAND and induce an increase in the level of national income, but the volume of exports itself is determined by any other country's propensity to import and not by the level of its own national income. Compare ENDOGENOUS VARIABLE.

expectations anticipations of future events in order to guide present economic acts. A major unresolved problem in economics is how to deal with the uncertainty the future holds, especially when individuals have different perceptions of that future.

Consequently, much economic analysis incorporates expectations in the various models as a given variable, usually under the heading CETERIS PARIBUS, or by assuming that an individual acts in accordance with the RATIONAL EXPECTATIONS HYPOTHESIS. A further problem is that expectations involve a time period and much economic analysis is static, that is, points of equilibrium may be observed but the route between them is considered irrelevant. A simple and instructive demonstration of expectations is given in the COBWEB THEOREM.

Nevertheless, expectations have played a significant part in economic theory, most notably in the work of Keynes. Expectations are a major variable, it is argued, in determining business cycles and affecting the SPECULATIVE DEMAND FOR MONEY. Expectations are also influential when dealing with the TERM STRUCTURE OF INTEREST RATES.

To incorporate expectations in economic theory, it is possible to treat individual behavior as adaptive, as illustrated in the ADAPTIVE EXPECTATIONS HYPOTHESIS. Although the concept is straightforward, future expectations being adapted from past and present experience, the attempts to reflect reality have led to formulation of complex structures.

See KEYNESIAN ECONOMICS, EXPECTATIONS-ADJUSTED/AUGMENTED PHILLIPS CURVE, SPECULATOR.

expectations-adjusted/augmented Phillips curve a reformulated PHILLIPS CURVE that allows for the effects of price EXPEC-
TATIONS on money wage increases. In the Phillips curve (see Fig.
70) $U^\star$ is the natural rate of unemployment or NONACCELERAT-
ING INFLATION RATE OF UNEMPLOYMENT (NAIRU). That is, the
rate of unemployment at which inflation is neither accelerating
nor decelerating. If the authorities attempt to reduce unemployment below the natural rate to, say, U_1 the inflation rate rises from
point A to point B on Phillips curve PC_1.

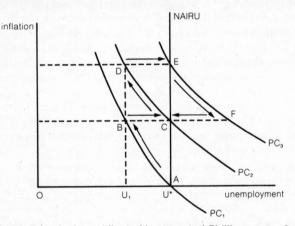

FIG. 70. **Expectations-adjusted/augmented Phillips curve.** See
entry.

Assuming that the increase in money wages exceeds the growth
of output per worker, labor prices itself out of jobs, and unemployment reverts to its natural level (point C) on a new Phillips curve
(PC_2), which is based on a higher expected rate of inflation. Starting now at point C, if the authorities again attempt to reduce
unemployment (to U_1), this will produce an acceleration in the
inflation rate to point D, but again the higher rate of money wages
will cause unemployment to revert to its natural level (point E) on
a new Phillips curve (PC_3) based on a yet higher expected rate of
inflation.

To get the inflation rate down, the authorities need to force unemployment above the natural rate temporarily, from point E to point F on the Phillips curve (PC_3), so as to reduce public expectations about the expected rate of inflation. As money wage rates fall, people are priced back into jobs and unemployment falls to its natural level, at point C on PC_2. See also INFLATIONARY SPIRAL.

expected value the quantitative results of uncertain events weighted by the probability of their occurrence. See RISK PROFILE, UTILITY INDEX.

expenditure approach to GNP see NATIONAL INCOME ACCOUNTS.

expenditure tax a form of INDIRECT TAX that is incorporated into the selling price of a product and borne by the consumer.

experience curve or **learning curve** the process whereby managers and employees learn through experience to operate new technologies more effectively over time so that growing familiarity with, and repetitive operation of, a new technology enables unit costs of production to be progressively reduced. See Fig. 71. See PRODUCTIVITY.

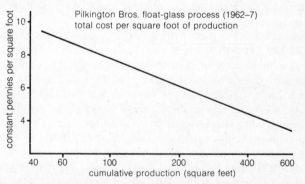

FIG. 71. **Experience curve.** The estimated reduction in total cost per square foot accruing from accumulated increases in the production of float glass using the revolutionary float glass process. Source: UK Monopolies Commission, *Float Glass* report, HMSO, 1968.

explicit cost a payment made by a company for use of FACTOR INPUTS (labor, capital) not owned by the company. Unlike IM-

PLICIT COSTS, which represent payments for the use of factor inputs owned by the company itself, explicit costs involve the company in purchasing inputs from outside FACTOR MARKETS.

exponential function a function in which a variable quantity is the power of a fixed number. Thus a^x and $(a + b)^x$ are exponential functions, with x the exponent. The former value can also be read "a to the power of x" and means that a is multiplied by itself the number of times the exponent states. In the exponential function $y = a^x$, if $a = 2$ and $x = 3$, then $y = 8$ (that is, $2 \times 2 \times 2$). Exponential functions transform into logarithms and vice versa. See LOGARITHMIC FUNCTION, LOG-LINEAR FUNCTION.

exponential smoothing see TIME-SERIES ANALYSIS.

export incentives the financial assistance given to domestic companies by a government as a means of promoting exports and helping the country's balance of payments. Export incentives may include direct subsidies to lower export prices (EXPORT SUBSIDY), tax concessions (remission of profits earned on exports), credit facilities (cheap export finance), and financial guarantees.

Export incentives are often viewed as an unfair trade practice by foreign countries and frequently result in retaliatory action being taken by them.

See COUNTERVAILING DUTY, BEGGAR-MY-NEIGHBOR POLICY.

export-led growth an expansion of an economy with exports serving as a leading sector. As exports rise, they inject additional income into the domestic economy and increase total demand for domestically produced output (see EXPORT MULTIPLIER). The increase in exports also enables a higher level of import absorption to be accommodated so that there is no BALANCE OF PAYMENTS constraint on achievement of sustained ECONOMIC GROWTH. See CIRCULAR FLOW OF NATIONAL INCOME MODEL.

export multiplier the ratio of increase in a country's NATIONAL INCOME to increase in the demand for the country's exports that brought it about. The INJECTION of increased exports into the CIRCULAR FLOW OF NATIONAL INCOME raises national income by some multiple of the original increase in exports. The value of the export multiplier depends on the country's MARGINAL PROPENSITY TO SAVE, MARGINAL PROPENSITY TO IMPORT, and MAR-

GINAL PROPENSITY TO TAX. The larger these propensities—that is, the larger the WITHDRAWALS from the income flow—the smaller will be the value of the export multiplier. See Fig. 72. See also MULTIPLIER, FOREIGN TRADE MULTIPLIER, EXPORT-LED GROWTH.

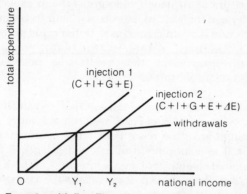

FIG. 72. **Export multiplier.** The effect of an increase in exports on national income. The additional exports (ΔE) serve to increase total injections and shift the injection schedule to the right, increasing national income by $Y_1 Y_2$.

export restraint agreement an arrangement between an exporting country and an importing country that limits the volume of trade in a particular product or products. Specifically, EXPORTS and IMPORTS between the two countries are limited to an agreed number of units, or percentage share of the importing country's domestic sales. An export restraint agreement is thus a protectionist measure (see PROTECTIONISM) designed to shield domestic producers in the importing country from foreign competition and help that country's balance of payments. See MULTI-FIBER ARRANGEMENT.

exports goods, services, and capital assets sold to foreign countries. Exports are important in two main respects: (a) together with imports, they make up a country's BALANCE OF PAYMENTS (a country must export in order to pay for its imports in foreign currency); (b) they represent an injection into the CIRCULAR FLOW OF NATIONAL INCOME, serving to raise real income and output. See EXPORT MULTIPLIER.

export subsidy a direct payment, or tax concession, made by a government to domestic companies to enable them to reduce their export prices. Although widespread use of export subsidies by a country can increase its exports and help its balance of payments, such subsidies are viewed as an unfair trade practice by the GENERAL AGREEMENT ON TARIFFS AND TRADE, and are likely to lead to retaliatory action by other countries. See COUNTERVAILING DUTY, BEGGAR-MY-NEIGHBOR POLICY.

ex post see EX ANTE.

external balance a situation of BALANCE-OF-PAYMENTS EQUILIB-RIUM that, over a number of years, results in a country's spending and investing abroad no more than other countries spend and invest in it. The achievement of external balance is one of the macroeconomic objectives of a government. Compare INTERNAL BALANCE. See also DEMAND MANAGEMENT, EXCHANGE RATES, MACROECONOMIC POLICY, INTERNAL-EXTERNAL BALANCE MODEL.

external diseconomies of scale the factors outside the influence of a single company that lead to increasing long-term AVER-AGE COSTS within all industry. For example, if a number of companies settle in a particular area, the additional road traffic they cause may slow up deliveries for some companies, increasing their transportation costs. See EXTERNAL ECONOMIES OF SCALE, DISECONOMIES OF SCALE.

external economies of scale the factors outside the influence of a single company that lead to decreasing long-term AVERAGE COSTS for all industry. For example, if a school concentrated on training large numbers of computer programmers to serve the needs of local computer businesses, the individual employer would have a supply of trained programmers available, with a resulting reduction in the company's own training costs. See EX-TERNAL DISECONOMIES OF SCALE, ECONOMIES OF SCALE, INTER-NAL ECONOMIES OF SCALE.

externalities factors not included in GROSS NATIONAL PRODUCT that affect human welfare. Pollution is a prime example of an external cost imposed on society: national output may only be maintained by allowing a certain degree of pollution that detracts from the quality of life. A company will include the PRIVATE COSTS of materials, labor, and capital used in producing goods and services but will not count the SOCIAL COSTS of pollution involved. On the other hand, positive externalities, such as the social benefits conferred by companies in training workers who become available for employment elsewhere, are not counted in national output. See WELFARE ECONOMICS, COST-BENEFIT ANALYSIS.

extrapolate to estimate an unknown (future) value by projecting from known (past) values (in TIME-SERIES ANALYSIS). This involves predicting a value for the DEPENDENT VARIABLE from a value of the INDEPENDENT VARIABLE that is beyond the range of observed independent variables, and outside the range the trend line may be inaccurate because the underlying relationship may be different over the broader range. By contrast, if we *interpolate*, that is, predict a value for the dependent variable from a value of the independent variable that lies within the range of observed independent variables, the prediction is likely to be more reliable. See FORECASTING.

F

face value see PAR VALUE.

factor 1. a FACTOR INPUT used in production (see NATURAL RE-
SOURCES, LABOR, CAPITAL). **2.** a business that buys in bulk and
performs a WHOLESALING function. **3.** a business that buys trade
debts from client companies at some agreed price below the nominal value of the debts and then arranges to recover them for itself.
See FACTOR MARKETS, FACTORING.

factor cost the value of goods and services produced as measured
in terms of the cost of the FACTOR INPUTS (materials, labor, etc.)
used to produce them, that is, excluding any indirect taxes levied
on products and any subsidies offered on products. For example,
a product costing $10 to produce (including normal profit) and
with a $1 indirect tax levied on it would have a market price of
$11 and a factor cost of $10. See FACTORS OF PRODUCTION.

factor income see NATIONAL INCOME.

factoring a financial undertaking in which a specialist finance company (the factor) purchases a company's ACCOUNTS RECEIVABLE
for an amount less than the book value of those accounts. The
factor's profit derives from the difference between the amounts
collected from the accounts purchased and the actual purchase
price of those accounts. The client company benefits by receiving
immediate cash from the factor rather than having to wait until
its customers eventually pay their debts, and avoids the trouble
and expense of pursuing tardy debtors. For example, if a company
has $100,000 of accounts receivable on its books, it may sell them
to a factoring company for, say, $80,000 cash, giving the factoring
company a discount of 20% and a potential profit of $20,000 if it
collects all the debts. Factoring companies may also advise on
credit ratings of individuals and companies, for which a fee is
charged. See DEBTORS, CREDIT CONTROLS.

FACTOR INPUTS

factor inputs FACTORS OF PRODUCTION (labor, capital, etc.) that are combined to produce OUTPUT of goods and services. See PRODUCTION FUNCTION, COST FUNCTION.

factor markets markets in which FACTORS OF PRODUCTION are bought and sold, and in which the prices of labor and other FACTOR INPUTS are determined by the interplay of demand and supply forces. See LABOR MARKET, CAPITAL MARKET, COMMODITY MARKET, DERIVED DEMAND

factors of production the resources used by companies as FACTOR INPUTS in producing a good or service. There are four main groups of factor inputs: NATURAL RESOURCES, LABOR, CAPITAL, and ENTERPRISE. Factors of production can be combined in different proportions to produce a given output (see PRODUCTION FUNCTION). It is assumed in the THEORY OF THE FIRM that companies will select the combination of inputs for any given level of output that minimizes the cost of producing the output (see COST FUNCTION). See also ENTREPRENEUR, MOBILITY.

fallacy of composition an error in logic that arises when it is assumed that what holds true for one individual or part must also hold true for the sum of the parts. For example, if a small number of people save more of their income, this may be considered to be good because more funds can be made available to finance investment. But if everybody attempts to save more, this will reduce total spending and income and may result in a fall in total saving. See PARADOX OF THRIFT.

FASB see FINANCIAL ACCOUNTING STANDARDS BOARD.

feasible region see LINEAR PROGRAMMING.

Federal Funds Rate see RATE OF INTEREST.

Federal Reserve System the US CENTRAL BANK. The Fed, as it is called almost universally, is a privately owned, government-created, nonprofit institution comprising 12 Federal Reserve Banks and some 5000 member banks. All nationally chartered banks must belong to the Fed, and many state-chartered banks are also in the system.

Governance of the system is in the hands of a Board of Governors, with members appointed by the US President. The board is assisted by committees of officers of banks, of which the most important is the Federal Open Market Committee. Private ownership of the Fed was established to prevent political control of the system, and there have been conflicts at various times between the Federal Administration and the Federal Reserve Banks.

The primary function of the Fed is to foster a flow of money and credit that facilitates orderly economic growth, stable currency, and long-run balance between US exports and imports. The principal means of achieving these goals are open market operations and adjustment of reserve requirements and discount rates.

The major tool of monetary policy is open market operations, meaning purchase and sale of US Government securities, usually short-term. The Committee sells to banks and to the public in order to damp price rises, and it pursues the opposite course to offset deflation. When banks or their customers purchase securities, the purchase causes the banks to lose an equivalent amount of their reserves and of their capacity to create money and credit. By contrast, sales to the Open Market Committee create additional reserves that enable the banks to expand money and credit.

The discount rate is the interest rate that the 12 Federal Reserve Banks charge banks that want to borrow *at the window*. To offset rising prices, the Fed may raise the discount rate, making it more expensive for banks to borrow and less profitable to lend or invest. This can lead to a reduction in money and credit. Lowering the discount rate would have the goal of offsetting deflationary tendencies.

Congress has given the Fed power to adjust, within established ranges, the rate of required reserves on demand deposits and on time deposits. In times of continuously rising prices, the Fed can be expected to raise the reserve requirements and to reduce the capacity of banks to create money and credit. Deflationary tendencies would lead to an opposite set of actions by the Fed.

Recent developments—proliferation of nonbanking financial institutions, decontrol of banking, removal of barriers to interstate and international banking—have diminished the ability of the Fed to control the supply of money directly.

In addition to the quantitative controls mentioned above, the Fed can employ certain qualitative controls to achieve its goals: establishing a maximum interest rate, establishing minimum down payments on so-called big-ticket consumer goods, establishing minimum down payments for purchase of securities, etc.

Other Fed responsibilities include supervision of member

banks, custodianship of required reserves, acting as fiscal agent for the Federal Government, and supplier of coins and currency. As is generally true of central banks, the Fed is a lender of last resort, ensuring that there is sufficient liquidity in the economy to prevent collapse of the banking system.

See DEMAND DEPOSIT CREATION, OPEN-MARKET OPERATION.

fees the payments to professional persons, such as lawyers and accountants, for performing services on behalf of clients.

fiat currency see FIDUCIARY ISSUE.

fiduciary issue or **fiat currency** currency issued by a government or bank that is not matched by holdings of gold or other securities. In the nineteenth century most currency issues were backed, at least in part, by gold, and people could exchange their paper money for gold on demand. Nowadays, most governments and banks have only minimal holdings of gold and other securities, insufficient to redeem their currency, so most of their currency issues generally are fiduciary. See MONEY SUPPLY.

final products GOODS and SERVICES that are consumed by end users, as opposed to INTERMEDIATE GOODS, which are used as FACTOR INPUTS in producing other goods and services. Thus, purchases of bread count as part of final demand but not purchases of the flour used to make the bread.

The total market value of all final products, which corresponds to total expenditure in the NATIONAL INCOME ACCOUNTS, corresponds to the total VALUE ADDED at each product stage for all products in the economy.

financial accounting the accounting activities directed toward preparation of annual reports to shareholders on their company's overall (profit) performance.

Financial Accounting Standards Board (FASB) an independent organization in the United States founded to establish and maintain generally accepted accounting principles.

financial institution an institution that acts primarily as a FINANCIAL INTERMEDIARY in channeling funds from lenders to borrowers (for example, COMMERCIAL BANKS, SAVINGS AND LOAN INSTITUTIONS), or from savers to investors (for example, PENSION FUNDS, INSURANCE COMPANIES). See FINANCIAL SYSTEM.

financial intermediary an organization that operates in financial markets linking lenders and borrowers or savers and investors. See FINANCIAL SYSTEM, COMMERCIAL BANK, SAVINGS BANK, PENSION FUND, INSURANCE COMPANY.

financial ratio see ACCOUNTING RATIO.

financial sector the part of the ECONOMY concerned with transactions of FINANCIAL INSTITUTIONS. Financial institutions provide money transmission services and loan facilities, and influence the workings of the real economy by acting as intermediaries in channeling SAVINGS and other funds into INVESTMENT uses. The financial sector, CORPORATE SECTOR, and PERSONAL SECTOR constitute the PRIVATE SECTOR. The private sector, PUBLIC (GOVERNMENT) SECTOR, and FOREIGN SECTOR make up the national economy.

financial security the financial instruments issued by companies, financial institutions, and government. Financial securities include STOCKS, DEBENTURES, BILLS OF EXCHANGE, TREASURY BILLS,and BONDS.

financial statement a representation of a company's assets and liabilities, derived from its accounting records.

financial system a network of financial institutions (BANKS, COMMERCIAL BANKS, SAVINGS AND LOAN INSITUTIONS, etc.) and markets (MONEY MARKET, STOCK EXCHANGE) dealing in a variety of financial instruments (BANK DEPOSITS, TREASURY BILLS, STOCKS, BONDS, etc.) that are engaged in money transmission and in lending and borrowing funds.

Financial institutions and markets occupy a key position in the economy as intermediaries in channeling savings and other funds to borrowers. In so doing one of their principal tasks is to reconcile the different requirements of savers and borrowers, thereby facilitating a higher level of saving and investment than would otherwise be the case. Savers in general look for a safe and relatively risk-free repository for their funds, which combines some degree of liquidity (ready access to their money) with a longer-term investment return that protects the real value of their wealth as well as providing current income. Borrowers, in general, require access to funds of varying amounts to finance current, medium-term, and long-term financial and capital commitments often, as is especially the case with business investments, under conditions of unavoidable uncertainty and high degrees of risk. The financial institutions help reconcile these requirements in three main ways:

(a) by pooling together the savings of a large number of individuals, thus making it possible in turn to make single loans running into millions of dollars;

(b) by holding a diversified portfolio of assets and lending for a variety of purposes to gain economies of scale by spreading their risks while still keeping profitability high; and

(c) by combining the resources of a large number of savers to provide both for an individual to remove funds at short notice, and for deposits to remain stable as a base for long-term lending.

fine-tuning a short-run interventionist approach to the economy that uses monetary and fiscal measures to control fluctuations in the level of AGGREGATE DEMAND, with the aim of minimizing deviations from MACROECONOMIC POLICY objectives. The application of fine-tuning is beset with the difficulty of accurately FORECASTING fluctuations in economic activity and in gauging the magnitude and timing of countercyclical measures. See DEMAND MANAGEMENT, STABILIZATION POLICY, MONETARY POLICY, FISCAL POLICY.

firm or **company** or **supplier** a transformation unit concerned with converting FACTOR INPUTS into higher-valued intermediate and final GOODS or SERVICES. The company or BUSINESS is the basic producing/supplying unit and is a vital building block in constructing a theory of the market to explain how companies interact and how their pricing and output decisions influence market supply and price (see THEORY OF THE FIRM, THEORY OF MARKETS).

The legal form of a firm consists of:

(a) a *sole proprietorship* a firm owned and controlled (managed) by one person.

(b) a *partnership* a firm owned and controlled by two or more persons who are parties to a partnership agreement.

(c) a *corporation* a firm owned by a group of common stockholders and whose capital is divided into a number of SHARES. See COOPERATIVE.

The economic form of a firm consists of:

(a) a *horizontal firm* one engaged in a single productive activity, for example, furniture finishing.

(b) a *vertical firm* one that undertakes two or more vertically linked productive activities, for example, the production of automobile components (clutches, chassis) and automobile assembly.

(c) a *diversified* or *conglomerate firm* one engaged in a number of unrelated productive activities, for example, automobile assembly, furniture finishing, and baking.

See HORIZONTAL INTEGRATION, VERTICAL INTEGRATION, DIVERSIFICATION.

firm location see COMPANY LOCATION.

firm objectives see COMPANY OBJECTIVES.

first-in first-out (FIFO) see INVENTORY VALUATION.

fiscal drag the restraining effect of PROGRESSIVE TAXATION on economic expansion. As NATIONAL INCOME rises, people move from lower to higher tax brackets, thereby increasing government TAX receipts. The increase in taxation constitutes a leakage from the CIRCULAR FLOW OF NATIONAL INCOME that will reduce the rate of expansion of AGGREGATE DEMAND below what would otherwise be the case. Governments may choose as part of FISCAL POLICY to adjust for the effects of fiscal drag by regularly increasing personal tax allowances or by increasing government expenditures.

Fiscal drag can also serve to automatically constrain the effect of the pressure of INFLATION in an economy, for with a high rate of inflation people will tend to move into higher tax brackets, thereby increasing their total tax payments, decreasing their disposal income, and reducing aggregate demand. This has the effect of reducing the pressure of DEMAND-PULL INFLATION. See AUTOMATIC STABILIZERS.

fiscal policy a tool of general MACROECONOMIC POLICY that seeks to influence the level of economic activity through control of government expenditure and taxation.

The use of deficit financing, that is, a BUDGET DEFICIT where the government spends more than its income from taxation, was advocated by KEYNES in the 1930s to effect a transition from a situation of mass unemployment to one approaching FULL EMPLOYMENT. Theoretically, an increase in government spending or reduction in taxes (an INJECTION into the economy) stimulates AGGREGATE DEMAND via the MULTIPLIER effect, thus creating jobs to satisfy that demand, raising national income (from Y to Y_1

in Fig. 73). If the level of economic activity is too high, that is, the economy is overheating, the government has the option of running a BUDGET SURPLUS, decreasing its expenditure, or increasing taxes (a WITHDRAWAL from the economy) to decrease aggregate demand.

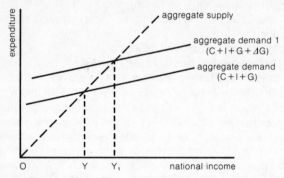

FIG. 73. **Fiscal policy.** The effect of an increase in government expenditure on aggregate demand and national income.

The main aim of fiscal policy is to effect a countercyclical policy so that BOOMS and DEPRESSIONS during the course of the BUSINESS CYCLE are offset. This leads fiscal policy to be used for the FINE-TUNING of an economy. Many economists believe that fiscal policy as a panacea for economic ills was misplaced, that it is more suited to conditions of depression that existed when Keynes wrote his *General Theory of Employment, Interest and Money* in 1936 than to inflationary economies. Consequently, in the late 1970s, during periods of so-called stagflation, it fell from favor somewhat and was replaced by greater faith in MONETARY POLICY to achieve a government's objectives. Recently, fiscal policies have reemerged and are now being received with more credibility by some economists than was apparent in the late 1970s. However, the debate still continues as to which are the most effective fine-tuning instruments to use.

See also CIRCULAR FLOW OF NATIONAL INCOME MODEL, DEFLATIONARY GAP, INFLATIONARY GAP, DEMAND MANAGEMENT.

fiscal year a business or government's accounting year. In the

United States, the government's fiscal year runs from October 1 to September 30 of the following calendar year. Different countries frequently have fiscal years differing from the normal calendar year.

Fisher effect an equation devised by Irving Fisher (1867—1947) in which the NOMINAL RATE OF INTEREST on a BOND is expressed as the sum of the *real* rate of interest and the rate of INFLATION expected over the duration of the bond. The equation is expressed as:

$$r = R + \propto + R \propto$$

where r = nominal rate of interest, R = real rate of interest, ∞ = rate of annual inflation over the life of the bond. $R \infty$ is a cross-product term that is usually dropped when the rate of inflation is low. This leaves what is now termed the Fisher effect formulation of:

$$r = R + \propto$$

Put another way, the interest rate must include an element to compensate lenders for the reduced value of present currency lent when it is returned by the borrower. This termed the inflation premium. For example, if inflation is 5% in 1 year, then nominal interest rates will rise by 5%, the real rate being unchanged. The Fisher effect suggests a one-to-one ratio between inflation and nominal interest rates. See INTERNATIONAL FISHER EFFECT.

Fisher equation see QUANTITY THEORY OF MONEY.

Fisher, Irving (1867—1947) characterized by Schumpeter among others as the greatest scientific economist in history. A founder of the Econometric Society, Fisher was innovative in employing the quantitative theory of money and was instrumental in introducing the use of index numbers.

fixed assets the assets, such as buildings and machinery, that are bought for long-term use by a company rather than for resale. Fixed assets are retained in the business for long periods, and generally each year a proportion of their original cost will be written off against profits for amortization [see DEPRECIATION(2)] to reflect the diminishing value of the assets. In a BALANCE SHEET, fixed assets are usually shown at cost less depreciation charged to date. Certain fixed assets, such as property, tend to appreciate in value [see APPRECIATION(2)] and need to be revalued periodically to help keep their BALANCE SHEET values in line with market values. See CURRENT ASSETS.

fixed costs or **overhead costs** any costs that in the short term do not vary with the level of output. See Fig. 74.

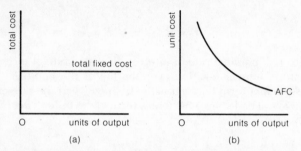

FIG. 74. **Fixed costs.** (a) The graph represents payments for use of FIXED FACTOR INPUTS (plant, equipment, etc.) that must be met whether output is high or low. (b) The graph represents the continuous decline in average fixed cost (AFC) as output rises with a given amount of fixed cost spread over an increasing number of units.

In the THEORY OF MARKETS a firm will leave a product market if in the long term it cannot earn sufficient TOTAL REVENUE to cover both total fixed costs and total VARIABLE COSTS. However, it will remain in a market in the near term as long as it can generate sufficient total revenue to cover total variable cost and make some contribution toward total fixed costs even though it is still making a loss, on the assumption that the loss situation is temporary. See MARKET EXIT.

fixed exchange-rate system a method of regulating EXCHANGE RATES between CURRENCIES. Under this system, currencies are assigned a fixed par value in terms of other currencies, and countries are committed to maintaining this value by support buying and selling. For example, between 1949 and 1967, under the INTERNATIONAL MONETARY FUND's (IMF) fixed exchange-rate regime, the United Kingdom maintained a rate of exchange of £1 = $2.80 with the US dollar. If the price of the pound rose in the FOREIGN EXCHANGE MARKET, the UK authorities bought dollars and sold pounds. If the price of the pound fell, the authorities sold dollars and bought pounds. See Fig. 75.

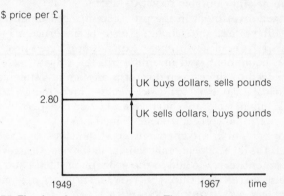

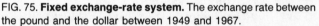

FIG. 75. **Fixed exchange-rate system.** The exchange rate between the pound and the dollar between 1949 and 1967.

With fixed exchange rates, trade and financial deals can be concluded in terms of known values. The disadvantage is that they often get out of line with underlying market trends and commit countries with serious balance-of-payments difficulties to defend unrealistic parities. For this reason the IMF system allowed for periodic DEVALUATIONS or REVALUATIONS of par values.

See BALANCE-OF-PAYMENTS EQUILIBRIUM, ADJUSTABLE PEG SYSTEM, GOLD COIN STANDARD, EUROPEAN MONETARY SYSTEM; see also FLOATING EXCHANGE-RATE SYSTEM.

fixed factor input a FACTOR INPUT to the production process that cannot be increased or reduced in the near term. This applies particularly to capital inputs, such as plant and equipment. See VARIABLE FACTOR INPUT, RETURNS TO THE VARIABLE FACTOR INPUT, FIXED COSTS.

fixed-interest financial securities any FINANCIAL SECURITIES that have a predetermined fixed RATE OF INTEREST attached to their PAR VALUE, for example, TREASURY BILLS, DEBENTURES, and PREFERRED STOCK. A debenture with a par value of $100 at 5% will pay out a fixed rate of interest of $5 a year until the expiration of the debenture, that is, the date of redemption. See BONDS.

fixed investment any investment in plant, machinery, equipment, or other durable CAPITAL GOODS.

Fixed investment in the provision of social products, such as roads, hospitals, and schools, is usually undertaken by governments as part of government expenditure. Fixed investment in plant, equipment, and machinery in the private sector will be influenced by the expected returns on such investments and the cost of capital needed to finance planned investments. Investment in the public sector may involve evaluation of expected returns in terms of social costs and social benefits.

Investment is a component of AGGREGATE DEMAND and so affects the level of economic activity in the near term, while fixed investment serves to add to the economic INFRASTRUCTURE and to raise POTENTIAL GROSS NATIONAL PRODUCT over the longer term. See INVENTORY INVESTMENT.

fixed overhead any indirect COSTS that do not vary with the level of output of a product. They include such items as rent and depreciation of fixed assets, whose total cost remains unchanged regardless of changes in the level of activity. Consequently, fixed overhead cost per unit of product will tend to fall as output increases, since OVERHEAD is spread over a larger output. See VARIABLE OVERHEAD.

fixed targets an approach to macroeconomic policy that sets specific target values for the objectives of FULL EMPLOYMENT, PRICE STABILITY, ECONOMIC GROWTH, and BALANCE-OF-PAYMENTS EQUILIBRIUM.

The essence of this approach can be illustrated simply by reference to the PHILLIPS CURVE trade-off between unemployment and inflation, as illustrated in Fig. 76. See MACROECONOMIC POLICY, OPTIMIZING.

flexible budget a budget that allows for the variation in costs associated with changes in output volume. The costs associated with running a manufacturing plant, for instance, at 50% of capacity, are different from costs incurred when running it at 70 or

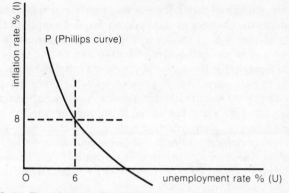

FIG. 76. **Fixed targets.** The Phillips curve shows that as unemployment (U) falls, inflation (I) increases, and vice versa. The Phillips curve is labeled P. Ideally, one might like the economy to be at the origin, point O, where full employment and complete price stability are simultaneously attained. The Phillips curve, however, sets a limit to the combinations of U and I that can be achieved in practice. Given this constraint, the task of governments is to specify acceptable target values for the two objectives. One could, for example, set a fixed target value for unemployment at 6% and a target value for inflation at 8% or, alternatively, a lower value for I and a higher value for U.

100% capacity. The budget must allow for the variation in plant utilization by distinguishing between fixed costs and variable costs and their relationship to output. See BUDGETARY CONTROL, BUDGETING.

floating debt any short-term FIXED-INTEREST FINANCIAL SECURITIES. Government floating debt is characterized by TREASURY BILLS or Treasury notes nearing maturity, and company floating debt by short-term bank loans. By means of a FUNDING operation, it is possible to convert short-term fixed interest debt into long-term fixed interest debt. See FUNDED DEBT.

floating exchange-rate system a system for determining EXCHANGE RATES between CURRENCIES by the interplay of market forces. Under a free float system, exchange rates between currencies are left to be determined entirely by market forces. Over time, the exchange rate between two currencies will alter in accordance with changes in the demand for and supply of the currencies concerned, as shown in Fig. 77a. In theory, this should always result in an equilibrium exchange rate, that is, a rate ensuring that a country achieves BALANCE-OF-PAYMENTS EQUILIBRIUM, leaving the country free to pursue desirable domestic policies without external constraints. In practice, however, the uncertainties associated with free floats tend to produce erratic and random exchange rate movements that will inhibit trade and produce destabilizing domestic effects. For these reasons countries prefer to manage their exchange rates, as shown in Fig. 77b. See PURCHASING-POWER PARITY THEORY, ASSET VALUE THEORY, INTERNATIONAL MONETARY FUND.

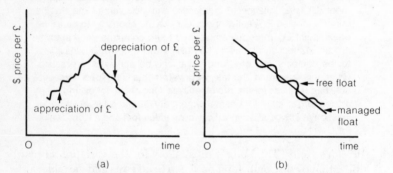

FIG. 77. **Floating exchange-rate system.** (a) If the United Kingdom's imports from the United States rise faster than the UK's exports to the US, in currency terms the UK's demand for dollars will increase relative to the demand in the US for pounds. This will cause the pound to fall against the dollar, making imports from the US to the UK more expensive and exports from the UK to the US cheaper. By contrast, if the UK's imports from the US rise more slowly than its exports to the US, in currency terms, its demand for dollars will be relatively smaller than the US demand for pounds. This will cause the poundd to rise, making imports from the US to the UK cheaper and exports from the UK to the US more expensive. (b) The graph shows how nations can manage the float by intervening in the currency market to buy and sell currencies, using their national currency reserves to moderate short-term fluctuation and smooth out the long-term trend line.

floor broker a member of a commodity or stock exchange who may execute orders for other brokers on the floor of the exchange.

flow a measurement of quantity over a specified period of time. Unlike inventory, for example, which is not a function of time, a flow measures quantity passing per minute, hour, day, or longer. A common analogy is made to a reservoir. The water entering and leaving the reservoir is a flow, but the water actually in the reservoir at any point in time is an inventory. INCOME is a flow but WEALTH is an inventory.

flow of funds analysis an analytical method that focuses on sources and uses of funds. Expenditures of one economic unit are incomes to other economic units, and every financial liability is someone's asset. This type of analysis is designed to show the interlocking nature of our financial system. The financial connections are traced among consumers, farms, factories, government agencies, and all the rest. The analysis can be read in the *Federal Reserve Bulletin*.

f.o.b. *abbreviation* for free-on-board. In BALANCE OF PAYMENTS terms, f.o.b means that only the basic prices of imports and exports of goods plus loading charges are counted, while cost-insurance-freight (C.I.F) charges incurred in transporting the goods from one country to another are excluded.

Food and Agricultural Organization (FAO) an international agency of the UNITED NATIONS, established in 1945. Its primary objective is to improve agricultural productivity and hence the nutritional standards of agrarian countries throughout the world. It works toward this objective by undertaking research on all aspects of farming, fishing, and forestry and by offering technical assistance to countries that require it. In addition, the FAO continually surveys world agricultural conditions and collects and issues statistics on human nutritional requirements and statistics on farming, fishing, forestry, and related topics.

forced saving or **involuntary saving** the enforced reduction of CONSUMPTION in an economy. This can be achieved directly by increasing taxation so that consumers' DISPOSABLE PERSONAL INCOME is reduced or it may occur indirectly as a consequence of INFLATION, which increases the prices of goods and services faster than consumers' money incomes increase.

Governments may deliberately increase taxes so as to secure a higher level of saving in order to obtain additional resources for investment in the public sector. A forced saving policy is often attractive for a developing country whose economic development is being held back by a shortage of savings, but it can have other uses. For example, it was used to help finance Great Britain during World War II.

forecasting the process of making predictions about future general economic and market conditions as a basis for making decisions in government and business. A number of forecasting methods can be used to estimate future economic conditions, varying greatly in terms of subjectivity, sophistication, data requirements, and cost:

(a) survey techniques, involving use of interviews or mailed questionnaires asking consumers or industrial buyers about their future buying intentions. Alternatively, members of a sales force may provide estimates of future market sales, or industry experts can offer forecasts of future market developments.

(b) experimental methods, providing demand forecasts for new products, etc., based either on the buying responses of small samples of panel consumers, or on large samples in test markets.

(c) EXTRAPOLATION methods, employing TIME-SERIES ANALYSIS, using past economic data to predict future economic trends. These methods implicitly assume that historical relationships that have held in the past will continue in the future, without examining causal relationships between the variables involved. Time-series data usually comprise a long-term secular trend, with certain medium-term cyclical fluctuations, and short-term seasonal variations, affected by irregular, random influences. Techniques such as moving averages or exponential smoothing can be used to analyze and project a time series, although they are generally unreliable in predicting sharp upturns or downturns in economic variables.

(d) leading indicator forecasts, to predict future values of economic variables from present values of statistical indicators that appear to have a consistent relationship with these economic variables. Such LEADING INDICATORS as business capital investment plans and new building starts can be used as a barometer for forecasting values, such as economic activity levels or product demand, and they can be useful for predicting sharp changes in these values.

(e) INPUT-OUTPUT ANALYSIS, using input-output tables to show relationships between industries and to analyze how changes in demand conditions in one industry will be affected by changes in demand and supply conditions in related industries. For example, automobile parts manufacturers will need to estimate the future demand for automobiles and the future production plans of the manufacturers that are their major customers.

(f) ECONOMETRIC methods, predicting future values of economic variables by examining other variables believed to be causally related to them. Econometric models link variables in the form of equations that can be estimated statistically and then used as a basis for forecasting. Judgment has to be used in identifying the INDEPENDENT VARIABLES that causally affect the DEPENDENT VARIABLE to be forecasted. For example, in order to predict future quantity of a product demanded (Qd), we would formulate an equation linking it to product price (P) and disposable income (Y):

$$Qd = a + bP + cY$$

then use past data to estimate the regression coefficients a, b, and c (see REGRESSION ANALYSIS). Econometric models may consist of just one equation like this, but in complex economic situations the independent variables in one equation often are themselves influenced by other variables, so that many equations may be necessary to represent all the causal relationships involved.

No forecasting method will yield completely accurate predictions, so when making any forecast we must allow for a *margin of error* in the forecast. In the situation illustrated in Fig. 78, we cannot make a precise estimate of the future value of an economic variable. Rather we must allow that there is a PROBABILITY DISTRIBUTION of possible future outcomes centered around the forecast value, showing a range of values with their associated probability distribution. Consequently, forecasters need to exercise judgment in predicting future economic conditions both in choosing the forecasting methods to use and in combining information from different forecasts.

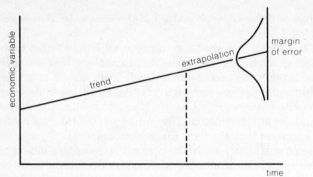

FIG. 78. **Forecasting.** The margin of error expected in economic forecasts.

foreign currency see FOREIGN EXCHANGE.

foreign exchange foreign currencies that are exchanged for a country's domestic CURRENCY in the financing of INTERNATIONAL TRADE and FOREIGN INVESTMENT. See FOREIGN EXCHANGE MARKET.

foreign exchange market a MARKET in which foreign currencies are bought and sold and EXCHANGE RATES between CURRENCIES are determined. Such a market is necessary because each country engaged in international trade and foreign investment and borrowing has its own currency, and this needs to be exchanged for trading partners' currencies in order to conclude trade, investment, and borrowing deals.

Currencies may be freely bought and sold (see FLOATING EXCHANGE-RATE SYSTEM), or subjected to government support buying and selling (FIXED EXCHANGE-RATE SYSTEM) and EXCHANGE CONTROLS.

The main centers for foreign exchange dealings are New York, London, Paris, Basel, Hong Kong, and Tokyo. See INTERNATIONAL DEBT.

foreign exchange reserves see INTERNATIONAL RESERVES.

foreign investment an investment by domestic residents (individuals, companies, financial institutions) in overseas physical assets and financial securities. Thus, for example, a MULTINA-

TIONAL FIRM may invest abroad by building a new overseas factory or by acquiring an established overseas company. Interest, profits, and dividends gained on these foreign investments may be repatriated or reinvested overseas. See CAPITAL MOVEMENTS, BALANCE OF PAYMENTS, CAPITAL INFLOW, CAPITAL OUTFLOW.

foreign sector the part of an economy concerned with transactions with overseas countries. The foreign sector includes IMPORTS and EXPORTS of goods and services as well as CAPITAL MOVEMENTS in connection with investment and banking transactions. The net balance of foreign transactions influences the level and composition of domestic economic activity and the state of the country's BALANCE OF PAYMENTS. The foreign sector, PERSONAL SECTOR, CORPORATE SECTOR, FINANCIAL SECTOR,and **PUBLIC** (GOVERNMENT) SECTOR make up the national economy. See also CIRCULAR FLOW OF NATIONAL INCOME MODEL and GROSS NATIONAL PRODUCT.

foreign trade multiplier the increase in a country's foreign trade resulting from expansion of domestic demand. The increase in domestic demand has a twofold effect. As well as directly increasing the demand for domestic products, it will (a) *directly* increase the demand for imports by an amount determined by the country's MARGINAL PROPENSITY TO IMPORT and (b) *indirectly* increase overseas demand for the country's EXPORTS by countries whose own incomes have now been increased by being able to export more to the country concerned.

The latter effect, however, is usually much less than the former, so the overall effect is to lower the value of the domestic MULTIPLIER, that is, the increase in net imports serves to partially offset the extra income created by increased spending on domestic products. See CIRCULAR FLOW OF NATIONAL INCOME MODEL.

forward exchange market see FUTURES MARKET.

forward integration the joining together in one company of two or more successive stages in a vertically related production/distribution process, for example, millers acquiring their own outlets for flour, such as bakeries. The main motives for forward integration by a company are to secure the market for its output and to obtain cost savings. See VERTICAL INTEGRATION.

franchise the assignment by one company to another (*exclusive* *franchise*) or others (*nonexclusive franchise*) of the right to supply its product. A franchise is a contractual arrangement entered into for a specified period of time, with the franchisee paying a ROYALTY to the franchisor for the rights assigned in addition to other possible considerations. Examples of franchises include the Kentucky Fried Chicken and McDonald chains. Individual franchisees are usually required to put up a large capital stake, with the franchisor providing training, technical assistance, specialized equipment, advertising, and promotion. Franchises enable franchisors to develop their business without raising large amounts of capital.

F ratio or **F statistic** the ratio of the variation *between* SAMPLE means and the variation *within* the samples. It is used in HYPOTHESIS TESTING when deciding whether observed differences between the means of several samples may reasonably be attributed to chance. Where the variation between sample means is much larger than the variation within the samples, then the variation between the means is too large to be accounted for by chance, since the variation within the samples provides a measure of chance variation. Under these circumstances, the null hypothesis that the sample means are not significantly different would be rejected.

It is possible to construct a PROBABILITY DISTRIBUTION for the F ratio, called the *F distribution*, to establish a level of significance for hypothesis testing. Customarily, the values chosen as significance criteria are the areas under the F distribution curve to one side of the 0.01 and 0.05 probabilities.

F ratios are used in formulating and testing hypotheses against sample data because of their value in analyzing variance. They enable us to analyze the total variation in data in two components: (a) variation between means or explicable variation, and (b) chance variation.

freedom of entry see CONDITION OF ENTRY.

free enterprise economy see PRIVATE ENTERPRISE ECONOMY.

free market economy see PRIVATE ENTERPRISE ECONOMY.

free port see FREE TRADE ZONE.

free rider a CONSUMER who deliberately understates a preference for a COLLECTIVE PRODUCT in the hope of being able to consume the product without having to pay the full economic price for it.

For example, when a number of homeowners seek to resurface their common private road, one of them may deliberately understate the value of the resurfaced road to himself on the grounds that the others will pay to have the entire road resurfaced anyway, and that he will therefore enjoy the benefit of it without having to pay toward resurfacing.

free trade the INTERNATIONAL TRADE that takes place without barriers, such as TARIFFS, QUOTAS, and EXCHANGE CONTROLS being placed on the free movement of goods and services between countries. The aim of free trade is to secure the benefits of international SPECIALIZATION. Free trade as a policy objective of the international community has been fostered both generally by the GENERAL AGREEMENT ON TARIFFS AND TRADE (GATT), and on a more limited regional basis by the establishment of various FREE TRADE AREAS, CUSTOMS UNIONS, and COMMON MARKETS.

free trade area a form of TRADE INTEGRATION between a number of countries, in which members eliminate all trade barriers (TARIFFS, etc.) among themselves on goods and services, but each continues to maintain barriers against trade with the rest of the world. The aim of a free trade area is to secure the benefits of international SPECIALIZATION, thereby improving members' real living standards.

free trade zone or **freeport** a designated area within the environs of an air or shipping port into which imports are allowed without payment of IMPORT DUTY (TARIFFS), provided the goods are to be subsequently exported either in their original form or as intermediate products within a final good. See ENTREPÔT TRADE.

frequency distribution often shortened to *distribution*, a means of summarizing large amounts of data by grouping statistical observations into convenient classes and then showing how these observations are distributed among the different classes. A numerical frequency distribution sorts data according to numerical size, for example, income bands as in Fig. 79a. A qualitative frequency distribution sorts data into categories according to some qualitative description such as industry group, as in Fig. 79c.

For certain purposes it is useful to have a numerical frequency distribution that groups observations in terms of cumulative ascending or descending size. This shows how many cases fall above

FRICTIONAL UNEMPLOYMENT

	Numerical distribution		Cumulative numerical distribution	
Weekly income ($)	number	Weekly income ($)	number
0–100	400	less than 100	400
101–200	300	less than 200	700
201–300	200	less than 300	900
301–400	100	less than 400	1,000
	1,000		
(a)		(b)	

Qualitative distribution

Industry	Numbers employed
Agriculture/Mining	100
Manufacturing	300
Construction/Building	200
Services/Retail	400

(c)

FIG. 79. **Frequency distribution.** See entry.

(more than) or below (less than) certain values. For example, Fig. 79b shows how a distribution, with cases falling into income classes, can be converted into a cumulative "less than" distribution. See HISTOGRAM.

frictional unemployment or **transitional unemployment** the unemployment experienced when people are changing jobs and are unemployed for a short time between jobs. Often people do not cease work, for whatever reason, and find another job immediately. The period of time between jobs, whether several days or even months, is seasonal *unemployment* of a frictional nature, that is, the markets do not operate smoothly. Frictional unemployment is only temporary and is thus usually ignored in estimating FULL EMPLOYMENT equilibrium.

Friedman, Milton (born 1912) American economist, for many years at the University of Chicago. He was awarded the Nobel Prize in Economic Sciences in 1976 for achievements in the fields of consumption analysis, monetary history, and theory, and for demonstration of the complexity of stabilization policy.

Friedman is a major contributor to contemporary economic analysis. His work on the consumption function led to formulation of the Permanent Income Hypothesis. He adapted Fisher's quantity theory of money to contemporary conditions and inspired what now is referred to as MONETARISM. He effectively stressed the limitations of Keynesian analysis. One of the founders of the so-called Chicago School, Friedman has consistently emphasized the advantages of a free market system.

fringe benefits any additional benefits offered to employees, such as use of a company car, free meals or luncheon vouchers, interest-free or low-interest loans, private health care insurance, pension plans, and stock purchase plans. In the case of senior managers, such benefits can be substantial in relation to salaries. Companies offer fringe benefits to attract employees and because such benefits may provide a low tax or no-tax means of rewarding employees compared with normally taxed salaries.

full capacity see CAPACITY.

full-cost pricing a method used by companies to price goods and services. See Fig. 80. The problem with this pricing method is that it takes no account of demand and hence the revenue implications of the price. Compare the marginal pricing method (see PROFIT MAXIMIZATION). See also COST-PLUS PRICING.

full employment the full utilization of all available labor and capital resources the economy is able to produce at the limits of its POTENTIAL GROSS NATIONAL PRODUCT. Full employment is one of the main objectives of MACROECONOMIC POLICY.

In practice 100% employment cannot be achieved. There always will be some unemployment due to labor turnover and people searching for and selecting new jobs, and because of structural changes in the economy—job losses in declining trades, which require people to transfer to new jobs created in expanding sectors. Accordingly, a more realistic interpretation of full employment suggests itself. Full employment is achieved when the number of unemployed people equals the number of job vacancies. Even this measure does not give an accurate estimate, however, because many groups, such as housewives and older workers, are too discouraged to seek work when job prospects are bleak, even though they wish to work (DISGUISED UNEMPLOYMENT).

For macroeconomic purposes, however, most governments

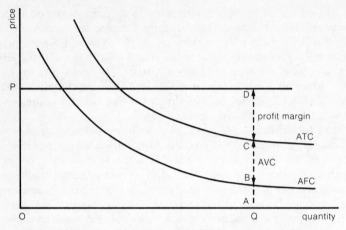

FIG. 80. **Full-cost pricing.** The price (OP) is made up of three elements: a contribution to cover part of the company's overhead costs (average FIXED COST)—AB; the actual unit cost (average VARIABLE COST) of producing a planned output of OQ units—BC; a PROFIT MARGIN expressed as a fixed percentage of total unit costs (average variable cost plus average fixed cost)—CD.

tend to specify their full employment objectives in terms of some targeted level of unemployment, for example, 5% of the total work force.

See UNEMPLOYMENT.

full employment equilibrium see EQUILIBRIUM LEVEL OF NATIONAL INCOME, POTENTIAL GROSS NATIONAL PRODUCT.

functional distribution of income the distribution of NATIONAL INCOME classified according to type of FACTOR INPUTfor example, labor, capital, wages, interest, rent, and profits. Here income is seen as a payment for the various factor inputs in contributing to the output of the economy. WAGES constitute by far the largest single element in factor payments, as Fig. 81 shows. See PERSONAL DISTRIBUTION OF INCOME.

functional notation a mathematical shorthand for expressing a relationship between two or more VARIABLES. To express the causality of relationship between the DEPENDENT VARIABLE (on the left-hand side of the equation) and the INDEPENDENT VARIA-

	Percentage
Compensation of Employees	73.9
Proprietors' Income	9.0
Rental Income	0.5
Corporate Profits	7.0
Net Interest	9.6
Total	100.0

FIG. 81. **Functional distribution of income.** The functional distribution of national income for the United States, 1987. Source: *Survey of Current Business*, July 1989, US Bureau of the Census, based on data from US Bureau of Economic Analysis.

BLE(s) (on the right-hand side of the equation), the usual terminology says one is a function of the other. For example, economists would suggest that demand for a product (D) is a function (*f*) of the price of that product (P), that is:

$$D = f(P)$$

fundamental disequilibrium a situation under a FIXED EXCHANGE-RATE SYSTEM, originally that operated by the INTERNATIONAL MONETARY FUND, in which a country is in a position of *persistent* BALANCE OF PAYMENTS deficit or surplus at a particular (fixed) exchange rate against other countries. The only practical course of action, given the inadequacy of internal measures, such as DEFLATION, to remedy the situation is a DEVALUATION to a lower exchange rate value in order to eliminate a deficit, and a REVALUATION to a higher exchange rate value to eliminate a surplus. See BALANCE-OF-PAYMENTS EQUILIBRIUM, INTERNAL-EXTERNAL BALANCE MODEL.

funded debt see FUNDING.

funding the process by which a government or company converts its short-term, fixed-interest debts into long-term, fixed-interest debts (*funded debts*). This involves persuading holders of short-term FIXED-INTEREST FINANCIAL SECURITIES to relinquish these in return for an equivalent amount of long-term, fixed-interest financial securities, and this usually can only be done by offering a more attractive rate of interest on the latter.

Funding is undertaken by monetary authorities as a means of

reducing the liquidity of the banking system, and by companies as a means of improving short-term liquidity. See FLOATING DEBT.

futures market or **forward exchange market** a MARKET for purchase and sale of COMMODITIES (wheat, pork bellies, etc.) and financial instruments (foreign currencies, common stocks, etc.) for delivery at some future time, as opposed to a SPOT MARKET, which provides for immediate delivery. Forward positions are taken by traders dealing in a particular commodity or financial instrument whose price can fluctuate greatly over time, in order to minimize the uncertainty and risk surrounding their long-term business dealings.

Traders minimize uncertainty about future prices by buying and selling *futures*—contracts that promise to sell or buy a commodity or financial instrument at a specified future date at a price agreed upon now. Unlike the spot market, in which commodities are traded in the physical sense, in the futures market only contracts are bought and sold. A dealer can enter into a contract agreeing to deliver a commodity at the agreed price (*take a short position*), or enter into a contract agreeing to accept the commodity and pay the agreed price on delivery (*take a long position*). Producers can contract to sell a commodity at a certain price at some time in the future in order to protect themselves against the risk of future adverse price changes. Buyers similarly can contract to buy a commodity at a certain price at some time in the future in order to protect themselves against the risk of future adverse price changes. Between the buyers and producers using futures as a hedge to minimize risk are dealers and SPECULATORS, who buy and sell futures, hoping to earn windfall profits by taking the risk of future price changes.

Many futures contracts take the form of OPTIONS, which are used to hedge against uncertainty about future prices. An option offers the right to sell or buy a commodity at an agreed price within some specified future time period and, once the option has been purchased, it can be exercised at the discretion of the option holder.

G

gains from trade the extra production and consumption benefits that countries can achieve through INTERNATIONAL TRADE. Countries trade with one another basically for the same reasons that individuals, companies, and regions engage in exchange of goods and services—to obtain the benefits of SPECIALIZATION. By exchanging some of its own products for those of other nations, a country can enjoy a much wider range of commodities and obtain them more cheaply than would otherwise be the case. International division of labor, with each country specializing in producing only some of the commodities it can produce, enables total world output to be increased and raises countries' real standards of living.

A country's choice of commodities to specialize in will be determined in large measure by its absolute and comparative advantages over its trading partners. See COMPARATIVE ADVANTAGE, THEORY OF INTERNATIONAL TRADE, TRADE INTEGRATION, TRADE CREATION.

Galbraith, John Kenneth (born 1908) economist, principally at Harvard University, whose views on the workings of the market economy have been expressed in a series of widely read books such as *The Affluent Society* (1958) and *The New Industrial State* (1967). Galbraith suggests that advanced industrial economies are made up of a competitive sector of small owner-managed businesses and a monopoly sector of large industrial companies managed by salaried technocrats, and he concentrates on the workings of the latter.

Galbraith argues that large companies plan their activities so as to minimize market uncertainty, seeking through advertising to create demand for new products before manufacturing them. This is a REVISED SEQUENCE, compared with the conventional economic view that consumers express innate wants and companies allocate resources to satisfying those wants. Nevertheless, Galbraith acknowledges that such large companies foster technical innovation and economies of scale that yield large gains in incomes. Furthermore, he sees the growth of large companies with original market power being balanced by COUNTERVAILING POWER on the other side of the market, for example, oligopoly against oligopsony. Where this does not occur, for example, in agricultural and labor markets, he suggests that government should intervene. Consequently, Galbraith argues, large companies should not be broken up but should be regulated by government to prevent abuse of their monopoly power, and government should attempt to increase the countervailing power of consumers and small businesses.

Galbraith also attacks the American market economy for devoting too few resources to the public sector while allowing private-sector activities to dominate, creating a situation of private affluence and public poverty.

game theory a technique that uses logical deduction to explore consequences of strategies that might be adopted by competing game players. Game theory can be used in economics to represent problems involved in formulating marketing strategy by small numbers of interdependent competitors.

An oligopolist (see OLIGOPOLY) needs to assess competitors' reactions to his own marketing policies to ensure that the payoff from any particular marketing strategy may be estimated. For example, consider a struggle for market share between companies X and Y where total market size is fixed, so that every percentage increase in the market share of one company is necessarily lost to the other (a ZERO-SUM GAME situation). Suppose company X has two strategy choices available, a price reduction (P) or a new advertising campaign (A), and that company Y has the same two strategies available. Any pair of strategies open to X and Y would result in a division of the market between them. If company X were to adopt strategy P, and Y were to adopt its strategy P, then X would gain 50% of the market, leaving 50% for Y. This 50%

market share is X's payoff. All such market share information can be summarized in the form of a *payoff matrix* as in Fig. 82.

Firm Y's strategy

		P	A
Firm X's	P	50	40
strategy	A	55	60

FIG. 82. **Game theory.** The payoff matrix between company X and company Y. (P represents price reduction, and A represents an advertising campaign.)

Each company must decide on its own best strategy, using the information in the table. If X adopts a cautious approach, it would assume that, in response to its strategy P, company Y would counter with strategy A, reducing X's payoff from its strategy P to its minimum value 40%, underscored in the matrix. Similarly, the fatalistic view of X's strategy A is that Y will counter with strategy P, reducing X's payoff from strategy A to its minimum value 55%, underscored in the matrix. Following this pessimistic view, X can make the best of the situation by aiming at the highest of these minimum payoffs, underscored in the matrix. In this case, the payoff of 55% is yielded by strategy A (a *maximum strategy*).

Company Y could employ a similar strategy, although for Y to assume the worst means that X receives a large market share so that Y, residually, receives very little. Thus, if company Y employs its strategy P, its worst possible payoff is 45% of the market, with 55% going to X, and this is marked by circling 55% in the matrix. If Y were to employ its strategy A, its worst possible payoff would be 40% of the market, with 60% going to X, and this 60% is also marked by a circle. The best of these pessimistic payoffs for company Y is the smaller of these circled figures, in this case 55% of the market going to X (a *minimax strategy*).

The outcome of this situation is that company X will choose its strategy A, and company Y its strategy P, and neither would be inclined to alter its choice of strategy.

GATT see GENERAL AGREEMENT ON TARIFFS AND TRADE.

GDP see GROSS DOMESTIC PRODUCT.

gearing see CAPITAL GEARING.

General Agreement on Tariffs and Trade (GATT) a multinational institution set up in 1947 to promote expansion of international trade through a coordinated program of trade liberalization. A major part of GATT's work has centered on negotiating multilateral tariff reductions and eliminating QUOTAS and other nontariff barriers to trade. GATT has supervised 10 conferences on tariff reductions, including the Kennedy Round of 1962—1967, which secured an average cut in tariff rates of 35%, and most recently the Uruguay Round of 1986. The Uruguay Round began with preliminary negotiations in the summer of 1986. In September of that year, a Ministerial Statement provided a strong foundation for further tariff reductions. Without stronger support from the heads of governments, however, it was predicted that little change would occur. By 1990, this prediction was still valid.

These GATT initiatives, together with the operations of the INTERNATIONAL MONETARY FUND and sustained economic growth in the developed countries, combined to bring about a record expansion of world trade down to the end of the 1960s. With the onset of recessionary conditions in 1973, however, much of the work of GATT was undermined by resurgence of PROTECTIONISM. The new protectionism, as it was commonly referred to, was based not on tariffs but on devices much less visible and hence more difficult to detect and control, for example, EXPORT RESTRAINT AGREEMENTS, import licensing procedures, local-content requirements, SUBSIDIZATION of domestic industries, etc. See GAINS FROM TRADE, MOST-FAVORED NATION CLAUSE, MULTIFIBER ARRANGEMENT.

general equilibrium analysis the analysis of the relationships between subsectors of an economy. General equilibrium analysis proceeds on the basis that events in one sector can have such a significant impact on other sectors that feedback effects, in turn, are likely to affect the functioning of the first sector. See Fig. 83.

Thus, in general equilibrium analysis, an attempt is made to determine the nature and strength of intersectoral linkages using, for example, INPUT-OUTPUT ANALYSIS. See PARTIAL EQUILIBRIUM ANALYSIS.

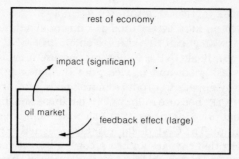

FIG. 83. **General equilibrium analysis.** An increase in the price of oil is likely to increase the cost structures of many other industrial sectors and hence serves to raise the general price level and related wage rates. This increase in prices and wages, in turn, increases input costs to the oil industry.

geometric progression a series of discrete values showing a growth pattern of the form:

$$a + ar + ar^2 + ar^3, \text{ etc.}$$

where a is the amount at the start and r is the amount added each time. Such a progression would show an accelerating growth trend over time. Geometric progressions can be used to analyze many problems in economics, such as COMPOUND INTEREST on loans (where a is the principal and r the interest rate), investment appraisal, and the MULTIPLIER. Compare ARITHMETIC PROGRESSION.

Giffen good a GOOD for which demand increases as its PRICE increases and vice versa, controverting the general theory of DEMAND. It only applies in the highly exceptional case of a good (see INFERIOR PRODUCT) that accounts for such a high proportion of households' budgets that an increase in price produces a large negative INCOME EFFECT that completely overcomes the normal SUBSTITUTION EFFECT. See PRICE EFFECT, UPWARD-SLOPING DEMAND CURVE.

Gini coefficient a measure of the degree of inequality in a distribution. See CONCENTRATION MEASURES.

GNP see GROSS NATIONAL PRODUCT.

GNP deflator a PRICE INDEX used as a means of adjusting money GROSS NATIONAL PRODUCT values to obtain *real* GNP values (see REAL VALUES). Real GNP is important because it represents output of physical goods and services, not their money values. An economy may appear to produce more goods and services (ECONOMIC GROWTH) because money GNP has increased, but this may simply reflect price increases (INFLATION) without any increase in physical output. The GNP deflator is thus designed to remove the influence of price changes and to record only real changes.

gold a monetary ASSET held by countries as part of their INTERNATIONAL RESERVES and sometimes used to finance BALANCE OF PAYMENTS deficits.

Formerly, many countries operated a GOLD COIN STANDARD system under which gold was used as the basis of a country's domestic MONEY SUPPLY, as well as to finance payments deficits. Gradually, however, the gold coin standard gave way to domestic monetary systems based on paper money and other metallic coins and, internationally, the gold-exchange standard in which currencies, such as the dollar and sterling, were used alongside gold as reserve assets.

In 1934 the price of gold was fixed at $35 a fine ounce by the United States, Britain, and France as part of a monetary pact by the three countries. This price was then officially adopted by member countries of the INTERNATIONAL MONETARY FUND on its formation in 1947. Gold was used as the numeraire of the Fund's fixed exchange rate system in setting par values for members' currencies, and members were required to pay a quarter of their quota subscriptions to the Fund in gold. Gold continued to serve as the linchpin of the IMF system, and its official price remained pegged at $35 an ounce down to 1971, when the Fund's fixed exchange-rate system gave way to floating rates. Countries had, however, found it increasingly difficult to hold the price of gold at the $35 an ounce level as world demand for gold as an industrial metal and for ornamental purposes continued to expand. In 1961 a gold pool was set up to regulate dealings in the metal, but in 1968 Fund members bowed to the inevitable, and a two-tier price structure was established. Gold continued to be priced at $35 an ounce for official transactions between central banks and the Fund, while the free market price of gold was left to be determined by market forces.

In 1972, gold was dropped as the numeraire of the Fund and replaced by the SPECIAL DRAWING RIGHT unit. Fund members were required to subscribe their quotas in a nongold form.

Outside the Fund, gold has continued to hold on to its status as the single most important component of international reserves. The attractiveness of gold as a reserve asset is underpinned by the fact that unlike national paper currencies, which are intrinsically worthless, it has a value in exchange as a commodity related to its use as an industrial base metal and for ornamental purposes. Gold holdings, however, suffer from the disadvantage that unlike other assets, such as stocks and bonds, they yield no interest.

gold coin standard an INTERNATIONAL MONETARY SYSTEM in which GOLD forms the basis of countries' domestic MONEY SUPPLY and is used to finance INTERNATIONAL TRADE and BALANCE OF PAYMENTS deficits.

Under the gold coin standard, EXCHANGE RATES were rigidly fixed in terms of gold. (The gold coin standard was widely adopted in the nineteenth century and operated down to the early 1930s.) In theory, the gold standard provided an automatic ADJUSTMENT MECHANISM for eliminating payment imbalances between countries, the specie-price-flow mechanism. Deficits were financed by outward gold transfers, which reduced the domestic MONEY SUPPLY. This in turn deflated the domestic price level, making imports relatively more expensive and exports relatively cheaper, thereby reducing volume of imports and increasing volume of exports. Surpluses were financed by inward gold transfers, which increased the domestic money supply. This in turn inflated the domestic price level, making imports relatively cheaper and exports relatively more expensive, and resulting in a fall in volume of exports and an increase in volume of imports. In this way both deficits and surpluses were removed and the BALANCE-OF-PAYMENTS EQUILIBRIUM restored. In practice, however, countries found that a combination of rigidly fixed exchange rates and complete subordination of domestic economic policy to the external situation was too onerous and opted for more flexible arrangements. Despite the experiments, a small group of economists urge a return to the gold coin standard.

See FIXED EXCHANGE-RATE SYSTEM, INTERNATIONAL MONETARY FUND.

golden parachute see TAKEOVER BID.

gold exchange standard a modified version of the GOLD COIN STANDARD, in which currencies such as the US dollar are used by countries in addition to gold to settle BALANCE OF PAYMENTS deficits. See INTERNATIONAL RESERVES.

goodness of fit see REGRESSION ANALYSIS.

goods or **commodities** any tangible economic products (washing machines, soap powders, tools, machines, etc.) that contribute directly or indirectly to the satisfaction of human wants. CONSUMER GOODS and PRODUCER GOODS are important components of GROSS NATIONAL PRODUCT. *Economic goods* are goods that are (a) scarce goods or (b) desirable goods that one would buy more of if one could.

goodwill the difference at a particular point in time between the market valuation of a company and the sum of its net assets computed in its BALANCE SHEET. If another company wishes to acquire the company, goodwill represents the premium the buyer must be prepared to pay for the company over and above its asset value, because of the company's trade contacts, reputation, management skill, and general know-how. When a company has a poor reputation, its market value as a going concern to a potential buyer may be less than the BALANCE SHEET value of its assets, in which case goodwill is said to be negative.

government (public) expenditure an important component of AGGREGATE DEMAND in the circular flow of income/expenditure. Government expenditure is used as an instrument of FISCAL POLICY in regulating the level of spending in the economy. However, short-term changes in government expenditure may be difficult to achieve because of administrative and political difficulties, especially when cuts in expenditure are being made with a view to contracting aggregate demand. For example, short-term cuts can be difficult to achieve in expenditures for health, education, etc., given the labor-intensive nature of these activities, without heavy firings and disruption of public services. Furthermore, when the brunt of such changes falls on public investment expenditures, the cuts can severely disrupt long-term investment projects and deplete the social infrastructure. In addition, when government expenditure includes spending on goods and services bought from businesses, changes can have dramatic effects on the prosperity of the private sector. See SOCIAL PRODUCTS, BUDGET (GOVERNMENT), COLLECTIVE PRODUCTS.

graph a means of portraying data in pictorial form showing the relationship between an INDEPENDENT VARIABLE and a DEPENDENT VARIABLE by labeling and scaling the two axes of the graph (see AXIS) to represent the two variables, plotting joint values of the two in the space between axes, and joining these values with a line. Graphs frequently show time as the independent variable, depicting by means of a line how the dependent variable has changed over time.

greenmail see TAKEOVER BID.

Gresham's law the economic hypothesis formulated by Sir Thomas Gresham (1519—1579) that "bad money forces good money out of circulation."

Where two media circulate together, and their relative intrinsic values in the market differ from their legally established values, the money with the higher intrinsic value will be hoarded. This occurred in the United States when the country was on a bimetallic standard, gold and silver both being standard money in 1837—1873. At various times, either gold or silver was hoarded, and the monetary system was destabilized.

gross domestic product (GDP) the value of all goods and services provided in a country by residents and nonresidents without regard to their allocation among domestic and foreign claims. This contrasts with GROSS NATIONAL PRODUCT, which is the sum of the domestic and foreign output of all residents of a country, including income received from abroad by residents for factor services rendered overseas, and after subtracting transfers to countries abroad

GROSS NATIONAL PRODUCT (GNP)

of income by residents of other countries. Among other problems is the difficulty of defining who is a resident.

International economic organizations tend to prefer to consider GDP rather than GNP. In the United States, government agencies seldom use GDP in their statistical studies even though there are limitations to using GNP. US economists appear to feel that even for international comparisons, GNP is superior.

gross national product (GNP) the market value of all final goods and services produced in a year. To derive GNP from the expenditure method, the following are added: personal consumption expenditures, gross private domestic investment, net exports of goods and services, and government purchases of goods and services.

To utilize GNP as a welfare indicator, GNP should be expressed in dollars of constant purchasing power and on a per capita basis. Recently, there have been attempts to qualify gross national product by calculating the social costs and social benefits associated with producing the GNP, for example, the social costs of pollution.

Gross National Product (in billions) for Selected Years in Nominal and Real Dollars (1982 = $100)

	Nominal	Real (1982)
1970	1,015.5	2,416.2
1975	1,598.4	2,695.0
1980	2,732.0	3,187.1
1982	3,166.0	3,166.0
1987	4,524.3	3,853.7

From *Economic Report of the President, January 1989*

gross private domestic investment the total spending on FIXED INVESTMENT (plant, equipment, etc.) in an economy over a one-year period. Gross domestic fixed capital formation is one component of GROSS NATIONAL PRODUCT. However, because of CAPITAL CONSUMPTION (fixed capital lost due to wear and tear) *net domestic fixed capital formation*, or *net investment*, may be considerably less than gross investment. In this case the net addition to the CAPITAL STOCK would be much smaller than the total

Gross National Product (in billions), 1987

I. Gross National Product	4,526.7
II. Personal Consumption	
A. Total	3,012.1
B. Durable Goods	421.9
C. Nondurable Goods	997.9
D. Services	1,592.3
III. Gross Private Domestic Investment	
A. Total	712.9
B. Fixed Investment	
1. Total	673.7
2. Nonresidential Total	446.8
3. Structures	139.5
4. Producers Equipment	307.3
5. Residential	226.9
C. Change in Business Inventories	39.2
IV. Net Exports of Goods and Services	
A. Net Exports	123.
B. Exports	428.
C. Imports	551.
V. Government Purchases of Goods and Services	
A. Total	924.7
B. Federal Total	382.
1. National Defense	295.3
2. Nondefense	86.7
C. State and Local	542.8
VI. Final Sales	4,487.5
VII. Gross Domestic Purchases	4,649.7

From *Economic Report of the President, 1959.*

figure unadjusted for capital depreciation. See NET NATIONAL PRODUCT.

gross profit the difference between SALES REVENUE and the COST OF GOODS SOLD. Gross profit less the operating expenses of the business equals NET PROFIT.

growth see ECONOMIC GROWTH.

H

hard currency in international finance, a currency in strong demand but short supply on the foreign exchange market. Hard currency status is usually associated with an economically strong country that is running a large surplus on its balance of payments. Demand for the currency is high to finance purchases of its exports, but the supply of the currency is relatively limited because the amount of it being made available for the purchase of imports is much lower. However, under a FLOATING EXCHANGE-RATE SYSTEM, the demand for, and supply of, the currency in theory should be brought into balance by an APPRECIATION of its EXCHANGE RATE value. Compare SOFT CURRENCY.

Harrod economic growth model a theoretical construct that examines the growth path of an economy. The model is concerned with the rate at which NATIONAL INCOME (Y) must grow in order to satisfy the Keynesian EQUILIBRIUM LEVEL OF NATIONAL INCOME condition:

$$\text{saving } (S_t) = \text{investment } (I_t) \qquad (1)$$

where t denotes a time period. In the model, S_t depends on national income:

$$S_t = sY_t \qquad (2)$$

that is, saving in each period depends on the income of the same period; s represents the AVERAGE PROPENSITY TO SAVE and MARGINAL PROPENSITY TO SAVE.

I_t depends on the *rate of change of income* from one period to the next, notationally Y_t (income in current time period), Y_{t-1} (income in previous time period), that is:

HARROD ECONOMIC GROWTH MODEL

$$I_t = \propto (Y_t - Y_{t-1}) \tag{3}$$

that is, investment is INDUCED INVESTMENT with the symbol ∞ representing the ACCELERATOR.

Given this assumed saving and investment behavior, what will the equilibrium condition represented in equation (1) require? By substituting equations (2) and (3) into equation (1) we obtain:

$$sY_t = \propto (Y_t - Y_{t-1}) \tag{4}$$

and by dividing both sides of equation (4) by ∞ Y_t we obtain:

$$\frac{s}{\propto} = (Y_t - Y_{t-1})Y_t . \tag{5}$$

If $(Y_t - Y_{t-1})$ is written as ΔY_t, then:

$$\frac{\Delta Y_t}{Y_t} = \frac{s}{\propto} \tag{6}$$

The left-hand expression is the percentage change in income. The right-hand side is the ratio of the marginal propensity to save to the accelerator. Since this is deduced from the condition for maintaining equilibrium in each time period, Harrod called the rate of change in income the warranted rate of growth.

If the actual rate of growth exceeds or is less than the warranted rate, income will be raised more or lowered more than is appropriate for maintaining equilibrium, causing a cumulative deviation from the equilibrium path.

Equation (6) determines the warranted rate of growth. The actual rate of growth is determined in the model by the rate of growth of the LABOR FORCE and the rate of growth of labor PRODUCTIVITY. Suppose that the labor force is growing at the rate of 1% a year and labor productivity at the rate of 2% a year. The actual (or natural rate of growth, as Harrod called it) attainable rate of growth of national income and output is thus 3% a year.

If the natural rate of growth exceeds the warranted rate of

growth, equation (5) indicates that the economy will experience a cumulative deviation from the warranted rate, with income growing at an excessive rate and causing secular expansion. By contrast, if the natural rate falls below that of the warranted rate, there will be SECULAR STAGNATION.

See DOMAR ECONOMIC GROWTH MODEL, SOLOW ECONOMIC GROWTH MODEL.

Heckscher-Ohlin factor proportions theory an explanation of COMPARATIVE ADVANTAGE in INTERNATIONAL TRADE that is based on differences in factor endowments between countries.

Consider a situation in which countries A and B produce goods X and Y. Country A, let us assume, has an abundance of labor and a scarcity of capital. By contrast, country B has an abundance of capital and a shortage of labor. Thus, the cost of labor is low relative to capital in country A, whereas the cost of capital is low relative to labor in country B. The production of good X, let us assume, is capital-intensive, and the production of good Y is labor-intensive.

Given these differences in labor and capital intensities, the following hypothesis about the structure of trade suggests itself: Country A has a comparative advantage in the production of good Y, because this uses much of its relatively cheap factor (labor). It will specialize in production of good Y, exporting Y in exchange for imports of X, the good in which it has a comparative disadvantage.

Country B has a comparative advantage in the production of good X because this uses much of its relatively cheap factor (capital). It will specialize in production of good X, exporting X in exchange for imports of Y, the good in which it has a comparative disadvantage.

The Heckscher-Ohlin theory presents a *static* supply-oriented interpretation of international trade that assumes that production functions are the same in all countries. The theory takes no account of the influence of dynamic technological change on comparative advantage. It also does not consider the effect of DEMAND and PRODUCT DIFFERENTIATION on the pattern of international trade flows.

See GAINS FROM TRADE, THEORY OF INTERNATIONAL TRADE.

HEDGING

hedging the process of reducing uncertainty about future market prices by effectively covering a bet through an offsetting bet. For example, in order to reduce exposure to losses from exchange-rate movements, a US company investing overseas may match the investment in a country with an equivalent amount of loans raised locally in that country. Then if an adverse exchange-rate movement reduces the dollar value of its overseas assets, it will simultaneously reduce the dollar value of its liabilities. OPTIONS are frequently used as an instrument for hedging. See FUTURES MARKET.

Herfindahl index a measure of the degree of SELLER CONCENTRATION in a market that takes into account the total number of companies in the market and their *relative* size distribution (share of total market output). See Fig. 84.

	Leading firm's share of market output (%)	5-firm concentration ratio (%)	Market share % per firm of remaining firms	Herfindahl index (H)
Firms	1 2 3 4 5			
Market A	12 12 12 12 12	60	5 8	0.104
Market B	40 5 5 5 5	60	8 5	0.190

FIG. 84. **Herfindahl index.** The Herfindahl index (H) is the sum of the squared company sizes, all measured as a proportion of total market size. In the figure, for market A, $H = (0.12)^2 \times 5 + (0.08)^2 \times 5 = 0.104$. If all companies in the market are the same size, the value of the index is equal to the reciprocal of the number of companies. Thus, if there are 10 companies all of the same size, $H = 0.1$. The upper limit of the index is 1, which occurs when there is a monopoly. The figure shows that market B ($H = 0.190$), with a single dominant company, is almost twice as concentrated as market A despite the fact that the latter has fewer companies. See CONCENTRATION MEASURES.

heteroscedasticity a statistical situation in which there is a pattern in the residual or error terms after an estimated regression equation has been calculated from sample observations of INDEPENDENT VARIABLES and DEPENDENT VARIABLES. If the estimated regression coefficients are good unbiased estimates of the true population coefficients of the independent variables, then the residual values should be randomly distributed and have a constant VARIANCE. If they are not, the estimated equation is an inaccurate fit or has overlooked other important independent variables that are affecting the dependent variable. Heteroscedastic error terms occur where the variance of the error term is not constant but grows or declines as the independent variable increases. Compare HOMOSCEDASTICITY. See also REGRESSION ANALYSIS.

hidden price reduction an increase in the amount or quality of a product offered at an unchanged price, for example, an increase in the weight of potato chips in a packet sold at the same price as before. Compare HIDDEN PRICE RISE.

hidden price rise a reduction in the quality or amount of a product offered at an unchanged price, for example, a reduction in the weight of a chocolate bar sold at the same price as before. Compare HIDDEN PRICE REDUCTION.

hidden reserve the undervaluation of the ASSETS or overvaluation of the LIABILITIES of a company in its BALANCE SHEET. For example, the value of a company's land and buildings may be shown in the balance sheet at HISTORIC COST or original cost, whereas the current market price of those assets may be considerably higher. Thus, if the assets were to be revalued to reflect current market values, the difference would be formally recorded in the balance sheet as an addition to capital reserves. See INFLATION ACCOUNTING.

hidden tax an INDIRECT TAX incorporated in the price of a good or service, but the consumer is not made fully aware of its existence or magnitude. For example, the amount of EXCISE DUTY included in the price of cigarettes and beer is not normally made known to the consumer. VALUE-ADDED TAX by contrast, is incorporated in the price of a product at specified rates.

hidden unemployment or **disguised unemployment** or **discouraged workers** a form of unemployment in which people able and willing to work do not seek work and do not appear in official unemployment data. Unless there are clear incentives for the hidden unemployed to make their presence known, unemployment statistics will be understated.

histogram or **bar chart** a graphical presentation of a FREQUENCY

HISTORIC COST

DISTRIBUTION in which the absolute and relative size of each category in a total is portrayed by means of the height of the bar or block representing that category. See Fig. 85.

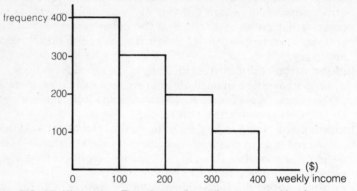

FIG. 85. **Histogram.** The *classes* (here shown as weekly after-tax income groups) are depicted on the horizontal axis, and the *class frequencies* on the vertical axis. The frequencies associated with the various classes are represented by the areas of the rectangles. For example, the area of the largest rectangle comprises 40% of the total area of the histogram, suggesting that 40% of all workers have a net income of $100 or less.

historic cost the original cost of purchasing an asset, such as an item of equipment. For accounting purposes, the asset is entered in a company's BALANCE SHEET at historic cost. However, allowance has to be made for the REPLACEMENT COST of the asset which, because of INFLATION, may well be considerably greater than the original price paid. Thus, DEPRECIATION provisions may be inadequate in a period of rapidly rising prices. See INFLATION ACCOUNTING, DEPRECIATION.

hoarding the nonproductive retention of money or products. A certain amount of money is held in currency form to finance day-to-day transactions, but this is turned over on a regular basis. Hoarding involves a deliberate abstention from current spending and investing and may occur because of an increase in LIQUIDITY PREFERENCE. Hoarding often occurs in less-developed countries, where people are unfamiliar with, or suspicious of, using the banking system as a savings repository.

holding company a company that controls one or more companies. Ownership may be complete (100%) or partial (ownership of 51% + of the voting shares in the company). Such ownership confers power to control the policies of subsidiary companies. The holding company may report the accounting results of its subsidiary companies as part of the accounting results for the group of companies.

Holding companies are used most frequently as a means of achieving diversified or conglomerate growth, with the company operating separate companies in different lines of production activity, but with each company subject to varying degrees of centralized control by the parent company.

See DIVERSIFICATION.

homogeneous products any goods offered in a market by competing suppliers and believed by buyers to be identical. Buyers will regard the products as perfect substitutes for one another and will have no preference for the products of particular suppliers. Homogeneity results in all suppliers having no ability to charge other than a common price for their products. See PERFECT COMPETITION, PRODUCT DIFFERENTIATION.

homoscedasticity a statistical situation in which there is no particular pattern in the residual or error terms after an estimated regression equation has been calculated from sample observations of INDEPENDENT VARIABLES and DEPENDENT VARIABLES. Homoscedastic residuals suggest that the estimated regression coefficients are good unbiased estimates of the true population coefficients of the independent variables. Compare HETEROSCEDASTICITY. See REGRESSION ANALYSIS.

horizontal integration the tendency for companies to SPECIALIZE at a particular level in the production and distribution of a product rather than engage in a number of successive stages (VERTICAL INTEGRATION). Also called *lateral integration.*

hot money short-term and volatile CAPITAL MOVEMENTS between countries that occur primarily in response to interest rate differentials between financial centers (ARBITRAGE), or in anticipation of likely DEVALUATION or DEPRECIATION and REVALUATION or

APPRECIATION of foreign currencies (SPECULATION). Speculative hot money flows are especially disruptive to the conduct of orderly exchange-rate management and the maintenance of balance-of-payments equilibrium and are thus frequently subjected to EXCHANGE CONTROL regulation by the authorities. See CAPITAL INFLOW, CAPITAL OUTFLOW.

households a group of individuals whose economic decision-making is interrelated. In economic theory, households perform two roles. On the one hand, they enter the marketplace as buyers or consumers of goods and services produced by companies. On the other hand, they provide FACTOR INPUTS to companies in order to produce those goods and services. The term "households" is used primarily in macro- (national income) analysis, while the term "consumers" is used in micro- (supply and demand) analysis. See CIRCULAR FLOW OF NATIONAL INCOME MODEL, PERSONAL SECTOR.

human capital the body of human knowledge that contributes know-how to productive activity. The knowledge base of a nation is added to by research and disseminated by teaching through general education and vocational training. Investment in human capital results in new, technically improved products and production processes that increase ECONOMIC EFFICIENCY, and human capital can be as significant as physical capital in promoting ECONOMIC GROWTH.

Investment in human beings, for example, by providing improved education and health care, has been shown to produce a large payout both in private and public areas. For example, number of years of schooling correlates closely with rising income. Research in the area of human capital indicates that great social benefits arise from investment in health, education, prison reform, improved housing, and the like. By applying what we already know and making the necessary investment, we should be able to increase productivity and reduce certain societal costs.

Research released in March 1989 by the House Select Committee on Children, Youth, and Families disclosed that US children are more likely to live in poverty, live with only one parent, or be killed before the age of 25 than are children in 11 other major industrial nations. The United States was 10th among these same countries, the USSR being 11th, in infant mortality rates. These and other data raise serious questions about deficiencies in investment in human capital. See ECONOMIC DEVELOPMENT.

hyperinflation a condition of chronic or runaway rates of INFLATION. Unlike CREEPING INFLATION, which usually has little ill effect on the functioning of an economy, hyperinflation reflects a situation in which people begin to lose confidence in the value of MONEY and revert to BARTER. At this point there is a serious danger of economic collapse accompanied by growing social disorder. Hyperinflation is an unusual phenomenon, but when it does occur, its causes are as much political as economic, for example, excessive printing of money to finance government spending—for wars in particular—or acute shortages of goods and services combined with a large pent-up demand, as in periods immediately following the ending of a war.

hypothesis a prediction derived from limited observation and theoretical analysis expressed precisely enough to be subjected to testing against empirical data. In economics, hypotheses are generated by a process of logical deduction from sets of initial insights and assumptions about the behavior of consumers, producers, etc. They are generally tested by collecting economic data and using statistical techniques to analyze them. This testing can lead to modification of the economic theory in light of the new economic data, or to abandonment of the theory in favor of an alternative theory that better explains the facts. See HYPOTHESIS TESTING.

hypothesis testing the development and use of statistical criteria to aid in making decisions about the validity of a HYPOTHESIS in uncertain conditions. In any such decision, there is a chance of making a correct choice and a risk of making a wrong choice. Hypothesis testing is concerned with evaluating these chances and providing criteria that minimize the likelihood of making wrong decisions.

For example, suppose we wanted to decide whether company size determines management remuneration and proceeded to formulate the hypothesis that average management remuneration is larger in bigger firms. This hypothesis can be either true or false and will be either accepted or rejected. The options are shown in the matrix below:

HYPOTHESIS TESTING

	Hypothesis is true	*Hypothesis is false*
Accept Hypothesis	correct decision	error (type 2)
Reject Hypothesis	error (type 1)	correct decision

If the hypothesis is true and we accept it, and if the hypothesis is false and we reject it, our decision will be correct. On the other hand, we could reject the hypothesis when it should be accepted (*type 1 error*), or we could accept a hypothesis that should be rejected (*type 2 error*). The risk of making such errors in testing a hypothesis using available sample data can be minimized. To avoid risk of a type 2 error, and to establish clear probabilities for risk of a type 1 error, careful formulation of the hypothesis is necessary. Often this involves formulating a *null hypothesis*, which assumes the exact opposite of what we want to prove. For example, in place of the earlier hypothesis that average management remuneration is larger in bigger firms, we would formulate the null hypothesis that average management remuneration is the same in large and small companies. Rejection of this null hypothesis is equivalent to acceptance of the original hypothesis. This null hypothesis can then be tested against sample data.

If repeated samples were taken from the population of firms, this sampling distribution can be approximated by a NORMAL DISTRIBUTION that in turn can be used to assess the PROBABILITY of making a type 1 error. This probability is called the *level of significance* at which a test of the significance of the null hypothesis will be conducted, customarily 0.01, 0.05, or 0.10. The level of significance is always specified before any test is made. For large samples, the level of significance established will be determined by the probability distribution of the normal distribution. For small samples, the level of significance will be based on the T DISTRIBUTION.

The final step involves the test of significance. Average management remuneration is calculated from sample data for small and large firms and compared with expected management remuneration which, according to our null hypothesis, should be the same in both small and big companies. If the difference between what we expect to find—average remuneration the same—and what we get is so large that it cannot reasonably be attributed to chance, we reject the null hypothesis on which our expectation is based. On the other hand, if the difference between what we expect—average remuneration the same—and what we get is so small that it reasonably may be attributed to chance, the results are not statistically significant. In the former case we would reject the null hypothesis and accept its mirror image, namely, management remuneration is larger in bigger firms. In the latter case we would reserve judgment on the issue of company size and management remuneration, since no clear link is either proved or disproved.

The statistical techniques of hypothesis testing are widely employed in empirical economic research.

I

identification problem a particular problem of applying REGRESSION ANALYSIS where it is difficult to identify the precise relationships between VARIABLES because all the variables change simultaneously. For example, the SCATTER DIAGRAMS in Fig. 86 show observations of the prices of a product and the quantities sold. Where the pattern of observations looks like those in Fig. 86a, and we have reason to believe that supply conditions have changed dramatically because of the effect of weather (food) or technology, while demand conditions have been relatively stable, it seems reasonable to assume that the data represent a demand curve (D_2) with changing supply conditions (S_1, S_2, S_3), so that any regression line fitted can be identified as a demand curve. Where the pattern of observations looks like those in Fig. 86b, and we have reason to believe that demand conditions have changed dramatically because of changes in disposable income or tastes, while supply conditions have been relatively stable, it seems reasonable to assume that the data represent a supply curve (S_2) with changing demand conditions (D_1, D_2, D_3), so that any regression line fitted can be identified as a supply curve. Where the pattern of observations looks like those in Fig. 86c, however, and both supply and demand conditions have been fluctuating dramatically, it is difficult to identify any clear pattern in the data, for changes in prices and quantities could have been caused by both supply and demand changes.

identity a means of arithmetically portraying the enduring equality between two or more VARIABLES that are equal by definition. For example, $\$1 = 100$ cents, and no matter how many dollars we have, they can always be converted into pennies cents by multiplying by 100. Identities are generally given a three-bar identity sign ($\equiv$) to indicate that the value to the left of the three bars is identical with the value to the right of the sign. The QUANTITY

ILLEGAL ACTIVITIES

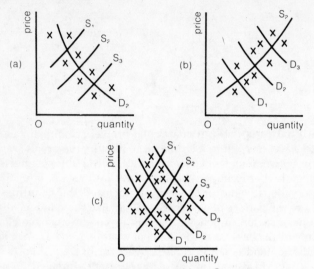

FIG. 86. **Identification problem.** See entry.

THEORY OF MONEY is one of the best examples of an identity in economics, written as

$$M.V. \equiv P.T$$

where M is the money stock, V is the velocity of circulation of money, P is the general price level, and T is the number of transactions undertaken. See EQUATION.

illegal activities any activities that are excluded from a country's NATIONAL INCOME ACCOUNTS because they are prohibited by law. For example, drug smuggling is illegal and therefore not included as part of legitimate economic activity. See BLACK ECONOMY, BLACK MARKET.

IMF see INTERNATIONAL MONETARY FUND.

immiserizing growth a situation in which a developing country's attempt to increase its growth potential through EXPORTS actually retards the increase. This is an exceptional situation, confined in *theory* only to a country whose export specialty—a mineral or agricultural crop—accounts for a preponderant share of world trade in that product. The country needs to export more to earn the foreign exchange to finance the capital imports it requires to underpin domestic growth. If all its export effort is concentrated on its specialty, this could lead to an oversupply of product, resulting in a deterioration of the country's TERMS OF TRADE. As a result the country's foreign exchange earnings will buy fewer imports, and domestic growth potential will be impaired. See ECONOMIC DEVELOPMENT.

imperfect competition see MONOPOLISTIC COMPETITION.

imperfect market see MONOPOLISTIC COMPETITION.

implicit cost or **imputed cost** the OPPORTUNITY COST to a firm or individual of using resources they own to produce an output. For example, if a company occupies a building it owns, it foregoes the opportunity of renting the building out. Thus, implicit costs represent the sacrifice of income that could have been earned by renting or selling the firm's resources to others.

To achieve an accurate measure of the total cost of producing goods or services, the company must *impute* a rent to itself based on the going market rate for renting the property.

See PROFIT, EXPLICIT COST, SHADOW PRICE.

import duty a tax levied by a government on imported products. Import duties are used to raise revenue for the government and to protect idomestic industries from foreign competition. See TARIFF, IMPORT RESTRICTIONS, PROTECTIONISM.

import penetration an increase in the proportion of domestic CONSUMPTION accounted for by imports. In some cases the displacement of domestic supply by imports may be beneficial insofar as it reflects COMPARATIVE ADVANTAGE, imports cheaper than domestic goods. Widespread import penetration across the economy not matched by an equivalent amount of exports can result in balance-of-payments difficulties and a fall in domestic income and output levels.

import quota see QUOTA.

import restrictions or **trade barriers** the limitation of imports into a country by a variety of techniques, for example, TARIFFS, QUOTAS, IMPORT SURCHARGES, EXPORT RESTRAINT AGREEMENTS, and EXCHANGE CONTROLS. The aim of import restrictions is to assist in removing a BALANCE OF PAYMENTS deficit and protect domestic industries against foreign competition. In general these practices are contrary to the rules of the GENERAL AGREEMENT ON TARIFFS AND TRADE, but GATT has been powerless to stop them in many cases. See PROTECTIONISM, BALANCE-OF-PAYMENTS EQUILIBRIUM.

imports the goods, services, and capital assets bought from foreign countries. Imports are important in two main respects. (a) Together with exports they make up a country's BALANCE OF TRADE. Imports must be financed (paid for in foreign currency) by an equivalent value of exports in order to maintain a payments equilibrium. (b) They represent a WITHDRAWAL from the CIRCULAR FLOW OF NATIONAL INCOME, serving to reduce real income and output. (See PROPENSITY TO IMPORT).

On the one hand, imports are beneficial in that they enable a country to enjoy the benefits of INTERNATIONAL TRADE, that is, obtain goods and services at lower prices; however, as indicated by (b) above, they are detrimental because they reduce income and output. It is important to maintain a *balance* between imports and exports. Imports are beneficial when matched by exports; that is, lost income on imports is restored by income gained on exports or by an inflow of funds from prior investments to maintain domestic income and output levels and, as indicated by (a) above, imports are financed by exports to preserve a BALANCE-OF-PAYMENTS EQUILIBRIUM.

See BALANCE OF PAYMENTS, INTERNAL-EXTERNAL BALANCE MODEL, GAINS FROM TRADE.

import schedule a schedule depicting the relationship between NATIONAL INCOME and the proportion of income spent on IMPORTS. (See AVERAGE PROPENSITY TO IMPORT.) The slope of the import schedule equals the MARGINAL PROPENSITY TO IMPORT.

import substitution a strategy pursued by a DEVELOPING COUNTRY as a means of promoting domestic INDUSTRIALIZATION and conserving scarce FOREIGN EXCHANGE resources. By limiting or removing competing IMPORTS through use of QUOTAS, TARIFFS, etc., the country aims to establish manufacturing industries that initially can be expanded to supply the domestic market, and later to develop an EXPORT trade. See INFANT INDUSTRY, ECONOMIC DEVELOPMENT.

import surcharge a special tax levied on IMPORTS over and above existing TARIFF rates. Import surcharges are employed primarily as a temporary means of assisting in removal of a balance of payments deficit. See IMPORT RESTRICTIONS, BALANCE-OF-PAYMENTS EQUILIBRIUM.

imputed cost see IMPLICIT COST.

incentive plan any form or system of rewarding an individual or group that increases effort or production. Such systems of reward include piecework payment systems, which are geared to individual or group effort and output; bonuses for reaching stipulated levels of production, for example, in mining; and profit-sharing schemes. See X-INEFFICIENCY, PRODUCTIVITY.

incidence of taxation the location of the ultimate payer of a tax. In the case of personal INCOME TAX, for example, it is the individual taxpayer who pays the tax. In other cases, due account must be taken of SHIFTS IN TAX. For example, suppose the tax authorities impose a PAYROLL TAX on companies that treat the tax as an increase in their input costs and raise their prices by an equivalent amount. Assuming no drop in sales, it is the consumers who bear the full burden of the tax, while the company bears only the temporary impact of the tax. See VALUE-ADDED TAX, PRINCIPLES OF TAXATION, LUMP-SUM TAXES.

income the flow of returns over a period of time derived from ownership of FACTORS OF PRODUCTION.

The returns to NATURAL RESOURCES, LABOR, and CAPITAL (the factors of production) are RENT, WAGES, and INTEREST, respectively. There is a fourth factor of production, *entrepreneurship*, which is rewarded with PROFIT. ENTREPRENEURS harness the other three factors of production to create income for themselves.

Care must be taken in using the term "income." It takes on different meanings according to the context in which it is used. Recipients of funds from government welfare programs in most cases do not have their income classified as part of NATIONAL INCOME because it is a TRANSFER PAYMENT. However, to recipients, the funds are income and would be treated as such in the THEORY OF DEMAND, where income is considered a constraint on consumption. See CIRCULAR FLOW OF NATIONAL INCOME MODEL.

income consumption curve a line depicting the relationship between consumer INCOME and the quantity of a product demanded on a graph. See Fig. 87. The slope of the income consumption curve reflects INCOME ELASTICITY OF DEMAND, a steeply sloping curve indicating inelastic demand with small changes in quantity demanded, which result from large changes in income, and vice versa.

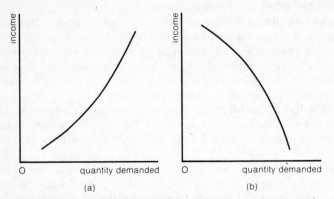

FIG. 87. **Income consumption curve.** (a) An income consumption curve for a NORMAL PRODUCT in which, as income rises, demand for the product also rises. (b) An income consumption curve for an INFERIOR PRODUCT in which, as income rises, buyers purchase less of the product, generally because they can now afford to buy more expensive alternatives. See INCOME ELASTICITY OF DEMAND.

income determination, theory of see EQUILIBRIUM LEVEL OF NATIONAL INCOME.

income distribution the apportionment of NATIONAL INCOME among the various FACTOR INPUTS (FUNCTIONAL DISTRIBUTION OF INCOME), or between factor input suppliers and other recipients (PERSONAL DISTRIBUTION OF INCOME).

income effect the change in consumers' real INCOME resulting from a change in product prices. A fall in the price of a good normally results in more of it being demanded. (See THEORY OF DEMAND.) Some of this increase is due to the *real income* effect, that is, income adjusted for changes in prices to reflect current purchasing power. If a consumer has a money income of, say, $100 and the price of good X is $10, he can buy 10 units of the product.

If the price of good X now falls to $5, he can buy the same 10 units for only $50. The consumer now has an extra $50 to spend on buying more of good X and other goods. The income effect, together with the SUBSTITUTION EFFECT, provides an explanation of why DEMAND CURVES usually slope downward. See CONSUMER EQUILIBRIUM, REVEALED PREFERENCE THEORY, PRICE EFFECT.

income elasticity of demand a measure of the degree of responsiveness of DEMAND to a given change in INCOME:

$$\frac{\text{income-elasticity}}{\text{of demand}} = \frac{\%\ \text{change in quantity demanded}}{\%\ \text{change in income}}$$

If a given change in income results in a more than proportional change in quantity demanded, demand is said to be *income elastic*. If a given change in income results in a less-than-proportional change in quantity demanded, demand is said to be *income inelastic*.

Income elasticity is positive for a NORMAL PRODUCT and negative for an INFERIOR PRODUCT. Products that have an income elasticity of demand of less than one are sometimes called STAPLE PRODUCTS. Those with an income elasticity of more than one are sometimes called LUXURY PRODUCTS. See ENGEL'S LAW, INCOME EFFECT, INCOME CONSUMPTION CURVE, DEMAND CURVE (SHIFT IN).

income expenditure model see EQUILIBRIUM LEVEL OF NATIONAL INCOME.

income per capita the NATIONAL INCOME of a country divided by its POPULATION. This gives the average income for every man, woman, and child in a country if it is all distributed equally. The distribution of income is not equal, and income per capita is therefore not necessarily a good indicator of typical living standards.

income redistribution a policy concerned with altering the pattern of INCOME DISTRIBUTION in an economy, mainly with social rather than economic objectives in mind. The general aim of such a policy is to achieve a more equitable distribution of income in the community so as to ensure that everybody is at least provided with some minimum standard of living. Transfer of income from

INCOMES POLICY

one section of a community to another is achieved primarily by use of a PROGRESSIVE TAXATION system and a variety of welfare provisions (subsidized housing, old-age pensions, etc.) See ABILITY-TO-PAY PRINCIPLE OF TAXATION, REDISTRIBUTION OF INCOME PRINCIPLE OF TAXATION.

incomes policy see PRICES AND INCOMES POLICY.

income support 1. a means of supplementing the incomes of poorer members of the community by means of TRANSFER PAYMENTS, such as supplementary benefits and unemployment pay. See NEGATIVE INCOME TAX, REDISTRIBUTION-OF-INCOME PRINCIPLE OF TAXATION. 2. a method of supporting the incomes of certain producers by providing direct payment where market prices are felt to yield insufficient income. See Fig. 88.

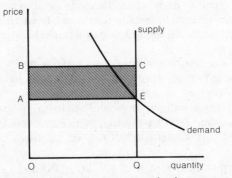

FIG. 88. **Income support.** In many countries income support systems are used specifically to assist the agricultural sector. In the graph, the equilibrium market price is OA. If this price is considered too low to recompense farmers adequately, the government will set a guaranteed price, say OB, and thus supplement farm incomes by a deficiency payment equal in the aggregate to the shaded area ABCE. Note that in contrast with the PRICE SUPPORT method, consumers still pay the market-determined price OA, and producers sell market-determined output OQ.

income tax a DIRECT TAX levied by the government on the INCOME (wages, rent, dividends) received by households in order to raise revenue and as an instrument of FISCAL POLICY. Income tax is usually paid on a progressive scale (see PROGRESSIVE TAX). Changes in income tax rates can be used as part of fiscal policy to regulate the level of AGGREGATE DEMAND. Increases serve to reduce DISPOSABLE PERSONAL INCOME available for consumption spending. Tax decreases increase disposable income. Income taxes can also be used to effect the distribution of incomes in society in line with the government's social policy. See TAXATION, PRINCIPLES OF TAXATION, CORPORATION TAX.

income velocity of circulation see QUANTITY THEORY OF MONEY.

increasing returns see RETURNS TO THE VARIABLE FACTOR INPUT.

independent variable a VARIABLE that affects some other variable in a model. For example, the price of a product will influence the demand for it. It is conventional to place the independent variable on the right-hand side of an EQUATION and, in the United States, to show the independent variable on the vertical axis of a GRAPH. In the example below, price (P) is the independent variable, and quantity demanded (D) the DEPENDENT VARIABLE:

$$D = f(P)$$

See FUNCTIONAL NOTATION.

indexation the automatic adjustment of an INCOME payment (for example, wages) or a value (for example, household contents insurance value) in proportion to changes in a general PRICE INDEX. Indexation is commonly used as a means of countering the effects of persistent price increases (INFLATION). See BASE PERIOD, INDEX-LINKED, INDEX NUMBER.

index-linked (of a variable) having a value determined in proportion to a specified index. For example, some pension plans are linked to the retail price index, so as retail prices increase year by year, pensions increase by the same proportion in order to maintain their value in real terms. In the United States, some private pensions, many public pensions, and all Social Security pension benefits are linked to changes (*adjustments*) in the *cost-of-living index (COLA)*. See BASE PERIOD, INDEXATION, INDEX NUMBER, PRICE INDEX, REAL VALUES.

index number a single numerical value that reflects the relative size of a VARIABLE in a period under review compared with its size in some predetermined BASE PERIOD. For example, a consumer price index may take the same sample of goods and services in each period and measure the average price of this typical basket of goods and services, showing this average price in the form of a single index number. The base period of an index is, by convention, given an index number of 100.

Regardless of whether the index is stated in terms of price, volume, or value, the principle of index numbers remains the same—to exhibit simply and concisely the measured change in a variable from one period to another.

See PRICE INDEX, INDEXATION, INDEX-LINKED.

indicative planning a method of controlling the economy that setting long-term objectives and mapping out programs of action designed to meet these objectives, using techniques such as INPUT-OUTPUT ANALYSIS. Unlike a CENTRALLY PLANNED ECONOMY, indicative planning works through the market (PRICE SYSTEM) rather than replaces it. To this end the planning process specifically brings together both sides of industry (the labor unions and management) and the government. The French have used indicative planning since the 1950s. See INDUSTRIAL POLICY.

indicators descriptive and anticipatory data used in analyzing business conditions and in economic forecasting. Best known of these indicators in the United States are the ones developed and regularly published by the Department of Commerce. These are the so-called leading, lagging, and coincident indicators.

The *leading indicators* are these: average workweek of production workers in manufacturing, average weekly claims for state unemployment insurance benefits, new orders for consumer goods and materials adjusted for inflation, vendor performance (companies receiving slower deliveries from suppliers), contracts and orders for plant and equipment adjusted for inflation, new building permits issued, changes in manufacturers' unfilled orders for durable goods, changes in sensitive materials prices, index of stock prices, money supply (M2 adjusted for inflation), and index of consumer expectations.

indifference curve a curve showing alternative combinations of two products, each of which gives the same UTILITY or satisfaction.

See Fig. 89. Indifference curves are used along with BUDGET LINES to determine a consumer's equilibrium purchases of two products and to analyze the effect of changes in the relative prices of these two products upon quantities demanded (see PRICE EFFECT). See CONSUMER EQUILIBRIUM, INDIFFERENCE MAP.

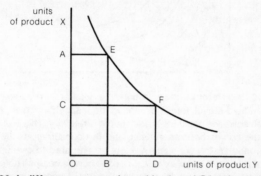

FIG. 89. **Indifference curve.** A combination of OA units of product X and OB units of product Y yields exactly as much satisfaction to the consumer as does the combination of OC units of product X and OD units of product Y.

Indifference curves slope downward, because consumers will always prefer more of both products and so will not be indifferent when offered two combinations of products with one combination offering more of both. Specifically, they will only give up one product if they receive more of another for it, showing indifference in choosing between combination E, which offers a lot of product X and little of product Y; and combination F, which offers less of product X and more of product Y (see ECONOMIC MAN).

indifference map a collection of ranked INDIFFERENCE CURVES that exhibit graphically an individual's increasing UTILITY, or satisfaction, when moving outward from the origin, consuming larger quantities of two products. See Fig. 90. Indifference curves are an ORDINAL UTILITY measure, and the numbers on the indifference curves in Fig. 90 *do not* indicate an absolute level of utility. Indifference curves never cross, because two crossing curves would imply inconsistent or irrational choices between the two products by the consumer (see ECONOMIC MAN).

indirect costs see OVERHEAD.

INDIRECT INVESTMENT

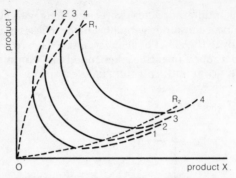

FIG. 90. **Indifference map.** In principle, indifference curves 1,2,3, etc. can take the full form indicated in the map, although in practice only the solid-line segment of each curve is relevant. This is because once the curves become vertical, and the consumer is fully sated with product Y, the consumer will not be prepared to give up extra units of product X to get extra Y. Once the curves become horizontal, and the consumer is fully sated with product X, the consumer will not be prepared to give up extra units of product Y to get extra X. The ridge lines R_1 and R_2 mark the boundaries of the effective segments of the indifference curves.

indirect investment any expenditure on FINANCIAL SECURITIES, such as STOCKS and BONDS. This is sometimes referred to as *financial* or *portfolio investment*. See INVESTMENT.

indirect tax a TAX levied by a government on goods and services in order to raise revenue and as an instrument of FISCAL POLICY. Indirect taxes have traditionally been regarded as shiftable, that is, the incidence and the impact of such taxes do not fall on the same people and the same firms. Examples of indirect taxes are SALES TAX and EXCISE DUTY.

Changes in indirect tax can be used as part of fiscal policy to regulate the level of AGGREGATE DEMAND, with increases in tax serving to reduce disposable income available for consumption spending, and decreases in tax increasing disposable income. Indirect taxes can be used to affect the shape of demand as well as its level, increases serving to discourage consumption of socially disapproved products like cigarettes and alcoholic drinks, and reductions encouraging consumption of socially approved products like food and books.

Unlike a DIRECT TAX, which varies according to the income of the taxpayer (PROGRESSIVE TAXATION), indirect taxes are regressive, insofar as the same amount is paid by all taxpaying consumers regardless of income. See TAXATION, REGRESSIVE TAXATION.

indivisibilities the minimum physical or technical size limitations on FACTOR INPUTS. For example, a company may want to purchase a machine that can perform 5000 operations a day. Due to design and technical difficulties, the smallest machine available optimally performs 10,000 operations a day. The machine is indivisible, since it cannot be reduced to two optimal half-machines. The AVERAGE COST of each unit of output is consequently greater than it would be if the manufacturer could produce at an output level at which the machine was optimally employed.

A manufacturer can achieve ECONOMIES OF SCALE by attaining a larger volume of production, but this can give rise to problems of combining large, indivisible inputs with different capacities. For example, if the manufacturer above needs to combine process A machines capable of carrying out 10,000 operations a day and process B machines capable of carrying out 4000 operations a day, only by producing 20,000 units a day in two process A machines and five process B machines would he be able to use both types of machines economically. Any other output level would result in underutilization of one or the other machine.

See PRODUCTION FUNCTION.

induced investment the part of an increase or decrease in real INVESTMENT brought about by a change in the level of NATIONAL INCOME. For example, a rise in national income accompanied by increased consumption spending, which may put pressure on existing supply capacity, may encourage businesses to invest in new plant and machinery. See ACCELERATOR, INVESTMENT SCHEDULE, AUTONOMOUS INVESTMENT.

industrial classification the grouping of economic activities of a similar nature into INDUSTRIES or MARKETS. A system used to group activities in this way is described as a *standard industrial classification.* Such a classification begins by identifying a wide spectrum of related groups' activities, for example, the manufacturing sector. Each group of activities then is subdivided into progressively narrower groups so that the classification can be used with varying amounts of detail for different purposes. Thus, within the manufacturing sector, a broad group such as textile manufacture may be subdivided first into different kinds of textile fabrics, such as wool, cotton, and synthetics, and these in turn into smaller subdivisions of activity, such as spinning, weaving, finishing, etc.

Industrial classifications are used for macroeconomic planning and COMPETITION POLICY purposes, and to obtain statistical information on output and employment. See STRUCTURE OF INDUSTRY, CROSS ELASTICITY OF DEMAND.

industrial democracy the participation of the work force, along with management, in making corporate decisions. See WORKER PARTICIPATION, LABOR UNION.

industrial economics or **industrial organization** the branch of economics concerned with the functioning of the PRICE SYSTEM. Industrial economics examines the relationships between MARKET STRUCTURE, MARKET CONDUCT, and MARKET PERFORMANCE, using the analytical framework of the THEORY OF MARKETS but within an empirical and dynamic setting. See MARKET STRUCTURE/CONDUCT-PERFORMANCE SCHEMA.

industrialization the extensive development of organized economic activity for the purpose of manufacture. Industrialization is characterized by transformation of a primarily agrarian economy into a more specialized, capital-intensive economy. Such a transformation was termed the *Industrial Revolution* in Western Europe and North America during the eighteenth and nineteenth centuries. Compare DEINDUSTRIALIZATION. See STRUCTURE OF INDUSTRY, ECONOMIC DEVELOPMENT.

industrial organization see INDUSTRIAL ECONOMICS.

industrial policy a series of measures undertaken by government to promote industrial EFFICIENCY, TECHNOLOGICAL PROGRESSIVENESS, and employment opportunities. Industrial policy is implemented both through selective intervention involving sponsorship and financial support of industries, companies, and projects, and through across-the-board programs designed to assist industrial regeneration and expansion.

In some countries, industrial policy has developed piecemeal and has varied in the degree of enthusiasm shown toward it from time to time. In other countries, industrial policy has been seen as an arm of INDICATIVE PLANNING and has been applied on a continuing and coordinated basis. See REGIONAL POLICY.

industrial property rights the ownership by a business of PATENTS on techniques and products, BRAND NAMES, and COPYRIGHTS giving legal entitlement and powers of redress against theft and unauthorized imitation. See PRODUCT DIFFERENTIATION.

industrial relations the practice of those processes, forces, and institutions through which employers and employees order and regulate their working lives. "Industrial relations" is an all-embracing term covering all aspects of the employment relationship and its associated institutions and social and economic environment. See LABOR UNION, COLLECTIVE BARGAINING, ARBITRATION, MEDIATION.

Industrial Revolution see INDUSTRIALIZATION.

industrial sector manufacturing—the part of an economy concerned with production of INTERMEDIATE GOODS (iron and steel, machinery and equipment, etc.) and FINAL PRODUCTS (washing machines, furniture, etc.). The industrial sector, together with the PRIMARY SECTOR and SERVICE SECTOR, forms an interlocking chain of economic activities that constitute a modern economy. See STRUCTURE OF INDUSTRY.

industry any economic activities classified by type of product or service provided: for example, the aircraft industry, the insurance industry. Industries are usually defined by reference to their principal products, but there often is disagreement with respect to how widely or narrowly industry boundaries are drawn. See MARKET, INDUSTRIAL CLASSIFICATION, MARKET STRUCTURE, CROSS ELASTICITY OF DEMAND.

inelastic relatively unresponsive to change. See PRICE ELASTICITY OF DEMAND, PRICE ELASTICITY OF SUPPLY, INCOME ELASTICITY OF DEMAND, CROSS ELASTICITY OF DEMAND.

inequality a means of arithmetically portraying a relationship between VARIABLES. For example, the inequality: $C \leq Y$ suggests that consumption expenditure (C) is less than, or at most equal to, disposable income (Y). Alternatively, we can write: $Y \geq C$, which suggests that disposable income is greater than, or at least equal to, consumption expenditure. See EQUATION.

infant industry a newly established industry, developed either by private enterprise or by a government, often in DEVELOPING COUNTRIES, as part of their INDUSTRIALIZATION programs. New industries are often subsidized by the government and/or protected from import competition in the hope that in due course they can exploit economies of scale and eventually withstand foreign competition.

Infant industries are often cited as legitimate areas for application of PROTECTIONISM, but policy in this area is open to abuse. See ECONOMIC DEVELOPMENT.

inferior product goods or services for which INCOME ELASTICITY OF DEMAND is negative; that is, as income rises, buyers purchase less of the product. Consequently, when the price of such a product falls, thereby effectively increasing consumers' real income, that price cut will have the INCOME EFFECT of tending to decrease the quantity demanded. This will tend to partially offset the SUBSTITUTION EFFECT of a price cut, which causes consumers to buy more of the product because it becomes relatively cheaper. This applies to a limited range of products. See PRICE EFFECT, NORMAL PRODUCT, INCOME CONSUMPTION CURVE, ENGEL'S LAW.

inflation an increase in the general level of prices in an economy that is sustained over a period of time. The annual increases in prices may be small or gradual (CREEPING INFLATION), or large and accelerating (HYPERINFLATION). The rate of inflation can be measured using, for example, a consumers' PRICE INDEX that shows the annual percentage change in consumer prices. See Fig. 91a. Inflation reduces the PURCHASING POWER of money (see REAL VALUES).

The avoidance of inflation has long been a main objective of MACROECONOMIC POLICY. Inflation is considered undesirable because of its adverse effects on income distribution (people on fixed incomes suffer), lending and borrowing (lenders lose, borrowers gain), speculation (diversion of saving away from industry into property and commodity speculation), and international trade competitiveness (exports become relatively more expensive, im-

	UK	W. Germany	US	Japan
1980	18.0	5.5	13.5	8.0
1981	11.9	6.3	10.4	4.9
1982	8.6	5.3	6.1	2.7
1983	4.6	3.3	3.2	1.9
1984	5.0	2.4	4.3	2.2
1985	6.1	2.2	3.5	2.1
1986	3.4	−0.2	2.0	0.4
1987	4.2	0.2	3.7	0.1
1988	4.9	1.2	4.1	0.7

(a)

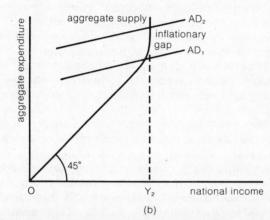

(b)

FIG. 91. **Inflation.** (a) National inflation rates, 1978—1986. Source: OECD *Economic Outlook,* 1988. (b) In the EQUILIBRIUM LEVEL OF NATIONAL INCOME model, inflation occurs whenever AGGREGATE DEMAND exceeds full employment aggregate supply, POTENTIAL GROSS NATIONAL PRODUCT. Equilibrium national income in the figure is OY_2, and if aggregate demand AD_2 exceeds full employment demand AD_1, an INFLATIONARY GAP develops. The traditional prescription for this situation is for the authorities to reduce spending by deflationary FISCAL POLICY and MONETARY POLICY measures—to shift aggregate demand from AD_2 to AD_1.

· ports cheaper). Inflation creates uncertainty and obstacles to future transactions. Hyperinflation is particularly serious because people lose confidence in the use of money for exchange purposes, and the economic system is apt to collapse.

There are two main explanations of why inflation occurs: (a) the presence of excess demand at the full employment level of national output, which pulls up prices (DEMAND-PULL INFLATION); (b) an increase in FACTOR INPUT input costs, which pushes up prices (COST-PUSH INFLATION). An alternative explanation of demand-pull inflation offered by MONETARISM blames excessive creation of money for inflation and prescribes restricting the rate of growth of money to match the growth of potential GNP. Economists who favor the cost-push explanation argue for PRICES AND INCOMES POLICY as the means of control inflation.

See INFLATIONARY SPIRAL, PURCHASING POWER, PHILLIPS CURVE, EXPECTATIONS-ADJUSTED/AUGMENTED PHILLIPS CURVE, ADAPTIVE EXPECTATIONS HYPOTHESIS, QUANTITY THEORY OF MONEY.

inflation accounting any adjustments in a company's accounts to allow for the effects of INFLATION and arrive at a view of the company's real profitability. In a period of rising prices, when the purchasing power of the money unit is declining, profit calculations based on HISTORIC COST of inventories and FIXED ASSETS are likely to overstate the real profit position. Various methods of allowing for the effects of inflation on a company's financial statements have been tried.

One relatively simple method of accounting that takes into account the effects of inflation is the *current purchasing-power method*. This method uses a PRICE INDEX number to adjust the calculated profit figure for a period and thereby to express profit realistically. A more detailed method is the *current cost-accounting method*. This method produces a supplementary financial statement and balance sheet. In these current-cost accounts, the deduction from revenue for COST OF GOODS SOLD is based on the REPLACEMENT COST of the goods sold, a cost-of-sales adjustment. DEPRECIATION is calculated on replacement cost of fixed assets used and not on their historic cost, a depreciation adjustment. See REVALUATION PROVISION, APPRECIATION(2).

inflationary gap the excess of total spending (AGGREGATE DE-MAND) at the full employment level of national income (POTEN-TIAL GROSS NATIONAL PRODUCT). As it is not possible to increase output further, the excess demand will cause prices to rise, that is, real output remains the same but the money or NOMINAL VALUE of that output will be inflated. See Fig. 92.

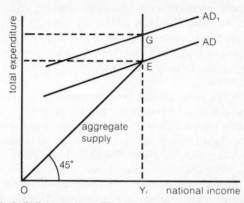

FIG. 92. **Inflationary gap.** The full employment level of national income/output is reached at output O Y_f, and at this output level the AGGREGATE SUPPLY SCHEDULE becomes vertical. If aggregate demand were at the level indicated by AD, the economy would be operating at full employment without inflation—at point E. However, if aggregate demand were at a higher level, such as AD_1, the excess aggregate demand would create an inflationary gap, equal to EG, pulling prices upward. See DEMAND-PULL INFLATION.

inflationary spiral or **price-wage spiral** a self-sustained increase in the rate of INFLATION brought about by interaction of rising final prices and rising input costs. For example, an initial sharp increase in the prices of goods and services caused by an increase in raw material costs can lead to a demand for higher MONEY WAGES by labor unions concerned with protecting their members' living standards. If the unions are successful, higher wage costs are soon likely to prompt manufacturers to raise their prices in order to maintain profit margins. The higher prices in turn produce further demand for wage increases, and so on. Once under way, price-cost increases tend to be self-reinforcing, and are exacerbated by EXPECTATIONS of even further increases. See ADAPTIVE EXPECTATIONS HYPOTHESIS, EXPECTATIONS-ADJUSTED/AUGMENTED PHILLIPS CURVE, MONEY ILLUSION.

infrastructure or **social overhead capital** a nation's roads, railways, housing, hospitals, schools, water supply, etc., accumulated earlier through INVESTMENT, usually by government or local authorities. It also includes such intangible items as a trained labor force created by investment in HUMAN CAPITAL.

Infrastructure plays an important role in improving a country's general living standards and in contributing to a high rate of ECONOMIC GROWTH.

inheritance tax a tax levied on a person's private assets when those assets are transferred to the person's heirs.

injections any expenditures on domestic goods and services originating from outside the household sector. In the basic CIRCULAR FLOW OF NATIONAL INCOME MODEL, all spending is done by households (CONSUMPTION expenditure). In the extended circular flow of income model, domestic output is also purchased by businesses, government, and overseas buyers. Thus, INVESTMENT, GOVERNMENT (PUBLIC) EXPENDITURE, and EXPORTS constitute injections into the income-spending flow. Compare WITHDRAWALS.

innovation the practical refinement and development of an original invention into a usable technique or product. Innovation is an important means of improving MARKET PERFORMANCE by, for example, lowering supply costs, improving product quality, and accelerating ECONOMIC GROWTH.

Innovation can be a lengthy and expensive process. For example, the original invention of the Xerox photocopying process came in 1948, but it took 10 years of additional development work before the first commercial version of the product was put on the market.

See TECHNOLOGICAL PROGRESSIVENESS, RESEARCH AND DEVELOPMENT.

input see FACTOR INPUTS.

input-output analysis or **interindustry analysis** the study and empirical measurement of the structural relationships between PRODUCTION sectors within an economy. The technique was devised by Wassily Leontief (born 1906) to measure the FACTOR INPUT required by different industries to achieve a given OUTPUT. A particular sector of the economy requires inputs from other sectors, perhaps raw materials, intermediate goods and services, or labor, in order to produce output. The dependence between industries or sectors is complex. That is, one sector does not produce, say, coal, for other sectors independent of the requirements of the coal industry for inputs from other sectors. For the mining sector, coal is an output. For the elctricity industry, coal is an input. By the same token, the coal industry requires inputs, including electricity, in order to produce the coal. The complexity of an economy can be gauged from this simple example. See VERTICAL INTEGRATION, INDICATIVE PLANNING, GENERAL EQUILIBRIUM ANALYSIS.

inside money see ENDOGENOUS MONEY.

insider trading any transactions in securities, such as STOCKS and BONDS, by persons having access to privileged information not as yet available to the general investing public, and who in consequence stand to gain financially from this knowledge. For example, a person employed by an underwriter and involved in working out details of a prospective TAKEOVER by a client of a company may himself or through other people—that is, by trading as an insider—arrange to purchase shares in the takeover target prior to public announcement of the takeover.

insolvency a condition under which an individual or company's LIABILITIES to creditors exceed ASSETS. The individual or company is therefore unable to discharge all accumulated liabilities from realizable assets.

Insolvency may occur after a period in which an individual's expenditures have exceeded his income, or a company's costs have exceeded its sales revenues. Frequently, an insolvent individual or company will become bankrupt and arrange for LIQUIDATION of available assets, the proceeds being distributed among creditors. See SHARE CAPITAL.

installment buying a contractual means of purchasing an ASSET in which an initial down payment is usually required, followed by monthly fixed payments that include interest charges for a specified time.

institutional investors the financial institutions that collect SAV-

INGS and other deposits and invest long-term in bonds and common stocks, government bonds, real estate, and foreign securities. Institutional investors include insurance companies, mutual funds, pension funds, and investment trust companies. In many countries, commercial banks are also major long-term investors.

Institutional investors have grown rapidly since the 1950s, encouraged both by favorable tax concessions granted by the government to contractual pension and life insurance plans, and the opportunities financial institutions provide to pool risks by investing in a variety of financial securities. Institutional investors now form the primary conduit for channeling personal savings into industrial and commercial investment, displacing direct investment by individual savers.

insurance a method of protecting a person or business against the financial consequences of loss of, and damage to, ASSETS through fire, theft, etc. (general insurance), and loss of life and limb (life and accident insurance). The term *assurance* is frequently used interchangeably with "insurance" to describe certain kinds of life insurance. See INSURANCE COMPANY, RISK AND UNCERTAINTY.

insurance company a financial institution that provides a range of insurance policies to protect individuals and businesses against the risk of financial losses in return for regular payment of PREMIUMS. An insurance company operates by pooling risks among a large number of contributors. From its past claims record, a company actuary can compute the probability of a particular event occurring, for example, a fire, and can assess the average financial loss associated with each event. Using this information, the actuary tries to calculate appropriate premiums and from the collective pool of premium income to meet outstanding financial claims. See FINANCIAL SYSTEM, INSTITUTIONAL INVESTORS, RISK AND UNCERTAINTY.

intangible assets nonphysical assets, such as GOODWILL, PATENTS, and TRADEMARKS, which have a money value.

intangibles costs and benefits usually associated with an investment project within the public sector, whether quantifiable or not, that cannot easily be valued in money terms. Examples include damage to scenery caused by projects, such as airport runway construction in rural areas, and the increased or decreased number of traffic deaths associated with road-building projects. Such intangibles are important, although they cannot easily be incorporated in an investment appraisal. See COST-BENEFIT ANALYSIS.

integration see HORIZONTAL INTEGRATION, VERTICAL INTEGRATION, DIVERSIFICATION, TRADE INTEGRATION.

intercept the point at which a line on a GRAPH intersects the vertical or horizontal AXIS. See LINEAR EQUATION.

interest a payment made by borrowers to lenders for use of their money both to finance physical and portfolio investment and to finance consumption. In aggregate terms, interest is a source of income and is thus included as a part of NATIONAL INCOME. (The exception is interest on the national debt, which is treated as a transfer payment.) In the THEORY OF SUPPLY, interest is a payment for the use of CAPITAL as a FACTOR OF PRODUCTION.

See also RATE OF INTEREST, NATIONAL INCOME ACCOUNTS, MARGINAL EFFICIENCY OF CAPITAL/INVESTMENT, DISCOUNT RATE, COST OF CAPITAL, TERM STRUCTURE OF INTEREST RATES, TIME PREFERENCE THEORY, NOMINAL RATE OF INTEREST, EFFECTIVE RATE OF INTEREST.

interest rate see RATE OF INTEREST.

intermediate goods the goods and services used as FACTOR INPUTS by businesses in producing other goods or services. An example is steel, which has a variety of end-uses, including car bodies, washing machine tubs, nuts and bolts, etc.

Intermediate goods are not counted as part of gross national product in the NATIONAL INCOME ACCOUNTS, in which final goods and services are measured. See FINAL PRODUCTS, VALUE ADDED.

intermediation the role of financial institutions in channeling SAVINGS and other deposits by LENDERS to BORROWERS. Financial intermediaries, such as COMMERCIAL BANKS and SAVINGS AND LOAN INSTITUTIONS, accept deposits from individuals and businesses and use these funds to make loans to credit-worthy customers. An intermediary's profit is the difference between rates paid for deposits and rates charged for loans. See FINANCIAL SYSTEM, DISINTERMEDIATION.

internal economies of scale a reduction in a company's AVERAGE COSTS of production as OUTPUT increases. Emphasis is often placed on technical economies, such as using plants at a greater capacity to reduce unit costs. It is widely recognized that large plants may facilitate a greater division of labor, but economies within the marketing, managerial, and financial spheres may also be obtained. Compare EXTERNAL ECONOMIES OF SCALE. See ECONOMIES OF SCALE, DISECONOMIES OF SCALE.

internal-external balance model a theoretical construct that seeks to integrate achievement of the MACROECONOMIC POLICY objectives of FULL EMPLOYMENT and PRICE STABILITY (internal balance) and BALANCE-OF-PAYMENTS EQUILIBRIUM (external balance).

A brief illustration of the model is given in Fig. 93a. The vertical axis shows the ratio of international prices to domestic prices. This is an index of the country's foreign competitive position. The farther one moves up the scale, the larger are exports and the smaller are imports. On the horizontal axis is domestic real demand, which increases from left to right. The two curves shown in the figure represent, respectively, external balance (EE) and internal balance (DD). The EE curve has a positive slope, indicating that the more unfavorable the international price ratio becomes, the lower domestic real demand must be to maintain balance-of-payments equilibrium. Positions to the left and above the curve represent payments surplus; to the right and below, deficit. The DD curve has a negative slope, indicating that the more unfavorable the international price ratio becomes, the higher domestic real demand must be to maintain full employment. Positions to the right and above the curve represent price inflation; to the left and below, unemployment.

Where the EE and DD curves intersect (point A), the country is in general equilibrium. All other positions represent disequilibrium. However, from only a few of these disequilibrium positions can the country attain the two policy objectives of internal and external equilibrium using just a single policy variable—specifically, from only those positions located on the horizontal and vertical dotted lines drawn through the intersection. In the situations shown by the horizontal line to the right of point A, for instance, the ratio of international to domestic prices is appropriate, but domestic real demand is too high, resulting in both inflation and a balance-of-payments deficit. DEFLATION of demand alone would

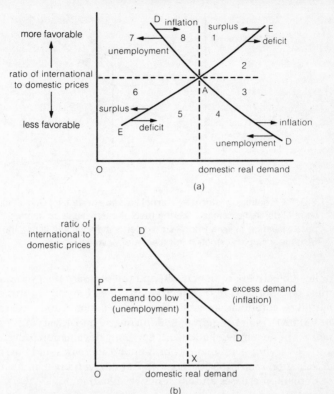

FIG. 93. **Internal-external balance model.** (a) See entry. (b) Given the ratio of international to domestic prices (P), domestic demand must be at level X to secure internal balance. If it is not, the result is unemployment or inflation.

therefore suffice to realize both goals. In situations shown by the vertical line below point A, domestic real demand is just right, but domestic prices are uncompetitive, resulting in both a balance-of-payments deficit and unemployment. A currency DEVALUATION alone would therefore suffice to realize both goals. However, these are special cases. In all other situations, both domestic demand and the international price ratio are inappropriate. As a result, the two

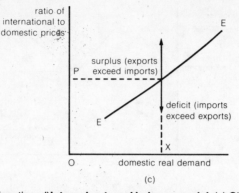

FIG. 93. (continued)**Internal-external balance model.** (c) Given the level of domestic demand (X), the ratio of international to domestic prices must be at level P to secure external balance. If it is not, the result is a surplus or deficit in balance of payments.

policy objectives are in conflict, and the separate policy variables must be combined to be effective. In zones 1 and 2, for instance, varying combinations of demand-deflation and currency REVALUATION are required, and in zones 3 and 4, varying combinations of demand-deflation and currency devaluation. In zones 5 and 6, varying combinations of demand increases and currency devaluation are required, in zones 7 and 8, varying combinations of demand increases and currency revaluation.

internal financing the ability to finance a company's growth from retained earnings. A company's NET PROFIT can be paid out in DIVIDENDS or retained for internal financing or some mixture of these two. Generally, stockholders look for some immediate income in the form of dividends and some growth in the capital value of their shares, which depends on growth. By paying out higher dividends, growth is slowed. Achieving the optimum solution between two conflicting objectives is an important area of study in managerial finance. See COST OF CAPITAL, RESERVES.

internalization the combining in one company of two or more related activities, as opposed to conducting the activities separately in different companies and then being synchronized through arms-length MARKET transactions. Economic theory postulates that a PROFIT MAXIMIZING firm will internalize a sequence of activities if the costs of doing so are lower than transacting the same activities through the market.

The most common example of internalization is that of VERTICAL INTEGRATION, combining a series of vertically related activities. Cost advantages accruing through vertical internalization include reduced production costs by linking together successive processes of manufacture, for example, iron and steel mills to avoid reheating, and avoidance of TRANSACTION COSTS incurred in imperfect markets, for example, monopoly surcharges imposed by input suppliers, unreliable sources of supply, and restrictions on sales outlets.

The concept of internalization is also relevant to HORIZONTAL INTEGRATION by multiplant domestic companies and multinational companies. In the latter case, establishment of production plants in overseas markets instead of servicing the markets by direct exporting occurs because of the transaction costs of market imperfections, such as TARIFFS, QUOTAS, and exchange rate restrictions as well as the fact that monopolistic advantages (a patented product, know-how, or a unique product) can be exploited and protected better by direct control.

internal rate of return see DISCOUNTED CASH FLOW.

Internal Revenue Service (IRS) the division of the US Department of the Treasury responsible for collecting internal revenue, including income taxes and excise taxes. It also enforces revenue laws.

International Bank for Reconstruction and Development see WORLD BANK.

international commodity agreement an agreement that attempts to stabilize prices of some internationally traded commodities, such as coffee or tin, with the objective of stabilizing foreign exchange earnings and producers' incomes, primarily in the DEVELOPING COUNTRIES. Although international commodity agreements are intended to further the interests of producing countries, they may also benefit consumers by removing uncertainties and inconveniences associated with erratic price movements.

International commodity agreements vary in format but one

typical approach involves establishment of an official price for the commodity, agreed on by member countries, which is then maintained over a period of time by use of a BUFFER STOCK. Surplus output is bought if market supply exceeds demand at the official price, and sold if demand exceeds market supply.

International commodity agreements have been promoted by the UNITED NATIONS CONFERENCE ON TRADE AND DEVELOPMENT as a means of enhancing the economic interests of the developing countries (see NEW INTERNATIONAL ECONOMIC ORDER), but serious difficulties are often encountered in ensuring their viability. For example, disagreements can occur between member countries concerning the official prices to set, arising out of differences in the degree of importance of the commodity to individual members' economies. The temptation is to set prices above market-determined rates, which places a financial strain on the buffer stock, eventually causing it to run out of money.

international competitiveness the ability of a country to compete successfully against other countries in INTERNATIONAL TRADE. Successful countries will maintain or increase their share of world exports and, by the same token, limit the extent of IMPORT PENETRATION into their domestic economies.

International competitiveness is reflected in two things: (a) *price competitiveness*, it is important that domestic suppliers are efficient and cost-effective and that governments can control domestic rates of INFLATION and maintain realistic EXCHANGE RATES for their currencies. (b) *nonprice competitiveness*, it is equally important that domestic suppliers offer export customers attractive new products, improve quality and performance of their products, meet delivery dates, etc.

international debt the money owed to the international community by borrowing countries. In the main, debtor countries are DEVELOPING COUNTRIES that have borrowed foreign exchange from advanced countries and private banks to finance economic development programs.

As can be seen from Fig. 94, DEBT SERVICING exceeded new lending in 1985. The problem of debt servicing has been especially acute for a number of countries that, because of a decline in foreign exchange earnings, have been forced in recent years to renege on or reschedule their foreign debts. This has reacted adversely on the willingness of some lenders to make further LOANS.

	$ Billions
Total debt outstanding	708
Disbursements, 1985	80
Debt repayments, 1985	102
Capital (50)	
Interest (52)	
Net transfer	−22

FIG. 94. **International debt.** The long-term debt (in US dollar billions) of 107 developing countries in 1985. Source: World Bank, 1986.

International Development Association see WORLD BANK.

International Finance Corporation see WORLD BANK.

international Fisher effect a situation in which NOMINAL RATE OF INTEREST differentials between countries reflect anticipated rates of change in the EXCHANGE RATE of their currencies (see FISHER EFFECT).

For example, if British investors anticipate that the US dollar will appreciate by, say, 5% a year against sterling, then in order to offset the expected change in parity between the two countries, they would be prepared to accept an interest rate of approximately 5% a year less on a dollar-denominated financial security than that which could be expected on an equivalent investment denominated in sterling. From a borrower's viewpoint, when the international Fisher effect holds, the cost of equivalent loans in alternative currencies will be the same regardless of the rate of interest.

The international Fisher effect can be contrasted with the *domestic Fisher effect* in which nominal interest rates reflect the anticipated real rate of interest and the anticipated rate of change in prices (INFLATION). The international equivalent of inflation is therefore changing exchange rates.

International Labor Organization (ILO) a special agency of the UNITED NATIONS whose objective is to promote improved living standards and working conditions throughout the world, thereby facilitating social justice as a basis for achieving world peace. The

ILO was originally founded in 1919 by the Treaty of Versailles and became affiliated with the UN in 1946, shortly after the UN was established.

The functions of the ILO encompass all aspects of social and economic conditions affecting employment throughout the world. It promotes national labor standards and work practices, but only in an advisory capacity, as it has no legislative powers. It provides technical assistance in manpower training, social policy, and administration and encourages cooperation between labor groups. The ILO is also concerned with collection and dissemination of international labor statistics and undertakes research on a variety of labor-related problems.

international liquidity or **international money** monetary assets that are generally acceptable as a means of financing INTERNATIONAL TRADE and/or as an INTERNATIONAL RESERVE asset with which to finance BALANCE OF PAYMENTS deficits. For example, the US dollar is used as the NUMERAIRE of the oil market and also serves as an important reserve asset. The SPECIAL DRAWING RIGHT is used only as a reserve asset.

International Monetary Fund (IMF) a multinational institution set up in 1947, following the Bretton Woods Conference of 1944 to supervise operation of a new international monetary regime— the ADJUSTABLE PEG SYSTEM. The Fund seeks to maintain cooperative and orderly currency arrangements between member countries, with the aim of promoting increased INTERNATIONAL TRADE and BALANCE-OF-PAYMENTS EQUILIBRIUM.

There are two different views on how international monetary cooperation should be approached. One holds that flexible exchange rates have led to excessive movements of exchange rates, which have made domestic macroeconomic management difficult. As a result, cooperative international agreements are essential for stabilizing exchange rates.

The other view stresses that domestic monetary stability should have the highest priority. Monetary authorities of the major industrial nations should pursue policies that ensure stable prices. When this is accomoplished, exchange rates will be predictable and economic cooperation made more likely.

The International Monetary Fund is active in two main areas:

(a) EXCHANGE RATES. Until 1971, countries established the FIXED EXCHANGE-RATE SYSTEM for their currencies in order to provide pivotal values for concluding trade transactions. A country, provided it first obtained the approval of the Fund, could alter its exchange rate, adjusting the rate upward (REVALUATION) or downward (DEVALUATION) to a new fixed level to correct a FUNDAMENTAL DISEQUILIBRIUM in its balance of payments—a situation of either chronic payments surplus or deficit. Since 1971, most of the world's leading currencies have been floating (see FLOATING EXCHANGE-RATE SYSTEM). This has resulted in the Fund's losing formal control over exchange rate movements, but member countries are still obliged to abide by certain rules of good conduct laid down by the Fund, avoiding in particular EXCHANGE CONTROLS and BEGGAR-MY-NEIGHBOR tactics.

(b) INTERNATIONAL LIQUIDITY. The Fund's resources consist of a pool of currencies and INTERNATIONAL RESERVE assets, excluding gold, subscribed by its members according to their allocated quotas. Each country pays 75% of its quota in its own currency and 25% in international reserve assets. Countries are given *borrowing* or *drawing rights* with the Fund that they can use, together with their own nationally held international reserves, to finance a balance-of-payments deficit.

Under the Fund's ordinary drawing-right facilities, members with balance of payments difficulties may draw, that is, purchase foreign currencies from the Fund with their own currencies, up to 125% of their quota. The first 25%, the so-called reserve *tranche*, or segment, may be drawn on demand. The remaining 100% is divided into four credit *tranches* of 25% each, and drawings here are conditional on members agreeing with the Fund on a program of measures for removing their payments deficit. Members are required to repay their drawings over a 3- to 5-year period.

In 1970 the Fund created a new international reserve asset, the SPECIAL DRAWING RIGHT (SDR) to augment the supply of international liquidity. It has also provided additional borrowing facilities for its poorer members. See also DOMESTIC CREDIT EXPANSION.

international monetary system a system for promoting INTERNATIONAL TRADE and SPECIALIZATION at the same time ensuring long-run individual BALANCE-OF-PAYMENTS EQUILIBRIUM. To be effective an international monetary system must be able to: (a) provide a system of EXCHANGE RATES between national currencies, (b) provide an ADJUSTMENT MECHANISM capable of removing payments imbalances, and (c) provide an amount of INTERNATIONAL RESERVES to finance payments deficits. Various international monetary systems have been tried, including the GOLD COIN STANDARD and, currently, the INTERNATIONAL MONETARY FUND system.

See FIXED EXCHANGE-RATE SYSTEM, FLOATING EXCHANGE-RATE SYSTEM, EUROPEAN MONETARY SYSTEM.

international money see INTERNATIONAL LIQUIDITY, INTERNATIONAL RESERVES.

international reserves or **foreign exchange reserves** financial assets used to settle BALANCE OF PAYMENTS deficits between countries. International reserves are made up of gold, foreign exchange, International Monetary Fund Drawing Rights, and SPECIAL DRAWING RIGHTS (SDRs). As Fig. 95 shows, gold and foreign exchange, particularly the US dollar, are the most important reserve assets. See EUROPEAN CURRENCY UNIT.

Reserve assets	Percentage of international reserves
Gold	42
Foreign exchange	53
Reserve position in	
International Monetary Fund	3
Special drawing rights	2

FIG. 95. **International reserves for 1986.**

international trade the exchange of goods and services between countries. International trade enables countries to obtain some goods and services more cheaply than they can produce them for themselves (COMPARATIVE ADVANTAGE), or be able to consume goods and services that would otherwise be unobtainable from domestic supply sources, for example, a scarce raw material or an advanced technology.

Through trade, countries can capitalize on their economic strengths, thereby improving their real living standards. However, the benefits of international SPECIALIZATION and trade may not be evenly distributed between countries. The manner in which world trading patterns have developed has not in fact benefited certain DEVELOPING COUNTRIES, which have specialized in a narrow range of commodities for which world demand has grown slowly. In addition, protectionist measures (see PROTECTIONISM) imposed by the advanced industrialized countries have also worked against the interests of the developing countries.

See GAINS FROM TRADE, THEORY OF INTERNATIONAL TRADE, FREE TRADE, TRADE INTEGRATION, GENERAL AGREEMENT ON TARIFFS AND TRADE.

interpersonal comparison see WELFARE ECONOMICS.

interpolate see EXTRAPOLATE.

invention the creation of new production techniques and processes and new products. Invention is an important aspect of MARKET PERFORMANCE and a contributing factor to ECONOMIC GROWTH. At the level of the individual market, inventions make it possible to lower supply costs and prices to consumers, and to provide consumers with improved products. In a more general way, invention can add to the growth of national income and output by the qualitative improvement of a country's CAPITAL STOCK as investment in new technologies improves PRODUCTIVITY.

See INNOVATION, MONOPOLY, TECHNOLOGICAL PROGRESSIVENESS, RESEARCH AND DEVELOPMENT.

inventory the part of a company's assets held in the form of raw materials, work in progress, and finished goods. Finished goods are held in inventory to ensure that goods are available when required by customers. Raw materials and components are held in inventory to prevent disruptions to production caused by lack of materials or components and to secure economies from bulk purchasing. The rate at which companies accumulate and deplete their inventories influences oscillations in economic activity (see INVENTORY VALUATION).

inventory cost the cost to companies of holding inventories of finished products and raw materials in order to provide immediate customer service or to prevent disruptions to production caused by lack of materials. Inventory costs include costs of warehouse space, insurance, deterioration and obsolescence of stored items, and interest on capital tied up in inventory. Such costs are roughly proportional to the value of the inventory, and to contain these costs, inventory levels must be kept low. On the other hand, companies also have costs for ordering and delivering goods for inventory, such as communicating with suppliers, accounting transactions, transportation, and unloading and inspecting goods. Some of these ordering and delivery costs may remain the same irrespective of the size of the order.

Since many ordering and delivery costs are fixed costs, to reduce them the company should place large orders at infrequent intervals. Such a policy will have the additional benefit of enabling the company to earn price discounts for bulk purchase. If orders are placed at infrequent intervals, however, inventory and its costs will be high. It is desirable to strike a balance between these two groups of costs in order to achieve the minimum inventory cost, as in Fig. 96, which shows the *optimum order quantity*, or *economical order quantity*, that serves to minimize total inventory cost. Order and delivery costs in Fig. 96 decrease as larger and less frequent deliveries are made. Larger deliveries at less frequent intervals involve a larger average inventory holding and, thus, higher costs. The optimum order quantity OB corresponds to the minimum point on the total inventory curve. For simple inventory situations, mathematical formulas can be used to determine the optimum order quantity.

In the simple model of Fig. 96, inventory costs are excluded, implying that replenishments of inventory can occur as soon as an order is placed, so that once inventories fall to zero, an order can be placed and the goods received. In actuality, there is usually a delay between placing an order and receiving delivery into inventory, and a company needs enough inventory cushion to cope with expected usage before replenishment can be achieved. Where there is some uncertainty about the rate of usage before inventory replenishment, or about the lead time required before replenishment can occur, there is risk of being out of inventory unless the company carries an adequate inventory cushion. The size of the cushion will seek to balance the extra costs associated with the extra inventory and the cost of running out of inventory.

inventory investment the investment in raw materials, WORK IN

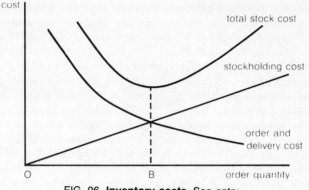

FIG. 96. **Inventory costs.** See entry.

PROGRESS, and finished goods. In contrast to FIXED INVESTMENT, inventories are constantly being turned over as the production cycle repeats itself, with raw materials being purchased, converted first into work in progress, then finished goods, then finally being sold.

The level of inventory investment made by a company will depend on its forecasts of future demand and its resulting output plans, and the amount of inventory it needs to allow for delivery delays on raw materials and production delays in serving customers, with appropriate buffer inventory to cover contingencies. Companies frequently find that actual levels of demand differ from their forecasts, so demand is less than expected and companies find that stocks of unsold goods build up (unintended inventory investment), or that demand exceeds expectations so that inventories run down (unintended inventory disinvestment). The cost of inventory investment includes order and delivery costs, deterioration and obsolescence of inventory, and interest charges on funds invested in inventory. Companies seek to minimize these costs by establishing economical order quantities and optimum inventory levels. See INVENTORY COST.

inventory valuation the placing of an appropriate money value on a company's inventory of raw materials, work in progress, and finished goods. When inflation causes the price of several different batches of finished goods to differ, the company has the problems of deciding: (a) what money value to place on the period-end physical inventory in the balance sheet, and (b) what cost to attach to the units sold in the period. The second decision has a direct bearing on the cost of goods sold and so on gross profit.

Formulas used to value inventory can lead to variations in the values shown in the balance sheet and in the cost of goods sold. For example, the *first-in, first-out (FIFO)* method assumes that goods are withdrawn from inventory in the order in which they were received, so the cost of goods sold is based on the cost of the oldest goods in inventory, while the value of closing inventory is based on the prices of the newest goods in inventory. By contrast, the *last-in, first-out (LIFO)* method assumes that the most recently purchased goods are theoretically withdrawn from inventory first. Thus, the cost of goods sold is based on the costs of the most recent purchases, while the value of closing inventory is based on the oldest goods on hand. LIFO gives a higher figure for cost of goods sold, one that closely approximates the replacement costs of goods sold, but it tends to understate the value of period-end inventory.

In the interests of prudence, a company would want to value inventory at cost or market value, whichever is lower, to avoid overstating profits. See INFLATION ACCOUNTING, HISTORIC COST, DEPRECIATION.

investment 1. expenditure on the purchase of FINANCIAL SECURITIES, such as STOCKS and BONDS. Also called *financial investment.* PORTFOLIO investment is undertaken by persons, firms, and financial institutions in the expectation of earning a return in the form of INTEREST or DIVIDENDS, or an appreciation in the capital value of the securities. **2.** capital expenditure on the purchase of physical assets, such as plant, machinery, equipment (fixed capital), and inventory (working capital), that is, *physical* or *real investment.* In economic analysis, unless otherwise indicated, the term "investment" relates specifically to physical investment. Physical investment creates *new* assets, thereby adding to a country's productive capacity, whereas financial investment only transfers the ownership of *existing* assets from one person or institution to another.

Investment from domestic savings requires that an amount of

current CONSUMPTION be forgone, that is, saved, so as to release the resources to finance it. Investment expenditure is a component of AGGREGATE DEMAND and an INJECTION into the CIRCULAR FLOW OF NATIONAL INCOME. In NATIONAL INCOME analysis, investment in provision of SOCIAL PRODUCTS, such as public roads, hospitals, and schools, is counted as part of GOVERNMENT (PUBLIC) EXPENDITURE. Thus, investment expenditure is normally defined as consisting only of private sector investment spending.

Investment can be split into gross and net investment: (a) gross investment is the total amount of investment undertaken in an economy over a specified time, usually one year; (b) net investment is gross investment less replacement investment or CAPITAL CONSUMPTION, that is, investment necessary to replace the part of the economy's existing capital stock used in producing this year's output.

The amount of investment undertaken depends on factors other than capital consumption considerations. In national income analysis, the MARGINAL EFFICIENCY OF CAPITAL/INVESTMENT and the RATE OF INTEREST are important determinants of the level of investment. The significance of investment lies in the contribution it makes to economic prosperity. Building new factories, adding new machinery and equipment, and investing in new techniques and products enable industry to supply a greater quantity of more sophisticated products and services to the consuming public. Similar investment in provision of social capital (schools, health, etc.) contributes vitally to upgrading general living standards. Compare DISINVESTMENT. See also ECONOMIC GROWTH, CAPITAL ACCUMULATION, CAPITAL DEEPENING, CAPITAL GOODS, CAPITAL WIDENING.

investment bank a bank whose function is provision of long-term equity and loan finance for industrial and other companies, particularly by underwriting new securities.

investment cycle see ACCELERATOR.

investment incentives inducements offered by a government or local authority to encourage capital INVESTMENT by the PRIVATE SECTOR either generally or in a specific area. Government inducements may take the form of capital grants toward the cost of equipment or tax reliefs on any profits earned. Local authority inducements usually take the form of tax reductions or exemptions and organizing the local infrastructure for the convenience of potential investors. The rationale for such incentives depends primarily on the government's objectives. It may want to reduce UNEMPLOYMENT in which case investment through the MULTIPLIER effect will help, or it may want to give certain DEVELOPMENT AREAS additional help in tackling local problems of unemployment or urban renewal. See REGIONAL POLICY.

investment schedule a schedule depicting the relationship between INVESTMENT and level of NATIONAL INCOME. The investment schedule is usually drawn with a positive slope as in Fig. 97 for two reasons: (a) as national income and output rise, a greater amount of REPLACEMENT INVESTMENT in absolute terms is required to maintain the economy's existing capital stock, viz.:

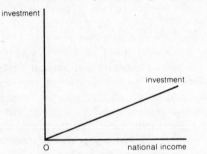

FIG. 97. **Investment schedule.** See entry.

	$	$
national income	1,000	2,000
capital stock	100	200
replacement investment (assumed to be 10%)	10	20

(b) increases in national income will bring about a greater amount of INDUCED INVESTMENT. Rising demand puts pressure on existing capacity and raises profitability, thereby encouraging businesses to invest more. See ACCELERATOR, EQUILIBRIUM LEVEL OF NATIONAL INCOME.

investment trust company a financial institution whose capital is subscribed by shareholders and which specializes in long-term investments in stocks, bonds, and government securities. See FINANCIAL SYSTEM, INSTITUTIONAL INVESTORS.

invisible exports and imports any services, such as banking, insurance, and tourism, that cannot be seen and recorded as they cross national boundaries. Invisible exports and imports, together with VISIBLE EXPORTS AND IMPORTS, make up the CURRENT ACCOUNT of a country's BALANCE OF PAYMENTS.

invisible hand a term devised by Adam SMITH to denote the way in which the market mechanism (PRICE SYSTEM) is capable of coordinating independent decisions of buyers and sellers without anyone being able to determine outcomes, that is, prices. According to Smith, this invisible hand, acting as the automatic equilibrating mechanism of the competitive market, maximizes individual welfare and economic efficiency. See PRIVATE ENTERPRISE ECONOMY.

involuntary saving see FORCED SAVING.

irredeemable bond or **annuity bond** a financial security issued for an indefinite period of time and never repayable.

irregular variations see TIME-SERIES ANALYSIS.

I.S. (investment-saving) schedule a schedule displaying the combinations of levels of NATIONAL INCOME and RATE OF INTEREST at which the equilibrium condition for the real economy (INVESTMENT = SAVINGS) holds (see EQUILIBRIUM LEVEL OF NATIONAL INCOME).

As shown in Fig. 98, the I.S. schedule slopes downward: a lower rate of interest stimulates a higher volume of investment (see MARGINAL EFFICIENCY OF CAPITAL/INVESTMENT), which in turn generates a higher level of output and income through a MULTIPLIER process. However, a higher volume of investment requires a higher volume of saving to keep the real economy in equilibrium (S = I). A higher volume of saving will only be forthcoming at a higher level of income, so a lower rate of interest requires a higher equilibrium level of income.

The I.S. schedule interacts with the L.M. SCHEDULE in determining a general equilibrium position for the economy as a whole.

I.S./L.M. model a theoretical construct that simultaneously integrates the real, I.S. (investment-saving), and the monetary, L.M.

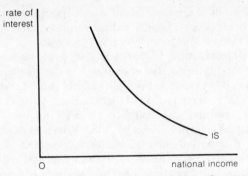

FIG. 98. **I.S. (investment saving) schedule.** See entry.

(demand for and supply of money), sides of the economy to present a general equilibrium position for the economy as a whole.

In the model, SAVING is a function of the level of NATIONAL INCOME, and INVESTMENT is a function of the RATE OF INTEREST and the MARGINAL EFFICIENCY OF CAPITAL/INVESTMENT. The I.S. SCHEDULE shows the combinations of levels of national income and rates of interest at which the equilibrium condition for the real economy $I = S$ holds (see EQUILIBRIUM LEVEL OF NATIONAL INCOME).

The demand for money, L, is a function of the level of national income (TRANSACTION DEMAND FOR MONEY) and the rate of interest (SPECULATIVE DEMAND FOR MONEY). The MONEY SUPPLY M, is given exogenously. The L.M. SCHEDULE shows the combinations of levels of national income and rates of interest at which the equilibrium condition for the monetary economy $L = M$ holds (see RATE OF INTEREST).

As shown in Fig. 99a, the I.S. schedule interacts with the L.M. schedule to determine a general equilibrium position, Y_e, for the economy as a whole.

The I.S./L.M. model, primarily a Keynesian construct, can be used to illustrate how FISCAL POLICY and MONETARY POLICY can be employed to alter the level of national income. For example, if the authorities wish to increase national income, they can increase the money supply. The increase in the money supply lowers the RATE OF INTEREST. The fall in the rate of interest in turn

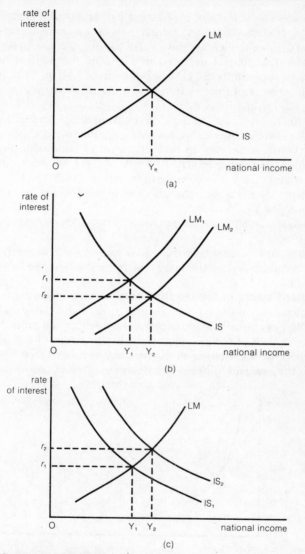

FIG. 99. **I.S./L.M. model.** (a) The general equilibrium position. (b) The effect of a shift in the L.M. schedule. (c) The effect of a shift in the I.S. schedule.

increases the volume of investment (see MARGINAL EFFICIENCY OF CAPITAL/INVESTMENT), which then, by means of MULTIPLIER effects, serves to increase the level of national income. In terms of the I.S./L.M. model depicted in Fig. 99b, the increase in the money supply shifts the L.M. schedule from LM_1 to LM_2, lowering interest rates from r_1 to r_2 and bringing about an increase in national income from Y_1 to Y_2.

Alternatively, the authorities could increase national income by, for example, increasing government investment, this increase in investment serving to raise the level of national income by means of multiplier effects. In terms of the I.S./L.M. model depicted in Fig. 99c, the increase in investment shifts the I.S. schedule from IS_1 to IS_2, bringing about an increase in national income from Y_1 to Y_2.

See also MONEY SUPPLY/SPENDING LINKAGES, KEYNESIAN ECONOMICS.

isocost line a line showing combinations of FACTOR INPUTS that can be purchased for the same total money outlay. See ISOQUANT CURVE.

isoquant curve or **isoproduct curve** a curve showing varying combinations of FACTORS OF PRODUCTION, such as labor and capital, that can be used to produce a given quantity of a product with a given state of technology, where FACTOR INPUTS can be substituted for one another in the production process. See Fig. 100.

If the isoquant in Fig. 100 reflects 100 units of production per

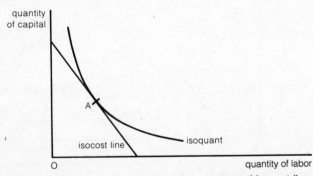

FIG. 100. **Isoquant curve.** The isoquant curve and isocost line.

period, then anywhere along that curve it is possible to determine the combination of factors required to produce 100 units. The slope of the isoquant reflects the substitutability of one factor for another in the production process (see MARGINAL RATE OF TECH-NICAL SUBSTITUTION, MRTS).

Isoquants slope downward to the right because the two inputs can be substituted for one another in the production process. The isoquants are convex to the origin, since the inputs are not perfect substitutes for one another but can be substituted for one another. Thus, the MRTS of X for Y declines as we move down any equal product curve from left to right.

Isoquants bear a marked similarity to INDIFFERENCE CURVES, combinations of two commodities yielding equal satisfaction to the consumer. But while there is no way of measuring satisfaction in physical units, so we can only talk of higher or lower indifference curves, we can measure physical output and say by how much production is greater on one equal-product contour than on another.

The ISOCOST LINE shows combinations of the two factor inputs that can be bought for the same total money outlay. Its slope reflects the *relative prices* of the two factors of production. Point A, where the isoquant is tangential to the isocost line, shows the lowest cost combination of inputs for producing 100 units of input. See PROCESS RAY, PRODUCTION FUNCTION, COST FUNCTION.

isoquant map a collection of ranked ISOQUANT CURVES that graphically exhibits a producer's increasing output per period when moving outward from the origin, using larger quantities of two FACTOR INPUTS, as in Fig. 101a. Isoquant curves are a cardinal measure, and the numbers on the isoquant curves in Fig. 101a indicate the absolute level of output per period. Isoquant curves never cross, because two crossing curves would imply inconsistent or irrational choices between the two factor inputs by the producer (see ECONOMIC MAN).

Although it is often possible to substitute factor inputs in production, substitution cannot continue indefinitely. Some minimum amount of both factors is required if production is to be maintained at a given level. For example, in order to produce 300 units in Fig. 101a, at least VL of X is required, and at least UT of

ISOQUANT MAP

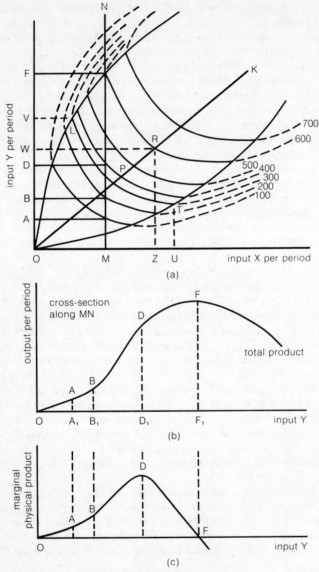

FIG. 101. **Isoquant map.** See entry.

Y. This is because at point T the isoquant is horizontal, indicating that at T the MARGINAL RATE OF TECHNICAL SUBSTITUTION of X for Y is zero. Similarly, at point L the isoquant is vertical, showing that beyond that point the substitution of Y for X would result in a decrease in output, indicated by the fact that the isoquant sheers away from the Y axis.

The ridge lines in Fig. 101a delineate the portions of the isoquants from which the company will make its choice of resource combinations. The top one joins all points at which isoquants become vertical, while the bottom one is the locus of all points at which isoquants become horizontal. The typical relations that will obtain between one isoquant and another can be shown by taking a cross section of the production contour map along the line MN. As we move up this line from M, we can read of the output that will be produced by increasing quantities of input Y when used with the company's plant and the given quantity OM of input X.

Not only does output increase as we move along MN, but the rate at which output rises follows a general pattern. In Fig. 101b, at output BB_1 an increase in input Y promises larger than proportional increases in output. At output DD_1 small percentage increases in use of Y promise equal percentage changes in output. At output FF_1 increases in factor Y promise less than proportional increases in output. This pattern is recognizable as the law of variable factor proportions (see RETURNS TO THE VARIABLE FACTOR INPUT).

The same pattern would be recognizable if we traced the behavior of output along a line such as OK in Fig. 101a. As we move toward K, the distances between successive isoquants reduce until point P is reached. After this point, the distances between successive isoquants become progressively larger. Along the line OK, increasing quantities of the two variable factors X and Y are being combined with the company's fixed plant and equipment.

The MARGINAL PHYSICAL PRODUCT curve for input Y shown in Fig. 101c is derived from the total product curve in Fig. 101b. As the amount of factor Y used increases from OA_1 to OD_1, its marginal physical product is rising. Then, for further increases in the use of factor Y, its marginal physical product is falling, becoming negative if more than OF_1 of Y is applied.

J

J-curve effect the tendency for a country's BALANCE OF PAYMENTS deficit to initially worsen following DEVALUATION of its currency before moving into surplus. This is because full adjustment of trade volumes to devaluation involves a time lag. Export prices fall immediately and import prices rise, so current exports earn less foreign exchange and current imports absorb more foreign exchange. This increases the size of the payment deficit (downturn of the J-curve). Over time, the lower export prices increase overseas demand, and export earnings rise. At the same time, higher import prices reduce domestic demand for imports, leading to improvement in balance of payments (upturn of the J-curve). See BALANCE-OF-PAYMENTS EQUILIBRIUM.

Jevons, William Stanley (1835—1882) English scientist and philosopher who developed the UTILITY theory in his book *The Theory of Political Economy* (1871). Jevons rejected the idea that the exchange value of a good depends on costs expended to produce it and argued instead that value depends on the individual consumer's subjective evaluation of the utility of a good. Jevons suggested that goods are valuable only if they provide utility and that labor and other factors of production become valuable when used to produce these goods. Specifically, he showed that a consumer will increase purchases of goods until the MARGINAL UTILITY gained from the last penny's worth of one good equals the marginal quality of the last penny's worth of every other good.

Jevons was also particularly interested in linking statistical analysis with theoretical analysis in economics, and he developed statistical series on production in Britain over a long period to try to determine the cause of BUSINESS CYCLES.

joint costs the COSTS involved in producing several products that are in JOINT SUPPLY, for example, gasoline, diesel fuel, kerosene, etc. produced from a common refining process. Operational joint costs, such as petroleum cracking costs, are difficult to allocate precisely between the different products in determining the exact cost of each.

joint demand see COMPLEMENTARY PRODUCTS.

joint profit maximization the possible situation of the optimization of industry profits by companies that coordinate their price and output policies rather than compete against each other. Joint profit maximization is typically associated with oligopolistic markets (see OLIGOPOLY) where firms, recognizing their MUTUAL INTERDEPENDENCE, operate PRICE LEADERSHIP systems and CARTELS.

joint supply a situation in which an increase or decrease in PRODUCTION of one good is inextricably linked to a greater or lesser extent with production of another. An example of joint supply is hides and beef. An increase in the DEMAND for hides increases the SUPPLY of cattle, which in turn brings about an autonomous increase in the SUPPLY CURVE of beef. As a result, if the demand for beef remains unchanged, its price will fall. See COMPLEMENTARY PRODUCTS.

joint venture a business owned jointly by two independent companies or by a company and a government. Joint ventures enable a greater total amount of resources to be employed in supply of a good or service, and can be especially effective in exploiting complementary resources with one party to the venture, for example, contributing production know-how, and the other contributing knowledge of the market.

junk bond a corporate bond with a low rating and a high yield. Such bonds often involve high risk and have been used in recent years in corporate takeovers and leveraged buyouts. The high interest costs entailed may have disastrous effects on companies issuing these bonds.

K

Keynes, John Maynard (1883—1946) English economist at Cambridge University who offered an explanation of mass unemployment and suggestions for government policy to cure unemployment in his influential book *The General Theory of Employment, Interest and Money* (1936). Before Keynes, CLASSICAL ECONOMICS had maintained that in a market economy the economic system would spontaneously tend to produce full employment of resources, because the exchange mechanism would ensure a correspondence between supply and demand (SAY'S LAW). Consequently, the classicists were confident that business recessions would cure themselves, with interest rates falling under the pressure of accumulating savings, and this would encourage businessmen to borrow and invest more. With wage rates falling, production costs would fall, encouraging businessmen to employ more workers. Keynes's concern about the extent and duration of the worldwide DEPRESSION of the 1930s and beyond led him to look for other explanations of recession.

Keynes argued that classical political economists were concerned with the relative shares in national output of the different factors of production, rather than the forces that determine the level of general economic activity, so their theories of value and distribution related only to the special case of full employment. Concentrating on the economic aggregates of NATIONAL INCOME, CONSUMPTION, SAVINGS, and INVESTMENT, Keynes provided a general theory for explaining the level of economic activity. He argued that there is no assurance that savings would accumulate during a depression and depress interest rates, since savings depend on income and incomes are low while unemployment is high.

Furthermore, he argued, investment depends primarily on

business confidence, which would be low during a depression, so investment would be unlikely to rise even if interest rates fell. Finally, he argued, wage rates would be unlikely to fall much during a depression given its stickiness, and even if they did fall would exacerbate the depression by reducing consumption.

Keynes saw the cause of a depression as reduced AGGREGATE DEMAND, and in the absence of any automatic stimulus to demand he argued that governments must intervene to increase aggregate demand and end depression. He suggested that governments stimulate consumption by putting money into consumers' pockets through tax cuts or directly increase governments' own expenditures to augment aggregate demand. See EQUILIBRIUM LEVEL OF NATIONAL INCOME.

Keynesian economics the view held by KEYNES of the way in which the aggregate economy works, subsequently refined and developed by his successors.

Much of what is today called Keynesian economics originated in his book *The General Theory of Employment, Interest and Money* (1936). Keynes gave economics a new direction and an explanation of the phenomenon of mass unemployment so prevalent in the 1930s. Economic doctrine before Keynes was based primarily on what is now termed MICROECONOMICS. Keynes switched from the classical concentration on individual prices and markets and individual demand functions, adopting aggregate analysis and introducing such new concepts as the CONSUMPTION FUNCTION.

Classical economists argued, and were officially supported by monetary authorities up to the time when they accepted Keynes's arguments, that FULL EMPLOYMENT is the result of a smooth-working PRIVATE ENTERPRISE ECONOMY. If unemployment occurred, wages would fall due to competition in labor markets to such an extent that unemployed labor would be rehired. (This was the neoclassical analysis that marginal productivity of labor would exceed or equal its marginal cost.) As employment fell, smaller payrolls would increase the supply of money, reduce interest rates, and increase investment opportunities. Keynes introduced the possibility of rigid wages in an attempt to explain what was inconceivable to classical and neoclassical economists, general equilibrium within the economy at less than full employment.

Keynes argued that INCOME depends on the volume of employment. The relationship between income and CONSUMPTION is defined by the PROPENSITY TO CONSUME.

Therefore, he argued, consumption depends on the related functions of income and employment. Anticipated expenditure on consumption and INVESTMENT is termed effective demand, and in a situation of equilibrium equals AGGREGATE SUPPLY. Keynes was of the opinion that in a state of equilibrium the volume of employment depended on aggregate supply, propensity to consume, and the amount of investment. The level of employment would therefore increase if either the propensity to consume increased, which Keynes held to be unlikely, or the level of investment increased, that is, greater demand for consumer and producer goods leads to an increase in supply. Increasing aggregate supply tends to lead to higher levels of employment.

Because of labor union pressure to maintain living standards, the difficulty of reducing wages means that rigidity of wages may lead to a situation of equilibrium at less than full employment. When this occurs, the government as a buyer of both consumer and producer goods can influence the level of AGGREGATE DEMAND in the economy. Aggregate demand may be increased by FISCAL POLICY or MONETARY POLICY. Keynes placed the emphasis on fiscal policy, whereby the government spends more than it collects in taxes. This is known as DEFICIT FINANCING and it stimulates aggregate demand. Through the MULTIPLIER effect, the stimulus to aggregate demand is several times larger than the initial expenditure. The effect is to move the economy toward full employment.

Certain Western economists began to question Keynesian economic ideas in the 1970s because of the occurrence of *stagflation*. Some of them embraced MONETARISM and began to look more kindly on the classical economic idea that government intervention is unnecessary and markets can ensure prosperity, provided that market rigidities are removed and the money supply is increased at the same rate as the gross national product.

KINKED DEMAND CURVE

See EQUILIBRIUM LEVEL OF NATIONAL INCOME, BUSINESS CYCLE, CIRCULAR FLOW OF NATIONAL INCOME MODEL, CLASSICAL ECONOMICS, DEFLATIONARY GAP, MONEY SUPPLY/SPENDING LINKAGES, QUANTITY THEORY OF MONEY, I.S./L.M. MODEL, SAY'S LAW, INFLATIONARY GAP, SUPPLY-SIDE ECONOMICS, BALANCED BUDGET.

kinked demand curve a curve that explains why prices charged by competing oligopolists (see OLIGOPOLY), once established, tend to be stable. In Fig. 102, DD is the DEMAND CURVE if all companies charge the *same* price. Starting from point K, if one company feels that if it were to charge a higher (unmatched) price than its rivals, it would lose sales to these rivals, then its relevant perceived demand curve becomes $D_H K$. On the other hand, the company may feel that if it were to charge a lower price, it would not gain sales from rivals because rivals would match price cuts along DD. Both price increases and decreases are thus seen to be self-defeating, and this produces a kinked demand curve, with prices tending to settle at K. The theory suggests that price K is likely to stick even though costs may change.

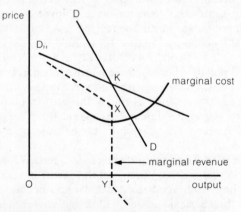

FIG. 102. **Kinked demand curve.** See entry.

It can be seen that there is a sharp step in the marginal revenue curve corresponding to the kink in the demand curve. In consequence, for a wide range of vertical shifts in the marginal cost curve, between points X and Y, K remains the selling price that maximizes profit. See GAME THEORY, MUTUAL INTERDEPENDENCE, PRICE LEADERSHIP.

Klein, Lawrence (born 1920) winner of the Nobel Memorial Prize in Economic Sciences, 1980, for creation of econometric models and their application to analysis of economic fluctuations and economic growth. He sought to develop practical uses for econometric models. With a graduate student, Arthur Goldburger, he developed the model that is regarded by many as the best early Keynesian model of a large economy. While teaching at the University of Pennsylvania, Klein continued to develop large macroeconomic models. These are the models that became the Wharton models, still in use for predicting changes in taxation, oil prices, and other economically significant parameters. Klein has also helped develop econometric models for the countries of Israel and Mexico, among others.

Kondratieff wave or **long-wave cycle** a theoretical long-term cycle ranging from boom to recession over a period of about 60 years, upon which shorter-term BUSINESS CYCLES are superimposed. Based on statistical observations by Kondratieff, explanations for these long waves in economic activity usually rely on a bunching of significant INNOVATIONS like gasoline engines, the digital computer, etc., which give an impetus to economic activity for decades before their impact wanes. This was an idea that later was developed further by Joseph SCHUMPETER.

Koopmans, Tjalling C. (1921—1985) winner of the Nobel Memorial Prize in Economics, 1975, with Leonid Kantorovich for contributions to the theory of optimal allocation of resources. The analytical technique Koopmans developed, called *activity analysis*, changed the way economists and production managers approach the allocation problem. He also developed mathematical techniques, many while at Yale University, that have been used by corporations and central planners.

Kuznets, Simon (born 1901) winner of the Nobel Memorial Prize in Economic Sciences, 1971, for his interpretation of economic growth, which has led to new and deepened insight into economic and social structure and process of development. In addition to analysis of economic development, Kuznets contributed to an understanding of business cycles and helped refine concepts of national income.

kurtosis the sharpness of the peak of a group of numerical observations summarized in a FREQUENCY DISTRIBUTION. Where such a distribution is depicted as a bell-shaped HISTOGRAM or CONTINUOUS DISTRIBUTION, kurtosis reflects the maximum height of the distribution, showing the largest values in the distribution.

L

---

labor the contribution to productive activity made by the work force both by hand, for example, in assembly of a car, and mentally, for example, in devising a computer program. Labor is one of the four main FACTORS OF PRODUCTION, the others being NATURAL RESOURCES, CAPITAL, and ENTREPRENEURSHIP. See also ECONOMIC GROWTH, HUMAN CAPITAL.

labor dispute a dispute between one or more employers, or organizations of employers, and one or more workers or labor unions, in which the dispute relates wholly or mainly to such matters as terms and conditions of employment; hiring, firing, or suspension of employment of workers; allocation of work among employees, matters of discipline, etc. Serious labor disputes may be characterized by strike action by workers and LOCKOUT of workers by management. Labor disputes may be settled in a number of ways, including voluntary agreement between concerned parties after COLLECTIVE BARGAINING or by recourse to ARBITRATION or MEDIATION.

labor force the total number of workers available for employment in an economy. Size of the labor force, quality of labor, and labor force participation, along with CAPITAL STOCK, determine a country's AGGREGATE SUPPLY potential. See POTENTIAL GROSS NATIONAL PRODUCT, ECONOMIC GROWTH.

labor-intensive firm/industry a company or industry that produces its output of goods or services using proportionately large inputs of LABOR and relatively small amounts of CAPITAL.

The proportions of labor and capital a company uses in production depend mainly on the relative prices of labor and capital inputs and their relative productivities. This in turn depends on the degree of standardization of the product achievable in fragmented markets in which consumers demand product variety, making it difficult to use large-scale capital-intensive production methods, which ordinarily facilitate ECONOMIES OF SCALE.

Clothing manufacture, plumbing installation and repair, and hairdressing are examples of labor-intensive industries. See BATCH PRODUCTION, CAPITAL-LABOR RATIO.

labor market a FACTOR MARKET that provides for an exchange of work for wages. The SUPPLY side of the market is represented by individual workers whose terms of employment may be influenced by unionism. The DEMAND side of the market is represented by companies requiring labor as a FACTOR INPUT in the production process (see MARGINAL PHYSICAL PRODUCT, MARGINAL REVENUE PRODUCT).

The labor market differs from other factor markets in that labor has certain peculiarities that make application of supply and demand difficult. There may be problems of intensity of effort, group morale, expense of job search, discrimination, and the like that can affect the supply of labor.

Since employers are not immune to the virus of discrimination, extra-economic concerns may distort the employers' demand for workers.

There are other peculiarities that characterize the act of exchange in the labor market and produce a situation in which the wage level and employment level are not uniquely determined by supply and demand. Rather, there is a range of indeterminacy over which rival power blocs within the labor market (unions, employers, and government) seek to further their economic and other objectives by bargaining.

See also COLLECTIVE BARGAINING, SUPPLY-SIDE ECONOMICS, WAGE RATE.

labor theory of value a doctrine developed by the classical economists, particularly Adam SMITH and David RICARDO. This theory endeavored to explain exchange value on the basis of labor time needed to create products.

In trying to explain exchange value and the determinants of income for the factors of production, Ricardo advanced a labor theory of value. His version of the theory made labor units a numeraire and did not lead him to conclude that labor under capitalism was universally exploited by capitalists.

Karl Marx took this suggestion of a labor theory of value to the point where he considered that labor is the source of all value. Employers buy labor power and pay it a subsistence rate. Suppose 8 hours of work are required to produce a product. Once the employer owns the worker's labor power, he can use it for more than 8 hours. If the worker puts in 10 hours, for example, he creates for the employer 2 hours of surplus value. It is not the capitalist that is the cause of exploitation, but the capitalist system. The worker is paid his proper exchange value, a subsistence wage. The capitalist sells the product for the proper exchange value (its price, 10 hours) and has 2 hours of truly unearned income.

The labor theory of value was replaced toward the end of the nineteenth century by the MARGINAL PRODUCTIVITY THEORY OF DISTRIBUTION, which took into account the contributions of all factor inputs into the production process, not just labor. See CLASSICAL ECONOMICS.

labor union an organization that represents the economic interests of a specific segment of the labor force. Unions come in a variety of forms, for example:

(a) *company union*, a union that represents every grade of labor within a single company and usually is not affiliated with other unions. This type of union is common in Japan. In the United States such unions tend to be dominated by the employer.

(b) *craft union* or *trade union*, a union that represents a particular group of skilled artisans, for example, electricians and plumbers, who may work in many different industries. This type of union is quite common in Great Britain, to a lesser extent in the United States.

(c) *industrial union*, a union that represents every grade of labor within a single industry. This type of union is common in Europe and in the mass production industries in the United States, for example, steel and automobiles.

(d) *general union*, a union that represents a broad spread of employees regardless of occupation or industry. These have become commonplace in the United States and Europe, often as a result of mergers between craft and industrial unions.

The prime objective of a union is to protect and advance the interests of its members by negotiating wages and conditions of employment, such as hours worked, job safety, and grounds for dismissal. As such, unions may have an important influence on the price of labor and supply costs in certain industries and in the broader macroeconomic context as well, since wage levels can affect the level of unemployment and inflation.

See LABOR MARKET, COLLECTIVE BARGAINING, PHILLIPS CURVE, WORKER PARTICIPATION, INDUSTRIAL RELATIONS.

Laffer curve a thesis shown graphically and representing that there exists an optimal tax rate, above which less revenue is produced because higher rates are said to discourage taxable enterprise. Conversely, lower tax rates are said to encourage taxable enterprise and produce more revenue. The advantages of low tax rates constitute one of the central claims of so-called supply-side economists.

lagged relationship the relationship between two or more variables in different time periods. For example, the current value of a variable such as consumption expenditure will depend on income in the previous time period. Time is denoted by the letter t, with t $-$ 1 being one period back and t $+$ 1 being one period forward. Such a relationship between income and consumption can be written in the notational form:

$$C_t = f(Y_{t-1})$$

where C_t = consumption in present period, $Y_t - 1$ = income in the previous period.

See also COBWEB THEOREM.

lagging indicator see LEADS AND LAGS.

laissez faire a doctrine of FREE TRADE and market competition dating from the time of Adam SMITH to the present. The implication of the theory is that private enterprise, competitive markets for factors and products, and unimpeded international commerce will lead to optimum consumer welfare and a rising standard of living. See CLASSICAL ECONOMICS, PRIVATE ENTERPRISE ECONOMY, PRICE SYSTEM.

land see NATURAL RESOURCES.

Laspeyres price index a weighted index number that uses base-year weights. For example, in calculating a PRICE INDEX, the respective quantities of various products bought in the base year would be noted and the prices of these products combined to form a single price index number. Later, the new prices of the products would be combined to form a new price index number with no allowance made for changes in relative quantities of the goods bought over time and their price changes. Also called *base-weighted index*. Compare CURRENT-WEIGHTED INDEX.

last-in first-out (LIFO) see INVENTORY VALUATION.

lateral integration see HORIZONTAL INTEGRATION.

law of diminishing marginal returns see DIMINISHING RETURNS.

law of large numbers the economic law stating that large groups tend to behave more uniformly than a single individual. For example, an individual consumer might buy more of a product whose price has risen, whereas most consumers would buy less. See DEMAND CURVE.

law of variable factor proportions see RETURNS TO THE VARIABLE FACTOR INPUT.

leading indicators the statistical TIME SERIES that experience has shown tends to reflect subsequent changes, and thus can be used to forecast changes because they precede the changes in a consistent manner and by a relatively constant time interval. For example, current birth statistics would provide a firm basis for predicting grade school enrollments 5 or 6 years ahead. Leading indicators such as orders for new machine tools, amount of overtime in manufacturing, and building starts are frequently used to forecast cyclical changes in macroeconomic variables, for example, GNP. See FORECASTING, TIME-SERIES ANALYSIS, INDICATORS.

leads and lags 1. the timing differences that exist between peaks and troughs of leading and lagging indicators, and the overall BUSINESS CYCLE. Thus, in a 7-year business cycle, if the peak of the cycle occurred in the middle year (year 4), then a leading indicator such as starts on new homes may have peaked in year 3. This indicator leads the business cycle by 1 year. Similarly, lagged variables (lagging indicators) will have peaks or troughs after the peak of the business cycle.

2. the time variation from standard payment practice when settling foreign trade debts. The variation results from the expec-

tations of traders that may influence the profitability of settling a debt early (lead) or late (lag). The most common factor contributing to this practice is expectation of a change in the EXCHANGE RATE. Traders in an importing country have an incentive to postpone settlement to manufacturers in the exporting nation if there is an expectation of a foreseeable devaluation in the rate of exchange of the exporting country's currency. Similarly, if an increase in exchange rate is in prospect, traders in the debtor nation can be expected to settle early.

See also J-CURVE EFFECT, LAGGED RELATIONSHIP, LEADING INDICATORS, COBWEB THEOREM.

learning curve see EXPERIENCE CURVE.

lease a legal contract under which the owner of an asset, such as a building or machinery, grants to someone else the right to use that asset for a specified period of time in return for periodic payments of rent. See LEASING, LEASEBACK.

leaseback an arrangement whereby the owner of an asset agrees to sell it to another person or company on condition that the asset can be leased to its original owner for a fixed term at a prearranged rent. Leaseback is normally undertaken to enable companies with valuable assets such as land to realize cash for use elsewhere in their business. See LEASE, LEASING.

leasing the purchase of an asset (buildings, machinery, airplanes, etc.) by a leasing company, which retains ownership of the assets and then leases them for use by clients who pay an agreed rent. Leasing is a useful source of INVESTMENT insofar as it enables individuals or companies to use assets without having to tie up large amounts of capital. See LEASE, OFF-BALANCE SHEET FINANCING.

least-squares estimation see REGRESSION ANALYSIS.

ledger the accounting records that keep track of the day-to-day financial transactions of a business with outside parties. For example, the *accounts payable ledger* would show the value of raw materials or services purchased from each supplier, payments made to suppliers for these, and any amounts still owing to suppliers. Similarly, the *accounts receivable ledger* would show the value of goods or services sold to each customer, amounts paid for these, and any amounts still owed by customers. In former times such

LEWIS, SIR W. ARTHUR

ledger accounts took the form of bound ledgers in which entries were recorded by hand. Today, they are generally kept as computer records. See ACCOUNTS PAYABLE, ACCOUNTS RECEIVABLE.

legal tender the part of a country's MONEY SUPPLY that is, in the eyes of the law, totally acceptable in payment for purchase of a good or service or repayment of a debt and taxes. CURRENCY (bills and coins) issued by the government fulfill this requirement. By contrast, a trader may refuse to accept as payment a check drawn against a BANK DEPOSIT.

lender a person, company, or institution that makes a LOAN to a BORROWER to enable the borrower to finance CONSUMPTION or INVESTMENT. Lenders frequently require borrowers to offer COLLATERAL SECURITY, for example, deeds to property, which lenders may retain if borrowers fail to repay the loan. See also CREDIT, FINANCIAL SYSTEM.

lender of last resort the role of a CENTRAL BANK in making money available to COMMERCIAL BANKS short of funds. When member banks find themselves with fewer liquid assets than they feel it is prudent for them to hold, that is, when they fall below their required reserves, they must improve their liquidity. They can do this by selling off TREASURY BILLS to the Federal Reserve Bank, calling in their short-term loans, borrowing Federal funds, or borrowing at the discount window of the Fed.

Leontief, Wassily (born 1906) winner of the Nobel Memorial Prize in Economic Sciences, 1973, for development of the input-output method and for its application to important economic problems. While he was at Harvard, his input-output tables were used to provide links between sectors of domestic and international markets. Leontief advanced the general equilibrium theory of Leon Walras and strengthened understanding of the interdependence of markets.

level of significance see HYPOTHESIS TESTING.

leverage see CAPITAL GEARING.

leveraged buyout see TAKEOVER BID.

Lewis, Sir W. Arthur (born 1915) winner with Theodore Schultz of the Nobel Memorial Prize for Economic Sciences, 1979, for contributions to the theory of ECONOMIC DEVELOPMENT. Lewis is the author of the seminal text *The Theory of Economic Growth*

(1955). He argued that although growth can bring positive benefits in improving living standards in DEVELOPING COUNTRIES, it can also disrupt those countries' cultures, especially where growth is too rapid. Lewis has emphasized the importance of economic infrastructure in developing countries and stressed the need for such social overhead capital as transport networks, communications systems, and educational facilities as prerequisites for growth.

liability a claim on the resources of an individual or business in respect to monies borrowed.

license 1. the grant by one company to another (*exclusive license*) or others (*nonexclusive license*) of the right to manufacture its product or to use its technology or distribution facilities. Similarly, the grant by the government to an authority, for example, a supplier of natural gas, or company of the right to supply a good or provide a service. The granting of a license in these cases is a CONTRACTUAL arrangement entered into usually for a specified period of time, with the licensee usually paying a ROYALTY or FEE for the rights assigned.

  2. a document that shows proof of legal ownership or entitlement and compliance with a statutory or private requirement for payment thereon, for example, a television station license or fishing license. Such licenses are issued primarily to raise revenue.

  3. a document issued as a means of ensuring that premises or persons are fit for the purposes in which they are engaged, for example, a licensed gambling casino.

life-cycle hypothesis the hypothesis that CONSUMPTION is not dependent solely on current DISPOSABLE PERSONAL INCOME, but is related to a person's anticipated lifetime earnings. For example, a person today may purchase a range of expensive products, such as an autombile, television set, etc., on extended credit terms, expecting that future income will rise as he or she moves up in earnings and will easily be able to pay interest and repayment charges. This hypothesis is similar to the PERMANENT INCOME HYPOTHESIS in that it gives greater breadth to the analysis of SAVING and consumption over and above the simplistic assumption that consumption is solely a function of current income.

limited liability a liability that limits the maximum LOSS a shareholder is liable for in the event of company failure. The principle of limited liability limits a shareholder's maximum loss to the original share capital invested, no further claims by creditors against the stockholder's other assets being permitted. As a result, people have been encouraged to invest in corporations, and corporations have become the dominant type of business structure.

When a business is subject to *unlimited liability,* as is the case with sole proprietors, unlimited partnerships, and unincorporated businesses, the owners of the business are liable in full for debts of the business if it fails. This may mean losing not only the capital they have put into the business, but also most of their personal assets.

limiting factor the critical constraint on a company's budgeted activity level. In most circumstances the limiting factor will be the amounts the company can sell, but in some cases the limiting factor may be shortage of production capacity, shortages of raw materials, or the like. Here planning will be aimed at devising a sales program that generates maximum profit from these limited resources. See BUDGET, BUDGETING, LINEAR PROGRAMMING.

limit order an order to buy or sell a specified number of shares of a security at a specified price.

limit pricing or **entry-forestalling price** a pricing strategy employed by established oligopolists (see OLIGOPOLY) in a market to exploit BARRIERS TO ENTRY in order to forestall new entry. A limit-pricing model is shown in Fig. 103, in which the barrier to entry is assumed to be ECONOMIES OF SCALE. Established firms produce a total output of OQ_1, which is sold at price OP_1. The MINIMUM EFFICIENT SCALE of output for the entrant to be just as cost-effective as established firms is $Q_1 Q_2$ (equal to OQ). It will be seen that as a result of the addition of this extra output to existing market supply OQ_1, the market price is lowered to OP_2, a price at which entry is unprofitable. Established firms are thus able to set an entry-limiting price of OP_1, thereby securing ABOVE-NORMAL PROFITS on the order of AB.

linear equation the relationship between two or more VARIABLES that takes the form of a straight line, for example:

$$Y = a + bX$$

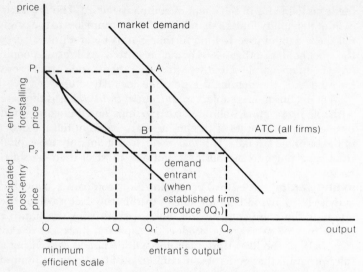

price

market demand

P_1 ----------- A

entry forestalling price

B

ATC (all firms)

P_2 -----------

anticipated post-entry price

demand entrant (when established firms produce $0Q_1$)

O   Q Q_1 Q_2 output

minimum efficient scale

entrant's output

FIG. 103. **Limit pricing.** See entry.

where a and b are constant PARAMETERS, X is the INDEPENDENT VARIABLE, and Y is the DEPENDENT VARIABLE. In the graphical representation of the equation, shown in Fig. 104, a is the intercept, that is, the point at which the line intersects the vertical axis, and b gives the slope of the line.

linear programming a mathematical technique useful in employing limited resources to meet a desired objective, such as minimizing cost or maximizing profit, where the resource limits are expressed as constraints.

For example, consider a firm making only two products, bookcases and chairs, and trying to decide how many of each to make. The company's output will be limited by the productive resources it has available, and these are depicted graphically in Fig. 105, in which quantities of bookcases are represented on the horizontal axis and quantities of chairs on the vertical axis. If the company has only 80 hours of machine time available each week, and it takes 5 hours of machine time to make a bookcase and 5 hours of ma-

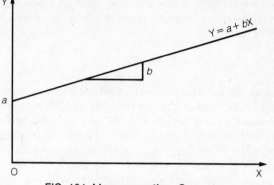

FIG. 104. **Linear equation.** See entry.

chine time to make a chair, then the maximum output with the available machine would be represented by line XY. Again, if there were only 84 man-hours of direct labor available, and each bookcase needs 7 hours of work, while each chair needs 3 hours, then the maximum output with the available direct labor force would be represented by line RT.

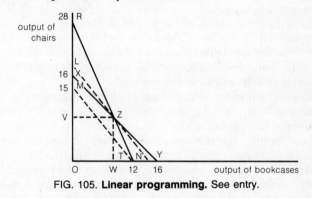

FIG. 105. **Linear programming.** See entry.

The area OXZT represents all feasible combinations of book-cases and chairs that can be produced with the limited machine hours and man-hours available (the *feasible region*).

LIQUIDATION

If each bookcase (b) sold makes a profit of $5, and each chair (c) $4, then in order to maximize profit the firm would seek to maximize output:

$$5b + 4c.$$

For example, in order to earn a profit of $60 the company could produce 12 bookcases or 15 chairs or some combination of the two, as represented by the broken line MT in Fig. 105. Combinations of bookcases and chairs corresponding to larger total profits can be represented by other lines, such as LN, which are parallel to MT but farther out from the origin 0. The line LN represents the largest profit the firm can earn with its available man-hours and machine-hours, since it is the highest broken line that just touches the resource constraints represented by the feasible region OXZT. The firm will therefore settle at point Z, producing OV chairs a week and OW bookcases a week in order to maximize its profits from available resources.

Linear programming also provides information about the value of additional resources to a company. For example, it shows how much extra profit could be earned by increasing the amount of machine-hours or man-hours available. It thus indicates the maximum amount the company should pay for additional units of these resources. These maximum amounts the company can afford without prejudicing profitability are called SHADOW PRICES of the machine-hours and man-hour resources.

When a company produces more than two outputs, two-dimensional graphical analysis is impossible. However, an optimum combination of outputs can still be calculated using a similar reasoning process through the mathematical approach called the *simplex method.* See PRODUCTION POSSIBILITY BOUNDARY.

liquidation the process by which a company's existence as a legal entity ceases. Such a process can be initiated at the behest of creditors when a company is insolvent (a compulsory liquidation), or by the company directors or shareholders, in which case it is known as a voluntary liquidation.

The person appointed liquidator, either by the company directors/shareholders or the creditors, sells off the company's assets for as much as they will realize. The proceeds of the sale are used to discharge any outstanding liabilities to the creditors of the company. If there are insufficient funds to pay all creditors (INSOLVENCY), preferential creditors are paid first, for example, the INTERNAL REVENUE SERVICE for taxes due, then ordinary creditors pro rata. If there is a surplus after payment of all creditors, it is distributed pro rata among the company shareholders. See also LIMITED LIABILITY.

liquidity a monetary asset (such as CURRENCY) that can be used directly as a means of payment. See MONEY, LIQUIDITY PREFERENCE.

liquidity preference a preference for holding money instead of investing it. KEYNES identified three motives for holding money: (a) TRANSACTION DEMAND FOR MONEY—money held day-to-day to finance current purchases; (b) PRECAUTIONARY DEMAND FOR MONEY—money held to meet unexpected future outlays; and (c) SPECULATIVE DEMAND FOR MONEY—money held in anticipation of a fall in the price of assets. In the Keynesian analysis, the amount of money held for these purposes depends mainly on the level of income and the interest rate.

liquidity ratio see RESERVE DEPOSIT RATIO.

liquidity trap a situation in which the RATE OF INTEREST is so low that people prefer to hold money or liquid assets (LIQUIDITY PREFERENCE) rather than buy bonds or other income-yielding assets. At low rates of interest the MONEY DEMAND SCHEDULE becomes infinitely elastic. In these circumstances any attempt by monetary policy to lower interest rates in order to stimulate more investment spending (see MONEY SUPPLY/SPENDING LINKAGES) will be futile and result in more money being held.

KEYNES argued that in a depressed economy experiencing a liquidity trap the only way to stimulate investment is to increase government expenditure or reduce taxes in order to increase AGGREGATE DEMAND and improve business confidence about future prosperity, encouraging companies to invest.

As yet, there is no evidence that there is a liquidity trap.

listed company a public CORPORATION whose shares are traded on one of the principal stock exchanges.

list price the published price of a good or service. The actual price paid by the buyer is often less than this, because suppliers are prepared to offer cash and trade DISCOUNTS. Many suppliers specify RECOMMENDED RETAIL PRICES for their products, but again the actual price paid can be much less than that recommended, depending on the strength of retail competition.

L.M. (liquidity-money) schedule a schedule showing the combinations of levels of NATIONAL INCOME and RATES OF INTEREST where the equilibrium condition for the monetary economy L = M holds. See Fig. 106.

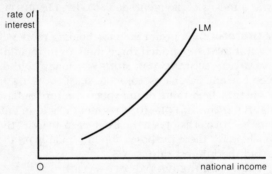

FIG. 106. **L.M. (liquidity-money) schedule.** The L.M. schedule slopes upward. With a given amount of money, a higher rate of interest leads to smaller demand for speculative balances, leaving more money available for transaction balances (SEE MONEY DEMAND SCHEDULE). If these transaction balances are to be demanded, national income will have to be higher, since the transaction demand for money is a function of the level of national income. Hence, to ensure that people willingly take up these balances at a higher rate of interest, a higher level of national income is required.

The L.M. schedule interacts with the I.S. SCHEDULE in determining a general equilibrium position for the economy as a whole.

See also I.S./L.M. MODEL, SPECULATIVE DEMAND FOR MONEY, TRANSACTION DEMAND FOR MONEY.

loan capital see DEBT CAPITAL.

loans the money advanced by COMMERCIAL BANKSand other institutions to business and personal borrowers and used to finance physical and financial INVESTMENT and purchases of current goods and services. See CONSUMER CREDIT, BANK LOAN.

location of industry the geographic spread of economic activity within an economy. Many factors may influence the location decisions of companies and industries, including proximity to raw materials, availability of labor, good communications, availability of trained engineers and scientists, and proximity to markets. Once an industry becomes established in a particular location, it tends to act as a focal point for further economic expansion, attracting directly the establishment of ancillary trades (component suppliers, backup services, etc.) and, indirectly, other firms and industries through EXTERNAL ECONOMIES OF SCALE and regional MULTIPLIER effects. REGIONAL POLICY also has a significant effect on industrial location.

lockout an illegal action taken by an employer to exclude employees from their place of work as part of a LABOR DISPUTE. See INDUSTRIAL RELATIONS, STRIKE.

locomotive principle the principle that in a world-wide RECESSION, one country, by expanding its AGGREGATE DEMAND, will increase its demand for IMPORTS, thus stimulating the EXPORTS of other countries and increasing economic activity in these other countries. In this way one country can act as a locomotive to pull other countries out of recession. When this occurs, it may result at the expense of the locomotive country's balance of payments.

logarithmic function a mathematical function that can be expressed in terms of its logarithm, such as y = log x. A logarithm is the index to which a fixed number, the base, must be raised to obtain a given number. It is customary to state which fixed number is being used so that the function can be expressed as:

$$y = \log_a x$$

where x and y are the variables and a is the base number. Common logarithms have a base of 10, whereas natural logarithms have a base of 2.71828, which is written:

$$y = \log_e x.$$

See LOG-LINEAR FUNCTION.

log-linear function a mathematical relationship of the form:

$$y = ax^b$$

which, when plotted on a logarithmic GRAPH, appears as a straight line. The relationship can be written:

$$\log y = \log a + b . \log x$$

log y being linearly related to log x. In this instance, x and y are the variables plotted on the horizontal and vertical axes, respectively, where a and b are constants. See EXPONENTIAL FUNCTION, LOGARITHMIC FUNCTION.

longitudinal of or relating to SAMPLE observations collected over a number of time periods. For example, we could collect data on changes in size of a sample of companies over a number of years and changes in remuneration of their chief executives over the same time periods, as a basis for investigating the relationship between executive remuneration and company size. Compare CROSS SECTIONAL.

long term an indefinite time period in the THEORY OF SUPPLY that is long enough for all FACTOR INPUTS to be varied, but within an existing technological framework—known production methods. Thus, a firm's plant size, which is fixed in the short term, can now be altered to allow for an increased scale of operations.

In the very long term, the technological framework itself changes as a result of new INVENTIONS and knowledge. Compare SHORT TERM. See also ECONOMIES OF SCALE, DISECONOMIES OF SCALE, RETURNS TO SCALE.

long-term capital employed any long-term funds (see FUNDING) employed in a business.

loophole a legal income tax deduction or tax credit, usually the result of legislation reducing the tax burdens of certain individuals or groups. The Tax Reform Act of 1986 in the United States eliminated many loopholes formerly enjoyed by certain industries and affluent people in exchange for lower tax rates. Among the most important loopholes still remaining is the deductibility of real property taxes and interest on home mortgages.

Lorenz curve see CONCENTRATION MEASURES.

loss the difference that arises when a firm's TOTAL REVENUES are less than TOTAL COSTS. In the SHORT TERM, when total revenues are insufficient to cover VARIABLE COSTS, a firm will probably exit from the market unless it perceives the situation as temporary. In these circumstances, when total revenues are sufficient to cover variable costs and make some contribution toward FIXED COSTS, a firm may continue to produce despite overall losses. In the LONG TERM, however, unless revenues are sufficient to cover both variable and fixed costs, overall losses will probably cause the firm to exit from the market. See MARKET EXIT, LOSS MINIMIZATION.

loss leader pricing the practice of some retailers who sell a particular product at a price below cost in order to attract customers into the store in hope that they will then be encouraged to make other purchases. See RESALE PRICE MAINTENANCE.

loss minimization the objective of a FIRM in the near term when confronted by adverse market conditions that prevent PROFIT MAXIMIZATION. Profit maximization or loss minimization requires the firm to produce at that level of output where MARGINAL COST equals MARGINAL REVENUE. For example, a firm under PERFECT COMPETITION would produce output OQ in Fig. 107. However, adverse short-term conditions may mean that at this level of output, price OP is insufficient to cover average total cost OC, so that the firm makes losses. In the near term, the firm will continue to produce this level of output as long as price (average revenue) is sufficient to cover AVERAGE VARIABLE COST (OC_1) and make some contribution toward FIXED COSTS, although in the LONG TERM, continued losses would force the firm to leave the market.

lump of labor the proposition that there is only so much work to be done in an economy, so if fewer people are needed to produce any given output, UNEMPLOYMENT must rise. It follows that labor-displacing technological change will inevitably lead to higher unemployment. The proposition is considered fallacious for the following reasons: (a) it assumes that the economy is already producing all the products society could possibly want, making no allowance for the possibility that labor displaced in one area of the economy can be redeployed to produce *more* goods and services elsewhere in the economy; (b) technological advance creates its own demand—it leads to higher PRODUCTIVITY, higher wages, and perhaps to new products, thereby increasing purchasing

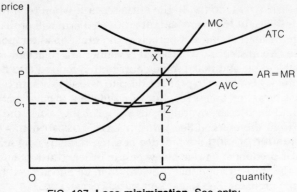

FIG. 107. **Loss minimization.** See entry.

power in the economy, which in turn increases output and employment.

lump-sum taxes taxes levied so that an individual cannot alter his or her liability, for example, poll taxes. These taxes raise revenue for a government without distorting resource allocation patterns. INDIRECT TAXES have a distorting effect because they cause consumers to rearrange their consumption patterns, and rearrangement represents a loss to consumers without corresponding gain to the government. Similarly, INCOME TAXES can distort choice patterns in affecting the choice between work and leisure. In practice there are few taxes that do not affect resource allocation. See TAXATION, INCIDENCE OF TAXATION, PRINCIPLES OF TAXATION.

luxury product any product that has an INCOME ELASTICITY OF DEMAND greater than one. This means that as incomes rise, proportionately more income is spent on such products. Products with an income elasticity of less than one are referred to as necessary or STAPLE PRODUCTS. See ENGEL'S LAW, NORMAL PRODUCT, INFERIOR PRODUCT, GIFFEN GOOD.

M

M1, M2, M3 see MONEY SUPPLY.

macroeconomic policy the setting of objectives by a government for the economy and the use of control instruments to achieve the objectives. Macroeconomic objectives include: FULL EMPLOYMENT, avoidance of INFLATION, ECONOMIC GROWTH, and BALANCE-OF-PAYMENTS EQUILIBRIUM. FISCAL POLICY and MONETARY POLICY are the main instruments used in trying to achieve these objectives.

macroeconomics the branch of economics concerned with study of aggregate economic activity. Macroeconomic analysis investigates how an economy as a whole works, and seeks to identify strategic determinants of the levels of national income and output, employment, and prices.

See also CIRCULAR FLOW OF NATIONAL INCOME MODEL, EQUILIBRIUM LEVEL OF NATIONAL INCOME, INTERNAL-EXTERNAL BALANCE MODEL, KEYNESIAN ECONOMICS.

Malthus, Thomas (1766—1834) English clergyman whose pessimistic ideas on the economic and social effects of population growth were published in his *Essay on the Principle of Population as It Affects the Future Improvement of Society* (1798). Malthus argued that land is finite and its productivity can increase at best only arithmetically (1,2,3,4, etc.), while population increases geometrically (1,2,4,8, etc.). In short, the increase in population tends to outrun the increase in food supply, and most people will be condemned to live in misery and poverty with only wars, epidemics, and famines serving to slow the growth of population.

Malthus's gloomy view of population growth contrasted sharply with the optimistic views about long-term economic development held by some of his contemporaries, leading Thomas Carlyle to term economics the *dismal science*. Although Malthus did not foresee the dramatic improvements in agricultural techniques that have occurred, nor the tendency for population growth to slow in industrialized countries, his ideas still cause concern, especially in DEVELOPING COUNTRIES.

Malthus made noteworthy contributions to economic thoery. He foreshadowed modern accounting of national income, improved the discussion of factor markets, raised the possibility of *general glut* (oversupply of goods and services), questioned whether trade has a beneficial outcome under all circumstances, and added to comprehension of differential rents. See DEMO-GRAPHIC TRANSITION.

managed float see FLOATING EXCHANGE-RATE SYSTEM.

management buyout the purchase of a business or division of a business by its management. In the former case, the shareholders may be prepared to accept management's financial terms of purchase, because their terms are better than those an outside bidder or merger partner is prepared to offer. In these cases, management buyouts are often defensively motivated, with the existing management fearing loss of their jobs following a hostile takeover. Sale of a subsidiary or division of a firm to its incumbent management is often undertaken as a means of DISINVESTMENT(2) by the parent firm from a particular line of business rather than resulting from a takeover or merger approach. Again, in the interests of shareholders, the financial details of such deals need to be carefully studied. Management buyouts are usually financed by outside interests, including VENTURE CAPITAL specialists and banks.

management-utility maximization a company objective in the THEORY OF THE FIRM that is used as an alternative to the traditional assumption of PROFIT MAXIMIZATION. The firm is assumed to seek to maximize management's utility or satisfactions, and the managerial preference function comprises three principal components: utility = F (staff, perquisites, investments).

Salaried managers prefer spending company money on these three things, called an *expense preference* by Oliver Williamson, because:

(a) additional staff can lead to managers getting more salary, since extra staff generally necessitates more tiers in the organization's hierarchy and so. Given the traditional salary differentials between tiers, this will increase the salaries of those at the top of the organization. In addition, extra staff means extra power, status, and prestige and may contribute to job security insofar as large departments in a company are less likely to be closed down.

(b) managerial perquisites, or perks, such as expense accounts, travel budgets, and company cars are valued as both low-taxed sources of indirect material income and because they boost status and prestige.

(c) discretionary investments above those that are economically essential enable managers to pursue pet projects and afford them status, prestige, and security through the amount of physical plant and equipment they control.

See also MANAGERIAL THEORIES OF THE FIRM, DIVORCE OF OWNERSHIP FROM CONTROL.

managerial theories of the firm the theories that substitute firm objectives, such as SALES-REVENUE MAXIMIZATION and ASSET-GROWTH MAXIMIZATION, for the traditional hypothesis of PROFIT MAXIMIZATION. These theories are based on two assumptions: (a) for large oligopolistic firms there is a DIVORCE OF OWNERSHIP FROM CONTROL that allows management, not shareholders, to set company objectives; (b) managers are more interested in sales and assets goals than profit maximization because the size of their salaries and their power and status (managerial utility) are linked chiefly to the size of the firm. Profits are still important, but seen as contributory to the attainment of some other objective rather than as an end in themselves.

The significance of the managerial theories as an extension of the THEORY OF THE FIRM lies in their usefulness as predictors of higher output levels and lower prices in comparison with the profit-maximizing theory.

manpower planning the continuing managerial process of identifying the requirement for human resources and implementing a strategy to optimally utilize and develop labor resources in line with strategic objectives. Manpower planning can be undertaken at corporate level, or it may be done at industry or national level. Manpower planning or human resource planning seeks to identify future manpower requirements and also embodies such other personnel management activities as recruitment, training, and promotion.

marginal analysis the examination of the effects of adding one unit to, or taking one unit from, some economic VARIABLE. See also all the following entries beginning with "marginal."

marginal cost the cost incurred in the near term in increasing OUTPUT by one unit. Given that FIXED COSTS do not vary with output, marginal costs (MC) are entirely marginal VARIABLE COSTS. MC falls at first, reflecting the fact that costs increase faster than output, as shown in Fig. 108, but then rises as decreasing returns set in.

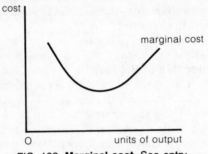

FIG. 108. **Marginal cost.** See entry.

MC together with MARGINAL REVENUE determines the level of output at which the firm attains PROFIT MAXIMIZATION.

marginal-cost/average-cost relationship the mathematical relationship between MARGINAL COST and AVERAGE COST. When average cost (AC) is falling, marginal cost (MC) is always below it. That is, if the cost of an extra unit of output lowers AC, it must itself be less than AC in order to drag the average down. When AC is rising, MC is above it. That is, if an extra unit of output increases AC, its cost must be more than AC in order to pull the average up. The MC curve cuts the AC curve at the minimum point on that curve, as shown in Fig. 109.

marginal cost pricing a pricing principle that argues for setting prices equal to the MARGINAL COST of production and distribution, ignoring whether or not FIXED COSTS are recouped from revenues. The principle has been advocated as a guide to the pricing and output policies of PUBLIC UTILITIES, on the grounds that prices reflecting the marginal cost to society of producing an extra

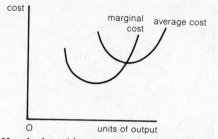

FIG. 109. **Marginal-cost/average-cost relationship.** See entry.

unit of output are socially desirable. The principle is particularly appealing when used for public facilities, where marginal costs are effectively zero, such as parks, bridges, and museums, because society can be improved by lowering the price of the facilities until they are fully used.

However, marginal cost pricing deals only with the near-term problem of generating an optimum price and output with existing capacity and ignores the long-term problem of ideal investment in new capacity. See Fig. 110. See also AVERAGE-COST PRICING, MARGINAL-COST/AVERAGE-COST RELATIONSHIP, NATIONALIZATION, PROFIT MAXIMIZATION.

marginal efficiency of capital/investment the RATE OF RETURN (PROFITS) expected on an extra dollar's worth of INVESTMENT. The marginal efficiency of investment decreases as the amount of investment increases (see Fig. 111a). This is because initial investments are concentrated on the best opportunities and yield high rates of return; later investments are less productive and secure progressively lower returns.

The amount of investment undertaken depends not only on expected returns but also on the cost of capital, that is, the RATE OF INTEREST. Investment will be profitable up to the point where the marginal efficiency of investment is equal to the COST OF CAPITAL. In Fig. 111a, at an interest rate of 20% only OX amount of investment is worthwhile. A fall in the interest rate to 10% increases the amount of profitable investment to OY.

It will be readily apparent from Fig. 111a that there is a link

MARGINAL FACTOR COST (MFC)

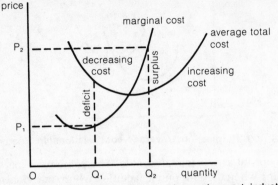

FIG. 110. **Marginal cost pricing.** In decreasing-cost industries, where marginal costs are below average total costs, setting a price equal to the marginal cost would result in losses that would have to be met from taxes or other sources (price OP_1). In increasing-cost industries, where marginal costs are greater than average total costs, marginal cost pricing would result in a surplus (price OP_2).

between the monetary side of the economy and the real economy. A fall in interest rates may stimulate more investment, which in turn will result in a higher level of national income. (See MONEY SUPPLY/SPENDING LINKAGES).

If expectations change and investors anticipate better returns from each investment because of technological progress, for example, then at any given rate of interest, such as 20%, more investment will be undertaken than before. That is, the marginal efficiency of investment will shift to the right, as shown in Fig. 111b, and investment will increase from OX to OZ.

marginal factor cost (MFC) the extra cost incurred by a firm in using an additional unit of a FACTOR INPUT. Marginal factor cost, together with the MARGINAL REVENUE PRODUCT of a factor, indicates to a firm how many factor inputs to employ in order to maximize profits.

marginal physical product the quantity of OUTPUT in the SHORT-TERM theory of supply produced by each extra unit of VARIABLE FACTOR INPUT in conjunction with a given amount of FIXED FACTOR INPUT. The marginal physical product curve, as

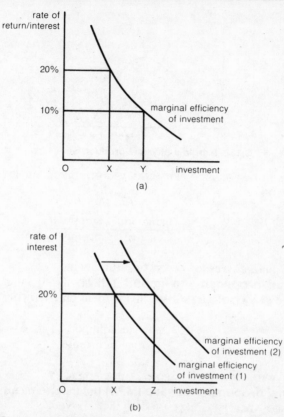

FIG. 111. **Marginal efficiency of capital/investment.** See entry.

shown in Fig. 112, rises steeply at first, reflecting increasing returns to the variable factor input, but then falls as DIMINISHING
RETURNS to the variable factor input set in.

marginal productivity theory of distribution a theory of the
FUNCTIONAL DISTRIBUTION OF INCOME in which FACTOR INPUTS
(labor, etc.) receive payment for their services (wages, etc.) that is
equal to their MARGINAL REVENUE PRODUCT.

marginal propensity to consume (MPC) the fraction of any

315

MARGINAL PROPENSITY TO IMPORT (MPM)

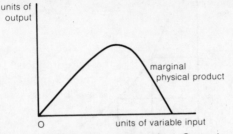

FIG. 112. **Marginal physical product.** See entry.

change in DISPOSABLE PERSONAL INCOME that is spent on CON-
SUMPTION:

$$MPC = \frac{\text{change in consumption}}{\text{change in income}}$$

See PROPENSITY TO CONSUME, MULTIPLIER.

marginal propensity to import (MPM) the fraction of any
change in NATIONAL INCOME that is spent on IMPORTS:

$$MPM = \frac{\text{change in imports}}{\text{change in income}}$$

See PROPENSITY TO IMPORT, MULTIPLIER.

marginal propensity to save (MPS) the fraction of any change
in DISPOSABLE PERSONAL INCOME that is saved:

$$MPS = \frac{\text{change in savings}}{\text{change in income}}$$

See PROPENSITY TO SAVE, MULTIPLIER.

marginal propensity to tax (MPT) the fraction of any change in
NATIONAL INCOME that is taken in TAXATION:

$$MPT = \frac{\text{change in tax}}{\text{change in income}}$$

See PROPENSITY TO TAX, MULTIPLIER, MARGINAL RATE OF TAXATION.

marginal rate of substitution a ratio of the MARGINAL UTILITIES of two products. It is measured by the slope of the consumer's INDIFFERENCE CURVE between the two products. To maximize utility, a consumer must equate the ratio of the marginal utilities of the two products to the ratio of their prices (see CONSUMER EQUILIBRIUM).

For an economy, the optimal distribution of national output is achieved when the marginal rate of substitution for all consumers is equal. See PARETO OPTIMALITY.

marginal rate of taxation the rate of TAXATION a person would pay on an incremental unit of INCOME.

In a steeply progressive income tax system, as income and average tax rates rise, marginal tax rates will rise more than average tax rates and take an increasing proportion of any additional income. Steep marginal tax rates may act as a disincentive and discourage people from working harder or making riskier investments. Such a reaction could lead to lower output, unemployment, and possibly lower tax revenues.

See AVERAGE RATE OF TAXATION, PROPENSITY TO TAX, PROPORTIONAL TAXATION, REGRESSIVE TAXATION, TAX REFORM ACT OF 1986.

marginal rate of technical substitution the ratio of the MARGINAL PHYSICAL PRODUCTS of two FACTOR INPUTS in the production process, that is, the amount by which it is possible to reduce factor input X and maintain output by substituting an extra unit of factor input Y. It is measured by the slope of the producer's ISOQUANT CURVE. In order to minimize production costs, a producer must equate the ratio of the marginal physical products of the two factor inputs, shown by the isoquant curve, to the ratio of their factor prices, shown by the ISOCOST LINE. See ISOQUANT MAP.

marginal rate of transformation a ratio of the MARGINAL COSTS of producing two products. It is measured by the slope of the PRODUCTION-POSSIBILITY BOUNDARY, which indicates the rate at which production of one product can be replaced by production of the other as a result of reallocation of inputs.

For an economy, the optimum composition of national output

is achieved when the marginal rate of transformation of the goods produced equals the ratio of their prices. See PARETO OPTIMALITY.

marginal revenue the addition to TOTAL REVENUE from the sale of one extra unit of output. Under conditions of PERFECT COMPETITION, the firm faces a horizontal DEMAND CURVE at the going market price (marginal revenue = price). See Fig. 113a. Marginal revenue interacts with MARGINAL COST in determining the level of output at which the firm achieves PROFIT MAXIMIZATION.

See AVERAGE REVENUE, ELASTICITY OF DEMAND, KINKED DEMAND CURVE, MONOPOLY.

marginal revenue product (MRP) the extra revenue obtained from using one more FACTOR INPUT to produce and sell additional units of OUTPUT. The marginal revenue product of a factor is given by the factor's MARGINAL PHYSICAL PRODUCT multiplied by the price of the product.

The marginal revenue product, together with the MARGINAL FACTOR COST, indicates to a firm how many factor inputs to employ in order to maximize profits. This can be illustrated by reference to the utilization of the labor input under PERFECT COMPETITION market conditions. In a competitive LABOR MARKET, the equilibrium WAGE RATE and numbers employed (W_e and Q_e, respectively, in Fig. 114a and b) are determined by the intersection of the market demand and supply curves for labor. Because each firm employs only a small fraction of the total labor force, it is unable to influence the wage rate. Thus, the wage rate and hence the marginal cost of labor (MFC) are constant for the firm—each extra worker adds exactly his or her wage rate to the firm's total factor cost. The firm's MRP declines because although under competitive conditions the product price remains constant, the marginal physical product falls due to DIMINISHING RETURNS to the labor input.

The firm will maximize profits by employing additional workers up to the point (Q_e in Fig. 114a) at which the last worker's contribution to revenue (MRP) is equal to the going wage rate (MFC).

marginal utility the increase in satisfaction (UTILITY) an individual derives from use or CONSUMPTION of one additional unit of a good

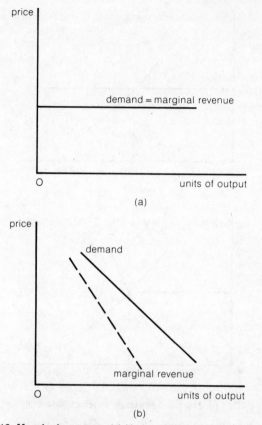

FIG. 113. **Marginal revenue.** (a) Under PERFECT COMPETITION each extra unit of output sold adds exactly the same amount to total revenue as each previous unit. (b) Under conditions of imperfect competition—for example, in MONOPOLISTIC COMPETITION—the firm faces a downward-sloping demand curve, and the price has to be lowered in order to sell more units. Marginal revenue is less than price. As price is lowered, each extra unit sold adds successively smaller amounts than previous units.

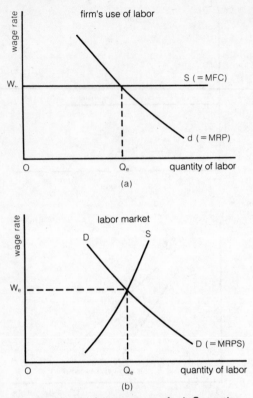

FIG. 114. **Marginal revenue product.** See entry.

or service. Marginal utility is concerned with the utility derived from each incremental unit used or consumed, and is therefore sometimes called *incremental utility*. For example, a person's TOTAL UTILITY (satisfaction) will increase if the person buys, say, an additional pair of shoes. If that person originally had three pairs of shoes, then the incremental unit will be one more pair, making four pairs. The marginal (incremental) utility is positive but *less* than the marginal utility derived from purchasing a third pair of shoes, the increment being from two pairs owned to three pairs owned after the purchase. This is known as DIMINISHING MAR-GINAL UTILITY.

Marginal utility is not to be confused with *total utility*. Total utility is the sum total of utility derived from *all* units used or consumed. Marginal utility is derived only from the *last* unit used or consumed. This difference in meaning explains what is known as the *value paradox*. Water has a high total utility but, due to its relative abundance, a low marginal one. Diamonds have a low total utility but, due to their relative scarcity, a high marginal one. Given the supply function of each, this determines price. The low marginal utility good (water) commands a low price while the high marginal utility good (diamonds) commands a high price.

Whenever a change in utility occurs, for example, the utility change from owning three to owning four pairs of shoes, the change can be calculated using mathematics. In calculus, such a change is called the first derivative, and as we are concerned with utility it is the first derivative of the total UTILITY FUNCTION. The *rate* of change of that change is the second derivative.

See CARDINAL UTILITY, ORDINAL UTILITY, CONSUMER EQUILIBRIUM, PARETO OPTIMALITY, PARADOX OF VALUE.

marginal utility of money the increase in satisfaction (UTILITY) an individual derives from spending an incremental unit of MONEY on goods or services.

margin of error see FORECASTING.

market an EXCHANGE mechanism that brings together sellers and buyers of a PRODUCT, FACTOR OF PRODUCTION, or FINANCIAL SECURITY.

Economists define a market as a group of products consumers view as being substitutes for one another, that is, they have a high CROSS ELASTICITY OF DEMAND. This concept of the market may not correspond exactly with INDUSTRIAL CLASSIFICATIONS, which group products in terms of their technical or production characteristics rather than consumer substitutability. For example, glass bottles and metal cans would be regarded by users as substitute packaging materials but are in fact allocated to different industrial classifications, the glass and metal industries, respectively. By contrast, the industrial classification category of steel products, for example, can encompass such diverse users as civil engineers (reinforcing bars), car manufacturers (car bodies), and appliance manufacturers (washing machines). However, in the absence of reliable cross elasticity of demand data, economists are often

MARKET CONCENTRATION

forced to fall back on industrial classifications as a best approximation of markets in empirical analysis.

The THEORY OF MARKETS distinguishes between markets according to their structural characteristics, in particular the number of sellers and buyers involved. A number of market situations can be identified, including:

PERFECT COMPETITION	=	many sellers, many buyers
OLIGOPOLY	=	few sellers, many buyers
OLIGOPSONY	=	many sellers, few buyers
BILATERAL OLIGOPOLY	=	few sellers, few buyers
MONOPOLY	=	one seller, many buyers
MONOPSONY	=	many sellers, one buyer
BILATERAL MONOPOLY	=	one seller, one buyer
DUOPOLY	=	two sellers, many buyers
DUOPSONY	=	many sellers, two buyers

Such a classification serves well for theoretical analysis, and there is no need to make fine distinctions relating to the boundaries of the market under consideration. However, from the point of view of applying policy, how widely or narrowly a market is defined depends largely on the particular issue the policy is concerned with and the degree of precision appropriate for that policy. For example, for macroplanning purposes it may be appropriate to refer broadly to the soft drinks market or food market.

See also LABOR MARKET, FOREIGN EXCHANGE MARKET, STOCK EXCHANGE, CAPITAL MARKET, COMMODITY MARKET.

market concentration see CONCENTRATION MEASURES.

market conduct the things done by firms in their capacity as suppliers and buyers of final and intermediate goods and services. Major facets of market conduct include: the objectives of firms and the policies they adopt with regard to prices, scale of output, product characteristics, etc., together with the effect of presence or absence of competing firms on formulation and implementation of those policies.

In the THEORY OF MARKETS, market conduct interacts with MARKET STRUCTURE in determining MARKET PERFORMANCE, while market structure and performance, in turn, affect market conduct.

See COMPANY OBJECTIVES, METHODS OF COMPETITION, MAR-
KET STRUCTURE/CONDUCT-PERFORMANCE SCHEMA, PERFECT
COMPETITION, MONOPOLISTIC COMPETITION.

market entry the entry into a market of a new firm or firms. In the
THEORY OF MARKETS, entrants are assumed to come into the market by establishing a new plant, thereby adding to the number of
competing suppliers in the market. New entry into a market occurs when established firms are earning above-normal or excess
profits. The entry of new firms plays an important role in enlarging
the supply capacity of a market and in removing above-normal
profits. In practice, new entry also takes place through TAKEOVER
of, or MERGER with, an established firm.

See CONDITION OF ENTRY, BARRIERS TO ENTRY, POTENTIAL
ENTRANT, CONTESTABLE MARKET, PERFECT COMPETITION,
MONOPOLISTIC COMPETITION, OLIGOPOLY, MONOPOLY, LIMIT
PRICING.

market exit or **exit** the withdrawal from a MARKET of a firm or
firms. In the THEORY OF MARKETS, a firm will leave a market if it
is unable to earn NORMAL PROFITS in the long run. Firm exit plays
an important role in eliminating EXCESS CAPACITY and reducing
total market supply. See also LOSS, AVERAGE COST(2).

marketing the managerial process of determining the requirements of a MARKET, that is, the CONSUMER'S needs, real or induced, and satisfying that DEMAND through production, distribution, pricing, promotion, and after-sales service. See MARKET
RESEARCH.

market maker a STOCK EXCHANGE firm that buys and sells STOCKS
and BONDS, thereby establishing a market for these securities.

market mechanism see PRICE SYSTEM.

market order on a stock exchange, an order to buy or sell a specified number of shares of a security at the best price available.

market performance the efficiency of MARKETS in utilizing
scarce resources to meet consumers' demand for goods and services, that is, how well the markets have contributed to optimization of economic welfare.

Five main performance criteria have been identified: (a) PRO-
DUCTIVE EFFICIENCY, (b) DISTRIBUTIVE EFFICIENCY, (c) ALLOCA-
TIVE EFFICIENCY, (d) TECHNOLOGICAL PROGRESSIVENESS, and (e)
PRODUCT PERFORMANCE. What is being sought is the ability of a

market to produce and distribute its existing products at the lowest possible cost and to charge consumers prices consistent with these costs. In a dynamic sense, market performance can also be judged in terms of whether firms introduce new cost-cutting production and distribution techniques, and better products over time.

In the THEORY OF MARKETS, market performance is determined by interaction of MARKET STRUCTURE and MARKET CONDUCT, while market performance itself affects market structure and conduct.

See also PARETO OPTIMALITY, RESOURCE ALLOCATION, MARKET STRUCTURE/CONDUCT-PERFORMANCE SCHEMA, PERFECT COMPETITION, MONOPOLISTIC COMPETITION, OLIGOPOLY, MONOPOLY.

market power the ability of a FIRM to administer within limits the supply price and terms of sale of its product without immediate competitive encroachment. The exercise of market power is typically associated with an OLIGOPOLY or MONOPOLY. See also ADMINISTERED PRICE, SELLER CONCENTRATION, CONDITION OF ENTRY.

market research the systematic collection, assimilation, and analysis of facts and opinions to assist managers in making decisions in order to identify market opportunities for a firm's existing or potential goods and services. See TEST MARKET.

market segmentation the division of a MARKET into subgroups of customers, each with their own buying characteristics, for example, men and women. Firms are thus able to adopt PRODUCT DIFFERENTIATION strategies to meet the needs of groups of buyers and enlarge their sales potential. See also PRICE DISCRIMINATION.

market share the proportion of total MARKET output or sales accounted for by an individual firm. Market-share data are used to measure the degree of SELLER CONCENTRATION in a market. See CONCENTRATION RATIO, CONCENTRATION MEASURES.

market structure the way in which a MARKET is organized. The THEORY OF MARKETS focuses especially on aspects of market structure that have an important influence on the behavior of firms and buyers and on MARKET PERFORMANCE. Structural features having a major strategic importance in relation to MARKET CONDUCT and performance include: (a) the degree of SELLER CON-

CENTRATION and BUYER CONCENTRATION as measured by the number of sellers and buyers and their relative size distribution; (b) the CONDITION OF ENTRY to the market—the extent to which established suppliers have advantages over potential new entrants because of BARRIERS TO ENTRY; and (c) the nature of the product supplied, whether it is a HOMOGENEOUS PRODUCT or one subject to PRODUCT DIFFERENTIATION.

Market structure, in turn, is affected by market conduct and performance. See VERTICAL INTEGRATION, DIVERSIFICATION, CONCENTRATION MEASURES, MARKET STRUCTURE/CONDUCT-PERFORMANCE SCHEMA.

market structure/conduct-performance schema an analytical framework for investigating the operation of market processes. Markets are ultimately judged on how well they have contributed to achievement of optimal economic efficiency. MARKET PERFORMANCE (see Fig. 115) is determined fundamentally by the interaction of MARKET STRUCTURE and MARKET CONDUCT. The schema attempts to identify structural and conduct parameters that have a strategic influence on market performance. These relationships have been formalized in the THEORY OF MARKETS.

The schema is useful to those who make public policy (see INDUSTRIAL POLICY), in particular framing measures designed to improve market performance.

market system see PRICE SYSTEM.

Marshall, Alfred (1842—1924) professor of political economy at Cambridge University and a dominant figure in Anglo-Saxon economics in late nineteenth and early twentieth centuries. His text *Principles of Economics* (1890) is still useful for graduate students.

Independently of the Austrian school, Marshall developed marginal utility analysis. He advanced the idea of diminishing marginal utility, an explanation of a downward-sloping demand curve, the relationship of income and substitution effects to demand curves, and the idea of elasticity of demand.

Marshall tried to incorporate classical long-run cost of production theories within contemporary marginal utility theory. Using the often-cited two blades of a scissors analogy, he suggested that both supply and demand determine prices, that is, neither blade of a pair of scissors is more important than the other.

Marshall argued that the forces of demand and supply deter-

MARSHALL-LERNER CONDITION

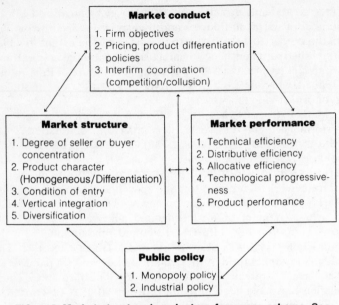

FIG. 115. Market structure/conduct-performance schema. See entry.

mine value, with demand determining price and output in the near term, and supply influencing price in the long term. He suggested that supply prices would depend on production costs and in analyzing near-term production cost showed how the marginal product of all resources tends to diminish as variable factor inputs are combined with fixed amounts of other resources (DIMINISHING RETURNS to the variable factor input). In the long run, Marshall suggested, industries would experience reducing costs and prices because of ECONOMIES OF SCALE resulting from greater specialization.

Marshall-Lerner condition the PRICE ELASTICITY OF DEMAND for imports and exports, a condition that must be satisfied if a DEVALUATION or REVALUATION is to be successful in removing a balance-of-payments deficit or surplus.

The elasticity values for a successful devaluation, for example, are:

demand for imports is price-elastic $(e \geq 1)$
demand for exports is price-elastic $(e \geq 1)$

How successful the devaluation is depends critically on the reaction of import and export volumes to the change in prices implied by the devaluation. If trade volumes are relatively elastic to price changes, the devaluation will be successful. That is, an increase in import prices results in a more than proportionate fall in import volume, reducing the total amount of foreign currency required to finance the import bill. The decrease in export prices results in a more than proportionate increase in export volume, bringing about an increase in total foreign currency earnings on exports.

By contrast, if trade volumes are relatively inelastic to price changes, the devaluation will not succeed. That is, an increase in import prices results in a less than proportionate fall in import volume, increasing the total amount of foreign currency required to finance the import bill. The decrease in export prices results in a less than proportionate increase in export volume, bringing about a fall in total foreign currency earnings on exports.

A number of other factors also influence the outcome of a devaluation, in particular the extent to which domestic resources are sufficiently mobile to be switched into export-producing and import-substitution industries.

See DEVALUATION, BALANCE-OF-PAYMENTS EQUILIBRIUM, PRICE ELASTICITY OF SUPPLY.

Marx, Karl (1818—1883) German philosopher who spent most of his life in England and produced a theory about historical change based on conflict between competing classes that is explained in his book *Das Kapital*. The first volume was published in 1867, and some of the remaining volumes, edited by Friedrich Engels and Karl Kautsky, were published posthumously in 1885, 1894, and later.

Marx argued that at each stage in history one class in society becomes powerful because of its ownership of the means of production. Meanwhile, however, another class is developing—the non-owners of means of production, with interests clashing with those of the dominant class. Finally, because of changes in the modes of production, the new class overturns the old and sets itself up as a new dominant group. For example, under feudalism the lords predominated because they controlled the land. That group gave way to the bourgeoisie, the capitalists who gained ascendancy because of their control of capital.

Capitalists, because they owned the means of production, determined wages. Exploitation of the working class and competition among capitalists enabled some factory owners to accumulate even greater wealth and gain monopoly power, while others fell into the proletariat class.

Workers produce goods and services of value, but because they are paid less than the value they create, capitalists are able to appropriate much of this value for themselves in the form of profits. Marx predicted that this exploitation and inherent contradictions in capitalism would lead to ever-worsening crises and eventually provoke a revolution in which the propertyless proletariat would overthrow the capitalist class and take over the means of production. Initially, under socialism, the nation's productive assets would be acquired and controlled by the government but eventually, when the problem of scarcity had been overcome, under COMMUNISM the workers themselves would collectively own the means of production, with goods and services being distributed according to peoples' needs. Their slogan would be: "From each according to his ability, to each according to his wants."

See also CENTRALLY PLANNED ECONOMY, LABOR THEORY OF VALUE.

mass production the manufacture of a PRODUCT in very large quantities, using continuous flow, capital-intensive methods of production. Mass production is typically found in industries where the product supplied is highly standardized, enabling automated machinery and processes to be substituted for labor. Mass-production industries are usually characterized by high levels of SELLER CONCENTRATION, difficult CONDITIONS OF ENTRY, and exploitation of ECONOMIES OF SCALE, which results in low unit costs of supply, Compare BATCH PRODUCTION.

mathematical economics the application of mathematical methods to problem-solving in economics.

matrix (*pl.* **matrices**) a rectangular array of elements displayed as rows and columns. Matrices may be of any dimension, for example, a matrix of three rows and two columns. Multiplying rows by columns gives the number of elements in a matrix, which in our example is six. Convention dictates that in all dealings with matrices the row is designated first. See also INPUT-OUTPUT ANALYSIS.

maximum strategy see GAME THEORY.

mean or **average** or **arithmetic mean** a method of representing the center or middle of a set of n numbers by a single number, that is, the sum of the n numbers divided by n. For example, if five people earn $100, $100, $150, $250, and $400 a day, then the mean income of the group is:

$$\$\frac{100 + 100 + 150 + 250 + 400}{5} = \$\frac{1,000}{5} = \$200$$

See also MEDIAN, MODE.

means test an examination of the personal and financial circumstances of an individual to assess his or her eligibility for benefits under a country's welfare system. The benefits being claimed are not regarded as a universal right, but are assessed under rules and regulations laid down by legislation and the government department concerned. The payment of the welfare benefit is considered a right only if an individual is within the limits of income, personal circumstance, etc., for the period of the claim.

median a means of representing the center or middle of a set of n numbers by a single number, that is, the value of the middle item when the items are arranged in increasing order of magnitude. For example, if five people earn $100, $100, $150, $250, and $400 a day, the median income of the group is $150 (the middle figure). See also MEAN, MODE.

mediation a procedure for settling disputes, most notably LABOR DISPUTES, in which a neutral third party meets with the disputants and endeavors to help them resolve their differences and reach agreement through continued negotiation. In some countries "conciliation" is distinguished from "mediation" by the degree of intervention exercised by conciliators or mediators in the process of encouraging the parties to settle their differences, with concilia-tors refraining from advancing, and mediators expected to ad-vance, proposals of their own for possible settlements.

In ARBITRATION, the neutral third parties make recommenda-tions and may decide disputes after listening to both sides.

See also COLLECTIVE BARGAINING, INDUSTRIAL RELATIONS.

medium of exchange the attribute of MONEY that encourages people to accept it in exchange for goods or services.

mercantilism a set of economic ideas and policies established in England and France during the seventeenth century, accompany-ing the rise of commercial capitalism. The mercantilists stressed the importance of trade and commerce as the source of the na-tion's wealth, and advocated policies to increase a nation's wealth and power by encouraging exports and discouraging imports in order to allow the country to amass quantities of gold. These pro-tectionist ideas (see PROTECTIONISM) were criticized by later clas-sical economists, such as Adam SMITH.

merchandising see SALES PROMOTION AND MERCHANDISING.

merchant bank so-called in Britain; in the United States more often called an investment bank, a specialist FINANCIAL INSTITU-TION that advises client companies on new stock issues and *under-writes* such issues, that is, guarantees to buy any shares unsold on the open market. They also advise companies in MERGER and TAKEOVER situations and may perform many other banking func-tions for large companies. See STOCK EXCHANGE.

merger or **amalgamation** the combining of two or more firms. Three broad categories of merger may be identified: (a) horizontal mergers between firms that are direct competitors in the same market, (b) vertical mergers between firms that stand in a sup-plier-customer relationship, and (c) conglomerate mergers be-tween firms operating in unrelated markets that are seeking to diversify their activities.

See WILLIAMSON TRADE-OFF MODEL, HORIZONTAL INTEGRA-TION, VERTICAL INTEGRATION, DIVERSIFICATION.

merit goods see SOCIAL PRODUCTS.

methods of competition an element of MARKET CONDUCT de-noting ways in which firms in a MARKET compete:

(a) Price. Sellers may attempt to secure buyer support by putting their product on sale at a lower price than that of rivals. They must bear in mind, however, that rivals may also lower their own prices. The result will be that all firms end up with lower profits.

(b) Nonprice competition, including (i) *physical* PRODUCT DIF-FERENTIATION. Sellers may try to differentiate technically similar products by altering their quality and design and by improving their performance. All these efforts are intended to secure buyer allegiance by causing buyers to regard these products as in some way better than competitive offerings. (ii) *product differentiation via selling techniques.* Competition in selling efforts includes advertising, general SALES PROMOTION (free trial offers, money-off coupons), personal sales promotion (representatives), and the creation of distribution outlets. These activities are directed at stimulating demand by emphasizing real and imaginary product attributes relative to products of their competitors. (iii) *New brand competition.* Given dynamic change (advances in technology, changes in consumer tastes), a firm's existing products may become obsolete. A supplier is then obliged to introduce new brands or redesign existing ones to remain competitive.

(c) Low-cost production as a means of competition. Although cost-effectiveness is not a direct means of competition, it is an essential way to strengthen the market position of a supplier. The ability to reduce costs opens up the possibility of (unmatched) price cuts, or enables firms to devote greater financial resources to differentiation activity.

See also MONOPOLISTIC COMPETITION, OLIGOPOLY, PRODUCT CHARACTERISTICS MODEL, PRODUCT LIFE CYCLE.

M-form (multidivisional form) organization an organizational structure adopted by firms in which management is decentralized, with separate groups or divisions of the firm responsible for groups of similar products or serving separate markets. Each group or division will have an autonomous management team and separate marketing, production, etc. functions. With such a structure, the top managers at the head office leave day-to-day running of the divisions to the managers responsible, although they monitor the profitability performance of the divisional managers and generally retain power over allocation of investment funds to the divisions. Oliver Williamson, who coined the term "M-form," argued that firms with M-form organizations were less likely to pursue nonprofit goals (MANAGEMENT-UTILITY MAXIMIZING) than firms with U-FORM (UNITARY-FORM) ORGANIZATIONS, because top managers could set clear profit goals for divisions and suffer little loss of control over their subordinates, compared with U-form firms. Williamson also argued that M-form organizations will gradually increase in popularity as firms grow, and will shed their U-form structures in favor of M-form structures. See also MANAGERIAL THEORIES OF THE FIRM, BEHAVIORAL THEORY OF THE FIRM.

microeconomics the branch of economics concerned with study of the behavior of consumers and firms and determination of the market prices and quantities transacted of FACTOR INPUTS and goods and services. Microeconomic analysis investigates how scarce economic resources are allocated between alternative ends and seeks to identify the strategic determinants of efficient use of resources. See also THEORY OF CONSUMER BEHAVIOR, THEORY OF THE FIRM, THEORY OF MARKETS, THEORY OF DEMAND, THEORY OF SUPPLY, MACROECONOMICS.

middleman a trader or company serving as intermediary between two parties, frequently producer and consumer or seller and purchaser. Wholesalers may be considered middlemen, for they frequently act as distributors from producers to retailers on a COMMISSION or fee basis. Real estate agents and insurance brokers are other examples. See WHOLESALING.

migration the movement of people into (immigration) and out of (emigration) a country, this movement serving to increase or decrease the country's population and labor force.

Mill, John Stuart (1806—1873) English economist who helped develop CLASSICAL ECONOMIC theory in his book *Principles of Political Economy with some of their Applications to Social Philosophy* (1848). Mill was a social reformer, and although he preferred to see the production and exchange of goods taking place in free markets, he argued that government intervention could improve the material well-being of the people through REDISTRIBUTION OF INCOME. Mill was the first to argue that educational barriers to labor mobility could create noncompeting groups of labor with permanent differences in wage rates between groups. He was also the first to analyze costs where two or more joint products are produced in fixed proportions.

minimax strategy see GAME THEORY.

minimum efficient scale the point on a firm's long-term AVER-
AGE COST curve at which ECONOMIES OF SCALE are exhausted and
constant returns to scale begin.

In the theory of costs, the long-term average cost is conventionally depicted as U-shaped, with economies of scale serving to reduce average cost as output increases to begin with, but
DISECONOMIES OF SCALE set in and average cost rises as output
increases. Statistical studies suggest, however, that for many industries long-term average cost curves are L-shaped, as shown in Fig.
116.

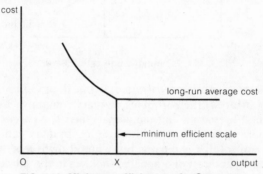

FIG. 116. **Minimum efficient scale.** See entry.

In industries in which the minimum efficient scale is large relative to total size of the market, we would expect to find high
degrees of SELLER CONCENTRATION, since the market might only
support a few firms of minimum efficient scale size. The potential
cost disadvantage to firms seeking to enter a market on a small
scale vis-a-vis large established firms, can also serve as a BARRIER
TO ENTRY in certain industries. See NATURAL MONOPOLY.

minimum wage the minimum rate of pay for LABOR, either established by the government (the Fair Labor Standards Act) or volun-
tarily agreed upon between labor unions and employers. Minimum wages are designed to ensure that workers are able to enjoy
some basic standard of living, although (as shown in Fig. 117), if
wage rates are set much above the equilibrium rate, W_e, the effect
is to reduce the demand for labor (from Q_e to Q_m). Thus, although

those who remain at work (OQ_m) are now better off, people who may be put out of work as wages rise ($Q_m Q_e$) are worse off.

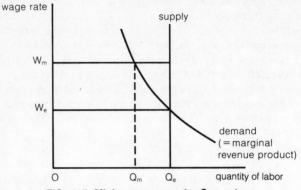

FIG. 117. **Minimum wage rate.** See entry.

See SUPPLY-SIDE ECONOMICS, MARGINAL-REVENUE PRODUCT.

minority interest the part of a subsidiary company's issued stock not owned by the parent company. When the parent company owns more than 50% of the stock of a subsidiary company, it is able to control that company, but when it owns less than 100%, the minority interest of other shareholders in the subsidiary company must be recognized.

mixed economy a method of organizing an economy to produce goods and services. Under this economic system, some goods and services are supplied by private enterprise, and others, typically basic INFRASTRUCTURE goods and services such as electricity, postal services, education, and water supply are usually provided by the government. In the United States, government regulation of public utilities is more likely than government ownership.

The mixed economy is a characteristic feature of most developed and developing countries, so-called pure or totally private-enterprise economies and centrally planned economies being rarely encountered. In almost all economies there are some forms of government regulation to offset some of the shortcomings of the market system, for example, the Pure Food and Drug Laws. The precise mix of private enterprise and government activities to be found in particular countries, however, does vary substantially between these two extremes and is much influenced by the political philosophy of the country concerned. See NATIONALIZATION, PRIVATIZATION.

mobility the degree to which a FACTOR OF PRODUCTION is willing or able to move between different locations or uses.

Of the four factors of production, *land* is geographically immobile, but not necessarily the uses to which land can be put, for example, industry or agriculture). *Labor* is both geographically and occupationally mobile but is not necessarily willing or able to move to another location or retrain for another occupation. *Capital (in the form of plant and machinery)* frequently is relatively immobile because it is difficult to find new uses for specialized plants and often difficult to change location due to the size and nature of such plants, for example, electrical generating machinery. *Finance capital (capital funds)*, however, is highly mobile and is increasingly able to penetrate international boundaries. See RESOURCE ALLOCATION.

mode a means of representing a set of n numbers by a single number that is the value occurring most often, that is, the one with the highest frequency. For example, if five people earn $100, $100, $150, $250, and $400 a day, the modal income is $100 (the most common income). The mode is useful in that it can be used to represent data grouped in the form of a qualitative FREQUENCY DISTRIBUTION. See also MEAN, MEDIAN.

model see ECONOMIC MODEL.

Modigliani, Franco (born 1918) winner of the Nobel Memorial Prize in Economic Sciences, 1985, for pioneer work in analyzing the behavior of household savers and the functioning of financial markets. Modigliani taught at the New School, in New York City, and at MIT for many years. He tried to reconcile some of the differences separating Keynesians and monetarists and developed a savings model known as the *life-cycle model*. With Merton Miller he advanced ideas on how firms distinguish between their investment and financial decisions.

While Modigliani has contributed to the emergence of the so-called rational expectations school, he rejected the argument that government can never improve the operation of the economy, because rational people will always anticipate a government's actions and negate their effects. With Lawrence Klein, another Nobelist, he helped design the MIT-University of Pennsylvania Model, a macroeconomic model.

monetarism a body of analysis relating to the influence of MONEY in the functioning of the economy. The theory emphasizes the importance of a balanced relationship between the amount of money available to finance purchases of goods and services, and the ability of the economy to produce such goods and services.

The theory provides an explanation of INFLATION centered on excessive increases in the MONEY SUPPLY. Monetarists argue that if the government spends more than it receives in taxes, increasing the need for the public sector to finance the shortfall, then the resulting increase in the money supply will increase spending and the rate of inflation. The pure QUANTITY THEORY OF MONEY (MV $\equiv$ PT) suggests that the ultimate cause of inflation is excessive monetary creation, that is, too much money chasing too little output. Thus, money creation is seen as a source of DEMAND-PULL INFLATION.

Monetarists suggest that cost-push is not a truly independent theory of inflation—increased spending has to be financed by money supply increases. Consider initially a given supply of money and given levels of output and prices. Assume now that costs increase, for example, higher wages, and this causes suppliers to raise prices. Monetarists argue that the increase in prices will not turn into an inflationary process—a persistent tendency for prices to rise—unless the money supply is increased. The given supply of money will buy fewer goods at the higher price level, and real demand will fall. But if the banking system increases the money supply, the same volume of goods can be purchased at the higher price level. If this process continues, COST-PUSH INFLATION is validated.

It is important to understand some of the differences between monetarists and Keynesians. They differ as to the determinants of changes in aggregate demand. For Keynesians, these are expenditures, with changes in the supply of money not of great significance. Monetarists, by contrast, place changes in the supply of money at the center of their analyses. This difference has been stated, probably overstated, as "Money doesn't matter. Money alone matters."

The policy implications of these differences have important consequences. Keynesians would rely primarily on fiscal policy; monetarists would employ changes in the money supply to produce economic stability. Further, there are differences over whether government intervention in markets is likely to be helpful or harmful. Monetarists are more likely to rely on competition in markets than on government intervention to promote stbility and growth of the economy.

See also MONEY SUPPLY/SPENDING LINKAGES, MONETARY POLICY, CHICAGO SCHOOL.

monetary base control the control of the monetary base of the financial system as a means of controlling a nation's MONEY SUPPLY. The monetary base is usually defined as bills and coins in circulation *plus* banks' cash on hand and their reserve balances at the Federal Reserve Banks. It is argued that if banks adhere to a well-defined required reserve ratio, then the Fed, by controlling this narrow monetary base, can control monetary growth. See DEMAND DEPOSIT CREATION.

monetary economy an economy characterized by money as a medium of exchange, standard of value, and store of value. This contrasts with a BARTER economy, in which a double coincidence of wants is essential for trade. In complex modern economies, it is difficult to picture a farmer giving, say, two sheep for a tractor tire. Although barter still exists on a small scale, most countries depend on money transactions as a means of conducting trade. Barter is sometimes the outcome of runaway inflation, with its attendant loss of confidence in money as a store of value.

monetary policy a tool of general MACROECONOMIC POLICY under control of the monetary authorities that seeks to attain government economic objectives by influencing the MONEY SUPPLY and/or RATE OF INTEREST—therefore credit.

The monetary authorities in the United States, the Federal Reserve System, attempt to achieve such objectives as price stability, low level of unemployment, and economic growth. The means of changing the money supply or rate of interest is by use of monetary instruments.

MONETARY SYSTEM

One problem in using monetary policy is that the rate of interest cannot be regulated without affecting money supply, and vice versa, so such changes have to be considered together. For example, if the Fed wishes to raise the interest rate, say, from Or_1 to Or_2 in Fig. 118, it can do so by reducing the money supply from OM_1 to OM_2. With the given demand curve for money, this would have the effect of raising interest rates as required. However, not all components of the money supply are under control of the Fed, and rising interest rates can, for example, encourage overseas lenders, swelling the domestic money supply and frustrating the Fed's attempts to restrict money supply.

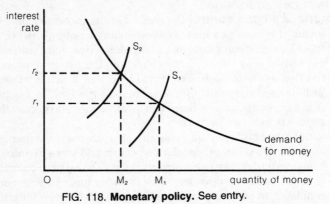

FIG. 118. **Monetary policy.** See entry.

Monetary policy has received greater emphasis in the late 1970s and early 1980s due in large part to stagflation and the growing influence of FRIEDMAN and the Chicago School, supplementing if not supplanting KEYNESIAN ECONOMICS.

See ECONOMIC POLICY, MONEY DEMAND SCHEDULE, MONEY SUPPLY/SPENDING LINKAGES, MONETARISM, QUANTITY THEORY OF MONEY, DEMAND DEPOSIT CREATION.

monetary system the policies and instruments employed by a country to regulate its MONEY SUPPLY. The physical form of the money supply (bills, coins, etc.), the denomination of the values of monetary units (dollars and cents, etc.), and the total size of the money supply are basic policy issues.

In the United States, the Federal Reserve authorities rely on three controls to influence the level of economic activity: (1) changes in bank reserve ratios, (2) changes in the discount rate, and (3) open market operations.

The monetary system also has an external dimension insofar as countries engage in international trade and investment, which involves interactive mechanisms, such as the EXCHANGE RATE, CONVERTIBILITY, and INTERNATIONAL RESERVES.

See also MONETARY POLICY, INTERNATIONAL MONETARY SYSTEM, RESERVES, OPEN-MARKET OPERATIONS, FEDERAL RESERVE SYSTEM.

monetary unit the standard unit of CURRENCY that forms the basis of a country's domestic MONEY SUPPLY, for example, the dollar (US), pound (UK), or franc (France). The monetary units of countries are related to each other for purposes of international trade and investment through their EXCHANGE RATE values. See MONEY.

money an ASSET generally acceptable as a medium of exchange. Goods, services, and other physical assets are priced in terms of money and are exchanged using money as a common denominator rather than having one GOOD etc. being exchanged for another, as in BARTER. The use of money as a means of payment enables an economy to produce more output, because it facilitates SPECIALIZATION in production and reduces time spent by sellers and buyers in arranging exchanges. Other important functions of money are its use as a store of purchasing power—money can be held over a period of time and used to finance future payments—and as a bookkeeping unit—money is used to measure and record the value of goods or services over time, for example, GROSS NATIONAL PRODUCT. See LEGAL TENDER.

money demand schedule a schedule that depicts the relationship between the quantity of MONEY demanded, Qd (LIQUIDITY PREFERENCE), and the RATE OF INTEREST (i) and the level of NATIONAL INCOME (Y):

$$Qd = f(i, Y)$$

If the rate of interest falls, the SPECULATIVE DEMAND FOR MONEY increases. This is the money held in anticipation of a fall in the price of investment assets, such as BONDS. The rate of interest varies inversely with the price of bonds. For example, if the nominal return on a bond is $100 and the price of the bond is $1000, then the effective interest rate is 10%. If the price of the bond falls to $50, the effective interest rate increases to 20%. Consequently, the lower the rate of interest, the higher the price of bonds. The higher the price of bonds, the less likely it is that bond prices will continue to rise and the greater the chance that prices will fall. Thus, as shown in Fig. 119a, the lower the rate of interest, the greater the inducement to hold cash for speculative purposes.

An increase in national income and product increases the precautionary and transaction demand for money, that is, money held day to day to finance current purchases of goods and services and for unpredictable circumstances. This shifts the money demand schedule outward to the right, from mds_1 to mds_2 in Fig. 119b.

The money-demand schedule interacts with the MONEY SUPPLY SCHEDULE to determine the equilibrium RATE OF INTEREST.

money illusion the illusion based on the failure of people to appreciate that a general increase in prices (INFLATION) reduces the real PURCHASING POWER of their income (REAL WAGES). In practice, however, this is unlikely to occur once people have become accustomed to living with inflation, and labor unions negotiate for increases in MONEY WAGES that allow for inflationary EXPECTATIONS. See also ADAPTIVE EXPECTATIONS HYPOTHESIS, INFLATIONARY SPIRAL.

money market a MARKET that deals in short-term lending and borrowing of money. Institutions involved in the money market include the Fed, commercial banks, and companies of many kinds. The main financial instruments dealt in are TREASURY BILLS and short-term notes.

money multiplier see DEMAND DEPOSIT CREATION.

money supply anything that fulfills the functions of money: medium of exchange, standard of value, standard of deferred payment, store of value. The Federal Reserve authorities, in establishing targets for the supply of money, use definitions of the stock of money based on liquidity. The *Economic Report of the President*

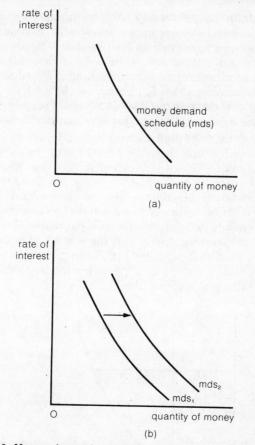

FIG. 119. **Money-demand schedule.** (a) With assumed constant national income. (b) The effect of an increase in national income.

for January 1989 describes the money stock for 1987 in *billions* and seasonally adjusted as follows:

M1 Narrow transaction money basic money supply: currency, demand deposits, traveler's checks, and other checkable deposits—$750.8

MONEY SUPPLY SCHEDULE

M2 Medium range money M1 plus savings and small time-deposits, repurchase agreements (overnight), Eurodollars (overnight), money market mutual fund balances—$2901.

M3 Wide range money M2 plus large denomination time-deposits, term repurchase agreements, term Eurodollars, institutions only money market fund balances—$3664.1

L Liquid and near-liquid assets M3 plus Treasury obligations, high-grade commercial paper, bankers' acceptances—$4328.

money supply schedule a schedule that depicts the amount of MONEY supplied and the RATE OF INTEREST. In some analyses, MONEY SUPPLY is drawn as a vertical straight line. That is, money supply is exogenously determined, being put into the economic system from outside by the government and nonbanking financial institutions. However, a significant part of the wider money supply is endogenously determined—for example, bank deposits are created by the banking system and these are highly interest-rate sensitive. Thus, in general, the higher the rate of interest—therefore, the higher the return on loanable funds—the greater the amount of money supplied (see Fig. 120).

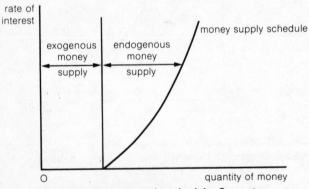

FIG. 120. **Money supply schedule.** See entry.

The money supply schedule interacts with the MONEY DEMAND SCHEDULE to determine the equilibrium rate of interest. See MONEY SUPPLY/SPENDING LINKAGES.

money supply/spending linkages 1. in the *Keynesian* view, the *indirect* link between MONEY SUPPLY and AGGREGATE DEMAND through the RATE OF INTEREST. In brief, an increase in the money supply, from M to M^1 in Fig. 121a, brings about a fall in the rate of interest from r to r^1, which results in an increase in planned INVESTMENT from I to I^1 (Fig. 121b). The rise in investment, in turn, increases aggregate demand and, via the MULTIPLIER effect, raises national income from Y to Y^1 (Fig. 121c). The fall in interest rates can also be shown to increase consumption expenditure. The lower cost of borrowing encourages people to use more loan financing to buy cars, television sets, etc. See KEYNES, KEYNESIAN ECONOMICS, EQUILIBRIUM LEVEL OF NATIONAL INCOME.

2. in the *monetarist* view, the *direct* link between money supply and level of aggregate demand. In brief, an increase in the money supply feeds directly into an increase in demand for final goods and services, and not just for investment goods. This proposition is based on the assumption that when households and businesses have more money than they need to hold, they will spend the excess on currently produced goods and services.

Briefly stated, traditional Keynesians expect an increase in the money supply to reduce interest rates, increase investment expenditures, and stimulate growth of the GNP. So-called pure monetarists expect an increase in the money supply to increase consumption and investment expenditures, raise interest rates, and cause inflation.

See also QUANTITY THEORY OF MONEY, MONETARISM, CROWDING-OUT EFFECT.

money wages the WAGE RATES expressed in terms of current money values. An increase in the general level of prices not matched by an equivalent rise in money wages, either because of MONEY ILLUSION on the part of the labor force or because employers refuse to grant money wage increases, will cause REAL WAGES to fall. That is, an unchanged wage rate will now buy fewer goods and services at the higher level of prices.

monopolistic competition or **imperfect competition** or **imperfect market** a type of MARKET STRUCTURE. A monopolistically competitive market is one that is characterized by:

MONOPOLISTIC COMPETITION

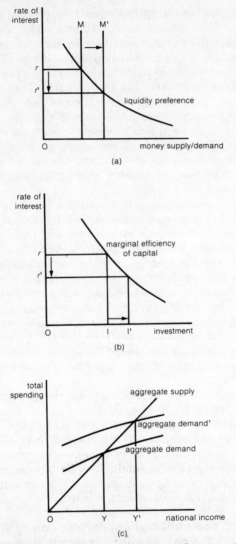

FIG. 121. **Money supply/spending linkages.** See entry. (a) Rate of interest. (b) Planned investment. (c) National income.

(a) *many firms and buyers*—the market comprises a large number of independently acting firms and buyers.

(b) *differentiated products*—the products offered by competing firms are differentiated from each other in one or more respects. These differences may be of a physical nature, involving functional features, or may be purely imaginary in the sense that artificial differences are created through ADVERTISING and SALES PROMOTION (see PRODUCT DIFFERENTIATION).

(c) *free market entry and exit*—there are no BARRIERS TO ENTRY preventing new firms from entering the market, or obstacles in the way of existing firms leaving the market. No allowance is made in the so-called theory of monopolistic competition for the fact that product differentiation by establishing strong BRAND LOYALTIES to established firms' products may act as a barrier to entry.

Apart from the product-differentiation aspects, monopolistic competition is structurally similar to PERFECT COMPETITION.

The analysis of an individual firm's equilibrium in monopolistic competition can be presented in terms of a representative firm; that is, all firms are assumed to face *identical* cost and demand conditions, and each is a profit maximizer (see PROFIT MAXIMIZATION), from which it is then possible to derive a market equilibrium position.

The significance of product differentiation is: (a) each firm has a market that is partially distinct from its competitors' markets. That is, each firm faces a downward-sloping demand curve (D in Fig. 122a), although the presence of vigorously competitive substitute products (high CROSS ELASTICITY OF DEMAND) will cause this curve to be relatively elastic; (b) the firms' cost structures (MARGINAL COST and AVERAGE COSTS) are raised as a result of incurring differentiation expenditures, that is, costs of selling.

The firm, being a profit maximizer, will aim to produce at the price (OP)—output (OQ) combination, shown in Fig. 122a, that equates marginal cost (MC) and MARGINAL REVENUE (MR). In the short term this may result in firms securing ABOVE-NORMAL PROFITS.

In the long term, above-normal profits will induce new firms to enter the market, thus depressing the demand curve faced by

MONOPOLISTIC COMPETITION

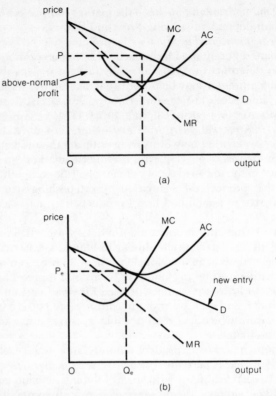

FIG. 122. **Monopolistic competition.** See entry. (a) Short-term equilibrium. (b) Long-term equilibrium.

established firms—pushing the demand curve leftward, thereby reducing the volume of sales associated with each price level. The process of new entry will continue until excess profits have been competed away. Figure 125b shows the long-term equilibrium position of the representative firm. It continues to maximize profits at a price (OP_e)—output (OQ_e) combination at which marginal cost equals marginal revenue, but now secures only a NORMAL PROFIT return. This normal profit position for the firm over time is similar to the long-term equilibrium position for a firm in perfect competition. However, monopolistic competition results in less efficient MARKET PERFORMANCE when compared with perfect competition. Monopolistically competitive firms tend to produce lower rates of output and sell output at higher prices than perfectly competitive firms. Since the demand curve slopes downward, it is necessarily tangent to the long-term average cost curve—which is higher than that of a perfectly competitive firm because of the addition of selling costs, to the left of the latter's minimum point. Firms thus operate a less than optimum scale of plant, and as a result there is EXCESS CAPACITY in the market.

monopoly a type of MARKET STRUCTURE characterized by: (a) *one firm and many buyers*—a market comprising a single supplier selling to a multitude of small, independently acting buyers; (b) *a lack of substitute products*—no close substitutes for the monopolist's product (CROSS ELASTICITY OF DEMAND is zero); and (c) *blocked entry*—BARRIERS TO ENTRY are so severe that it is impossible for new firms to enter the market.

In *static monopoly* the monopolist is in a position to set the market price. However, unlike a perfectly competitive producer (see PERFECT COMPETITION), the monopolist has marginal and average revenue curves that are not identical. The monopolist faces a downward-sloping demand curve (D in Fig. 123a) and in order to sell additional units of product, sellers must reduce the price at which all units must be sold. The objective of the monopolist, like that of the competitive firm, is assumed to be PROFIT MAXIMIZATION, and the monopolist operates with complete knowledge of relevant cost and demand data. Accordingly, the monopolist will aim to produce at the price-output combination that equates MARGINAL COST and MARGINAL REVENUE. Figure 123b indicates the short-term equilibrium position for the monopolist. The monopolist will supply Q_e output at a price of P_e. At the equilibrium price, the monopolist secures ABOVE-NORMAL PROFITS. Unlike the competitive firm situation, in which entry is unfettered, entry barriers in monopoly are assumed to be so great as to shut out new suppliers. There is no possibility of additional productive resources entering the industry, and in consequence the monopolist will continue to earn above-normal profits over the long term, until such time when supply and demand conditions change radically. Market theory predicts that given identical cost and demand conditions, monopoly leads to a higher price and a lower output than does perfect competition.

In a static monopoly, a fundamental assumption is that costs of production increase at relatively low output levels. The implication of this is that the firm reaches an equilibrium position at a size of operation that is small relative to the market. Suppose, however, that production in an industry is characterized by significant economies of scale. That is, individual firms can continue to lower unit costs by producing much larger quantities. We may illustrate this by assuming that a perfectly competitive industry is taken over by a monopolist. It is unlikely in this instance that costs would be unaffected by the change in scale of operations. Figure 123c illustrates the case in which reduction in unit costs as a result of the economies of single ownership gives rise to greater output and lower price than the original perfect competition situation.

The fall in unit costs as a result of monopolization moves the marginal cost curve of the monopolist (MC_m) to the right of the original supply curve (S_{pc}), so that more is produced (Q_m) at the lower price (P_m). We still make the assumption that marginal costs are rising over the relevant range of output. Over time, this expectation follows from the proposition that at some size economies of large scale are exhausted and diseconomies of scale set in. The diseconomies are usually associated with administrative and managerial difficulties that arise in large, complex organizations. However, there is growing evidence to the effect that the long-term average cost curve (and hence MC curve) for many capital-intensive industries is L-shaped. In these industries total demand and individual market shares, not cost considerations, limit the size of the firm. It thus may grow and find a level of output such that further expansion would be unprofitable. In doing so, however, it may become so large relative to the market that it attains a degree of power over price. This is not to deny that the monopolist could further increase output and lower price were the monopolist not trying to maximize profit. Such a position would not, however, be the result of a return to perfect competition. What has happened is that the firm, seeking its best profit position, has abandoned the

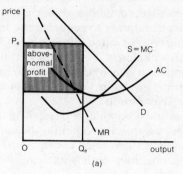

(a)

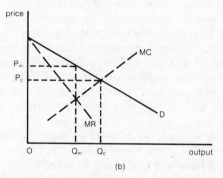

(b)

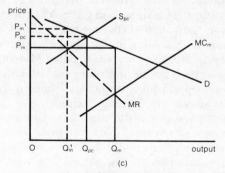

(c)

FIG. 123. **Monopoly.** See entry.

status of insignificant small competitor. It has not necessarily done so through a systematic attempt to dominate the market. On the contrary, underlying cost conditions of the market have impelled this growth. In such an industry it is possible that small, competitive-sized firms cannot survive. Moreover, to the extent that unit costs are lower at higher production levels, the large firm is a *technically more efficient* entity.

The case of significant economies of scale, then, may be characterized as one in which atomistic competition becomes technically impossible and, under an efficiency criterion, undesirable. The demonstration of competitive optimality implicitly negates this kind of complication.

The analysis developed above also neglects dynamic aspects of the market system. According to an influential group of economists, major improvements in consumer welfare occur largely as a result of technological innovations. The growth of resources and development of new techniques and products over time rather than adjustments provide maximum output from a given (static) input. Also, monopolistic elements function as a precondition and protection of innovating effort. Perfectly competitive firms certainly have the motivation to employ the most efficient known production techniques, since this is necessary to their survival. But their inability to sustain above-normal profits limits both their resources and incentive to develop new technology. By contrast, the pure monopolist, earning above-normal profits, will have greater financial resources to promote technical advance but only a weak *incentive* to innovate given the lack of effective competition. However, technological advance is a means of lowering unit costs and thereby expanding profits, and these profits will not be of a transitory nature, given barriers to entry. Moreover, technical superiority may itself be one of the monopolist's barriers to entry; hence, the monopolist must persist and succeed in the area of technological advance to maintain dominance.

SCHUMPETER was one of the most important advocates of the possibility that an industry exhibiting strong monopolistic elements may employ productive techniques superior to those of its competitive counterpart. To the extent that innovation of processes and products is centered in the large oligopolistic firm, a comparison of oligopoly/monopoly with perfect competition at a fixed technological position understates systematically the social contribution of the former.

Diagrammatically, Schumpeter's contention can be illustrated by using Fig. 123c. The competitive market produces Q_{pc}, where short-term marginal cost equals price. If this industry were monopolized, the ordinary expectation would be a price rise to $P_m{}^1$ and an output decrease to $Q_m{}^1$. However, if the monopolist in such an industry introduces cost-reduction innovations, the entire marginal cost curve may fall so that the monopolist may actually produce more (Q_m) at a lower price (P_m) than the original competitive industry, even if the monopolist fully exploits his market power.

It is, of course, possible that society will remain worse off under monopoly, even if the monopoly innovates. The benefits of innovation may not outweigh the costs of monopolistic exploitation.

See also OLIGOPOLY, MONOPOLISTIC COMPETITION, DISCRIMINATING MONOPOLIST, CONSUMERS' SURPLUS, CONCENTRATION MEASURES, PERFECT COMPETITION.

monopoly firm see DOMINANT COMPANY.

monopoly laws see ANTITRUST POLICY.

monopoly of scale see DOMINANT COMPANY.

monopoly profit the long-term ABOVE-NORMAL PROFITS accruing to a monopolist. See MONOPOLY.

monopsony a form of BUYER CONCENTRATION, that is, a MARKET situation in which a single buyer confronts many small suppliers. See MONOPOLY, BILATERAL MONOPOLY.

monotonic function a function that either increases or decreases continuously along its range. An increasing function cannot decrease below its previous stated value and vice versa for a decreasing function. For example, if disposable income has increased every year over the past 10 years, it may be considered a monotonic function because each year has seen an increase over the previous year without falling below whatever the previous year's disposable income was.

Monte Carlo simulation see SIMULATION.

moonlighter a person, either employed or unemployed and perhaps drawing unemployment benefits, who takes paid work on the side to gain extra income. For example, an out-of-work painter may paint someone's house, be paid in cash for the job, and not report the income when filing tax returns. The term "moonlighter" is also applied to people who work a second job, are paid by check, and do report the income.

moratorium the suspension of repayment of debt or interest for a specified time—for example, the freezing of debt repayment obligations extended by the government of an advanced country and by private banks to a developing country experiencing acute balance-of-payments difficulties, or the suspension of debt payments to dealers in a commodity or other market after a dramatic price collapse. See DEBT SERVICING, INTERNATIONAL DEBT.

mortgage the conveyance of an ASSET by a BORROWER (mortgagor) to a LENDER (mortgagee) as security for a loan. On completion of the obligations imposed by the legal mortgage agreement, the mortgagor has the right to have the assets reconveyed from the mortgagee. Unless the mortgagor defaults on the agreement, the mortgagee does not have the right of possession of the assets pledged for security.

most-favored nation clause an underlying principle of the GENERAL AGREEMENT ON TARIFFS AND TRADE (GATT) under which each country undertakes to apply the same rate of TARIFF to *all* its trading partners. This general principle of nondiscrimination evolved out of earlier GATT endorsement of bilateral trade treaties in which, if country A negotiated a tariff cut with country B, and country B subsequently negotiated an even more favorable tariff cut with country C, then the tariff rate applying in the second case would also be extended to A.

moving average see TIME-SERIES ANALYSIS.

multicollinearity a statistical situation in which a number of INDEPENDENT VARIABLES are highly correlated (see CORRELATION) so that they all vary together. In such situations it is impossible to disentangle the effect of any one of these independent variables on the DEPENDENT VARIABLE in REGRESSION ANALYSIS.

Multi-Fiber Arrangement (MFA) a trade pact between some 80 developed and DEVELOPING COUNTRIES that regulates INTERNATIONAL TRADE in textiles and clothing. Its purpose is to give poor countries guaranteed and growing access to markets in Europe and North America, but at the same time to ensure that this growth does not disrupt the older established textile clothing industries of the developed countries. MFA 1 (1974) allowed imports to grow by 6% a year in real terms. MFA 2 (1978) and MFA 3 (1982) involved a series of bilateral arrangements, negotiated country-to-country, product-by-product, to restrict imports of certain items where imports disrupt local market. The MFA now contains more than 3000 quotas for various countries and products.

The MFA appears to be a form of PROTECTIONISM that discriminates against the interests of the less-developed countries, many of which are highly dependent on the textile industries as a leading sector in promoting their ECONOMIC DEVELOPMENT. MFA is clearly contrary to the principles of the GENERAL AGREEMENT ON TARIFFS AND TRADE, but has been conveniently exempted from that body's rules of good conduct.

multilateral trade the INTERNATIONAL TRADE between all countries engaged in export and import of goods and services. Compare BILATERAL TRADE.

multinational firm a FIRM that produces and sells in a number of countries as distinct from a firm that produces in one country and exports to overseas markets. Direct investment by multinational firms to establish of overseas production units occurs because of the greater cost-effectiveness and profitability resulting from:

(a) *firm-specific advantages.* A firm may have a monopolistic advantage over its competitors, a patented technology or unique product, that can better be exploited and protected by direct control rather than shared with overseas producers and distributors.

(b) *locational advantages.* Direct investment enables a firm to reduce transportation costs and to keep in closer touch with local market conditions—changes in consumer tastes, competitors' actions, etc.

(c) *country-specific advantages.* Direct investment enables a firm both to avoid governmental restrictions on market access, such as TARIFFS and QUOTAS, and to take advantage of lower labor and other input costs and local investment inducements, such as cash grants and tax write-offs.

See also INTERNALIZATION, TRANSFER PRICE.

multiple-correlation coefficient a measure of the goodness of fit of an estimated multiple regression equation to the sample observations. See CORRELATION COEFFICIENT, REGRESSION ANALYSIS.

multiple linear regression see REGRESSION ANALYSIS.

multiplier the ratio of an induced change in the EQUILIBRIUM LEVEL OF NATIONAL INCOME to an initial change in level of spending. The multiplier effect denotes the phenomenon whereby some initial increase or decrease in rate of spending will bring about a more than proportionate increase or decrease in national income.

Two important features of the multiplier need to be noted: (a) it is a cumulative process rather than instantaneous effect, and as such is best viewed in terms of a series of successive additions to income; (b) the value of the multiplier depends on the fraction of extra INCOME spent on CONSUMPTION (the MARGINAL PROPENSITY TO CONSUME) (MPC) at each successive addition. The multiplier is the reciprocal of marginal propensity to save.

For simplicity, assume that all income is either consumed or withdrawn as SAVINGS. That is, the MPC and MARGINAL PROPENSITY TO SAVE (MPS) together $= 1$. The value of the multiplier (K) is then given by the formula

$$K = \frac{1}{1 - MPC} \text{ or } \frac{1}{MPS}$$

The larger an increase in consumption from an increment of income, the larger the multiplier. Thus, if MPC is 0.9, MPS is 0.1, and the multiplier value is 10. If MPC is 0.75, MPS is 0.25, and the multiplier value is only 4.

The multiplier effect is illustrated in Fig. 124a and b. With a multiplier value of 4, an initial $500 million of extra spending results in a $2 billion increase in national income, as Fig. 124a shows. In each round of spending increase, a proportion of the additional income created is saved and so leaks from the circular flow, failing to get passed on as additional consumption expenditure in the next round. When the cumulative total of these savings leakages is equal to the initial increase in spending, the multiplier process ceases and the economy reaches a new equilibrium.

Figure 124b demonstrates the multiplier effect graphically.

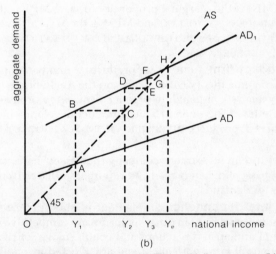

Round	Change in national income (in $ millions)	Change in consumption MPC= 0.75	Change in saving MPS= 0.25
1. Initial Increase in Spending	500	375	125
2.	375	281	94
3.	281	211	70
4.	211	158	53
5.	158	119	39
All later Rounds	475	356	119
Totals	2.000	1,500	500

(a)

(b)

FIG. 124. **Multiplier.** See entry. (a) The multiplier process. (b) The multiplier effect of increased spending on national income.

Starting at national income level OY_1, if AGGREGATE DEMAND increases from AD to AD_1, the initial injection of extra spending AB would serve to increase output and income by Y_1Y_2. This additional income would induce yet more spending (CD), which in turn would increase output and income by Y_2Y_3. This additional income would induce yet more spending (EF), which in turn would increase output and income further by Y_3Y_4, and so on. The process ends when the new equilibrium level of income Y_e is reached.

Of course, in addition to the savings withdrawal from the income flow, there are also TAXATION and IMPORT withdrawals, which further reduce the value of the multiplier. Thus, the more sophisticated multiplier is given by the formula:

$$K = \frac{1}{MPS + MPT + MPM}$$

where MPS is the marginal propensity to save, MPT is the MARGINAL PROPENSITY TO TAX, and MPM is the MARGINAL PROPENSITY TO IMPORT. See also CIRCULAR FLOW OF NATIONAL INCOME MODEL, ACCELERATOR.

multiproduct firm a FIRM that produces a number of products. Basic economic theory concentrates on the single-product firm to simplify analysis, although in practice firms often produce different varieties of the same product (product development) or several different products (DIVERSIFICATION). See PRODUCT-MARKET MATRIX.

mutual fund an investment company that issues shares on a continuing basis and stands ready to repurchase shares from shareholders on demand.

mutual interdependence an element of MARKET CONDUCT in which some or all firms in a market formulate competitive strategy in light of anticipated reactions and countermoves of rival firms. The actions of firms both affect and are affected by one another. For example, a price cut may appear to be advantageous to one firm considered in isolation, but if this results in other firms also cutting their prices to protect their sales, all firms may suffer reduced profits. Accordingly, firms may seek to avoid price competition, employing such mechanisms as PRICE LEADERSHIP to coordinate their prices. The same mutual interdependency considerations may apply to other areas of competition. For example, if one firm increases its advertising expenditures, others may follow suit to protect their market shares.

Such interdependency exists in market situations, typically in an oligopolistic market (see OLIGOPOLY), in which leading firms supply significant proportions of total market supply.

See also CARTEL, PRICE WAR, DUOPOLY, PRODUCT DIFFERENTIATION, GAME THEORY, KINKED DEMAND CURVE THEORY, LIMIT PRICING.

mutual savings banks state-chartered institutions operated for the benefit of the depositors. Their assets have traditionally been in mortgages and high-grade corporate and government securities.

Myrdal, Gunnar (1898—1987) winner of the Nobel Memorial Prize in Economic Sciences with Friedrich A. von Hayek, 1974, for pioneering work in the theory of money and penetrating analysis of the interdependence of economics, social phenomena, and institutional phenomena. In this, Myrdal foreshadowed Keynesian models of macroeconomic activity.

For the Carnegie Corporation he conducted an important study, *An American Dilemma: The Negro Problem and Modern Democracy*, 1944, which inspired further study and was cited by the US Supreme Court in desegregation decisions. In a 10-year study, *Asian Drama*, 1968, Myrdal sought to establish that only extensive reforms in population control, agricultural land distribution, health care, and education can bring about sustained growth.

N

national debt the money owed by a national government to domestic and foreign lenders. A national debt arises when a government spends more than it takes in from taxation and other receipts (BUDGET DEFICIT). This may arise, for example, because of a one-time occurrence such as the financing of a war, or it may reflect a government's commitment to an expansionary FISCAL POLICY or overestimation of revenues and underestimation of expenditures.

Concern over the size of the US national debt has been expressed ever since the period called the Great Depression, and the debt has grown especially fast in the most recent decade. In 1979 the federal government owed the public $625 billion. By the middle of 1989, the debt had grown to $2.1 trillion. To the latter sum might be added the $590 billion that state and local governments owe. How dangerous is this situation?

The burden of a debt should not be assessed by the size of the debt but by the debtor's capacity to pay. In the case of the federal government, the best measure of capacity to pay is the size of the debt in relation to the gross national product (GNP). In 1933 the national debt was about 42% of GNP, and approximately the same ratio held at the end of 1988. As a result of World War II, the national debt rose to 53% of GNP. Yet, by 1974 the ratio of debt to GNP had fallen to 24%, the lowest point since 1929.

It can be stated, therefore, that the size of the present national debt need not be frightening. At 42% of GNP, the national debt is where we have been as a nation several times in the last 50 years.

At the same time, the interest costs of the national debt can be a burden and may lead to distortion in allocating scarce resources. At the end of World War II, interest on the national debt was 7% of the federal budget and 1.5% of the GNP. In 1989, interest costs and percentage of national debt were not much more than twice those numbers at the end of World War II.

Although it is also true that about 14% of the Federal budget goes for interest on the national debt, pointing this out does not give a balanced picture of the burden. The federal government currently collects about $200 billion annually in interest owed the government.

It has been said in the past that the national debt should not be a source of worry, since it is money we owe ourselves. Indeed, US investors traditionally have held about 98% of the debt, and by 1978 foreigners held 25% of the publicly held national debt. By 1989, however, foreigners actually held less, about 19%, or about $340 billion. So, generally speaking, we still owe the money to ourselves and we should take comfort from that fact.

See BURDEN OF DEBT, GROSS NATIONAL PRODUCT.

national income the total money income received by households in return for supplying FACTOR INPUTS to business over a period of time. National income is equal to NET NATIONAL PRODUCT and consists of the total money value of goods and services produced over the time period (GROSS NATIONAL PRODUCT) less CAPITAL CONSUMPTION. See CIRCULAR FLOW OF NATIONAL INCOME MODEL.

national income accounts the most important global record for one year of the activity of an economy. These figures are computed in two ways. The *expenditure viewpoint* explains flow of product. The *income viewpoint* explains flow of costs.

The differences between the two approaches can be presented in tabular form:

Income Viewpoint	*Expenditure Viewpoint*
(FLOW OF COSTS)	(FLOW OF PRODUCT)
National Income (at factor cost)	Household Sector
	Personal Consumption
Wages	Expenditures
Rent	+
Interest	Government Sector
Profit	Purchases of Goods and Services
+	+
Nonincome Items (expense items)	Business Sector
	Gross Private Domestic

Indirect Business Taxes	Investment
Capital Consumption	+
(depreciation)	Foreign Sector
	Net Export of Goods and Services
=	=
TOTAL GROSS NATIONAL INCOME IN $	TOTAL GROSS NATIONAL PRODUCT IN $

In practice, and to avoid double counting in using the expenditure approach, the value-added method is used, that is, counting only what each stage of production has added to the final value of goods and services. For example, a farmer sells some wheat to a miller for 60 cents. The miller sells the flour he makes from it to a baker for 90 cents. The baker sells the bread he bakes from it for $1. The contribution to gross national product is $1, and not 60 cents plus 90 cents plus $1. The value added is 60 cents plus 30 cents plus 10 cents = $1.

If the national income figures are corrected for size of population and stated in real rather than money terms, international comparisons can be drawn, and a crude measure of welfare can be derived. Many international agencies prefer to use gross domestic product (GDP) in place of GNP.

Gross National Product (GNP)
    minus
Capital Consumption Allowances (depreciation) (CCA)
    equals
Net National Product (NNP)
    minus
        Indirect Business Taxes (IBT)
           equals
        National Income (NI)
    minus
                Income Earned But Not Received
           Corporate Income Taxes (CIT)
           Undistributed Corporate Profit (UCP)
           Social Insurance Contributions (SIC)
              plus
                Income Received But Not Earned

           Transfer Payments (TP)
   equals
      Personal Income (PI)
   minus
      Personal Taxes (PT)
   equals
      Disposable Personal Income (DPI)
         out of which come
            Personal Consumption Expenditure (PCE)
            Personal Savings (PS)
   Expressed symbolically:
   GNP − CCA = NNP
   NNP − IBT = NI
   NI − CIT + UCP + SIC + TP = PI
   PI − PT = DPI
   DPI = DCE + PS

nationalization the public ownership of industry. In a CENTRALLY PLANNED ECONOMY, most or all of the country's industries are owned by the government. Resources are allocated, and the supply of goods and services determined in accordance with a NATIONAL PLAN. In a MIXED ECONOMY, some industries are owned by the government, but the supply of most goods and services is undertaken by PRIVATE ENTERPRISE ECONOMY industries operating through the MARKET mechanism. The extent of public ownership of industry depends on political ideology, with advocates of central planning seeking more nationalization, and proponents of private enterprise favoring little or no nationalization.

The main economic justification for nationalization in nonsocialist societies relies heavily on the NATURAL MONOPOLY argument. Some goods and services can be provided more efficiently by a monopoly supplier, because ECONOMIES OF SCALE are so great that only by organizing the industry on a single-supplier basis can full advantage be taken of cost savings. Natural monopolies are particularly likely to arise where the provision of a good or service requires an interlocking supply network as, for example, in gas, electricity, and water distribution, and railroad services. In these cases laying down competing pipelines and train tracks would involve unnecessary duplication of resources and extra expense. Significant production economies of scale are associated with capital-intensive industries, such as iron and steel manufacture. In other instances, however, the economic case for nationalization is far less convincing. Industries or individual firms may be taken over because they are losing money and need to be reorganized, or because there is political concern over loss of jobs.

A private enterprise MONOPOLY could, of course, also secure the same efficiency gains in production and distribution as a government monopoly, but the danger exists that it might abuse its position of market power by monopoly pricing. The government monopolist, by contrast, may seek to promote the interests of consumers by charging fair prices. Opponents of nationalization argue, however, that government monopolists are likely to dissipate the cost savings arising from economies of scale by internal inefficiencies (bureaucratic rigidities and control problems giving rise to X-INEFFICIENCY), and the danger is that such inefficiencies could be exacerbated over time by government subsidy of unprofitable activities.

The problem of reconciling supply efficiency with other economic and social objectives of governments further complicates the picture. For example, the government may force nationalized industries to hold down their prices to help in controlling inflation, but by squeezing the industries' cash flow, the longer term effects of this might be to reduce their investment programs. Nationalized industries may be charged with social obligations. For example, they may be required by the government to provide train, postal, and telephone services to remote rural communities even though these are totally uneconomic.

Thus, assessing the overall relative merits and demerits of nationalization is difficult. See MARGINAL COST PRICING, AVERAGE COST PRICING, PUBLIC UTILITY, PRIVATIZATION.

National Labor Relations Act known better as the *Wagner Act* of 1935, the basic federal law governing labor relations. This act, which applies only to workers who produce goods for interstate commerce, identifies unfair labor practices of employers that can interfere with the right of self-organization of employees. It provides a mechanism whereby employees can choose their representatives in a union election, and for a National Labor Relations Board to enforce the provisions of the Wagner Act.

The Wagner Act assisted the *CIO* (Committee for Industrial Organization) in its effort to organize workers in the mass production industries, and the years from 1935 to 1940 witnessed the most rapid growth of union membership in US history.

During World War II, however, there were some disruptive strikes and the attitude became prevalent that unions had become too powerful. As a result, in 1947, Congress passed a series of amendments to the National Labor Relations Act, collectively known as the *Taft-Hartley Act*, designed to reduce the power of unions.

national plan a long-term plan for development of an economy. Such plans usually cover a period of 5 years or more and attempt to remove bottlenecks to economic development by coordinating growth of various sectors of the economy through appropriate investment and manpower planning. National plans are formulated by government agencies in CENTRALLY PLANNED ECONOMIES, and by collaboration between government, industry, and labor unions in MIXED ECONOMIES. See also INDICATIVE PLANNING.

national product the total money value of goods and services produced in a country over a given time (GROSS NATIONAL PRODUCT). Gross national product less CAPITAL CONSUMPTION or depreciation is called NET NATIONAL PRODUCT, which is equal to NATIONAL INCOME.

natural monopoly a situation in which ECONOMIES OF SCALE are so significant that costs can only be minimized when the entire output of an industry is supplied by a single producer, making supply costs lower under MONOPOLY than under conditions of PERFECT COMPETITION and OLIGOPOLY. The natural monopoly proposition is the principal justification for the NATIONALIZATION of industries, such as electricity and gas. See MINIMUM EFFICIENT SCALE.

natural rate of economic growth see HARROD ECONOMIC GROWTH MODEL.

natural rate of unemployment see NONACCELERATING INFLATION RATE OF UNEMPLOYMENT.

natural resources the contribution to productive activity made by land, for example, a factory site or farm, and basic raw materials such as iron ore, timber, oil, and wheat. Natural resources are one of the three main FACTORS OF PRODUCTION, the other two being LABOR and CAPITAL.

near money any easily salable (liquid) ASSETS that perform the function of MONEY as a STORE OF VALUE, but not that of a universally acceptable MEDIUM OF EXCHANGE. Debate continues on the extent to which liquid assets are money. See MONEY SUPPLY.

necessary condition a condition indispensable for achieving an objective. A necessary condition is usually contrasted with a *sufficient condition,* which is viewed as the adequacy of a condition to achieve an objective.

For example, an increase in INVESTMENT is a necessary condition in achieving higher rates of ECONOMIC GROWTH, but it is not a sufficient condition to generate growth insofar as other factors, such as an increase in the LABOR FORCE, also contribute to raising growth rates.

negative income tax a proposed tax system aimed at linking taxation and welfare payments systems for low-income or no-income members of society. This would be done by replacing the separate systems for collecting taxes and for providing welfare benefits by a single system that combines the two by establishing a common stipulated minimum income level, taxing those above it and giving *tax credits* to those below it.

Proponents of the negative income tax point to its advantages in encouraging people to work and in making labor markets more flexible. See POVERTY TRAP.

neoclassical economics a school of economic ideas based on the writings of MARSHALL et al. that superseded CLASSICAL ECONOMIC doctrines toward the end of the nineteenth century. Frequently referred to as the marginal revolution, neoclassical economics involved a shift in emphasis away from classical economic concern with the source of wealth and its division between labor, landowners, and capitalists toward study of the principles governing optimal allocation of scarce resources to given wants. The principles of DIMINISHING MARGINAL UTILITY were founded in this new school of economic thought.

neo-Keynesians those economists who tend to support to a greater or lesser degree the main thrust of KEYNES'S arguments and who have subsequently revised and built on the theory Keynes propounded. See DOMAR ECONOMIC GROWTH MODEL, HARROD ECONOMIC GROWTH MODEL.

net book value the accounting value of a FIXED ASSET in a firm's BALANCE SHEET that represents its original cost less cumulative DEPRECIATION charged to date.

net national product the GROSS NATIONAL PRODUCT less CAPITAL CONSUMPTION or depreciation. It takes into account the fact that a proportion of a country's CAPITAL STOCK is used up in producing this year's output.

net present value see DISCOUNTED CASH FLOW.

net profit the difference between a firm's TOTAL REVENUE and all EXPLICIT COSTS. In accounting terms, net profit is the difference between GROSS PROFIT and the costs involved in running a firm.

net worth in accounting terms, total assets minus total liabilities. Net worth is the amount of money that would result from company LIQUIDATION.

New International Economic Order (NIEO) an economic and political concept that advocates fundamental changes in the conduct of INTERNATIONAL TRADE and ECONOMIC DEVELOPMENT to redress the economic imbalance between DEVELOPED COUNTRIES and DEVELOPING COUNTRIES. The United Nations responded to the call of developing countries for such a change by issuing the *Declaration and Program of Action on the Establishment of a New International Economic Order* in 1974, which laid down principles and measures designed to improve the relative position of the developing countries. These initiatives have centered on promotion of schemes, such as (a) INTERNATIONAL COMMODITY AGREEMENTS to support developing countries' primary produce exports; (b) negotiation of special trade concessions to enable developing countries' manufactured exports to gain greater access to markets of developed countries; (c) encouragement of a financial and real resource transfer program of ECONOMIC AID; and (d) increased economic cooperation between developing countries.

These aspirations have been pursued primarily through the

UNITED NATIONS CONFERENCE ON TRADE AND DEVELOPMENT, but as yet have met with little success.

new issue market see CAPITAL MARKET.

newly industrializing country a DEVELOPING COUNTRY that has moved away from exclusive reliance on primary economic activities, mineral extraction and agricultural and animal produce, by establishing manufacturing capabilities as a part of a long-term program of INDUSTRIALIZATION. Brazil, Mexico, and Hong Kong are examples of newly industrializing countries. See STRUCTURE OF INDUSTRY, ECONOMIC DEVELOPMENT.

new protectionism the use of such devices as EXPORT RESTRAINT AGREEMENTS, local content requirements, and import licensing arrangements, which serve to restrict INTERNATIONAL TRADE. See GENERAL AGREEMENT ON TARIFFS AND TRADE, PROTECTIONISM, BEGGAR-MY-NEIGHBOR POLICY.

Nobel Memorial Prize in Economic Sciences the most prestigious international award in economics. In the 22 years that the prize has been awarded, 1969—1990, 17 American economists have received the prize.

nominal price 1. a PRICE that is minimal in relation to the true worth of a PRODUCT or FACTOR INPUT. There are a number of reasons why a token price may not reflect true market value. It could be that no market exists in which a price can be determined. Again, limited amounts of a product may deliberately be priced at much less than the product's true market value, as part of a special sales promotion. 2. a price of a FINANCIAL SECURITY. See PAR VALUE.

nominal (coupon) rate of interest the RATE OF INTEREST payable on the face value of a BOND. For example, a $1000 bond with a 5% nominal rate of interest would generate a nominal return of $50 a year. See EFFECTIVE RATE OF INTEREST.

nominal rate of protection the actual amount of PROTECTION accorded domestic suppliers of a final product when a TARIFF is applied to a competing imported final product. For example, assume that initially the same domestic product and imported product are both priced at $100. If an AD VALOREM TAX of 10% is now applied to the imported product, its price will increase to $110.

This allows domestic VALUE ADDED and prices to rise by up to $10, with the domestic product still remaining fully competitive with the imported product. The nominal rate of protection accorded to domestic suppliers is thus 10% of the price of the imports. Compare EFFECTIVE RATE OF PROTECTION.

nominal values the measurement of an economic aggregate, for example, GROSS DOMESTIC PRODUCT, in terms of current prices. Because of price changes from year to year, observations based on current prices can obscure an underlying trend. See REAL VALUES.

nonaccelerating inflation rate of unemployment (NAIRU) or **natural rate of unemployment** the underlying level of UNEMPLOYMENT consistent with a stable rate of INFLATION. Development of inflationary EXPECTATIONS among those who conduct union/management negotiations may have caused the nonaccelerating inflation rate of unemployment to rise over recent decades. See PHILLIPS CURVE, EXPECTATIONS-ADJUSTED/AUGMENTED PHILLIPS CURVE.

nondiscretionary monopoly policy a policy on the control of MONOPOLY that involves stipulation of acceptable standards of MARKET STRUCTURE and MARKET CONDUCT and prohibits any breach of these standards. See MONOPOLY POLICY.

nonmarketed economic activity any economic activity that, although usually legal, is not recorded in the NATIONAL INCOME ACCOUNTS of a nation. Labor and other inputs used in such activities are not paid cash for the work done and are therefore unrecorded. Examples of such activities are unpaid cooking and cleaning by housewives and unpaid charity work by voluntary organizations. Such omissions distort international comparisons of gross national income figures not least because rural areas tend to be more self-sustaining, whereas urbanized areas tend to purchase what they need rather than make it themselves, for example, milk, bread, etc. See BLACK ECONOMY.

nonparametric statistics a branch of STATISTICS in which the PARAMETERS of a POPULATION distribution are *not* predetermined. That is, no assumptions have to be made about the shape of the population distribution before the technique can be used. Nonparametric statistical tests can be undertaken on data not truly numerical. For instance, on ordinal scale data, tests can be carried out on the ranking of variables. Such tests are sometimes called ranking tests. Compare PARAMETRIC STATISTICS.

nonprice competition see METHODS OF COMPETITION, PRODUCT DIFFERENTIATION.

nonsystematic risk the part of total risk within the CAPITAL ASSET PRICING MODEL uniquely attributable to holding a specific security. Unlike SYSTEMATIC RISK or market risk, nonsystematic risk is independent of general market variations. Events unique to a security may result from corporate decisions, such as dividend policy, changes in capital structure, and recruitment of top personnel. Changes in a firm's share price may be positive or negative depending on the opinion of investors. The argument is that such nonsystematic variations occur randomly, so if a sufficiently large and well diversified portfolio of stocks is held, variations will cancel each other out, that is, tend toward zero. This means that if investors can eliminate unique risk by diversifying their portfolio, their concern about the riskiness of holding an asset is represented totally by the linear relationship of the BETA COEFFICIENT of systematic risk. The two components of risk, systematic and nonsystematic, are sometimes referred to as *nondiversifiable* and *diversifiable*, respectively, for the reasons outlined. See also RANDOM WALK.

normal curve see NORMAL DISTRIBUTION.

normal distribution a special kind of PROBABILITY DISTRIBUTION whose CONTINUOUS DISTRIBUTION (the *normal curve*) has a bell-shaped symmetrical pattern that extends indefinitely at both ends. The normal curve has the special property of being definable in terms of its MEAN and STANDARD DEVIATION. Once these are known, it is possible to calculate the height of the curve (the frequency) corresponding to any numerical value. As with other continuous distributions, it is also possible to estimate the probability of getting a numerical value between two numbers by the corresponding area under the curve.

The standard normal distribution is a normal distribution whose scale has been changed so that it has a normal curve with a zero mean and unit standard deviation (see Fig. 125). This standard normal curve has a total area equal to 1.0, and the probability of getting a particular numerical value that is a given number of standard deviations to the left or right of the mean can be estimated directly from the area under the curve (as in Fig. 125). Where distributions can be approximated by a standard normal curve, about 68% of cases fall within one standard deviation of the mean; 95% of cases fall within two standard deviations of the mean; and 99% of cases fall within three standard deviations of the mean.

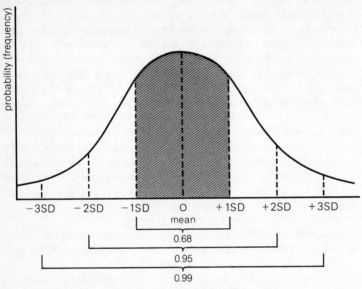

FIG. 125. Normal distribution. See entry.

The normal curve is widely used in analyzing economic data, especially in HYPOTHESIS TESTING.

normal product a good or sevice for which the INCOME ELASTICITY OF DEMAND is positive; that is, as income rises, buyers purchase more of the product. Consequently, when the price of such a product falls, thereby effectively increasing consumers' real income, the price cut will have the INCOME EFFECT of tending to increase quantity demanded. This will tend to reinforce the SUBSTITUTION EFFECT of a price cut, which will cause consumers to buy more of the product because it has become relatively cheaper.

This applies to most products with the exception of INFERIOR PRODUCTS, for which the income effect is negative. See PRICE EFFECT.

normal profit a PROFIT just sufficient to ensure that a firm will continue to supply its good or service, because the profit is sufficient to cover both fixed and variable costs. In the THEORY OF MARKETS, firms' COST curves thus include normal profit as an integral part of supply costs (see ALLOCATIVE EFFICIENCY).

If the level of profit earned in a particular market is too low to generate a return on capital employed comparable to that obtainable in other equally risky markets, the firm's resources will be transferred to some other use.

See OPPORTUNITY COST, MARKET EXIT, ABOVE-NORMAL PROFIT.

normative economics the study of what ought to be in economic theory, rather than what is provable. For example, the statement that people who earn high incomes *ought* to pay more income tax than people who earn low incomes is a normative statement. Normative statements reflect peoples' subjective value judgments of what is good or bad and depend on ethical considerations, such as fairness, rather than on strict economic rationale. The actual economic effects of a structure that taxes the rich more heavily than the poor, for example, on spending and saving, is a matter for POSITIVE ECONOMICS. See WELFARE ECONOMICS, PROGRESSIVE INCOME TAX, MARGINAL RATE OF TAXATION.

null hypothesis see HYPOTHESIS TESTING.

numeraire a monetary unit used as the basis for denominating international exchanges in a product or commodity, and financial settlements, on a common basis. For example, the US dollar is used as the numeraire of the oil trade; the SPECIAL DRAWING RIGHT unit is used as the numeraire of the internal financial transactions of the INTERNATIONAL MONETARY FUND, and the EUROPEAN CURRENCY UNIT is used to denominate financial transactions within the EUROPEAN MONETARY SYSTEM.

O

odd lot in a stock market transaction, a quantity of stock smaller than the established 100-share unit for active issues or the 10-share unit for specified inactive issues.

OECD see ORGANIZATION FOR ECONOMIC COOPERATION AND DEVELOPMENT.

off-balance sheet financing the payment for use of an ASSET by LEASING rather than buying it. If a company wishes to install a new $50,000 photocopier, for example, it may enter into a lease agreement and agree to pay $12,000 a year over 5 years rather than buy the copier. Each year $12,000 is charged against profits in the company's financial statement. The copier does not appear in the BALANCE SHEET as a FIXED ASSET, because the firm does not own it. Instead it shows up as an annual operating cost that can be offset against PROFIT for TAXATION purposes. Off-balance sheet financing enables a company to use expensive assets without investing large sums of money to buy them. It also enables a company to keep its LONG-TERM CAPITAL EMPLOYED as small as possible, improving its return on investment. See LEASEBACK.

offer curve see EDGEWORTH BOX.

official financing see BALANCE OF PAYMENTS.

Ohlin, Bertil (1899—1979) winner of the Nobel Memorial Prize in Economic Sciences with James Meade, 1977, for their contribution to the theory of international trade and international capital movements. Ohlin's work indicated that countries will export goods that would be relatively cheap without trade, and import goods that would be relatively expensive without trade. See HECKSCHER-OHLIN FACTOR PROPORTIONS THEORY.

Okun's Law one of the more reliable statistical associations between unemployment rates and changes in real gross national product, named for Arthur Okun (1929—1979). Okun's Law postulates that a 1% drop in unemployment will be associated with a 3% rise in real gross national product.

oligopoly a type of MARKET STRUCTURE characterized by:

(a) *few firms and many buyers*—the bulk of market supply is in the hands of relatively few large firms that sell to many small buyers.

(b) *homogeneous or differentiated products*—the products offered by suppliers may be identical or, more commonly, differentiated from each other in one or more respects. These differences may be of a physical nature, involving functional features, or may be purely imaginary in the sense that artificial differences are created through ADVERTISING and SALES PROMOTION AND MERCHANDISING (see PRODUCT DIFFERENTIATION).

(c) *difficult market entry*—high BARRIERS OF ENTRY make it difficult for new firms to enter the market.

The primary characteristic associated with the condition of fewness is known as MUTUAL INTERDEPENDENCE. Basically, when deciding on prices and other market strategies, firms must take into account the likely reactions and countermoves of competitors in response to its own moves. A price cut, for example, may appear to be advantageous to one firm considered in isolation, but if this results in other firms cutting their prices to protect sales, all firms may suffer reduced profits. Accordingly, oligopolists tend to avoid price competition, employing various mechanisms (PRICE LEADERSHIP, CARTELS) to coordinate prices.

Oligopolists compete against each other by using various product differentiation strategies (advertising and sales promotion, new product launches) to preserve and enhance profitability. Price cuts are easily matched, whereas product differentiation is more difficult to duplicate, thereby offering the chance of a more permanent increase in market share. Differentiation expands sales at existing prices, or the extra costs involved can be passed on to consumers. Differentiation by developing brand loyalty to existing suppliers makes it difficult for new firms to enter the market.

Traditional (static) market theory shows oligopoly to result in MONOPOLY-like suboptimal MARKET PERFORMANCE. Output is restricted to levels below cost minimization; inefficient firms are cushioned by a reluctance to engage in price competition; differentiation competition increases supply costs; and prices are set above minimum supply costs, yielding oligopolists ABOVE-NOR-MAL PROFITS protected by barriers to entry. As with monopoly, however, this analysis makes no allowance for the contribution that ECONOMIES OF SCALE may make to reducing industry costs and prices and the important contribution of oligopolistic competition to INNOVATION and new product development.

See KINKED DEMAND CURVE, LIMIT PRICING, PERFECT COMPETITION, MONOPOLISTIC COMPETITION, DUOPOLY, GAME THEORY.

oligopsony a form of BUYER CONCENTRATION in a market situation in which a few large buyers confront many small suppliers. See also OLIGOPOLY, BILATERAL OLIGOPOLY, COUNTERVAILING POWER.

OPEC see ORGANIZATION OF PETROLEUM EXPORTING COUNTRIES.

open economy an economy heavily dependent on INTERNATIONAL TRADE, EXPORTS and IMPORTS being large in relation to the size of the economy's NATIONAL INCOME. For such economies, analysis of the CIRCULAR FLOW OF NATIONAL INCOME MODEL must allow for the influence of exports and imports. Compare CLOSED ECONOMY.

open-market operation an instrument of MONETARY POLICY involving sale or purchase of government TREASURY BILLS and BONDS as a means of controlling the MONEY SUPPLY. If, for example, monetary authorities wish to *increase* the money supply, they will buy Treasury bills from banks and the general public. The money paid out to banks and members of the public will increase bank reserves. As money flows into the banking system, the banks' excess reserves enable them to increase their lending. This results in the multiple creation of new bank deposits and, hence, expansion of the money supply. See DEMAND DEPOSIT CREATION, RESERVES, MONEY MULTIPLIER.

operational research the study of practical problems to achieve optimum utilization of available resources for stated objectives. Industry has found many of the mathematical techniques that have been developed to be particularly applicable to practical problems it faces. Techniques such as LINEAR PROGRAMMING, CRITICAL PATH ANALYSIS, and decision theory all help in finding the optimal solution among many possibilities. Operational research has been applied in areas such as PRODUCTION, MARKET-ING, distribution, finance, and inventory control, drawing on the skills of economists, mathematicians, statisticians, accountants, and engineers.

opportunity cost or **economic cost** a measure of the economic cost of using scarce resources (FACTOR INPUTS) to produce a good or service in terms of the alternatives thereby forgone. For example, if more resources are used to produce food, fewer resources are then available to provide alcoholic drink. Thus, in Fig. 126, the PRODUCTION POSSIBILITY BOUNDARY (PP) shows the quantity of food and drink that can be produced with society's scarce resources. If society decides to increase production of food from OF_1 to OF_2, it will have fewer resources to produce drink, so that drink production will decline from OD_1 to OD_2. The slope of the production possibility boundary shows the MARGINAL RATE OF TRANSFORMATION, the ratio of the MARGINAL COST of producing one good and the marginal cost of producing the other. In practice, not all resources can be switched readily from one end use to another.

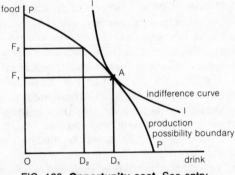

FIG. 126. **Opportunity cost.** See entry.

In the same way, if a person with limited income chooses to buy more of one good or service, he or she can only do so by forgoing consumption of other goods or services. The preference between food and drink is reflected in that person's INDIFFERENCE CURVE II in Fig. 126. The slope of the indifference curve shows the consumer's MARGINAL RATE OF SUBSTITUTION—how much of one good he or she is prepared to give up in order to release income that can be used to acquire an extra unit of the other good.

If indifference curve II is typical of all consumers' preferences between food and drink, society would settle for OF_1 of food and OD_1 of drinks, for only at point A would the opportunity cost of deploying resources (the slope of PP) correspond to the opportunity cost of spending limited income (the slope of II). See also PARETO OPTIMALITY.

optimal factor combination see DIMINISHING RETURNS.

optimal scale see PRODUCTIVE EFFICIENCY.

optimizing the maximization of society's economic welfare with respect to the macroeconomic objectives of FULL EMPLOYMENT, PRICE STABILITY, ECONOMIC GROWTH, and BALANCE-OF-PAYMENTS EQUILIBRIUM.

To simplify matters, the essence of this approach can be illustrated by reference to the PHILLIPS CURVE trade-off between unemployment (U) and inflation (I). The Phillips curve in Fig. 127 shows that inflation increases as unemployment falls and vice versa.

optimum the best possible outcome within a given set of circumstances. For example, in the theory of CONSUMER EQUILIBRIUM, a consumer with a given income who is facing set prices for products will adjust purchases of these products so as to maximize the utility or satisfaction to be derived from spending his or her limited income. Similarly, a business confronted by a given market price for its product will adjust output of that product to maximize profits. See also PROFIT MAXIMIZATION, OPTIMIZING, PARETO OPTIMALITY.

option the right to sell (*put option*) or buy (*call option*) a COMMODITY, for example, pork bellies or soy beans, or a financial ASSET, for example foreign currency or securities, at an agreed price at some future time within a stated period. Options are used primarily in connection with FUTURES MARKETS in commodities and financial assets, where prices are apt to fluctuate greatly over time and can be an effective means of HEDGING or SPECULATING.

ordinal utility a UTILITY determined by the ordering of a CONSUMER'S preferences on an ordinal scale. The consumer ranks

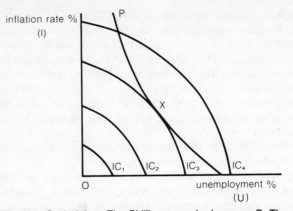

FIG. 127. **Optimizing.** The Phillips curve is drawn as P. The economic welfare of society is represented by a family of INDIFFERENCE CURVES—IC_1, IC_2, IC_3, IC_4 — indicating successively higher levels of economic welfare as the origin, O, is approached. The optimum point is at the origin, because there full employment and complete price stability are theoretically attained simultaneously. However, the Phillips curve sets a limit to the combinations of U and I that can be achieved in practice. Given this constraint, the task of the authorities is to select the combination of U and I that maximizes society's economic welfare. This occurs at point X, where the Phillips curve is tangential to indifference curve IC_3. See FIXED TARGETS.

bundles of goods and services in order of preference, the first preference giving the greatest satisfaction or utility, down to the last, which gives least.

In an ordinal scale, the magnitude between ranks is not uniform. That is, the utility gained or lost between bundles ranked one and two, is not necessarily the same as between bundles two and three, and so forth. In arithmetic scales, the difference between one inch and two inches is one inch, and between two inches and three inches is also one inch. Ordinal scales take on different and usually unmeasurable magnitudes between numbers.

Within a particular bundle of goods, the consumer is indifferent to various combinations, as shown by an INDIFFERENCE CURVE. The important thing is that rational consumer behavior must be assumed, meaning that consumers would always choose the bundle with greater utility rather than the one with lesser utility.

From this concept of ordinal utility are derived INDIFFERENCE MAPS, which are frequently used to construct DEMAND CURVES. See also CARDINAL UTILITY, DIMINISHING MARGINAL UTILITY, ECONOMIC MAN.

ordinary least squares see REGRESSION ANALYSIS.

organizational slack any organizational resources devoted to satisfying claims by subunits within the business organization in excess of the resources the subunits need to complete company tasks. Organizations tend to build up a degree of organizational slack when they operate in less competitive, oligopolistic markets (see OLIGOPOLY) in the form of excess staffing, etc. This slack provides a pool of emergency resources the organization can draw on during bad times. When confronted with a deteriorating economic environment, the organization can exert pressure on its subunits to trim organizational slack and enable the organization to continue to achieve its main goals. Faced with increasing market competition, the organization will increasingly run a tight ship as slack is trimmed, until in the limiting case of PERFECT COMPETITION, organizational slack will be zero and PROFIT MAXIMIZATION becomes the rule.

The concept of organizational slack is a particular feature of the BEHAVIORAL THEORY OF THE FIRM and is similar in many respects to the concept of X-INEFFICIENCY. See also PRODUCTIVITY.

Organization for Economic Cooperation and Development (OECD) an organization established in 1961, taking over from the Organization for European Economic Cooperation (OEEC), which was set up in 1948 to assist economic recovery in Europe after World War II as a result of the Marshall Plan. Membership in OECD numbered 24 in 1989 and included all major European countries and the United States, Canada, Australia, and Japan.

OECD provides a multinational forum for discussing economic affairs of mutual concern, particularly promotion of economic growth and international trade. OECD also coordinates provision of ECONOMIC AID to less developed countries. OECD is a primary source of international economic data and regularly publishes comparative statistics.

Organization of Petroleum Exporting Countries (OPEC) an

organization established in 1960 to look after the oil interests of Iran, Iraq, Kuwait, Saudi Arabia, and Venezuela. By 1973, eight more countries had joined the OPEC ranks: Qatar, Indonesia, Libya, Abu Dhabi, Algeria, Nigeria, Ecuador, and Gabon.

The year 1973 was to prove a watershed for the world economy. Since the early 1950s, growth rates in both the advanced and less-developed countries had been accelerating and international trade had increased even more rapidly, stimulated by expansionary policies in the advanced countries and trade liberalization (see GENERAL AGREEMENT ON TARIFFS AND TRADE). In 1973, however, OPEC wrested the initiative in controlling oil prices away from American oil companies, and the price of oil quadrupled from $2.50 to over $11.50 a barrel. The effect was to produce balance-of-payments deficits in most oil-consuming countries and with them a protracted world recession. As the recession bit, oil revenues began to fall, to which OPEC responded by increasing prices sharply again in 1979 from under $15 a barrel to about $28 a barrel.

OPEC is often cited as an example of a successful producers' CARTEL. In a classical cartel, market supply is deliberately restrained in order to force prices up by allocating production QUOTAS to each member. Interestingly, in OPEC's case because of political difficulties, formal quotas have not been used successfully to cut production until recently. The main reason it was able to increase prices in the past was that the demand for oil is highly price-inelastic. Most recently, however, OPEC has been under pressure for two reasons: (a) the total demand for oil has fallen, partly due to a world recession but also due to the fact that its high price has made it economical to substitute alternative forms of energy, coal, in particular, so oil is now less price-inelastic than formerly; (b) the increased profitability of oil production has led to a high rate of investment in new oil fields, the North Sea in particular, and this has weakened the control of OPEC over world supplies. These factors have led to a dramatic fall in the price of oil—as low as $10 a barrel in 1986—which has exacerbated pressures already evident within OPEC itself, with members disagreeing on responses to the new situation.

organization theory a behavioral framework for analysis of decision-making within large, complex organizations. Economic analysis frequently considers a FIRM to be a single autonomous unit seeking to maximize profit. By contrast, organization theory suggests that in large organizations decisions are often decentralized, that decisions are influenced by other than economic motives, and that the decision process is influenced by the company's internal structure, or organization. Nonoptimal, or *satisficing*, decisions are the result, rather than maximized profits See PROFIT MAXIMIZATION, COMPANY OBJECTIVES, SATISFICING THEORY, BEHAVIORAL THEORY OF THE FIRM.

output the GOODS and SERVICES produced using a combination of FACTOR INPUTS.

output per man-hour see PRODUCTIVITY.

outside money see EXOGENOUS MONEY.

overdraft see BANK LOAN.

overhead costs see FIXED COSTS.

overhead or **indirect costs** any COSTS not directly associated with a product, that is, all costs other than DIRECT MATERIALS cost and DIRECT LABOR cost. Production overhead (factory overhead) includes the cost of INDIRECT MATERIALS and INDIRECT LABOR along with other production expenses, such as factory heat, light, power, and depreciation of plant and machinery. The cost of factory departments, such as maintenance, materials storage, and the cafeteria that serves producing departments, are similarly part of production overhead. All selling, distribution, and administrative costs are also counted as overhead since they cannot be directly related to units of product. See also FIXED COST.

overstaffing the employment of more LABOR than strictly required to perform an economic activity efficiently. This can arise through bad work organization on the part of management or through RESTRICTIVE LABOR PRACTICES, called *featherbedding*.

oversubscription a situation in which the number of SHARES applied for in a new stock issue exceeds the numbers to be issued. This requires the underwriter responsible for handling the issue to devise a formula for allocating the shares. By contrast, *undersubscription* occurs when the number of shares applied for falls short of the number on offer, requiring the underwriter to buy the surplus shares. See CAPITAL MARKET.

over-the-counter market a secondary stock market for company STOCKS and certain government securities, for example, local authority bonds, that are not traded on the New York or the American Stock Exchange.

overtime the hours of work that are additional to those formally agreed on by the labor force as constituting the basic work week. Employers use overtime work to meet sudden increases in business activity, viewing overtime by the existing labor force as a more flexible alternative to taking on extra workers. Agreements between unions and management sometimes stipulate overtime rates. Since 1938, Federal Wage and Hour Law has required overtime pay, and overtime pay rates can be one and one half to three times the basic hourly rate.

P

Pac Man defense see TAKEOVER BID.

paradox of thrift the paradox of savings, proposing that there is an inconsistency between the apparently virtuous nature of household SAVINGS and the potentially undesirable consequences of such saving. If most households decide to save a larger proportion of their incomes, they will consume less. The resulting reduced expenditure, unless offset by increased government or investment expenditure, will lower AGGREGATE DEMAND and lead to lower levels of output and employment. Thus, an increase in savings may reduce the level of national income.

Thrift or saving is beneficial to an economy because it releases resources from the production of consumer goods to the production of investment goods. However, if households attempt to save more than businesses plan to invest at a given level of income—that is, withdrawals exceed injections in the CIRCULAR FLOW OF NATIONAL INCOME MODEL—this may cause the EQUILIBRIUM LEVEL OF NATIONAL INCOME to decline, also reducing the actual amounts saved and invested. See FALLACY OF COMPOSITION and Fig. 128.

paradox of value the proposition that the value (PRICE) of a good is determined by its relative scarcity rather than by its usefulness. Water is extremely useful and its TOTAL UTILITY is high but, because water is so abundant, its MARGINAL UTILITY (hence, its price) is low. Diamonds, by contrast, are much less useful than water, yet their great scarcity makes their marginal utility (hence, their price) high.

parameter or **coefficient** the CONSTANT terms in an EQUATION that specify the precise relationship between VARIABLES. For example, in the LINEAR EQUATION:

PARAMETRIC STATISTICS

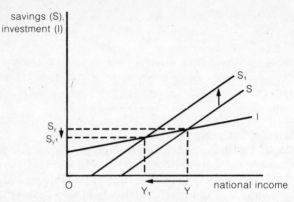

FIG. 128. **Paradox of thrift.** The savings schedule rises from S to S_1, but the rise serves to reduce the equilibrium level of national income from Y to Y_1, and the actual amount saved from S_y to S_{y1}.

$$Y = a + bX$$

the constants a and b are parameters depicting the relationship between the INDEPENDENT VARIABLE X and the DEPENDENT VARIABLE Y. Parameter a shows the value Y will take if X is zero. Parameter b shows by how much the dependent variable Y will change as the independent variable X changes. See REGRESSION ANALYSIS.

parametric statistics a branch of STATISTICS in which the parameters of a POPULATION distribution are predetermined. That is, a particular type of population distribution is assumed to be associated with the analysis. Such a technique of statistical inference may assume, for instance, that a sample was drawn from a normally distributed population. Compare NONPARAMETRIC STATISTICS.

Pareto, Vilfredo (1848—1923) Italian engineer who later became professor of economics at Lausanne University. Pareto used the mathematical principles applicable to equilibrium in mechanical systems to construct a general theory of economic equilibrium in his book *Mannuale di Economica Politica* (1906). Pareto acknowledged that utility was not measurable and argued that a purely ordinal conception of utility (see ORDINAL UTILITY) was sufficient to formulate a theory of choice. This led Pareto to use INDIFFERENCE CURVES to show how an individual's scale of preferences can be represented by an indifference map. Pareto was also known for his ideas on income distribution. See PARETO OPTIMALITY.

Pareto optimality the maximization of the economic welfare of the community.

Three conditions must hold for a Pareto optimum to be attained.

Consider a simplified economy in which two goods are produced (X and Y) and there are two consumers (A and B).

(a) *Optimal distribution of goods between consumers* requires that:

$$\frac{MU_{XA}}{MU_{YA}} = \frac{MU_{XB}}{MU_{YB}}$$

where MU_{XA} is the MARGINAL UTILITY of good X to consumer A, MU_{YA} is the marginal utility of good Y to consumer A, and so forth. This condition states that the MARGINAL RATE OF SUBSTITUTION between two goods, the ratio of their marginal utilities, must be the same for each consumer. If this were not the case, the consumers could improve their positions by exchanging goods. The consumer who values X highly relative to Y could trade some of his or her Y to the consumer who values Y highly relative to X. Only when the utility ratios are the same for both consumers is such mutually beneficial trade impossible.

(b) *Optimal allocation of inputs in productive uses*, employing two inputs, i and j, in the production of goods X and Y. Optimal utilization of inputs requires that the ratio of the MARGINAL PHYSICAL PRODUCTS of i and j employed in producing X be the same as the ratio of their marginal physical products in producing Y. That is:

$$\frac{MP_{iX}}{MP_{jX}} = \frac{MP_{iY}}{MP_{jY}}$$

PARETO OPTIMALITY

If this equality is not satisfied, one input is relatively more efficient in producing one output, and the other input therefore is relatively less efficient in producing the same output. It will thus benefit the community to divert more of the first input into its more efficient use and to divert the other input from that use. This will permit the community to expand production of one output at a constant level of resource use. Only when the marginal product ratios are the same can the community not gain by reallocating its inputs among competing uses.

(c) *Optimal amounts of output*, illustrated in Fig. 129, which depicts a transformation curve showing the quantities of goods X and Y that can be produced by using the resources of the community fully. The slope of the curve represents the MARGINAL RATE OF TRANSFORMATION, that is, the ratio of the MARGINAL COST of good X to the marginal cost of good Y. Optimal output for any pair of goods, X and Y, requires that the goods be produced in quantities such that:

$$\frac{MU_X}{MC_X} = \frac{MU_Y}{MC_Y}$$

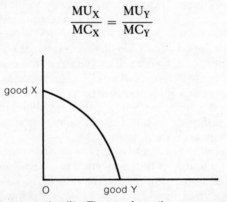

FIG. 129. **Pareto optimality.** The transformation curve or production possibility boundary.

That is, the ratio of marginal cost to marginal utility must be the same for each good, so the last dollar's worth of good X generates the same utility as the last dollar's worth of good Y, etc. This condition will be satisfied if the slope of the transformation curve, the marginal cost ratio between X and Y, is equal to the marginal utility ratio between X and Y, the marginal rate of substitution. If the ratios were unequal, the community would benefit by producing more of the good that yields the higher marginal utility per unit of marginal cost.

If all these conditions are met, it would be impossible to improve the welfare of one or more individuals without simultaneously reducing the welfare of another or others. See PRODUCTION POSSIBILITY BOUNDARY, WELFARE ECONOMICS.

Parkinson's law a satirical observation by Professor C. Northcote Parkinson suggesting that work expands according to the time available in which to do it. If this observation holds, the inefficiency it creates poses a serious organizational problem for businesses of any significant size. See ORGANIZATION THEORY, X-INEFFICIENCY.

partial correlation coefficient a measure of the strength of relationship between two VARIABLES while the influence of other variables is held fixed. Where three or more variables are correlated, the relationship between two of them may be influenced in turn by their relationship to the third variable, so the ordinary correlation coefficient between the two can give misleading indications of their precise relationship. The partial correlation coefficient shows the isolated relationship between the two variables by eliminating the interference of the third variable. Partial correlation coefficients help us examine economic data on the relationship between variables on a CETERIS PARIBUS, other things being equal, basis.

See CORRELATION COEFFICIENT, DIFFERENTIAL CALCULUS, BETA COEFFICIENTS.

partial derivative see DIFFERENTIAL CALCULUS.

partial equilibrium analysis the analysis of relationships within a subsector of an economy, for example, an individual market. The analysis proceeds on the basis that events in this sector have so insignificant an impact on other sectors that feedback effects will be negligible or nonexistent. For example, an increase in the price of carrots is unlikely to have much effect on the general price level, so any possible feedback effects can be safely ignored for purposes of analyzing the market for carrots. Thus, in partial equilibrium analysis, each subsector is treated as a self-contained entity. See GENERAL EQUILIBRIUM ANALYSIS.

participation rate the proportion of the labor force or a particular subgroup within it, such as married women, holding jobs.

par value the price printed on the face of a stock certificate, bond, or other financial instrument. For example, a corporation may issue ordinary shares with a par value of, say, $1, but its market price on the STOCK EXCHANGE may be higher or lower than this par value, depending on current demand and supply for it. Also called *face value*.

patent the grant by a government of temporary MONOPOLY rights and control over new products, processes, and techniques to their INVENTORS. Patent protection is seen as an important means of fostering TECHNOLOGICAL PROGRESS by providing an opportunity for inventors and INNOVATORS to recoup development expenses and secure a profit reward for taking risks. To minimize the danger of monopolistic exploitation, patents are granted only for limited time periods. See also PATENT OFFICE, INDUSTRIAL PROPERTY RIGHTS.

Patent Office a US governmental agency within the Department of Commerce that administers matters relating to PATENTSand TRADEMARKS.

payback 1. the period it takes for an INVESTMENT to generate sufficient cash to recover in full its original capital outlay. For example, a machine that costs $1000 and generates a net cash inflow of $250 a year will have a payback of 4 years. **2.** The return on the amount invested. See also DISCOUNTED CASH FLOW.

payoff matrix see GAME THEORY.

payroll tax a tax on a company's payroll expenditure. The tax is paid entirely by the company. Insofar as such a tax alters the relative price of LABOR and CAPITAL, it may result in the company's substitution of capital for labor. See COST FUNCTION.

penetration price a pricing policy that involves charging a comparatively low price for a product in order to secure growing sales and a high market share. This policy will be adopted by a firm when consumers are expected to be price-sensitive, that is, demand is price-elastic. See also DUMPING, SKIMMING PRICE.

pension any payment to people who have retired from paid employment, in the form of a lump sum or regular income. There are two main types of pension plans: (a) government retirement pensions under which employees and employers pay SOCIAL SECURITY TAXES over the working lives of the employees, and providing a minimum retirement income for all workers and some of their dependents. (b) occupational pensions operated by private sector employers and occasionally by unions, under which employees and employers, or employers alone, make regular contributions to a PENSION FUND or INSURANCE COMPANY plan. The amount of occupational pension workers receive depends on the amount of the regular contributions and the number of years employees have worked. Pensions are paid by pension funds and insurance companies out of the income they earn by investing in financial securities and the like. Occupational pensions may provide additional income over and above social security payments.

pension fund a financial institution concerned with management and administration of personal, company, and governmental contractual and voluntary retirement plans. Pension funds collect regular contributions from employers and sometimes their working members as well and make payments to retired beneficiaries. Pension funds specialize in long-term investments in stocks and bonds, government securities, and property. See also FINANCIAL SYSTEM, INSTITUTIONAL INVESTORS.

per capita income see INCOME PER CAPITA.

percentiles the numerical values that divide a group of numerical observations into 100 parts, each containing an equal number of observations. Compare QUARTILES, DECILES.

perfect competition or **atomistic competition** a type of MARKET STRUCTURE characterized by: (a) *many firms and buyers,* that is, a large number of independently acting firms and buyers, each firm and buyer being sufficiently small to be unable to influence the price of the product bought or sold; (b) *homogeneous products,* that is, products offered by competing firms are identical not only in physical attributes but also are regarded as identical by buyers, who have no preference between the products of various producers; (c) *free market entry and exit,* that is, there are no BARRIERS TO ENTRY— hindrances to entry of new firms—or impediments to

PERFECT COMPETITION

exit of existing sellers; (d) *perfect knowledge* of the market by buyers and sellers; and *mobility* with access of all buyer to sellers. See Fig. 130. See also ALLOCATIVE EFFICIENCY and MONOPOLISTIC COMPETITION.

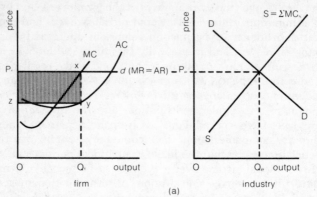

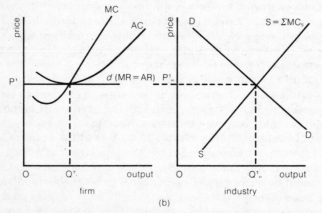

FIG. 130. **Perfect competition.** See entry. (a) Short-term equilibrium. (b) Long-term equilibrium.

perfect market see PERFECT COMPETITION.

permanent income hypothesis a hypothesis suggesting that consumption by an individual depends on his or her permanent income derived from work or from investment income. More specifically, the hypothesis, which has been proposed by Milton Friedman, suggests that an individual consumes a constant proportion of the present value of his or her income flow from work and wealth, called *permanent income*, while holding intact the wealth itself.

The annual figure for permanent income would be the total income a consumer expects to receive divided by a consumer's life expectancy in years. Permanent consumption is similar to permanent income, the relationship being essentially one of proportionality. It would include expenditure on mortgage payments, heating, lighting, and the like. Permanent income and consumption constitute the anticipated and planned elements of income and consumption.

Transitory income reflects all other factors that occur through chance or accident, such as windfalls or negative transitory income resulting from illness. Transitory consumption is the part of consumption that is not permanent, for example, expenditure on an extra holiday out of a windfall inheritance. Since individuals seek to consume a constant proportion of their permanent incomes, the result of windfall gains or losses will be changes in savings.

Friedman argues that transitory income and transitory consumption are totally unrelated to permanent income and permanent consumption and that both permanent and transitory aspects need to be investigated in order to determine the total relationship between consumption and income.

See also KEYNESIAN ECONOMICS, CONSUMPTION FUNCTION, DISPOSABLE PERSONAL INCOME, LIFE-CYCLE HYPOTHESIS, FRIEDMAN, MONETARISM.

personal distribution of income the distribution of NATIONAL INCOME classified according to the size of income received by individuals or households. The sizes of peoples' incomes differ for a variety of reasons, including differences in natural ability, educational attainment, special skills, and ownership of WEALTH. The personal distribution of original income is very unequal. For example, in 1987, 41.5% of people in the United States with a college degree earned $50,000 or more, while 0.8% of people with 6 years of schooling earned that much.

Distribution of Personal Income

Family Rank (by fifths)	% Share of Income 1973	% Share of Income 1980	% Share of Income 1987
Lowest Fifth	6	5.1	4.6
Second Fifth	12	11.6	10.8
Third Fifth	17	17.5	16.9
Fourth Fifth	24	24.3	24.1
Highest Fifth	41	41.6	43.7

From *Statistical Handbook, 1989.*

See also REDISTRIBUTION-OF-INCOME PRINCIPLE OF TAXATION, PRINCIPLES OF TAXATION, FUNCTIONAL DISTRIBUTION OF INCOME.

personal sector the part of the economy concerned with the transactions of HOUSEHOLDS. Households receive income from supplying factor inputs to other sectors of the economy and influence the workings of the economy through their spending on goods and services and SAVINGS decisions. The personal sector, CORPORATE SECTOR, and FINANCIAL SECTOR constitute the PRIVATE SECTOR. The private sector, PUBLIC (GOVERNMENT) SECTOR, and FOREIGN SECTOR make up the national economy. See also CIRCULAR FLOW OF NATIONAL INCOME MODEL.

Phillips curve a curve depicting an empirical observation, based on the work of the British economist A. W. Phillips, of the relationship between the level of UNEMPLOYMENT and the rate of change of MONEY WAGES and, by inference, the rate of change of prices (INFLATION). A fall in unemployment from A to B in Fig. 131 due to an increase in the level of AGGREGATE DEMAND brings about an acceleration in the rate of increase of money wages from C to D, reflecting employers' greater willingness to grant wage increases as the demand for their products expands. By contrast, rising unemployment and falling demand lead to a slowing in the rate of increase of money wages. The curve thus suggests there is a trade-off between unemployment and DEMAND-PULL INFLATION. However, while there has been strong empirical support of the Phillips curve relationship in the past, unemployment and inflation in recent years have tended to coexist (see STAGFLATION). This has led to attempts to reformulate the Phillips curve to allow, for example, for the effect of price expectations on money wage increases. See also EXPECTATIONS-ADJUSTED/AUGMENTED PHILLIPS CURVE.

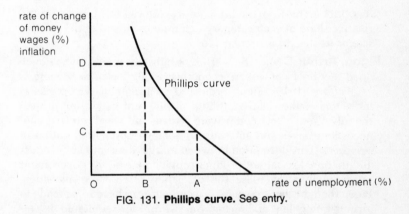

FIG. 131. **Phillips curve.** See entry.

physiocracy a school of thought or set of economic ideas based on the writings of QUESNAY and other eighteenth-century French economists and philosophers. The physiocrats felt that land was the sole source of income and wealth in society, capable of producing a so-called net product. They also believed in the idea of a natural order in society that harmonized the interests of individual citizens with the common interests of society. This made physiocrats strong proponents of individual liberty and strong opponents of government intervention in society (*laissez faire*) other than to protect individuals and their property rights.

Adam SMITH was strongly influenced by physiocratic ideas and in his hands the natural order was spelled out in the form of the workings of the market mechanism. See also PRIVATE ENTERPRISE ECONOMY.

picket a person on STRIKE or supporting a strike who seeks to discourage entry into a place of work where a labor dispute is in progress.

piecework payments any wage payments made to a person based solely on the amount of goods he or she produces. This type of wage system has declined in popularity. See also WAGE RATE, X-INEFFICIENCY.

pie chart a chart portraying data in pictorial form, showing the relative share of each category in a total by means of the relative size of its slice of a circular pie.

Pigou, Arthur Cecil (1877—1959) English economist who developed the theory of welfare economics in his book *The Economics of Welfare* (1919). Pigou preferred to accept market prices as indicators of the relative utilities of different goods, but argued that divergence between private returns and social returns could necessitate taxes and subsidies to achieve optimal allocation of resources. This distinction between marginal private net product and marginal social net product provided a case for government intervention to increase the efficiency of resource allocation. Pigou thought that interpersonal comparisons have to be made in formulating policy, and he made a case for more equitable DISTRIBUTION OF INCOME on the ground of diminishing marginal utility of income. See REAL BALANCE EFFECT.

planned economy see CENTRALLY PLANNED ECONOMY.

point elasticity a precise measure of the responsiveness of DEMAND or SUPPLY to small changes in PRICE, INCOME, etc. Taking PRICE ELASTICITY OF DEMAND (E), point elasticity may be defined as:

$$E = (-1)\frac{\%\Delta Q}{\%\Delta P}$$

where E = price elasticity of demand, %ΔQ = percentage change in quantity demanded, %ΔP = percentage change in price.

Since the DEMAND CURVE slopes downward from left to right, the ΔQ has the opposite sign to ΔP, so (−1) is added to the equation to generate a positive value for the elasticity figure. The numerical value of E signifies the degree of elasticity, that is, it lies between zero and infinity. An example of the measurement of point elasticity is given in Fig. 132.

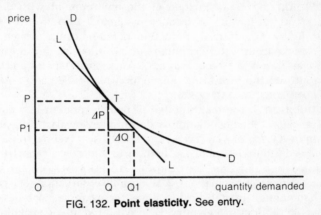

FIG. 132. **Point elasticity.** See entry.

To measure elasticity at a price P, we need to measure the slope of the demand curve at point T, where the demand curve is tangential to the straight line LL. The slope of the tangent LL is equal to ΔQ/ΔP, where the increment in output (ΔQ) is very small. This gives the formula for point elasticity:

$$E = \frac{\Delta Q}{\Delta P} \times \frac{Q}{P}$$

Where the calculated value of E is greater than 1, demand is described as elastic. Where E is less than one, but greater than zero, demand is inelastic. See also ELASTICITY OF DEMAND.

poison pill see TAKEOVER BID.

political economy until recently the common name for the study of economics, since economists were somewhat more concerned than those who followed them with the relationship between pure theory and practical action. For example, MARSHALL (1842—1924) visited the poor areas of several cities and "resolved to make as thorough a study as I could of political economy" instead of continuing in studies of mathematics.

poll tax a tax levied at a fixed rate per capita. See LUMP-SUM TAXES.

pollution the contamination of the environment with dirty or harmful substances. A frequently quoted EXTERNALITY when dealing with industrial production, pollution can take such forms as smoke from factory chimneys or hazardous chemical waste. It is considered to be a cost of ECONOMIC GROWTH and a negative input into the measure of economic welfare. See also WELFARE ECONOMICS, SOCIAL COSTS.

population 1. the total number of people resident in a country. The size of the population is determined by past and present BIRTH RATES, DEATH RATES, and MIGRATION trends. In most advanced industrial countries, both birth and death rates have declined for a long time (see DEMOGRAPHIC TRANSITION), producing slow growth of populations. **2.** all possible observations of a certain phenomenon in statistical analysis, for example, incomes of all people resident in a country. Where it is too time-consuming and expensive to record all possible observations, it is necessary to take a SAMPLE, for example, the incomes of 1000 citizens, and generalize about the incomes of all citizens from this sample. See also STATISTICAL INFERENCE.

population census see CENSUS.

population trap a situation in which a country's rate of POPULATION growth is greater than its attainable rate of ECONOMIC GROWTH. As a consequence INCOME PER CAPITA declines, and the problem of alleviating mass poverty is made worse. To remedy this situation, it may be necessary for a government to try to influence population growth. See DEMOGRAPHIC TRANSITION.

portfolio the set of FINANCIAL SECURITIES held by an investor or institution. Typically, investors will want to hold a variety of financial securities to spread their risks. They may also seek a mixture of types of financial securities, some offering high short-term DIVIDEND payments and others offering long-term capital appreciation when their market prices rise significantly. See PORTFOLIO THEORY.

portfolio theory the study of the way in which an individual investor may theoretically achieve maximum expected return from a varied PORTFOLIO of FINANCIAL SECURITIES with a given level of RISK AND UNCERTAINTY. Alternatively, the portfolio may achieve for the investor a minimum amount of risk for a given level of expected return. Return on a security comprises INTEREST or DIVIDEND, plus or minus any CAPITAL GAIN or loss from holding the security over a given time period. The *expected* return on securities within the portfolio is the weighted average of the expected returns on individual INVESTMENTS in the portfolio. The important thing, however, is that the risk attaching to a portfolio— its STANDARD DEVIATION—is less than the weighted average risk of each individual investment.

See also CAPITAL ASSET PRICING MODEL, EFFICIENT MARKET HYPOTHESIS.

positive economics the study of what can be verified rather than what ought to be. For example, the statement that a cut in personal taxes increases consumption spending in the economy is a statement that can be confirmed or refuted by examining available empirical evidence on the effects of taxation on spending. Positive economics seeks to identify relationships between economic variables, quantify and measure these relationships, and make predictions of what will happen if a variable changes. Compare NORMATIVE ECONOMICS.

potential entrant a FIRM willing and able to enter a MARKET under the right conditions. In the THEORY OF MARKETS, potential entry turns into actual entry into a market when (a) existing firms in the market are earning ABOVE-NORMAL PROFITS and (b) newcomers are able to overcome any BARRIERS TO ENTRY.

Actual new entry plays an important regulatory role in a market in removing above-normal profits and in expanding market supply. (See, for example, PERFECT COMPETITION.) However, the mere threat of potential entry may in itself be sufficient to ensure that existing firms supply the market efficiently and set prices consistent with supply costs.

Potential entrants to a market may be newly established firms, firms that currently supply the market with inputs or are currently its customers (*vertical entry*), or firms that currently operate in other markets and want to expand their activities in new directions (*diversified entry*).

See also CONDITION OF ENTRY, MARKET ENTRY, VERTICAL INTEGRATION, DIVERSIFICATION, CONTESTABLE MARKET.

potential gross national product (GNP) the maximum level of OUTPUT an economy is capable of producing at a point in time by fully utilizing all available FACTOR INPUTS. Productive potential depends on the size of the LABOR FORCE and the average level of labor PRODUCTIVITY, that is, output per worker. The level of productivity itself depends on the current state of technology, the amount of CAPITAL STOCK per worker, and the CAPITAL-OUTPUT RATIO. See Fig. 133.

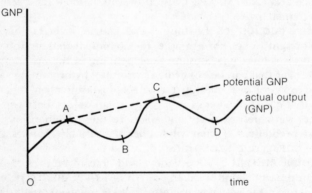

FIG. 133. **Potential gross national product.** The difference between potential GNP and actual GNP.

In practice the level and rate of growth of potential GNP are difficult to measure. See BUSINESS CYCLE, EQUILIBRIUM LEVEL OF NATIONAL INCOME, GROSS NATIONAL PRODUCT.

pound the standard CURRENCY unit of Britain and a number of other countries, mainly current and former members of the British Commonwealth. When used in international transactions, the UK pound is referred to as STERLING to distinguish it from any other country's pound, such as the Lebanese or Egyptian pound.

poverty a widening area of economic research. In addition to welfare costs, there are large social costs associated with the numbers of people having low incomes, for example, cost of crime, cost of poor health, and low productivity associated with low levels of education. The importance of studying human capital has been reinforced by increasing concern over poverty, so studies of the sources and consequences of poverty now occupy a niche in economic analysis.

poverty trap a situation in which unemployed persons receiving welfare payments are not encouraged to seek work because their after-tax earnings potential in work is *less* than the benefits currently obtained by not working. Given that welfare benefits may represent some minimum standard of living, the problem is how to reconcile this with the so-called work ethic. One suggested way is for a government to provide employers with subsidies that enable them to pay wages higher than the minimum level of welfare payment, even though the MARGINAL REVENUE PRODUCT of the work undertaken does not warrant it. It will thus be to people's economic advantage to obtain employment, and in so doing they may acquire work experience and skills that improve their long-term earnings potential.

Alternatively, the overlap between entitlement to welfare payments, based on one set of income scales, and the threshold level of income at which people begin to pay taxes, based on a different set of income scales, can be removed by introduction of a NEGATIVE INCOME TAX. Such a unitary tax system replaces means-tested welfare entitlement on the one hand, and PROGRESSIVE TAXATION on the other. Under this unitary tax system, people pay taxes when they are employed and earning more than a stipulated minimum income, and they receive a tax rebate to bring their income up to the stipulated minimum level when unemployed or when earning less than the minimum. See also SUPPLY-SIDE ECONOMICS.

precautionary demand for money in the Keynesian analysis, a demand for money balances to be held by individuals and firms to provide a safety net for the uncertainties of everyday life, for example, repairing storm damage to one's home or, in the case of a firm, incurring a particularly large or unexpected bad debt. Precautionary and transaction balances are sometimes considered together, since they are both a positive function of INCOME, the balances tending to increase as income increases. Compare TRANSACTION DEMAND FOR MONEY, SPECULATIVE DEMAND FOR MONEY. See also MONEY DEMAND SCHEDULE, LIQUIDITY PREFERENCE, L.M. SCHEDULE.

predatory pricing a pricing policy pursued by a firm or group of firms with the intention of harming rival suppliers or exploiting the consumer. Examples of the former include PRICE SQUEEZING and selective price cuts to drive competitors out of the market, while exploitation of the consumer comes about through overpricing by MONOPOLY suppliers and CARTELS.

preference/similarity theory an explanation of INTERNATIONAL TRADE in manufactured products based on consumer demand for product variety, for example, the EXPORT from West Germany of cars to, and the import of cars from, Japan.

The theory postulates that domestic suppliers specialize in manufacture of the kinds of products demanded by the majority of domestic consumers, but are able to export some of their output to countries where such products appeal to a minority of consumers. By the same token, the minority of domestic consumers may have slightly different demands, which can be satisfied by imports from countries where such tastes are those of the majority. Since the kinds of products demanded in a country are determined in large measure by level of per capita income, most exchanges of manufactures take place between countries of a similar industrial structure, each exporting and importing essentially similar products. Through trade, the variety of manufactured products available to consumers is extended, and the gain from trade derives not from lower prices, as emphasized by the conventional theory of COMPARATIVE ADVANTAGE, but from being able to consume the precise brand or variety of product demanded.

See also INTRA-INDUSTRY TRADE, THEORY OF INTERNATIONAL TRADE.

preferred stock a FINANCIAL SECURITY issued to individuals and institutions that provides long-term financing for corporations. Preferred stock pays a fixed dividend and generally is given priority over common stock in payment of dividends. In the event the corporation is liquidated, holders of preferred stock have first claim on assets of the business reamining after all creditors have been paid. Generally, preferred stockholders have no voting rights at company ANNUAL MEETINGS.

premium **1.** an addition to the published LIST PRICE of a good or service charged by a supplier to customers. **2.** the sale of stocks and bonds at a price above nominal value. In markets where shares have no nominal value, it involves sale of shares above current market price. **3.** the purchase of a particular company's issued stock or bonds at a price above the average market price of those of other companies operating in the same area. The higher price reflects investors' optimism about the company's prospects. **4.** a general rise in prices of all stocks and bonds to higher levels in anticipation of an upturn in the economy. **5.** the extent to which a foreign currency's market EXCHANGE RATE rises above its official exchange rate under a FIXED EXCHANGE-RATE SYSTEM. **6.** the payment made to an insurance company for an insurance policy. See also SPECULATIVE DEMAND FOR MONEY.

present value see DISCOUNTED CASH FLOW.

price the money value of a unit of a GOOD, SERVICE, ASSET, or FACTOR INPUT. In some markets, for example, see PERFECT COMPETITION, price will be determined entirely by the forces of DEMAND and SUPPLY. In other markets, for example, MONOPOLY markets, powerful suppliers have considerable discretion over the prices they charge. In certain circumstances, prices may be subjected to governmental PRICE CONTROL or regulated by means of PRICES AND INCOMES POLICY. See also EQUILIBRIUM MARKET PRICE, ADMINISTERED PRICE.

price competition a form of rivalry between suppliers involving an attempt to win customers by offering a product at a lower price than competitors offer.

Price competition is especially beneficial to consumers insofar as it results in establishment of prices consistent with the real costs of supplying the product improves the RESOURCE ALLOCATION

PRICE CONTROLS

efficiency of the market by eliminating inefficient, high-cost suppliers (see PERFECT COMPETITION). From the suppliers' point of view, price competition may be something to be resisted, because it reduces the profitability of the market and so, where conditions permit, for example, in an OLIGOPOLY, suppliers may attempt to avoid price competition.

See PRICE LEADERSHIP, PRICE PARALLELISM, COLLUSION, METHODS OF COMPETITION.

price controls the specification by a government of minimum and/or maximum prices for goods and services. Price may be fixed at a level below the EQUILIBRIUM MARKET PRICE or above it, depending on the objective in mind. In the former case, for example, the government may wish to keep the price of some essential good such as food down as a means of assisting poor consumers. In the latter case, the aim may be to ensure that producers receive an adequate return (see PRICE SUPPORT). More generally, price controls may be applied across a wide range of goods and services as part of a PRICES AND INCOMES POLICY aimed at combatting INFLATION. See also RATIONING.

price discrimination the ability of a supplier to sell the *same* product in a number of separate MARKETS at *different* prices. Markets can be separated in a number of ways, including by geographical location, for example, domestic and foreign; the nature of the product itself, for example, original and replacement parts for automobiles; and users' requirements, for example, industrial and household electricity consumption.

Price discrimination can be both beneficial and detrimental, for example, discriminating prices may be used as a means of ensuring that a plant produces at full capacity, thereby enabling economies of large-scale production to be attained. On the other hand, price discrimination may be used as a means of increasing monopoly profits. See DISCRIMINATING MONOPOLIST.

price-earnings ratio a ratio used to appraise a quoted public company's profit performance that expresses the market PRICE of the company's stock as a multiple of its profit. For example, if a company's profit amounts to $1 a share and the stock is selling for $10, its price-earnings ratio is 10:1. When a company's prospects are considered by the stock exchange to be good, it is likely that the company's stock price will rise above the average to yield a higher price-earnings ratio. See EARNINGS PER SHARE.

price effect the effect of a change in price on the quantity demanded of a product. See Fig. 134.

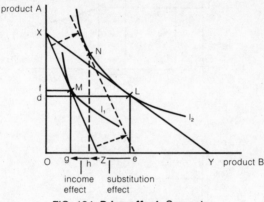

FIG. 134. **Price effect.** See entry.

See also GIFFEN GOOD, CONSUMER EQUILIBRIUM, THEORY OF DEMAND, INCOME EFFECT, SUBSTITUTION EFFECT, NORMAL PRODUCT.

price elasticity of demand a measure of the degree of responsiveness of DEMAND to a given change in price:

$$\text{elasticity of demand} = \frac{\% \text{ change in quantity demanded}}{\% \text{ change in price}}$$

If a change in price results in a more than proportionate change in quantity demanded, then demand is *price-elastic* (Fig. 135a). If a change in price produces a less than proportionate change in the quantity demanded, then demand is *price-inelastic* (Fig. 135b).

At the extremes, demand can be perfectly price-inelastic, that is, price changes have no effect on quantity demanded, which shows up as a straight-line vertical demand curve; or demand can

PRICE ELASTICITY OF DEMAND

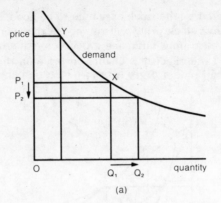

(a)

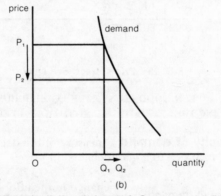

(b)

FIG. 135. **Price elasticity of demand.** See entry. (a) Elastic demand. (b) Inelastic demand.

be perfectly price-elastic, that is, any amount will be demanded at the prevailing price, which shows up as a straight-line horizontal demand curve.

TOTAL REVENUE—price times quantity demanded—will be affected by price changes. Where demand is price-elastic, a small cut in price will generate a large increase in quantity demanded, so a price cut will serve to increase total revenue and a price rise will serve to reduce total revenue. By contrast, where demand is price-inelastic, a large cut in price will generate only a small increase in quantity demanded, so a price cut will serve to reduce total revenue, and a price rise will serve to increase total revenue. Where demand has *unitary elasticity*, the percentage price cut will be matched by an offsetting percentage change in quantity demanded and total revenue remains the same.

It must be stressed, however, that the price elasticity of demand can vary along the length of a given demand curve. For example, although in Fig. 135a the demand curve as a whole is elastic in configuration, it is more elastic at point X than at point Y.

The concept of demand elasticity is useful to firms in setting product prices, including PRICE DISCRIMINATION, and to governments in setting rates of indirect taxes to raise revenue. See also PRICE ELASTICITY OF SUPPLY, POINT ELASTICITY.

price elasticity of supply a measure of the responsiveness of SUPPLY to a change in PRICE:

$$\text{elasticity of supply} = \frac{\%\ \text{change in quantity supplied}}{\%\ \text{change in price}}$$

If a change in price results in a more than proportionate change in quantity supplied, supply is price-elastic (Fig. 136a). If a change in price produces a less than proportionate change in the quantity supplied, supply is price-inelastic (Fig. 136b).

At the extremes, supply can be perfectly price-inelastic, that is, price changes have no effect at all on quantity supplied, which shows up as a straight-line vertical supply curve; or supply can be perfectly price-elastic, that is, any amount will be supplied at the prevailing price, which shows up as a straight-line horizontal supply curve.

The degree of responsiveness of supply to changes in price is affected by the length of time involved. In the near term, when full capacity is being utilized, supply can only be increased in response to an increase in demand/price by working existing plants more intensively, but this usually adds only marginally to

PRICE ELASTICITY OF SUPPLY

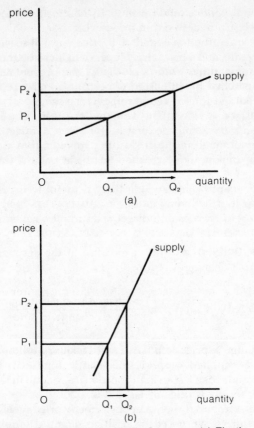

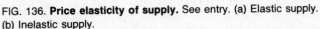

FIG. 136. **Price elasticity of supply.** See entry. (a) Elastic supply.
(b) Inelastic supply.

total market supply. Thus, in the near term the supply curve tends
to be relatively price-inelastic. Over time, however, firms are able
to enlarge supply capacities by building additional plants and by
extending existing ones. As a result, supply conditions tend to be
more price-elastic over the long term. However, in some cases (for
example, petrochemicals) supply responses may not occur until
passage of 5 years or more.

price equilibrium see EQUILIBRIUM MARKET PRICE.

price fixing the establishment of a common price for a good or service by a group of suppliers acting together, as opposed to suppliers setting their prices independently. Price fixing is often a feature of an unregulated OLIGOPOLY market. See RESTRICTIVE TRADE AGREEMENT, COLLUSION, CARTEL, ADMINISTERED PRICE.

price index a weighted average of prices of all goods and services produced in an economy measured over time. Price indices can be used to measure the rate of INFLATION and as a GNP DEFLATOR.

A commonly used price index in the United States is the *Consumer Price Index (CPI)*, which measures the average level of the prices of a fixed basket of goods and services bought by final consumers. Each item in the index is weighted according to its relative importance in total consumers' expenditure. Starting from a selected base year (index value = 100), price changes are then reflected in changes in the index value over time. Thus, if 1970 = 100 and in 1995 the index value were to stand at 200, this would indicate that retail prices on average had doubled between the two dates.

It should be noted that beginning with the winter of 1988, the base period of the CPI has been reset as 1982—1984 = 100. See also PURCHASING POWER.

price leader a firm that establishes the market price for a good or service and initiates price changes that then are followed by competing suppliers. Two forms of price leadership have been identified: (a) DOMINANT COMPANIES, whose powerful positions in a market enable them to secure compliance with their prices by smaller rivals; (b) *barometric price leaders*, whose recognized adeptness at establishing prices fully reflective of market conditions makes other suppliers willing to accept their price changes.

Leader-follower relationships are a typical feature of OLIGOPOLY markets in coordinating price changes, and tend to result in a strong degree of PRICE PARALLELISM. See PRICE LEADERSHIP.

price leadership a means of coordinating oligopolistic price behavior (see OLIGOPOLY), enabling firms to secure high profits. One example of price leadership is that of leadership by a DOMINANT COMPANY having cost advantages over competitors. In Fig. 137, firm A is the low-cost supplier, with a MARGINAL COST curve MC_A, and firm B has higher costs, with a marginal cost curve MC_B. The individual demand curve of each firm is dd when they set *identical* prices (that is, it is assumed that total industry sales at any price are divided equally between the two firms), and mr is the associated MARGINAL REVENUE curve. Firm A can maximize profits by producing output OQ_A (where $MC_A = mr$) at a price of OP_A. Firm B would like to charge a higher price (OP_B), but the best it can do is accept the price set by firm A, even though this means less than maximum profit. Given firm B's conjecture about reactions of firm A to any price change by B, any alternative course of action would mean even less profit. If B were to charge a higher price than P_A, it would lose sales to firm A, whose price is unchanged, moving left along a new kinked demand curve segment KP_B. If B were to cut its price below P_A, firm A would undertake matching price cuts, moving right along the demand-curve segment Kd. Firm B could not hope to win such a PRICE WAR because of its higher costs. Thus, firm B's best course of action is to charge the same price as that established by firm A.

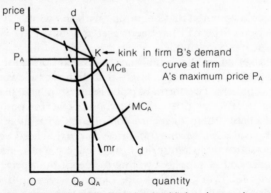

FIG. 137. **Price leadership.** Price leadership by a low-cost company. See entry.

Two additional types of price leadership may be seen: (1) *barometric price leadership*, in which the price leader may change—as the weather changes; and (2) *collusive price leadership*, in which under conditions of oligopoly, firms with somewhat similar market shares and demand and cost conditions do not choose to contest the wishes of others in setting prices for their market.

price level the general level of prices in an economy, as measured by a PRICE INDEX. Price levels in consecutive time periods are often compared as an indication of INFLATION rates.

price parallelism the tendency in an OLIGOPOLY market for suppliers to charge identical prices. Parallel prices may come about because suppliers, recognizing their MUTUAL DEPENDENCE, desire to avoid price competition, which reduces their profits, or they may come about as a result of deliberate COLLUSION between suppliers to fix prices, which maximizes their profits.

See also PRICE LEADERSHIP, CARTEL.

prices and incomes policy a policy concerned with controlling INFLATION by *directly* attempting to halt or slow down the INFLATIONARY SPIRAL of price and pay increases, in contrast with deflationary MONETARY POLICY and FISCAL POLICY, which may work *indirectly* to achieve the same result. The basic rationale advanced for a prices and incomes policy is that whereas deflationary monetary and fiscal policies can only control inflation by increasing the rate of unemployment, a rigorously applied prices and incomes policy can check inflation *and* maintain high levels of employment.

A prices and incomes policy can be operated on a voluntary or a compulsory basis. In the former case, an appeal is made to the collective responsibilities of firms not to increase prices unduly and for labor unions to moderate demands for wage increases. Such exhortations, however, are easily ignored. A compulsory policy has more chance of success, certainly in the medium term, if it is backed by strong penalties for noncompliance. Typical elements of the compulsory approach include: (a) an initial, brief freeze (6 months—1 year) on all price and wage increases; (b) a following period, usually phased to allow for gradual relaxation of controls, in which either (i) general norms are laid down for permitted prices and wages, for example, limiting them to 3% a year, or (ii), more specifically, the establishment of formulas for linking permitted price and wage increases—in the case of a price rise to nonabsorbable cost increases, and in the case of a wage rise to increases in productivity. The latter approach requires establishment of some regulatory body to ensure that proposed price and wage increases are justified.

Proponents of a prices and incomes policy see it as a useful way of defusing inflationary expectations, thereby removing the danger of accelerating inflation rates. It must be recognized that because such a policy interferes with the operation of market forces, it is likely to produce distortions in factor and product markets. See MACROECONOMIC POLICY, ALLOCATIVE EFFICIENCY, INFLATION.

price squeezing a type of RESTRICTIVE TRADE AGREEMENT in which vertically integrated firms (see VERTICAL INTEGRATION) are able to injure nonintegrated competitors. This arises when integrated firms produce both a raw material and finished goods, while the nonintegrated firms produce only finished goods and must rely on the integrated firms for their raw material supplies. A squeeze is applied if the integrated firms charge the nonintegrated firms a high price for the raw material and sell the finished product at a price that allows nonintegrated firms only minimal profits or forces losses on them.

Situations can also arise in which integrated firms produce raw materials and finished goods, while nonintegrated firms produce only the raw material but have to rely on the integrated firms as a market for their raw materials. A squeeze is applied if the integrated firms pay a low price for the raw material from nonintegrated firms, but a high price for the raw material from integrated firms, allowing the nonintegrated firms only minimal profits or forcing losses on them.

price stability the maintenance of an unchanged general level of prices over time in an economy. Price stability, especially the avoidance of rising prices, is one of the main objectives of MACROECONOMIC POLICY.

price support a means of supporting the incomes of certain producers by administratively maintaining the prices of their products above market price. In many countries, price support systems are used to assist the agricultural sector by ensuring an adequate level of total farm incomes. In Fig. 138, the EQUILIBRIUM MARKET PRICE is OA. If this price is considered too low to remunerate farmers adequately, the government will set a support price, say OB, at which it is prepared to buy up any unsold output. At the support price of OB, the government is then committed to acquiring the unsold output of CF at a total cost equal to the shaded area CFGH. The main problems with the price support method are that it penalizes consumers and results in wasteful overproduction. The price support method is used as the basis of the common AGRICULTURAL POLICY of the EEC. Compare INCOME SUPPORT.

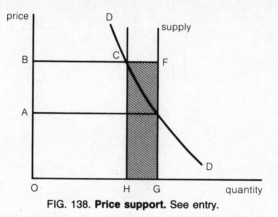

FIG. 138. **Price support.** See entry.

price system or **market mechanism** a characteristic of an economy in which basic decisions about what to produce, how to produce it, and how products (incomes) are to be distributed are determined by interaction of buyers and sellers in product and factor markets, as indicated in Fig. 139a.

In a PRIVATE ENTERPRISE ECONOMY, or a MIXED ECONOMY with a significant private sector, the current levels of output and consumption of products are the result of the decisions of households and firms being put into operation through the price system as they carry out transactions in markets. The firm is a key element in the market system operating in product markets in which it sells products, and in factor markets in which it buys or hires resources. The price system embraces both types of markets and broadly operates so as to ensure that resources are allocated in accordance with consumer demand, that is, under conditions of consumer sovereignty.

The price system can provide a sophisticated mechanism for

PRICE SYSTEM

(a)

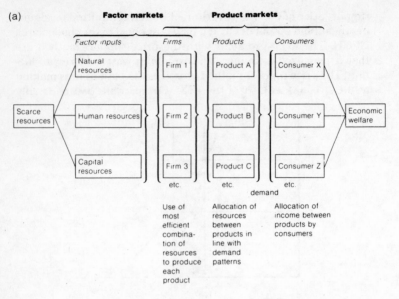

(b)

	Product markets		**Factor markets**	
	Pea market	Carrot market	Pea inputs	Carrot inputs
Short Run	D = S	D = S	DF = SF	DF = SF
	D↑	D↓		
	D > S	D < S		
	P↑	P↓		
	Pr↑	Pr↓		
Long Run	market entry	market exit	DF↑	DF↓
	S↑	S↓	DF > SF	DF < SF
	P↓	P↑	Pf↑	Pf↓
	Pr↓	Pr↑		
	D = S	D = S		

Key: D = product demand; S = product supply; P = price of products;
Pr = profits of suppliers; Pf = price of factor input; SF = factor
supply; DF = factor demand

FIG. 139. **Price system.** See entry.

allocating resources in an automatic way. However, it is not necessarily as nearly perfect a resource allocator as it may appear. First, the response of supply within the price system to changes in consumer demand may be slow and painful, because less efficient firms are not eliminated quickly but continue in business making losses. Secondly, resources are not always as mobile occupationally or geographically as the model implies, especially when workers require significant training to acquire appropriate skills. Thirdly, the price system cannot ensure provision of certain COLLECTIVE PRODUCTS such as highways, which are enjoyed in common by all consumers, because no markets exist for such products. Finally, efficient functioning of the price system depends crucially on the structural characteristics of product and factor markets. With PERFECT COMPETITION in product and factor markets, the price system might well operate along the lines of the previous example. By contrast, where markets are characterized by MONOPOLY or OLIGOPOLY with high BARRIERS TO ENTRY, firms are not free to enter or leave product markets at will in response to profit opportunities. For example, if a particular market is dominated by a monopoly supplier, when faced with an increase in demand, the monopolist may decide not to expand supply, preferring to exploit the increased demand by raising selling price. In the long term, consequently, the monopolist earns above-normal profits, and no extra factor inputs are devoted to production as consumer demand requires. See CENTRALLY PLANNED ECONOMY, THEORY OF MARKETS.

price taker a business that sells its output at a fixed price determined by market forces, as in PERFECT COMPETITION, or by government-imposed PRICE CONTROLS.

price theory the subject matter of MICROECONOMICS and to a lesser degree of MACROECONOMICS, price theory is concerned with the determinants of exchange values in product and factor markets. The efforts of price theorists are directed at explaining the prices firms must pay to factors of production, and the prices consumers must pay in the product market. They consider how prices are shaped by the structure and practices of an industry and its factor and product markets. Further, they must consider the forces that determine the general domestic price levels of a country as well as price levels in international trade.

PRICE WAR

See THEORY OF DEMAND, THEORY OF SUPPLY, THEORY OF MARKETS, THEORY OF CONSUMER BEHAVIOR, THEORY OF THE FIRM, OLIGOPOLY, MONOPOLY.

price war any competition between rival suppliers centered on aggressive price cutting. Price wars may break out when demand for a product is depressed and there is EXCESS SUPPLY capacity in the market. Again, if FIXED COSTS are a high proportion of total costs, suppliers may be tempted to cut their prices to maintain full working capacity.

Price warfare is beneficial to the consumer and to RESOURCE ALLOCATION within the market insofar as it serves to eliminate inefficient, high-cost suppliers. The problem from the suppliers' point of view is that cutthroat price competition reduces the profitability of the market and everybody finishes up worse off. For this reason suppliers, particularly OLIGOPOLY suppliers, will normally try to avoid price wars and direct their competitive efforts into PRODUCT DIFFERENTIATION. See METHODS OF COMPETITION.

primary sector the part of the economy concerned with extraction of raw materials and provision of food. The primary sector, INDUSTRIAL SECTOR, and SERVICE SECTOR form an interlocking chain of economic activities that constitute a modern economy. See STRUCTURE OF INDUSTRY.

prime cost or **direct cost** the sum of direct materials cost and direct labor cost of a product. Prime cost tends to vary proportionately with the level of output.

prime rate the RATE OF INTEREST charged by COMMERCIAL BANKS for short-term LOANS to their best customers. The prime rate is somewhat lower than other commercial borrowing rates but only applies to so-called blue-chip companies, generally large companies with the highest credit ratings. See BANK LOAN.

principles of taxation the rationale underlying use of the various methods of TAXATION. There are three main principles of taxation: ABILITY-TO-PAY PRINCIPLE OF TAXATION, BENEFITS-RECEIVED PRINCIPLE OF TAXATIONand REDISTRIBUTION-OF-INCOME PRINCIPLE OF TAXATION.

private costs the costs—EXPLICIT COSTS and IMPLICIT COSTS—incurred by firms for the use of FACTOR INPUTS in producing their OUTPUTS. Compare SOCIAL COSTS.

private enterprise economy or **free market economy** or

capitalism a method of organizing an economy to produce GOODS and SERVICES. Under this ECONOMIC SYSTEM, the means of production are privately held by individuals and firms. Economic decision-making is highly decentralized, and resources are allocated through a large number of goods and services markets. The MARKET synchronizes decisions of buyers and sellers and, by establishing an EQUILIBRIUM PRICE, determines how much of a good will be produced and sold and which factors will be employed.

See CENTRALLY PLANNED ECONOMY, MIXED ECONOMY, NATIONALIZATION, PRIVATIZATION, PRICE SYSTEM.

private placement the issuance of new securities, bonds, etc., to a selected group of investors rather than to the investing public at large. See CAPITAL MARKET.

private sector the part of the economy concerned with transactions of private individuals, businesses, and institutions (the PERSONAL SECTOR, the CORPORATE SECTOR, and the FINANCIAL SECTOR, respectively). The private sector and PUBLIC SECTOR make up the domestic economy, and together with the FOREIGN SECTOR make up a nation's economy.

privatization the denationalization of an industry, transferring it from public to private ownership. The extent of government ownership of industry depends much on political ideology, with CENTRALLY PLANNED ECONOMY proponents seeking more NATIONALIZATION, and advocates of PRIVATE ENTERPRISE ECONOMY favoring little or no nationalization.

probability the likelihood of a particular uncertain event occurring, measured on a scale from 0.0 (impossible) to 1.0 (inevitable). People generally estimate probabilities on the basis of the relative frequency with which an event has occurred in the past under given circumstances, and generalize from this experience. In some circumstances it is easy to estimate the proportion of occasions on which an event occurs. For example, the probability of getting heads when flipping a balanced coin is 0.5, because with such a coin in the long run we would get 50% heads and 50% tails. In estimating probabilities in business situations, however, there may be no experiences or only a few that are useful in gauging the relative frequency of an event. See also RISK AND UNCERTAINTY.

PROBABILITY DISTRIBUTION

probability distribution a theoretical FREQUENCY DISTRIBUTION showing the expected frequency with which a particular event is likely to occur on average. For example, the PROBABILITY distribution for the likelihood of getting a head when flipping a balanced coin would be:

number of heads	probability
0	0.5
1	0.5

See NORMAL DISTRIBUTION, BINOMIAL DISTRIBUTION.

process ray a line depicting the path a firm can follow in expanding OUTPUT where technical constraints mean that FACTOR INPUTS must be used in fixed proportions in a given production process. Figure 140 shows the production options open to a firm that has a choice between processes A, B, and C, each of which uses capital and labor in fixed proportions. If this firm wanted to produce, say, 100 units of output per period then it could produce 100 units by settling at point d using process A, or point e using process B, or point f using process C. However, it cannot choose any combination of inputs along the lines joining d, e, and f because such intermediate combinations are not technically feasible. See ISOQUANT CURVE.

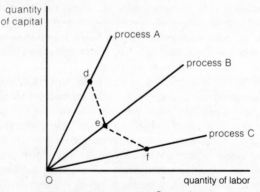

FIG. 140. **Process ray.** See entry.

producer or **supplier** the basic producing-supplying unit of economic theory. In economic theory, a producing unit is usually a

416

FIRM, although some government organizations also produce goods and services.

producer goods CAPITAL GOODS and other goods such as fuel and lubricants, which are used as FACTOR INPUTS in the production of other products, as opposed to being sold directly to consumers. Compare CONSUMER GOODS.

producer price index the oldest continuous statistical data series of the Bureau of Labor Statistics. It is designed to measure average changes in prices by producers of all commodities at all stages of processing. It is based currently on 3400 commodity price series and uses, with 1982 as the base year.

producers' surplus the excess of actual earnings by a producer from a given quantity of output, over and above the amount the producer would be prepared to offer before withdrawing from the market altogether. Alfred MARSHALL considered that such excess earnings occurred over the earnings of the marginal firm in an industry, which led to various producers in the industry obtaining ECONOMIC RENTS and QUASI-RENTS in the short term. Quasi-rents are sometimes included in economic rents. Producers' surplus is directly analogous to CONSUMERS' SURPLUS and is shown in Fig. 141.

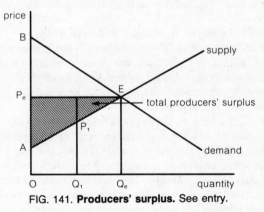

FIG. 141. **Producers' surplus.** See entry.

At any point along the segment of the supply curve AE, the producer would be willing to supply the appropriate quantity and

PRODUCT

would still receive a greater price, OP_e (the EQUILIBRIUM MAR-
KET PRICE), than he or she would be prepared to sell at. For
example, the producer would be prepared to supply the intramarginal quantity OQ_1 at a price of OP_1, although in fact receiving
the market price OP_e, yielding a producers' surplus, $P_1 P_e$. The
total of all such producers' surpluses is indicated by the shaded
area $AP_e E$. Under conditions of PERFECT COMPETITION, the individual producer faces a perfectly horizontal DEMAND CURVE, and
as long as firms produce a combined output of OQ_e, no producers'
surplus will accrue. The corollary is that producers must operate
in imperfectly competitive markets (MONOPOLISTIC COMPETI-
TION, OLIGOPOLY, and MONOPOLY) to achieve a producers' surplus. Consumers' surplus is the triangle bounded by $P_e BE$. Both
producer and consumer surpluses have implications for ALLOCA-
TIVE EFFICIENCY and WELFARE ECONOMICS.

product a generic term covering both GOODS and SERVICES.

product characteristics model a THEORY OF CONSUMER BE-
HAVIOR that shows how CONSUMERS choose between a number of
brands of a product, each of which offers particular product characteristics in fixed proportions. For example, consumers buying
prune juice may be looking for two principal product characteristics—flavor and vitamin content. Three brands of prune juice are
available—Brand A, Brand B, and Brand C—each of which is differentiated insofar as it places a different emphasis on the two
product characteristics. The three brands are represented by the
rays in Fig. 142, which show the fixed proportions of product
characteristics in each brand. Brand A, for example, has high vitamin content but little flavor. Brand C, by contrast, has a lot of
flavor but low vitamin content.

Points a, b, and c on these rays show how much of each brand
of juice can be bought for a given unit of expenditure at the
prevailing prices of the three brands. To find the consumer's utility maximizing choices, it is necessary to introduce a set of indifference curves, I_1, I_2, and I_3, showing the consumer's preferences
between the two product characteristics. The consumer's final
choice will be Brand B, as he or she settles at point b on the highest
indifference curve, I_3, consistent with limited expenditure.

See CONSUMER EQUILIBRIUM, INDIFFERENCE CURVES, PROD-
UCT DIFFERENTIATION.

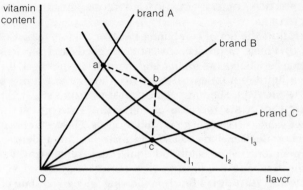

FIG. 142. **Product characteristics model.** See entry.

product differentiation an element of MARKET CONDUCT denoting the ways in which suppliers may distinguish their own product from the products of competitors. Product differentiation is a form of nonprice competition (see MARKET COMPETITION). On the supply side, products may be differentiated according to differences in quality, location, performance, innovative or novel features, design, styling, and packaging. On the demand side, imaginary differences may be cultivated between products, through ADVERTISING emphasizing imputed or subjective qualities: better than, cleaner and whiter than, etc. The more ignorant buyers are of the relative qualities and performance of competing brands, the more susceptible they are likely to be to persuasive advertising.

The purpose of such differentiating activity is to secure an initial demand for the firm's products and, by cultivating BRAND LOYALTIES, ensure that sales are increased or at least maintained. The significance of product differentiation is that it increases the possibilities of competitive action, with firms facing off on quality, advertising, etc., rather than price alone.

Although product differentiation is often referred to as a form of market imperfection, this should not be interpreted to mean that heterogeneity is bad. Genuine differences among products in particular imply great diversity and more choices for consumers. See also PRODUCT CHARACTERISTICS MODEL, MONOPOLISTIC

PRODUCTION

COMPETITION, OLIGOPOLY, HOMOGENEOUS PRODUCTS, MARKET STRUCTURE.

production the act of combining FACTOR INPUTS (labor, capital, etc.) by FIRMS to produce OUTPUTS of goods and services. The relationship between inputs and outputs in physical terms is shown by the PRODUCTION FUNCTION and in cost terms by the COST FUNCTION. See FACTORS OF PRODUCTION.

production costs the costs of converting FACTOR INPUTS into higher value OUTPUTS of goods and services. The costs of manufacturing products include costs of raw materials, labor, depreciation and maintenance of plant and equipment, rent, taxes, lighting, and heating. See also PRODUCTION FUNCTION, COST FUNCTION.

production function a function showing for a given state of technological knowledge the relationship between physical quantities of FACTOR INPUTS and physical quantities of OUTPUT involved in producing a good or service. Since the amount of output depends on the quantities of inputs used, the relationship can be depicted thus in FUNCTIONAL NOTATION:

$$Q = f(I_1, I_2 \ldots I_n)$$

where Q = output of a product and I_1, I_2, etc., are quantities of the various factor inputs 1, 2, etc. used in producing that output.

It is important to emphasize that factor inputs can be combined in a number of different ways to produce the same amount of output. A method that is technically the most efficient is the one that may use only small amounts of labor, while another method may employ large quantities of labor and little capital. In physical terms, the method that is *technically the most efficient* is the one that uses the fewest inputs. Economists, however, are more concerned with the cost aspects of the input-output relationship, specifically the least costly way of producing a given output. See also COST FUNCTION, COBB-DOUGLAS PRODUCTION FUNCTION.

production possibility boundary or **transformation curve** a method of illustrating the economic problem of SCARCITY. The production possibility boundary shows the maximum amount of goods and services that can be produced by an economy at a given period of time with available resources and technology. Figure

143 shows a production possibility boundary for cars and hospitals, assuming that all resources are fully employed in the most efficient way. Point A represents the maximum production of cars if no hospitals are produced. Point B represents the maximum production of hospitals if no cars are produced. At any point along the boundary, such as C, there is a trade-off between the two goods. Car production can be expanded *only* by taking resources away from production of hospitals.

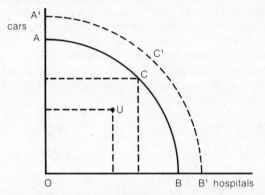

FIG. 143. **Production possibility boundary.** See entry.

The boundary is curved rather than a straight line because not all resources are equally efficient in producing the two goods. Thus, near point A, where a large number of cars are being produced and few hospitals, large numbers of construction workers have been diverted from hospital construction to make cars. As it is unlikely they will be as efficient working on an assembly line as in construction, when we move from point C to point A, the production possibility curve flattens. By contrast, near point B where large numbers of hospitals are being built and few cars, large numbers of workers have been diverted from making cars to doing construction work, and since they are likely to be less efficient at the latter than the former, as we move from point C to point B the boundary steepens.

The point labeled U indicates UNEMPLOYMENT. More of both

goods can be produced as idle resources are employed up to the limit set by the production possibility boundary. The broken line A^1B^1 shows how the production possibility boundary tends to move outward over time as a result of long-term ECONOMIC GROWTH, which increases potential output. How far out the boundary moves and how quickly depend on the rate of economic growth.

See also OPPORTUNITY COST, LINEAR PROGRAMMING.

productive efficiency an aspect of MARKET PERFORMANCE denoting the efficiency of a market in producing current products at lowest possible cost in the long term, using existing technology. Productive efficiency is achieved when output is produced in plants of optimal scale and when there is a long-term balance of market supply and demand. See Fig. 144. See also MINIMUM EFFICIENT SCALE, TECHNOLOGICAL PROGRESSIVENESS, EXCESS CAPACITY, RATIONALIZATION.

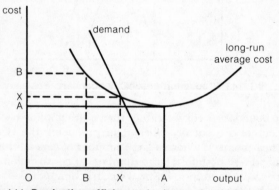

FIG. 144. **Productive efficiency.** In the graph, which assumes a U-shaped long-term AVERAGE COST curve, plant size OA results in minimum cost. If plant sizes are suboptimal (OB) or if optimal-sized plants (OA) are underutilized because of a shortfall in demand (OX), then actual supply costs will be higher than attainable costs.

productive potential see POTENTIAL GROSS NATIONAL PRODUCT.

productivity the relationship between the OUTPUT of an economic unit and the FACTOR INPUTS that have gone into producing the output. Productivity is usually measured in terms of *output per man-hour* to facilitate interfirm, interindustry, and intercountry comparisons. Productivity increases when output per man-hour is raised. The main source of productivity increases is the use of more efficient workers and more and better CAPITAL STOCK (see CAPITAL WIDENING and CAPITAL DEEPENING).

This important point can be illustrated in the following three stages. (a) Suppose, initially, that the assembly of a car is a labor-intensive operation; it takes a team of 10 men working with a minimal amount of capital—wrenches and screwdrivers only— one whole day to assemble one car. (b) The firm now invests in hydraulic lifting gear (CAPITAL DEEPENING), and this cuts down considerably the amount of time needed for aligning parts for assembly, reducing the time it takes to complete the assembly operation to, say, a tenth of a day. The same team of men now can assemble 10 cars a day—their productivity has gone up tenfold. (c) The firm introduces a continuous flow assembly line with automatically controlled machines (again, capital deepening) that one man can operate. Output increases to, say, 50 cars a day, and productivity of the remaining man has increased from 1 car a day (a tenth of 10 cars) to 50.

Just as importantly, nine men have been released from the team. Either they all can be put to work on a similar automated assembly line (capital widening), in which case the total output of the 10 men would be 500 cars a day (10×50), compared with 50 before, or they can be redeployed outside the automobile industry, thereby helping to increase output in other sectors of the economy. Studies have demonstrated that investment in human capital can have a potent effect on increasing productivity.

Increased productivity thus makes an important contribution to the achievement of higher rates of ECONOMIC GROWTH.

See also CAPITAL-OUTPUT RATIO, SPECIALIZATION, QUALITY CONTROL, RESTRICTIVE LABOR PRACTICE, WORK STUDY, X-INEFFICIENCY, ORGANIZATIONAL SLACK, HUMAN CAPITAL.

product life cycle the assumption that a typical sales pattern is followed by a product over time as changing consumer tastes and technological INNOVATION cause new products to emerge that supersede existing products. The typical life cycle followed by a product introduced into a market is depicted in Fig. 145. It has four main phases:

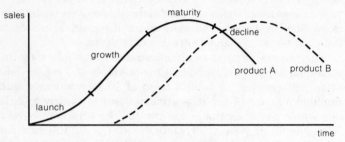

FIG. 145. **Product life cycle.** See entry.

(a) *product launch*, which follows successful development of a new product and proceeds to national launch. When the product is first put on the market, sales volume will be low until consumer resistance has been overcome, and at this stage the market is frequently limited to high-income consumers.

(b) *product growth phase*, in which the product gains market acceptance and sales grow rapidly as the product reaches the mass market. During this phase competitors may begin to enter the field with rival products, so the distinctiveness of the original product fades.

(c) *product maturity*, in which sales are largely limited to repeat purchases by existing customers, since the majority of potential customers have already made their first purchases. At this stage the market is saturated, so competitors are unable to benefit from market growth and must compete intensely to maintain or increase their share of the constant market.

(d) *product decline*, in which sales begin to decline as consumer tastes change or superior products are launched. If left to follow this downward trend, the product will eventually die as sales fall to low levels, although managers may decide to phase out the product long before this.

Most companies market a number of products and must formulate a product-range strategy, providing for a regulated process of new product launches, with new products, such as B in Fig. 145, growing while older products, such as A, reach maturity. This enables companies to maintain an appropriate PRODUCT MIX of newly launched products, growth products, and mature lines.

A company's pricing policy for a product may be related to the stages of the product's life cycle. During the launch phase, managers will tend to opt for a high *skimming price*, which capitalizes on the new and distinctive nature of the product and the temporary monopoly power it provides. In this early stage, demand for the product is likely to be less price-elastic (see PRICE ELASTICITY OF DEMAND), for high prices will not deter high-income pioneer consumers. Furthermore, a high price will reinforce the quality image of the largely untried product as well as recouping research and development costs and heavy promotion expenditures. During the growth phase, managers may change to a low *penetration price*, lowering price to bring the product within reach of the mass of consumers. At this stage, demand is likely to be more price-elastic, for the average consumer is more price-conscious than the pioneer consumer. By lowering price, the firm can expand sales appreciably, gaining cost savings from large-scale production, and can maintain a large market share in the face of entry by competitors. Once the maturity phase is reached with several similar products firmly established in the market, prices will tend to stay in line, for any attempt by one firm to reduce its price and expand its market share will provoke retaliation as competitors fight to maintain market share.

Similarly, other elements of the marketing mix, such as advertising and sales promotion, need to be adapted to the phases of the product life cycle. But it should be kept in mind that recent research has disclosed that the theory does not have as much significance as originally suggested. See also PRODUCT PERFORMANCE.

product life cycle theory a theory seeking to explain changes in the pattern of INTERNATIONAL TRADE over time, which is based on a dynamic sequence of product INNOVATION and diffusion. Four phases of the cycle can be postulated. (a) As new products are introduced, the consuming country is likely to be the producing country because of the close association between innovation and demand. This original producing country, typically an advanced industrial country, becomes an exporter to other high-income countries. (b) Production begins in other leading industrial coun-tries, and the innovating country's exports to these markets are displaced. (c) As these countries' own demand for the product reaches sufficient size to enable producers to take advantage of economies of scale, they too become net exporters, displacing the innovating country's exports in nonproducing countries. (d) Fi-nally, as the technology and product become increasingly stan-dardized to the point where relatively unskilled labor can be used in the production process, DEVELOPING COUNTRIES with lower costs become exporters of the product, further displacing the in-novating country's exports. Meanwhile, however, the innovating country has moved on to the production of new products. See also TECHNOLOGICAL GAP THEORY, THEORY OF INTERNATIONAL TRADE.

product-market matrix a matrix for analyzing the scope for change in a firm's product-market strategy. Figure 146 shows the matrix, which depicts products on one axis and markets on the other. A firm seeking to achieve profit and growth in changing market conditions has four major strategies available: (a) more effective penetration of existing markets by existing products, in-creasing the firm's market share; (b) development of new markets for its existing products, capitalizing on the firm's production strengths; (c) development of new products for its existing mar-kets, exploiting the firm's marketing strengths; and (d) develop-ment of new products for new markets, that is, DIVERSIFICATION. This last strategy has generally the highest-risk, since it takes the firm furthest from its production and marketing expertise. See also PRODUCT MIX.

		Market	
		Present	New
Product	Present	1. market penetration	2. market development
	New	3. product development	4. diversification

FIG. 146. **Product-market matrix.** See entry.

product mix the mixture of PRODUCTS offered by a FIRM. Since products sometimes tend to follow a typical PRODUCT LIFE CYCLE, it is expedient for companies to maintain an appropriate mix of newly launched products, growth products, and mature lines. In addition, the firm may choose to offer a range of similar products to appeal to different sectors of the market as part of a MARKET SEGMENTATION strategy. A firm will generally consider its product mix in the context of its broader marketing mix, embracing price, advertising, etc. See also PRODUCT-MARKET MATRIX.

product performance an aspect of MARKET PERFORMANCE denoting the quality and performance of existing products and a company's record with respect to development of new products. Introduction of new products and qualitative improvement of existing products may enhance consumer welfare by providing consumers with better value for their money in terms of price/quality trade-offs. See Fig. 147.

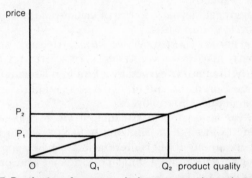

FIG. 147. **Product performance.** An improvement in product quality from OQ_1 to OQ_2 can enable the firm producing the product to charge a higher price to reflect this improvement, increasing price from OP_1 to OP_2. If price is raised less than proportionately with the increase in product quality, as in the figure, the consumer receives a net benefit from product improvement.

See also PRODUCT DIFFERENTIATION, TECHNOLOGICAL PROGRESSIVENESS, INVENTION, INNOVATION, RESEARCH AND DEVELOPMENT, PRODUCT LIFE CYCLE.

profit the difference arising when a firm's TOTAL REVENUE exceeds its TOTAL COSTS. This definition of economic profit differs from that used conventionally by business people (*accounting profit*) in that accounting profit only takes into account explicit costs. Economic profit can be viewed in terms of:

(a) the return accruing to entrepreneurs after payment of all EXPLICIT COSTS—payments such as wages to outside factor-input suppliers— and all IMPLICIT COSTS—payments for use of factor inputs—that is, capital and labor supplied by the owners themselves.

(b) a residual return to owners of a firm for providing capital and for taking a risk.

(c) the reward to entrepreneurs for organizing productive activity, for innovating new products, etc. and for taking risks.

(d) the prime mover of a PRIVATE ENTERPRISE ECONOMY serving to allocate resources between competing end uses in line with consumer demands.

(e) in aggregate terms, a source of income and thus included as part of NATIONAL INCOME.

See also PROFIT MAXIMIZATION, NORMAL PROFIT, ABOVE-NORMAL PROFIT, RISK AND UNCERTAINTY, OPPORTUNITY COST.

profitability the PROFIT earned by a firm in relation to the size of the firm, measured in terms of total ASSETS employed, long-term capital, or number of employees.

profit center an organizational subunit given responsibility for minimizing COSTS and maximizing REVENUE within its limited sphere of operations. Profit centers facilitate management control by helping to determine a unit's performance and profitability. See also COST CENTER.

profit margin the difference between the selling price of a product and its PRODUCTION COST plus selling cost. The size of the profit margin will depend on the percentage profit markup a firm adds to costs in determining its selling price. The size of the profit margin is measured by the PROFIT-TO-SALES RATIO. See also FULL-COST PRICING.

profit maximization the objective of a firm in the traditional THEORY OF THE FIRM and the THEORY OF MARKETS. Firms seek to establish their price-output combination that yields the maximum profit. Achievement of profit maximization can be depicted in two ways.

(a) Where TOTAL REVENUE (TR) exceeds TOTAL COST (TC) by the greatest amount. In Fig. 148, this occurs at the output level where the slopes of the two curves are identical, and tangents to each curve are consequently parallel, as at Q_e. At any output level below Q_e, the relevant tangents would be diverging—the TR and TC curves would still be moving apart and profits would still be rising. At any output level beyond Q_e, on the other hand, the relevant tangents would be converging and the profit surplus of TR over TC would be falling. Thus, Q_e is the optimum point, for there the distance between the total revenue and total cost curves is maximized (equal to AB). The difference between the two curves shows up in the total profit curve, which becomes positive at output OQ_1, reaches a maximum at output OQ_e (where profit CD = AB), and becomes negative beyond output OQ_2.

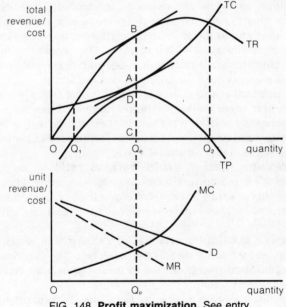

FIG. 148. **Profit maximization.** See entry.

(b) Profit maximization can be shown to occur where MAR-GINAL REVENUE (MR) equals MARGINAL COST (MC)—at output OQ_e in the figure. At all output rates above OQ_e, additional units add more to cost than revenue, so total profits are reduced. At all output rates less than OQ_e, additional units add more to revenue than cost, thereby expanding total profits. Only where MR = MC are profits maximized. See also ECONOMIC MAN.

profit motive a company's objective, to ensure that revenue exceeds costs. The term is usually associated with the COMPANY OBJECTIVE of PROFIT MAXIMIZATION, but a profit motive would still exist where only satisfactory profits were aimed for. See also PROFIT, SATISFICING THEORY.

profit sharing any payment system in which employees receive a proportion of their pay in the form of profit-related payments. Advocates of such procedures suggest that they can help reduce unemployment by making wages more variable. They hold that unemployment occurs because the price of labor is stuck at too high a level and argue that profit-related income programs can build some flexibility into labor markets. They argue that because of the automatic profit-related cushion, employers will be slower to lay off workers during a recession and quicker to hire workers when conditions are good. In addition, it is held that workers who participate in profit sharing are better motivated than wage earners to improve PRODUCTIVITY within their companies, since they share in any additional profits created. See also SUPPLY-SIDE ECONOMICS, WAGE RATE, MINIMUM WAGE.

profit-to-sales ratio or **profit-margins ratio** an accounting measure of a firm's PROFIT MARGINS, which expresses PROFITS as a percentage of SALES REVENUE. Competitive pressure on selling prices or cost increases serve to squeeze profit margins and affect profits.

progressive taxation a structure of TAXATION in which tax is levied at an increasing rate as INCOME rises. The marginal incidence of taxation rises therefore to some upper limit on earned income.

Virtually all western economies have some form of progressive taxation structure as a means of supporting government expenses in which the biggest individual burdens are placed on those most capable of paying. This ABILITY-TO-PAY PRINCIPLE OF TAXATION is regarded, as far as earned personal incomes are concerned, as the most equitable form of taxation. Compare REGRESSIVE TAXATION, PROPORTIONAL TAXATION. See also INCIDENCE OF TAXATION, REDISTRIBUTION-OF-INCOME PRINCIPLE OF TAXATION, TAX REFORM ACT OF 1986.

progress payments a contractual arrangement common in construction projects whereby payment for work done is made at predetermined stages along the route to completion.

propensity to consume the proportion of DISPOSABLE PERSONAL INCOME spent by households on CONSUMPTION of final goods and services. The average propensity to consume (APC) is given by:

$$\frac{\text{total consumption}}{\text{total income.}}$$

The marginal propensity to consume (MPC) is the fraction of any change in income that is spent:

$$\frac{\text{marginal propensity}}{\text{to consume (MPC)}} = \frac{\text{change in consumption}}{\text{change in income.}}$$

In the simple CIRCULAR FLOW OF NATIONAL INCOME MODEL, all disposable income is either consumed or saved. It follows that the sum of the MPC and the MARGINAL PROPENSITY TO SAVE is always one.

A rise in the propensity to consume increases consumption expenditure for a given income level—increases the consumption injection into the circular flow of national income. This results in an increase in aggregate demand and national income, as Fig. 149 shows.

propensity to import the proportion of NATIONAL INCOME spent on IMPORTS. The average propensity to import (APM) is given by:

$$\frac{\text{total imports}}{\text{total income.}}$$

PROPENSITY TO SAVE

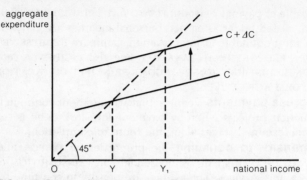

FIG. 149. **Propensity to consume.** The effect on national income of an increase in the propensity to consume. See MULTIPLIER.

The marginal propensity to import (MPM) is the fraction of any change in income spent on imports:

$$\text{marginal propensity to import (MPM)} = \frac{\text{change in imports}}{\text{change in income.}}$$

A rise in the propensity to import decreases consumption expenditure on domestically produced output for a given income level. That is, it increases the imports withdrawal from the CIRCULAR FLOW OF NATIONAL INCOME. This increase reduces national income, as Fig. 150 shows. See MULTIPLIER.

propensity to save the proportion of DISPOSABLE PERSONAL INCOME saved by households (see SAVINGS). The average propensity to save (APS) is given by:

$$\frac{\text{total saving}}{\text{total income.}}$$

The marginal propensity to save (MPS) is the fraction of any change in income that is saved:

$$\text{marginal propensity to save (MPS)} = \frac{\text{change in saving}}{\text{change in income.}}$$

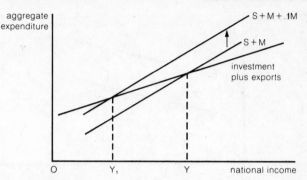

FIG. 150. **Propensity to import.** The effect on national income of
an increase in imports.

In the simple CIRCULAR FLOW OF NATIONAL INCOME MODEL,
all disposable income is either consumed or saved by households.
It follows that MARGINAL PROPENSITY TO CONSUME and MPS add
up to one. (Note that "saving" is defined as all disposable income
not spent by consumers regardless of whether savings are placed
in banks, hidden under the bed, or whatever.)

A rise in the propensity to save decreases consumption expenditure for a given income level. That is, it increases savings withdrawal from the circular flow of national income and results in a
decrease in aggregate demand and national income, as Fig. 151
shows. See MULTIPLIER.

propensity to tax the proportion of NATIONAL INCOME taken in
TAXATION by government. The average propensity to tax (APT) is
given by:

$$\frac{\text{total taxation}}{\text{total income.}}$$

The marginal propensity to tax (MPT) is the fraction of any
change in income that is taken in taxation:

$$\text{marginal propensity} \atop \text{to tax (MPT)} = \frac{\text{change in taxation}}{\text{change in income.}}$$

433

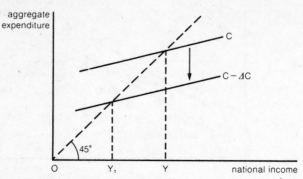

FIG. 151. Propensity to save. The effect on national income of an increase in the propensity to save.

Direct taxes reduce total income to (net of tax) DISPOSABLE PERSONAL INCOME. Thereafter, a proportion of this disposable income will be spent, and indirect taxes on goods and services bought will reduce still further the proportion of income returned to the business sector as factor returns.

See MULTIPLIER.

A rise in the propensity to tax decreases disposable income for a given income level, that is, increases taxation withdrawal from the CIRCULAR FLOW OF NATIONAL INCOME. This decreases consumption expenditure, which results in a decrease in AGGREGATE DEMAND and NATIONAL INCOME.

property taxation the local property taxes paid by businesses and homeowners that finance provision of local services.

proportional taxation a structure of TAXATION in which taxes are levied at a constant rate as INCOME rises, for example, 10% of each increment of income as income rises. This form of taxation takes the same proportion of tax from a low-income taxpayer as from a high-income taxpayer. Compare PROGRESSIVE TAXATION, REGRESSIVE TAXATION.

protectionism a deliberate policy on the part of governments to erect trade barriers, such as TARIFFS and QUOTAS, in order to protect domestic industries from foreign competition.

While there are arguments for protection especially appealing to sectional interests, protectionism for the most part cannot be vindicated as being in the best interests of national and international communities. For example, take the often-cited contention that tariffs are needed to equalize wages between countries. US and British textile industries complain that their domestic positions are undermined by foreign suppliers who employ cheap labor. It should be noted, however, that for the economy as a whole high wage rates are the *result,* not the cause of productive efficiency. Other industries successfully meet foreign competition in both domestic and foreign markets despite higher wages. This is because they rank higher in the order of COMPARATIVE ADVANTAGE. Protection of industries that stand low in the order of comparative advantage distorts the industrial ranking and leads to inefficient resource utilization. Foreign competition would force contraction of the textile industries, and the resources released from textiles could then be devoted to products in which the United States and United Kingdom have a comparative advantage.

Protection might be necessary in the short term to enable orderly restructuring of industries, particularly where manpower resources are highly localized, but there is the danger that such protection might become permanent.

Other arguments for protection, while superficially appealing, can usually be achieved more effectively by alternative means. Thus, selective tariffs and quotas may assist in restoring BALANCE-OF-PAYMENTS EQUILIBRIUM but distort the ordering of industries by comparative advantage. By contrast, aggregate fiscal and monetary policies and adjustments in exchange rates affect all foreign transactions.

There are some seemingly respectable arguments for protection. From the viewpoint of the welfare of the world as a whole, the most popular claim made for tariffs etc. is the so-called INFANT INDUSTRY argument. Protection can be effective in stimulating development of an industry well suited to a country in terms of potential comparative advantage but that finds it impossible to get started without protection from imports. Over time and suitably protected, such an industry is able to acquire internal economies of scale, that is, lower costs through exploiting a larger domestic market and take advantage of various external economies—a trained labor force or the learning-by-doing effect. Eventually, the new industry is able to become equally efficient or more efficient than its older competitors. The tariff can then be removed, leaving behind a viable and competitive industry.

Such temporary protection of industries does not conflict with the goal of free traders, which is maximum specialization on the basis of comparative advantage. It is only through the temporary equalization of competitive conditions that the industry is able to reach a stage of development that enables it to realize its full potential.

Yet there are problems. Industries are frequently selected for protection not on the basis of a favorable comparative advantage but for nationalistic reasons, for example, diversification of the economy. "Infant industry" becomes a shibboleth to justify promiscuous protection without regard for merit. The protection afforded may be excessive and may continue for longer than necessary.

In some circumstances, tariffs can be used to improve a country's TERMS OF TRADE by forcing down prices in exporting countries. This applies especially to major importers large enough to exercise buying power. It is to be noted, however, that the gain from cheaper imports may be offset by two adverse effects of tariffs: diversion of resources to less productive uses and the fact that trading partners are likely to retaliate by imposing tariffs of their own.

See also IMPORT RESTRICTIONS, NOMINAL RATE OF PROTECTION, EFFECTIVE RATE OF PROTECTION, BEGGAR-MY-NEIGHBOR POLICY, GENERAL AGREEMENT ON TARIFFS AND TRADE, MULTIFIBER ARRANGEMENT.

provision also called *sinking fund*, the amounts charged in accounting against a firm's profits in anticipation of costs likely to arise in the future. The most common of these is the provision for doubtful DEBTS, which is established in anticipation of failure of some customers to pay what they owe. In addition, a firm may make a specific provision against, say, a damages claim that is not yet settled. Provisions are aimed at trying to ensure that PROFITS are not overstated by making sure that all a firm's costs are charged, even those whose precise amount is not yet certain. See REVALUATION PROVISION.

proxy an authorization to a person or firm to act in place of another. Prior to a CORPORATION'sannual meeting, for example, a SHAREHOLDER unable to attend and vote on items contained in the agenda may give written authorization for someone else to attend and vote at the meeting in his or her stead. A shareholder's proxy is frequently given to the incumbent board of directors to vote with as they see fit, hence the term "proxy vote."

public company see CORPORATION.

public debt the NATIONAL DEBT and other miscellaneous debt for which the government is ultimately accountable. Such miscellaneous debt would include, for example, the accumulated debts of industries that the government operates.

public expenditure see GOVERNMENT (PUBLIC) EXPENDITURE.

public finance the branch of economics concerned with the income and expenditure of public authorities, the relationship of one to the other, and their effect upon the economy in general. When the CLASSICAL ECONOMISTS wrote on the subject of public finance they concentrated on the income side, TAXATION. Since the Keynesian era of the 1930s, more emphasis has been given to the expenditure side and the effect of FISCAL POLICY on the economy. When government income and expenditure in a year are equal, we are said to have a BALANCED BUDGET. When expenditure exceeds income, we have a BUDGET DEFICIT and vice versa for a BUDGET SURPLUS. See also KEYNESIAN ECONOMICS, PROGRESSIVE TAXATION.

public goods see SOCIAL PRODUCTS.

public ownership see NATIONALIZATION.

public sector or **government sector** the part of the economy concerned with transactions of the government. Government receives income from TAXATION and other sources and influences the workings of the economy through its own spending and investment decisions [GOVERNMENT (PUBLIC) EXPENDITURE] and through its control (via MONETARY POLICY and FISCAL POLICY) of spending and investment decisions of other sectors of the economy. The public sector, together with the PERSONAL SECTOR, FINANCIAL SECTOR, CORPORATE SECTOR, and FOREIGN SECTOR, makes up the national economy. See CIRCULAR FLOW OF NATIONAL INCOME MODEL.

public utility an enterprise that provides certain essential goods or services such as water, electricity, and gas. What makes these firms public is that their market structures and technology preclude their being purely competitive. In the United States and some other countries, most of these goods and services are provided by privately owned, but publicly regulated, companies. In other countries, for instance, Great Britain, most of these products are provided by publicly owned corporations (nationalized industries), although this policy has begun to be reversed in recent years under a policy known as *privatization*. See MARGINAL COST PRICING, NATIONALIZATION, NATURAL MONOPOLY.

public works any expenditure by government on social INFRA-STRUCTURE, such as roads, airports, hospitals, and sewers. Such expenditure was strongly advocated by KEYNES during the DE-PRESSION of the 1930s to alleviate the problem of UNEMPLOY-MENT and stimulate AGGREGATE DEMAND via the MULTIPLIER effect. See KEYNESIAN ECONOMICS, MACROECONOMIC POLICY, GOVERNMENT (PUBLIC) EXPENDITURE.

pump priming any GOVERNMENT (PUBLIC) EXPENDITURE designed to stimulate AGGREGATE DEMAND and, through the MULTI-PLIER effect, create a much larger increase in NATIONAL INCOME. When an economy finds itself with a DEFLATIONARY GAP, it is thought that government need not undertake the closing of that gap by itself. Only a small part of the deflationary gap need be filled by the government in order to induce and encourage optimism in the economy. Thereafter, according to some economists, additional private sector expenditure will lead toward full employment through increased aggregate demand. See STABILIZATION POLICY, DEMAND MANAGEMENT.

purchasing power the extent to which a given monetary unit can buy goods and services. The greater the amount of goods and services purchased with say, $10, the greater is its purchasing power. Purchasing power is directly linked to the CONSUMER PRICE INDEX and can be used to compare the material wealth of an average person from a previous time with the wealth of a person living at present. Changes in purchasing power are inversely related to changes in prices. See INFLATION, PURCHASING-POWER PARITY THEORY.

purchasing power parity theory a theory of EXCHANGE RATE determination postulating that under a FLOATING EXCHANGE-RATE SYSTEM, exchange rates adjust to offset differential rates of INFLATION between countries that are trading partners in such a way as to restore BALANCE-OF-PAYMENTS EQUILIBRIUM. Differential rates of inflation can bring about exchange rate changes in two principal ways. The first relates to the effect of changes of relative prices on import and export demand. As the prices of country A's products rise relative to those of country B, purchasers of these products tend to move away from A and toward B, decreasing demand for A's currency and increasing demand for B's currency. This leads to DEPRECIATION of the bilateral exchange rate of currency A for currency B. Thus, a higher level of domestic prices in country A is offset by a fall in external value of its currency.

A second way that exchange rates can change in response to differential rates of inflation is through currency SPECULATION. As prices rise in country A relative to country B, managers of foreign-currency portfolios and speculators anticipate an eventual lowering of the real value of A's currency in terms of its purchasing power and tend to move away from it in their holdings, again causing a depreciation of currency A.

This theory predicts, therefore, that differential rates of inflation lead to compensating exchange rate changes. However, it is also possible that exchange rate changes themselves can lead to differential rates of inflation. For example, if import demand is highly price-inelastic, an exchange rate depreciation may lead to an increase in domestic inflation. There is, thus, a problem in respect to causality (see DEPRECIATION). See also ASSET-VALUE THEORY.

Q

quality control a discipline concerned with improving the quality of goods and services produced. Quality control is intended to prevent faulty components or faulty finished goods from being produced, and it uses a variety of devices to help achieve this aim. Techniques of statistical sampling and testing can be used to identify faulty materials and products. Statistical variability limits can be used to ensure, for example, that machines continue to hold their tolerances in producing goods. See also PRODUCTIVITY, PRODUCT PERFORMANCE, PRODUCT DIFFERENTIATION.

quantity theory of money a theory positing a direct relationship between MONEY SUPPLY and general PRICE LEVEL in an economy.

The basic identity underlying the quantity theory was first published by Irving Fisher (1867—1947) in 1911. The Fisher equation states that:

$$MV \equiv PT$$

where M is the money stock, V is the VELOCITY OF CIRCULATION of money (average number of times each $ changes hands in financing transactions during a year), P is the general price level, and T is the number of transactions or total amount of goods and services supplied.

The above relationship is true by definition, because total money expenditure on goods and services (MV) in a period must equal the money value of goods and services supplied by sellers (PT), and the four terms are defined in such a way that the identity must hold. However, the identity can be converted into a testable equation by assuming that the velocity of circulation of money is constant or changes slowly.

Economists at Cambridge University reformulated the traditional quantity theory of money to emphasize the relationship between the stock of money in an economy (M) and final income (Y). The income velocity of circulation, called the Cambridge equation, is thus:

$$V = \frac{Y}{M}$$

where V is the average number of times the money stock of an economy changes hands in the purchase of final goods and services. For example, taking Y as gross national product, if a country has a GNP of $5 billion and an average money stock (M) over a year of $1 billion, then V is 5. Velocity cannot be observed directly and is thus determined using Y and M, figures that can be calculated from government statistics.

The term V in the Cambridge equation is not the same as V in Fisher's traditional quantity theory of money. In Fisher's equation, $MV \equiv PT$, rearranged to give:

$$V = \frac{PT}{M}$$

The number of transactions in the period, T, includes *all* transactions for real goods and services plus financial transactions. In the Cambridge equation, PT (where P = average price level) is replaced by Y, which contains not *all* transactions, but only those generating final income. This formulation enabled the Cambridge economists to emphasize real income, that is, final goods and services.

The classical economists argued that velocity of circulation was constant, because consumers have relatively constant spending habits and so turn over money at a steady rate. This argument converts the identity into an equation that leads to the *quantity theory*, which expresses a relationship between supply of money and general price level. If V and T are constant then:

$$M = P \quad \text{and} \quad \Delta M = \Delta P.$$

The modern exponents of the quantity theory (see MONETA-RISM) do not necessarily hold that the velocity of circulation is fixed, but they argue that it will change slowly over time as a result of financial innovations like the spread of bank accounts, check payments, and credit cards. They also point out that in a fully employed economy, a maximum amount of goods and services is produced and can be exchanged, so the number of transactions, T, is determined by supply considerations such as productivity trends. With V and T fixed or slowly changing, the price level is determined by the money supply (M). Any increase in the money supply feeds directly into an increase in demand for goods and services (aggregate demand). It follows that if the money supply (M), and hence aggregate demand, increase *over time* faster than the supply capacity of the economy (T), the result will be a rise in the general price level, P (INFLATION). By contrast, Keynesian economists argue that the velocity of circulation is unstable, changes rapidly, and may offset changes in the money supply.

See also MONEY SUPPLY/SPENDING LINKAGES, MONETARY POLICY, MONETARISM.

quartiles the numerical values that divide a group of numerical observations into four parts, each with an equal number of observations. Quartiles are frequently applied to data arranged in decreasing numerical order. Thus, for example, one quarter of the eight observations below exceed the first quartile (9); one half exceed the second quartile (6); and three quarters exceed the third quartile (3).

Quartiles example: 11,10/8,7/5,4/2,1

Compare DECILES, PERCENTILES.

quasi-rent the additional reward to a FACTOR OF PRODUCTION that is in short-term fixed supply, over and above VARIABLE COSTS. In the long term, the reward to the factor of production will equate to TRANSFER EARNINGS. The principle of quasi-rent is illustrated in Fig. 152.

In the original situation demand is shown by DD, and a given quantity Q is produced at price P. If there is an increase in demand from DD to D_1D_1, quantity cannot be increased in the short term.

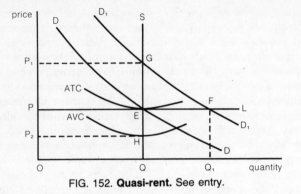

FIG. 152. **Quasi-rent.** See entry.

The supply curve becomes PES. Consequently, the excess of demand over supply raises price to P_1 at quantity Q. The section of the supply curve from E to S is vertical and is thus said to be perfectly inelastic.

Assume that a firm covers its average total costs, ATC, a necessary long-term requirement, at point E. In the short term the firm need only cover its average variable costs, AVC, at point H. The quasi-rent will be the area $P_1 P_2 HG$. In the long term, the supply curve PL is horizontal (infinitely elastic), and additional productive capacity will be brought to bear to produce quantity Q_1. At this point, additional units Q to Q_1 are produced at the same cost per unit, and quasi-rent disappears. Note that fixed costs, the difference between average variable costs and average total cost, are essential parts of long-term costs of production and include the necessary return for factors of production to be maintained at their present level rather than transferred elsewhere (see TRANSFER EARNINGS).

See AVERAGE COST, MARGINAL COST, ECONOMIC RENT.

Quesnay, François (1694—1774) French surgeon whose economic writings helped lay the foundation for the physiocratic school of thought (see PHYSIOCRACY). Quesnay suggested that agriculture was the sole source of wealth, with the productive class (tenant farmers) creating an economic surplus over and above what they need for their own subsistence. This net product is then available to meet the needs of landowners, artisans, and merchants. Quesnay wrote *Tableau Économique* (1758) to show how the net product is produced and circulates among farmers, landlords, and merchants, which was in effect an INPUT-OUTPUT ANALYSIS and a foreshadowing of circular flow.

queuing the delays caused to customers waiting for service. Where numerous service channels are provided, customers will experience few delays even when many customers arrive simultaneously for service. On the other hand, providing numerous service channels involves large labor costs, as in the case of supermarket checkout cashiers; or large investment in physical facilities, such as tanker berths or airport runways. Queuing models employing statistical techniques can be used to analyze queues and to balance the cost of resources used to provide service against the cost of time lost by customers waiting for service or customers lost as a result of excessive time spent in queues. See also SIMULATION.

quota an administrative device to limit (a) output or (b) trade.

(a) Under a producer's CARTEL arrangement, each supplier is given a fixed output to produce. Quotas are used by the cartel to establish monopoly prices by ensuring that the total output of all the firms is restricted relative to market demand.

(b) Under a trade quota system, the government directly restricts the volume of permissible imports to a specified maximum level (the *import quota*) in order to protect domestic industries against foreign competition. As a protectionist device, a quota is more effective than TARIFFS, especially when import demand is price-inelastic. (When import demand is price-inelastic, increasing import prices has little effect on the volume of imports.) In these cases the only certain way of limiting imports is through use of physical controls. See also PROTECTIONISM.

quota sample a form of STRATIFIED SAMPLE in which the interviewer or sampler selects items in proportion to the relative size of each subgroup within the total POPULATION. Quota samples are frequently used in market research, opinion polls, and other statistical survey work because they are generally quicker and less expensive than RANDOM SAMPLES.

quoted company a public corporation whose shares are traded on a major stock exchange or on related secondary markets, such as the OVER-THE-COUNTER MARKET. See LISTED COMPANY.

R

---

raider or **corporate raider** a person or group that seizes or threatens to seize control of a publicly owned company, for example, by buying its stock secretly and by gathering proxies. See DAWN RAID.

R and D see RESEARCH AND DEVELOPMENT.

random sample a SAMPLE selected by chance in which every item in the POPULATION has an equal chance of being included. Compare QUOTA SAMPLE, STRATIFIED SAMPLE.

random walk the statistical requirement that, given the same distribution parameters—MEAN and VARIANCE, for example—successive decisions over time are independent and taken from the same distribution. In terms of stock prices, for example, Kendall observed that they wandered randomly. The prices were said to follow a random walk because successive changes in value were independent.

This means there is an equal chance that a stock will rise or fall in value. This behavior of stock prices has been incorporated into the CAPITAL ASSET PRICING MODEL in the form of NONSYSTEMATIC RISK. The EFFICIENT MARKET HYPOTHESIS in its weak form asserts that because investors, in establishing stock prices, are in a perfectly competitive market, they have taken into account SYSTEMATIC RISK, the risk inherent in the economy in general. The shocks that occur through nonsystematic risk are randomly generated, indicating an equal likelihood of increasing or decreasing values, which can be eliminated by holding a diversified PORTFOLIO. See DIVERSIFICATION.

range a measure of variation within a group of numerical observations, that is, the difference between the largest observation and the smallest observation. For example, if five products had prices of $5, $4, $3, $2, and $1, then the range of prices would be $5 —

$1 = $4. The range provides a quick indication of the variability of a set of data, although not an accurate indication, because it considers only the two extreme values in the group and ignores the dispersion of the remaining observations, which lie between the extremes. See also AVERAGE DEVIATION, STANDARD DEVIATION.

rank correlation coefficient a measure of the strength of relationship between pairs of sample observations based on their ordinal ranking within the sample rather than their precise numerical values. If there were a perfect positive relationship between variables X and Y ($r = +1$), the largest value of X should be associated with the largest value of Y; the second largest value of X should be linked with the second largest value of Y, and so on. Any departure from these rankings would show a weaker relationship between X and Y, reflected in a smaller CORRELATION COEFFICIENT. See also NONPARAMETRIC STATISTICS.

ratchet effect an effect analogous to an everyday mechanical ratchet which, having gone forward one notch, will not move backward.

The ratchet effect exists in a number of areas in economics, most notably CONSUMPTION, INFLATION, and WAGES. With consumption, for example, it has been argued that when a household income falls, the household tries hard to maintain consumption at its previous highest level. This means people will use their savings or borrow to maintain their previous levels of consumption expenditure. Once income rises again, the household moves forward to attain a higher plateau of consumption. The CONSUMPTION FUNCTION is thus not reversible. See also PERMANENT INCOME HYPOTHESIS.

rate of exchange see EXCHANGE RATE.

rate of interest the price paid for use of money and credit. There are many interest rates. The benchmark for long-term rates is the price of US Treasury bonds with maturities of 10 years or more. The federal funds rate, which is the rate most financial institutions charge one another for overnight loans, is the short-term benchmark.

Interest must be paid because money and credit are scarce and useful. Interest can be paid because borrowed funds can increase the borrowers' incomes. How much interest will be paid is a source of controversy. Depending on how one defines money, there are several competing explanations of the determinants of interest rates. One of these is the loanable funds theory.

The lower the cost of borrowing money, the more money will be demanded by consumers and businesses. The higher the rate of interest, the greater the supply of loanable funds. The equilibrium rate of interest is determined by the intersection of the demand for (D_m), and supply of (S_m); loanable funds—interest rate R in Fig. 153a. In theory, monetary authorities can control the rate of interest by changes in the MONEY SUPPLY and, through the rate of interest, the level of total spending (aggregate demand) in the economy. If the money supply is increased from S_m to $S_m^{\ 1}$, as in Fig. 153b, the effect is to lower the equilibrium rate of interest from R to R^1.

There is some controversy about the interest sensitivity of the demand for money and supply of money schedules. Keynesians (see KEYNESIAN ECONOMICS) would argue that saving is largely a function of the level of income rather than the rate of interest, so the supply of loanable funds is relatively interest inelastic. Keynesians also argue that investment plans are primarily determined by businessmens' expectations about future levels of economic activity, which are linked with the cost of capital, so the demand for loanable funds is also relatively interest inelastic. This means that even large changes in interest rates are considered unlikely to have much effect on the amounts of money demanded and supplied, and thus on levels of consumer and investment spending.

By contrast, monetarists (see MONETARISM) would argue that both the supply of and demand for loanable funds are relatively interest elastic, so even small changes in interest rates can have a large effect on consumer and investment spending.

See MONEY SUPPLY/SPENDING LINKAGES, EFFECTIVE RATE OF INTEREST, MONEY DEMAND SCHEDULE, MONEY SUPPLY SCHEDULE, MARGINAL EFFICIENCY OF CAPITAL/INVESTMENT, DISCOUNT RATE, MONETARISM.

rate of return the PROFITS earned by a business, measured as a percentage of the ASSETS employed in the business. See NORMAL PROFIT, ABOVE-NORMAL PROFIT, RATE-OF-RETURN REGULATION.

rational behavior see ECONOMIC MAN.

RATIONAL EXPECTATIONS HYPOTHESIS

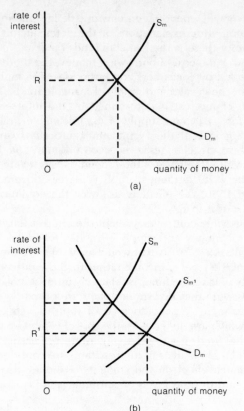

FIG. 153. **Rate of interest.** See entry.

rational expectations hypothesis a HYPOTHESIS suggesting that firms and people predict future events without bias and with full access to relevant information at the time a decision is to be made. Only new information will have an effect on EXPECTATIONS or behavior.

Business expenditure on investment and inventory is affected greatly by expectations that businessmen have of the future. These expectations are major contributory elements in determining the BUSINESS CYCLE. If business people operated under conditions of total knowledge, then the business cycle in its present form would perhaps cease to exist. Expectations play a major part in wage negotiations, in which employers and employees have to anticipate future events, such as the rate of inflation. MONEY ILLUSION would not exist, and employment would be based on real wages at all times.

From a statistical point of view, the hypothesis does not assert that expectations are always accurate. Forecasting errors will occur but will be neither biased nor predictable. Expectations in essence take the form of a PROBABILITY DISTRIBUTION with a MEAN and a VARIANCE, although it is with the former that the hypothesis is primarily concerned.

The rational expectation model may be more applicable to markets approaching perfect competition and less successful when applied to modern macroeconomic problems.

See also ECONOMIC MAN.

rationalization the reorganization of an industry or firm to enable it to use its resources more efficiently. Rationalization usually involves closing high-cost plants, either through merging of firms or their exit from the industry, which then enables output to be concentrated in plants of MINIMUM EFFICIENT SCALE and enables a better balance to be achieved between industry supply and demand. See also PRODUCTIVE EFFICIENCY.

rationing a physical method of allocating a product in short supply relative to demand (EXCESS DEMAND). In a free market this situation would not arise—the excess demand would be choked off by an increase in price of the product (see EQUILIBRIUM MARKET PRICE). But if the price is fixed below its equilibrium rate, for example, by the government wishing to hold down the prices of key products, such as food, the use of ration tickets provides a practical means of allocating available supply among consumers equitably.

In Fig. 154, for example, if the price of a product is fixed by the government at O_r, it is necessary to ration the amount of output producers are willing to supply, OQ_r, at this price among consumers who are demanding the greater amount of OQ_s.

See also BLACK MARKET, PRICE CONTROLS.

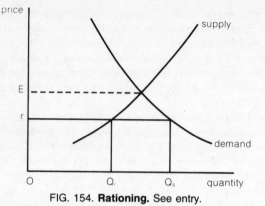

FIG. 154. **Rationing.** See entry.

real balance effect or **Pigou effect** the mechanism by which an increase in the REAL VALUE of MONEY balances leads to an increase in the level of AGGREGATE DEMAND.

Assume that wages and prices are perfectly flexible, both upward and downward, in an economy at less than full employment. A decrease in wages and prices increases the real value of a household's wealth. Asset wealth, for example, land and durable goods, decreases in line with other prices, so real wealth remains constant in asset terms. Other wealth is in the form of cash holdings—the obverse being debt, or negative wealth—so to the extent that money maintains its original PURCHASING POWER, a decrease in price will increase a household's wealth, thus stimulating consumption.

If the Pigou mechanism occurred at the point of full employment, an increase in real money wealth would lead to greater consumer demand. This could not be satisfied, because the economy is already operating at full employment. Prices would therefore increase until real money balances were restored to their original level.

The Pigou effect is probably of mainly theoretical interest, for labor unions would resist any decrease in nominal wage rates and try at least to maintain *real* wage rates. In any case, except where specifically tied to a COLA, wages are set for a sufficiently long period not to be readily adjusted to changes in prices. Few employers would agree to raise wages, with the exception already noted, simply because prices have risen, and few employees would agree to accept cuts in pay, as Keynes stated, because prices have fallen. Maintaining full employment without inflation by depending on stable real wages appears to be a forlorn hope.

real balances the real PURCHASING POWER of MONEY balances held. The true value of money lies not in its nominal denomination but in its ability to purchase goods to satisfy wants. If prices and incomes both doubled, the real value of money would remain constant. See REAL VALUES, REAL BALANCE EFFECT.

real income or **real wages** the MONEY WAGE rate (W) divided by the general PRICE LEVEL of products. Notationally, this is written W/P. If wages and prices both rise by 10% from an initial index number of 100, the original ratio of W/P is 100/100 = 1, and the new ratio of 110/110—that is, 100 plus 10% rise for both W and P—is also 1. An increase in real wages occurs when W rises more quickly than P, or P remains constant. In the latter instance, a rise in W of 10% would give the ratio 110/100 = 1.1, making wage earners 10% better off because they can purchase 10% more products with their new wages.

Analysis of real and money wages in relation to employment and output is a continuing central theme within economics, although it is generally thought to be real wages that determine the level of employment rather than money wages.

See CLASSICAL ECONOMICS, KEYNESIAN ECONOMICS, MONEY ILLUSION.

real values the measurement of an economic aggregate, for example, GROSS NATIONAL PRODUCT corrected for changes in the PRICE LEVEL over time, thus expressing the value in terms of constant prices. As reported in the *Survey of Current Business, May 1989*, there was a substantial increase in real value of GNP between 1980 and 1987—from $3,167.1 billions in constant dollars to $3,847 billions in constant dollars. See GNP DEFLATOR.

real wages see REAL INCOME.

recession a phase of the BUSINESS CYCLE characterized by a modest downturn in the level of economic activity. Real output and investment fall, resulting in rising unemployment. See DEFLA-

TIONARY GAP, DEMAND MANAGEMENT, INFLATION, STABILIZA-
TION POLICY.

reciprocal the inverse function of a stated value, frequently written as a negative exponential, such as:

$$Y = ax^{-1}$$

If $a = 3$ and $x = 5$, the equation becomes:

$$Y = 3 \cdot \frac{1}{5}$$

Therefore, 1/5 is the reciprocal of 5. The numerator becomes 1,
and the denominator the value in question—5 in this case.

recommended retail price a practice of manufacturers indicating a resale PRICE for their products. Unlike RESALE PRICE MAIN-
TENANCE, the recommended retail price is seen merely as a reference point for retailers in setting their own price. Subject to
competitive conditions, the actual price paid by consumers is in
most cases much less than the recommended price. See LIST
PRICE.

recovery a phase of the BUSINESS CYCLE characterized by an upturn in the level of economic activity. Real output and investment
increase, and unemployment falls. A recovery in economic activity usually depends on there being an increase in AGGREGATE
DEMAND, which may come about autonomously or be induced by
expansionary FISCAL POLICY and MONETARY POLICY. See also DE-
MAND MANAGEMENT, STABILIZATION POLICY.

rectangular hyperbola a curve of the mathematical form $Y = a/x$, the area under which is constant at any point along it. The
curve is asymptotic to the axes, approaching but never touching
the axes.

For example, a DEMAND CURVE of unitary PRICE ELASTICITY
OF DEMAND—an elasticity of 1—is a rectangular hyperbola, as
shown in Fig. 155.

redeemable financial security a financial security, such as a
DEBENTURE or PREFERRED STOCK, which is issued for a fixed period of time and is repayable on maturity.

REDISTRIBUTION-OF-INCOME PRINCIPLE OF TAXATION

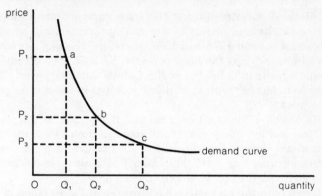

FIG. 155. **Rectangular hyperbola.** At point a, the area beneath the curve is $OP_1 \times OQ_1$. At point b, the area under the curve is $OP_2 \times OQ_2$. At point c, the area under the curve is $OP_3 \times OQ_3$. The area of each rectangle is exactly the same as that of any other, and each would give the same TOTAL REVENUE (price $\times$ quantity).

redeployment of labor the movement of LABOR from one firm to another, or from one industry to another, usually made necessary by technical change, such as introduction of labor-saving machinery, or by structural change, such as decline of an industry. Redeployment often requires a high degree of labor MOBILITY, both geographically and in terms of acquiring new job skills. See also RESOURCE ALLOCATION.

redistribution-of-income principle of taxation the principle that TAXATION and TRANSFER PAYMENTS can be used to decrease the amount of inequality of income.

Since 1980, a number of influences have combined to increase the inequality of income in the United States. The *Tax Reform Act of 1986* reduced the number of tax brackets, eliminated loopholes, and excused the poorest from paying taxes. Unfortunately, it also had the effect of reducing the progressivity of the tax system and caused much damage among those least equipped to pay taxes.

Increases in the Social Security tax, which is a regressive tax, have offset the reduction in rates of the 1986 Act, so more than half the wage earners now pay more in payroll taxes than in income taxes. In 1987, as a result, the real average hourly earnings of nonsupervisory workers were lower than in any year since 1966.

REDUCING-BALANCE METHOD

The federal government and the state governments, in effect, reduced welfare payments by not raising them enough to offset inflation. Between 1978 and 1987, therefore, the number of impoverished working families increased by 23%. The 20 million people who in 1989 fell below the Census Bureau's poverty line were from families with at least one member in full-time or part-time work.

By March 1990, the Congressional Budget Office calculated that the average family's pretax income had risen 14% since 1977 in constant dollars. But the lowest 40% of families, those with annual incomes below $17,000, had actually lost ground as wages stagnated and transfer payments declined.

Changes in the tax system have worsened the situation in recent years. Since 1977, the richest 10% of the US population have enjoyed an 8% cut in federal taxes, and the poorest 20% have suffered a 3% increase. The second poorest 20%, who consider themselves part of the middle class, pay 10% higher taxes.

See also PROGRESSIVE TAXATION, ABILITY-TO-PAY PRINCIPLE OF TAXATION, TRANSFER PAYMENTS, TAX REFORM ACT OF 1986.

reducing-balance method see DEPRECIATION(2).

regional policy a policy concerned with removing significant imbalances between regions of an economy because of unemployment rates and levels of INCOME PER CAPITA. The main approach adopted may be that of spreading industrial activity around the regions so as to avoid unemployment of labor and capital resources in the DEPRESSED AREAS and undue congestion in the more prosperous ones. A particular emphasis of regional policy may be the regeneration of areas that have fallen into industrial decline by encouraging new firms and industries to locate and invest in these areas. This is the so-called *inward investment approach*, which involves taking work to the workers.

Another approach is to encourage people to move out of depressed regions. This is the so-called *taking the workers to the work approach*, which has not found favor. Not only does it tend to accentuate the problems of the depressed areas themselves—loss of skilled workers, reduced local spending and incomes, etc.—but it also creates difficulties for receiving areas, particularly if they are already congested with respect to housing, schools, etc.

See also ENTERPRISE ZONE, STRUCTURAL UNEMPLOYMENT, DEINDUSTRIALIZATION, LOCATION OF INDUSTRY, COMPANY LOCATION.

registered trader a full-time employee of a stock exchange member organization who has met the requirements of the exchange with respect to background and knowledge of the securities industry. Traders buy and sell securities for their own accounts and, when called on, they must make a bid or an offer to sell that will narrow the existing quoted spread in the price of a security or increase the depth of an existing quote.

regression analysis a statistical technique for estimating the EQUATION that best fits sets of observations of DEPENDENT VARIABLES and INDEPENDENT VARIABLES in order to make the best estimate of the true underlying relationship between these variables. From this estimated equation, it is possible to predict what the (unknown) dependent variable(s) will be for a given value of the (known) independent variable(s).

Taking the simplest example of a linear equation with just one independent variable and a dependent variable (disposable income and consumption expenditure), the problem is to fit a straight line to a set of data consisting of pairs of observations of income (Y) and consumption (C). Figure 156 shows such a set of paired observations plotted in graph form, and we need to find the equation of the line that provides the best possible fit to our data, for this line will yield the best predictions of the dependent variable. The line of best fit to the data should be chosen so that the sum of the squares of the vertical deviations (distances) between the points and the line should be as small as possible. This method of *ordinary least squares* is applied in most regressions. The *goodness of fit* of the regression line to the sample observations is measured by the CORRELATION COEFFICIENT.

In arithmetic terms, the line depicted in Fig. 156 is a linear equation of the form:

$$C = a + bY$$

where the coefficients of the equation, *a* and *b,* are estimates based on single observations of the true population parameters.

REGRESSION ANALYSIS

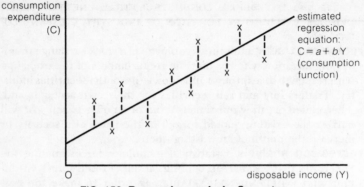

FIG. 156. **Regression analysis.** See entry.

These constants, *a* and *b,* obtained with the method of ordinary least squares, are called the estimated regression coefficients. Once their numerical values have been determined, they can be used to predict values of dependent variable C from values of independent variable Y. For example, if the estimated regression coefficient of *a* and *b* were 1000 and 0.9, respectively, the regression equation would be C = 1000 + 0.9 Y, and we could predict that for a disposable income of $10,000, consumer expenditure would be:

$$C = a + bY$$
$$C = 1,000 + 0.9Y$$
$$= 1,000 + 0.9 \ 10,000$$
$$= 10,000$$

The regression coefficient of the slope of the linear regression, *b,* is particularly important in economics, for it shows the change in the dependent variable—in this case consumption—associated with a unit change in the independent variable—in this case income. For example, a *b* value of 0.9 suggests that consumers will spend 90% of any extra disposable income.

The regression equation will not provide an exact prediction of the dependent variable for any given value of the independent variable. This is because the regression coefficients estimated from sample observations are merely the best estimate of the true population parameters and so are subject to chance variations. Consequently, it is possible to construct a CONDITIONAL DISTRIBUTION showing likely values of dependent variable C predicted by the regression equation for a given value of independent variable Y. The standard deviation of this conditional distribution gives an indication of the limits between which we would expect consumption expenditure to fall for a given level of disposable income. This is reflected in a statistic called the STANDARD ERROR of the estimate, which shows estimated limits within which we could expect C to fall for a given Y with a predetermined probability of say 0.99 or 0.95. For example, if the standard error in the above example for a 0.95 probability were 500, then we could be confident that on 95% of occasions the true consumption figure for an income of $10,000 would lie within the range:

$$\$10,000 - 500 \quad \text{and} \quad \$10,000 + 500$$

To acknowledge the imperfections in any estimated regression equation based on a sample in depicting the true underlying relationship in the population as a whole, the regression equation is generally written as:

$$C = a + bY + e$$

with the addition of a *residual* or *error term, e,* to reflect the residual effect of chance variations and the effects of other independent variables, for example, interest rates on consumer credit, which influence consumption spending but are not explicitly included in the regression equation.

When it is felt that more than one independent variable has a significant effect on the dependent variable, the technique of *multiple linear regression* will be employed. The technique involves formulating a multiple linear regression equation involving two or more independent variables, such as:

$$C = a + bY + dI + e$$

459

REGRESSIVE TAXATION

where I is the interest rate on consumer credit and d is an additional regression coefficient attached to this extra independent variable. Estimation of this multiple linear regression equation by the method of ordinary least squares involves fitting a three-dimensional plane, or surface, to a set of sample observations of consumer spending, disposable income, and interest rates in such a way as to minimize the squared deviations of the observations from the plane. In arithmetic terms, the sample observations can be used to make numerical estimates of the three regression coefficients (a, b, and d) in the above equation.

When the underlying relationships between independent and dependent variables are not linear, techniques of linear regression cannot be applied. However, when relationships are curvilinear, they often can be transformed into linear relationships by such devices as taking the natural logarithms of the variables in order to make them amenable to linear regression analysis. See also IDENTIFICATION PROBLEM.

regressive taxation a structure of TAXATION in which taxes rise as a percentage of the taxpayer's income as that income declines. Indirect taxes, such as sales taxes or excise duties, become regressive when taken as a proportion of total net income. For example, if an item costs $100 and sales tax is 10%, then $10 in relation to $200 a week net pay is greater than $10 to a person earning $600 a week net. The burden of taxation, therefore, is proportionately greater on less affluent members of society and cannot be considered an equitable tax. Compare PROGRESSIVE TAXATION, PROPORTIONAL TAXATION. See also ABILITY-TO-PAY PRINCIPLE OF TAXATION, INCIDENCE OF TAXATION, REDISTRIBUTION-OF-INCOME PRINCIPLE OF TAXATION.

relative concentration measure see CONCENTRATION MEASURES.

relative income hypothesis the HYPOTHESIS that it is not a person or nation's absolute income that matters but relative income, that is, how it compares with the income of others. If this is so, since all individuals or countries cannot become *relatively* better off, the pursuit of growth for growth's sake becomes futile. See also CONSPICUOUS CONSUMPTION.

relative price see INDIFFERENCE CURVE, ISOQUANT CURVE.

relativities any comparisons between the WAGES or SALARIES of workers in the same firm, the same industry, or between different industries. Such relativities reflect differences in training requirements, skill levels, and responsibilities. See also WAGE DIFFEREN-TIALS.

rent the periodic payments made to the owners of ASSETS for use of their land or other assets as FACTORS OF PRODUCTION. In aggregate terms, rents are a source of income and are included as a part of NATIONAL INCOME. See also ECONOMIC RENT, QUASI-RENT.

replacement cost the cost of replacing an ASSET, such as an item of machinery. Unlike HISTORIC COST—the original cost of acquiring an asset—replacement cost takes into account the effects of INFLATION in increasing asset prices over time. See also REVALUATION PROVISION, INFLATION ACCOUNTING, APPRECIATION(2).

replacement investment the INVESTMENT undertaken to replace a firm's plant and equipment or an economy's CAPITAL STOCK that has become worn out or obsolete. See CAPITAL CONSUMPTION.

representative firm a concept devised by Alfred MARSHALL for use in market analysis. The representative firm is a hypothetical business organization rather than an actual production unit. Because it is an abstract concept, it is not based on a typical business unit of the time and is representative primarily with respect to average costs rather than firm size. Marshall argued that most firms are able to take advantage of INTERNAL ECONOMIES OF SCALE to reduce costs, which in turn leads to growth of individual firms and of the industry itself. In addition, as firms grow larger, EXTERNAL ECONOMIES OF SCALE become increasingly important. The representative firm has middling access to such economies.

Marshall encountered a number of difficulties in his analysis and reverted to one of the most famous analogies in economics, that of a tree representing a firm. Firms grow from seedlings through youth and maturity, and finally die, with new firms replacing the output of the dying firms. These firms are thus indicative of the supply curve for the whole industry. The industry may therefore be in equilibrium (the forest) but each of the constituent firms (the trees) is not required to be so. The representative firm can therefore be seen as the typical tree in the forest.

See also MONOPOLISTIC COMPETITION.

resale price maintenance (rpm) a type of RESTRICTIVE TRADE

RESEARCH AND DEVELOPMENT (R AND D)

AGREEMENT in which a supplier prescribes the PRICE at which retailers are to sell the product to final buyers. The main objection to rpm centers on the fact that it restricts or eliminates retail price competition and, by prescribing uniform retail margins, serves to cushion inefficient retailers. The existence of this practice is frequently challenged in the courts.

research and development (R and D) any scientific investigation leading to discovery of new techniques and products (INVENTION) and their commercial application (INNOVATION), together with refinement and improvement of existing technologies and products.

R and D contributes to the competitive strength of a firm and the nation by promoting a higher rate of ECONOMIC GROWTH.

See TECHNOLOGICAL PROGRESSIVENESS, PRODUCT PERFORMANCE, PRODUCT LIFE CYCLE.

reserve deposit ratio or **liquidity ratio** see LEGAL RESERVES.

reserve base currency and demand deposits under control of the banking system plus money held by the public. The base is often referred to as high-powered money, because any increase in bank reserves or increase of money in circulation that finds its way into the banking system provides a basis for expansion of money and credit.

reserves 1. any additional claims of company shareholders that reflect increases in the value of company ASSETS in the BALANCE SHEET. Revenue reserves arise when some after-tax profit is retained in the business to finance acquisition of extra assets, rather than being paid out as DIVIDENDS. Capital reserves arise when company assets, such as buildings, are revalued to reflect increased market value due to inflation. Reserves serve to increase SHAREHOLDERS' CAPITAL EMPLOYED in a company. See also RETAINED PROFITS, APPRECIATION(2), REVALUATION PROVISION, INFLATION ACCOUNTING.

2. Since 1980, all depository institutions in the United States have had to maintain as reserves certain specified assets to support their deposits. Legal reserves, currency, and checks that are counted as reserves must be in the bank tills or on deposit in a Federal Reserve Bank. Required reserves are the specified percentages that must be held against deposits. Excess reserves are currency and checks, legal reserves that exceed the required amount. The key to understanding how banks can apparently create money rests on an appreciation of the fact that the US banking system is a *fractional reserve system*. When banks acquire deposits, they keep only a fraction of the currency and checks deposited as a reserve and lend out the rest. Assume, for example, a required reserve rate of 20%. If a bank acquires a deposit of $1000, it must keep $200 as a required reserve, but it will seek to make loans and investments of $800. If all the money thus created remains within the banking system, the system now has $1000 in required reserves.

3. monetary assets held by countries to finance balance of payments deficits. See INTERNATIONAL RESERVES, FEDERAL RESERVE SYSTEM, DEMAND DEPOSIT CREATION.

reserve tranche see INTERNATIONAL MONETARY FUND.

residual see REGRESSION ANALYSIS.

resource allocation the allocation of an economy's FACTORS OF PRODUCTION between alternative uses in line with patterns of consumer demand, which in turn reflect a given size and distribution of national income. Resources are optimally allocated when the proportions in which factor inputs are combined to produce GOODS and SERVICES reflect their relative costs so as to minimize costs of production, and when the output of goods and services fully reflects the distribution of consumer preferences as between those goods and services. (See PARETO OPTIMALITY.)

More specifically, resources are optimally allocated when in each market the price paid for the good or service fully reflects the *lowest* economic cost of supplying it.

See ALLOCATIVE EFFICIENCY, PRODUCTIVE EFFICIENCY, DISTRIBUTIVE EFFICIENCY, MOBILITY, PRICE SYSTEM, THEORY OF MARKETS.

resources see FACTORS OF PRODUCTION.

restraint of trade see RESTRICTIVE TRADE AGREEMENT.

restrictive labor practice a practice, usually operated by a LABOR UNION in the interests of its members, that has the effect of reducing productive efficiency. For example, a union may insist that a specified number of people work on a particular activity even though it involves employing more people than strictly required to undertake the activity efficiently (*featherbedding*); different unions operating in the same plant may lay down rules specifying which tasks their members may work on and which they may not, which has the effect of limiting job interchangeability; and unions may resist the installation of new machinery, especially if the new machinery will result in job losses. See also PRODUCTIVITY, X-INEFFICIENCY.

restrictive trade agreement a form of COLLUSION between suppliers aimed at removing competition wholly or in part. For the most part, such agreements concentrate on fixing common prices and discounts, but may also stipulate production quotas, sharing of markets, and coordinated capacity adjustments. The main objection to restrictive agreements is that they tend to raise prices above competitive levels and serve to protect inefficient suppliers from the rigors of competition. Most countries take a tough line on restrictive agreements, either prohibiting them outright or allowing them to continue only in exceptional circumstances.

retailing the purchasing of products from manufacturers or independent wholesalers and reselling the products to final consumers. Retailing organizations range from single stores to multiple-branch CHAIN STORES, including DEPARTMENT STORES, SPECIALIST SHOPS, DISCOUNT STORES and COOPERATIVES.

retail price index or **consumer price index (CPI)** a measure of the change in prices of a market basket of goods and services purchased either by urban wage earners and clerical workers or by all urban consumers. From time to time the commodities in the basket and their weights or amounts are changed to reflect changes in consumption patterns. The current CPI employs a base period of 1982—1984 = 100 and reflects the results of studies of what was bought in day-to-day living in those years. See PRICE INDEX.

retained profits or **undistributed profits** any after-tax PROFITS that are reinvested (*plowed back*) rather than being paid out to firm owners in DIVIDENDS. Such retained earnings form a valuable source of capital to be INVESTED in additional FIXED ASSETS and CURRENT ASSETS. They serve to swell the value of the firm to shareholders by adding to revenue RESERVES.

returns to scale the relationship between OUTPUT of a product and the quantities of FACTOR INPUTS used to produce it in the long term. For example, when doubling the quantity of factor inputs used results in doubling output, constant returns to scale are experienced. When ECONOMIES OF SCALE are present, a doubling of factor inputs results in a more than proportionate increase in output. By contrast, when DISECONOMIES OF SCALE are encountered, a doubling of factor inputs results in a less than proportionate increase in output.

returns to the variable factor input the rate of change of OUTPUT within the SHORT TERM theory of supply, resulting from changes in the VARIABLE FACTOR INPUT in a plant of a given (fixed) size. See AVERAGE COSTS, DIMINISHING RETURNS.

revaluation an administered increase in the value of one CURRENCY against other currencies under a FIXED EXCHANGE-RATE SYSTEM, as in Fig. 157. The objectives of a revaluation are to assist in removal of a surplus in a country's BALANCE OF PAYMENTS and reduction of excessive accumulation of INTERNATIONAL RESERVES. A revaluation makes IMPORTS cheaper and EXPORTS more expensive, thereby encouraging additional imports and lowering export demand.

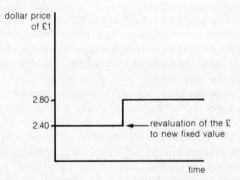

FIG. 157. **Revaluation.** A revaluation of the pound against the dollar.

How successful a revaluation is in removing a payments surplus depends on the reactions of export and import volumes to the change in relative prices, that is, the PRICE ELASTICITY OF DEMAND for exports and imports. If these values are low, that is, if demand is inelastic, trade volumes will not change very much, and the revaluation may in fact make the surplus larger. On the other hand, if export and import demand is elastic, the change in trade volumes will operate to remove the surplus. BALANCE-OF-PAYMENTS EQUILIBRIUM will be restored if the sum of export and import elasticities is greater than unity (the MARSHALL-LERNER CONDITION).

See DEVALUATION, INTERNAL-EXTERNAL BALANCE MODEL.

revaluation provision an accounting provision made for the increased cost of replacing a FIXED ASSET over and above its HISTORIC COST. DEPRECIATION charges spread the original cost of a fixed asset over its estimated life, preventing the cost of the asset from being ignored in calculating net profit and so preventing the firm's LONG-TERM CAPITAL EMPLOYED from being distributed as DIVIDENDS. However, where the REPLACEMENT COST of a fixed asset is expected to exceed its original cost, a prudent firm may withhold additional profits instead of distributing them, in anticipation of having to pay this additional sum. See INFLATION ACCOUNTING.

revealed preference theory an alternative explanation for an individual consumer's downward-sloping DEMAND CURVE, requiring the consumer to reveal what his or her preferences are in given sets of circumstances. The preferences given may be between two or more goods, but where more than two goods exist, money is taken to represent all other goods for ease of graphical analysis, as in Fig. 158.

If a consumer prefers a combination of money (OM_1) and good X (OX_1), he or she will be at point a on the BUDGET LINE (or relative price line) MX. If good X becomes cheaper, so more can be had, the consumer's *real* income increases and he or she can move to budget line MX_2. The combination of goods the consumer prefers is now at, say, b.

However, not all the change is due to increasing real income caused by the fall in the price of good X. Some of it is due to substitution of the now cheaper good X for others, and this effect is always positive, that is, it is not possible to purchase less of the now cheaper good X after the change to MX_2, than when on the budget line MX.

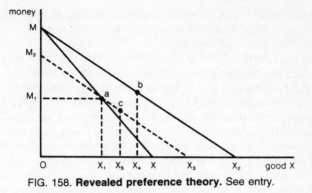

FIG. 158. **Revealed preference theory.** See entry.

If the consumer's new configuration of goods at b is reduced proportionately, by introducing a hypothetical decrease in income in the form of an inward parallel shift of the budget line to position $M_2 X_3$, then the consumer will choose a new position, say, point c. The SUBSTITUTION EFFECT is from X_1 to X_5, while X_5 to X_4 is the INCOME EFFECT.

See CONSUMER EQUILIBRIUM, INDIFFERENCE CURVE, PRICE EFFECT.

revenue the money received by a firm from selling its output of GOODS or SERVICES (SALES REVENUE), or money received by government from TAXATION. See AVERAGE REVENUE, MARGINAL REVENUE, TOTAL REVENUE.

reverse takeover a situation in which a smaller but dynamic company, wishing to expand rapidly, takes over a larger but unprogressive company and issues stock, junk bonds, or other securities to raise the necessary funds to purchase the shares of the larger company. See TAKEOVER.

revised sequence the idea that the traditionally held view in economic theory of companies responding to a unidirectional flow of instruction from consumers in the marketplace (CONSUMER SOVEREIGNTY) may be inappropriate in a modern economy characterized by large companies. Instead, GALBRAITH suggests, large corporations may have the means and ability to influence consumers' market behavior just as much as consumers affect corporate market behavior. In perfectly competitive markets, the traditional theory—that of accepted sequence—may still be valid, but in an OLIGOPOLY or MONOPOLY it is no longer valid.

Ricardo, David (1772—1823) English stockbroker who amassed a fortune before retiring early to study economics. In his *Principles of Political Economy and Taxation* (1817), Ricardo stated that the exchange value of products is measured by the amount of labor needed to produce them. He developed a theory of distribution to explain how this value is shared between major classes in society. Ricardo suggested that however prosperous the economy, wages could never rise above subsistence level. As workers became more prosperous, they would have more children and, as these children grew up, this additional labor supply would force wages down, because there would not be a proportionate increase in output, the result being his *iron law of wages*.

Ricardo argued that nonfarm producers would not benefit much from economic progress either, since competition would keep their prices at long-run normal profits, and wage payments would cut into their profits. He regarded landlords as being the only real beneficiaries of economic progress, since with a finite amount of arable land and a growing population to feed, rental incomes would grow and the value of land would rise. Rising rents would raise the cost of food produced, and workers would need higher wages to pay for food, eroding capitalists' profits.

Ricardo formulated the theory of comparative advantage, which established that as long as there were differences in cost structures, international trade would be mutually advantageous. See ECONOMIC RENT, COMPARATIVE ADVANTAGE.

ridge lines see INDIFFERENCE MAP.

rights issue the issue by a corporation of additional stock to existing SHAREHOLDERS at a price generally a little below current market price. Rights are issued to existing shareholders in proportion to their existing shareholdings, and shareholders may sell their rights if they do not wish to subscribe for extra shares.

risk analysis the systematic analysis of the degree of risk attaching to capital projects. Risk reflects the variability of expected future returns from a capital INVESTMENT, so the statistical technique of PROBABILITY can be applied to assist in arriving at a decision. See also CAPITAL BUDGETING, RISK AND UNCERTAINTY, DECISION TREE.

risk and uncertainty a situation of potential LOSS of a firm's IN-VESTMENT resulting from operating in an uncertain business environment. Certain risks are insurable, for example, the risk of fire or theft, but not the firm's ability to survive and prosper. The firm itself must assume the risks of the marketplace: if it cannot sell its products, it will go bankrupt; if it is successful, it will make profits. Thus, risk taking is to be viewed as an integral part of the process of supplying GOODS and SERVICES and in innovating new products. PROFITS, in part, are a reward for successful risk-taking.

Since managers do not know for certain what the future holds, they are forced to guess what the most likely outcome of any decision will be, effectively assigning a statistical PROBABILITY to the likelihood of future events occurring. All such estimates of the likelihood of future events occurring must, by their very nature, be subjective, although some estimates are likely to be better than others, depending on the amount of information available. When large amounts of information are available on which to base estimates of likelihood, so that accurate statistical probabilities can be formulated, we may talk of risk rather than uncertainty. For example, an insurance company dealing with fire insurance policies and claims for large numbers of manufacturers, will be able to compile detailed statistics about numbers of fires and the amount of damage done by each, and can use this information to predict the likelihood of a business experiencing a fire. This detailed statistical information enables the insurance company to charge manufacturers premiums for indemnifying them against fire losses and to make a profit by so doing. By contrast, a single manufacturer would find it difficult to predict the likelihood of premises being damaged by fire and the amount of damage, since such an event would tend to be a rare experience for the manufacturer.

Faced with a possibility of fire, the manufacturer can either choose to bear the risk of losses resulting from a serious fire or can avoid the full cost of fire damage by paying an insurance company a premium to share the risk. The company, in doing so, has diluted the risk, which is now shared by all holding fire with that insurance company. Again, the manufacturer can take the risk that the prices of its main raw materials will be much higher in the next year, or it can contract through a commodity FUTURES MARKET to buy raw materials supplies for future delivery at a fixed price.

Uncertainty, unlike risk, arises from changes difficult to predict or from events whose likelihood cannot be accurately estimated. Unfortunately, many management decisions fall into this category, since they are rarely repetitive and past data are not available to act as a guide to the future. Such market uncertainty as to the likelihood and extent of losses that might arise in launching a new product can only be gauged by managers through combining the limited available data with their own judgment and experience.

Managers can improve on their subjective estimates about the future by collecting information from forecasts, market research, feasibility studies, etc., but they need to balance the cost of collecting such information against its value in improving decisions. Where costs of information are prohibitive, managers may turn to various RULES OF THUMB, such as full-cost pricing, which yield reasonably good decisions.

The traditional THEORY OF THE FIRM envisaged a firm armed with perfect knowledge about its future costs and revenues, making pricing and output decisions on the basis of a marginal weighting of costs and revenues. This cognitive assumption of perfect knowledge is open to criticism in light of what appears above.

See ENTREPRENEUR, HEDGING, DECISION TREE, RISK PROFILE, SCHUMPETER.

risk capital any business capital subscribed by an individual EN-TREPRENEUR or group of ordinary SHAREHOLDERS that entails some risk of loss in the event the enterprise fails. See RISK AND UNCERTAINTY.

risk premium see RISK PROFILE.

risk profile or **risk premium** a depiction of the attitudes toward risk displayed by those who make decisions, based on von Neumann and Morgenstern's concept of the expected UTILITY INDEX. For example, you could ask business people how much they would be prepared to pay to play a game of chance offering a 50/50 chance of winning $1 or nothing. If they were neutral in attitude toward risk, they might be prepared to pay 50 cents to play such a game (see point A in Fig. 159). This suggests that they regard 50 cents as being the certainty equivalent of a 50/50 chance of winning $1 or nothing. Where such a neutral attitude to risk exists, the term *expected money value* is used to denote the certainty equivalent of a risk. It is found by taking the money value of each outcome and weighting it by the PROBABILITY of its occurrence. Thus, $0.5 \times \$1 + 0.5 \times \$0 = 50$ cents.

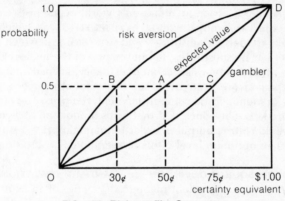

FIG. 159. **Risk profile.** See entry.

However, if the business people were averse to risk, then when confronted with the same game offering a chance of $1 or nothing, they might be prepared to pay, say, only 30 cents rather than 50 cents to play (see point B in Fig. 159). Here the difference between the 50 cents certainty equivalent based on the expected value criterion, and the 30 cents certainty equivalent of the cautious business people, represents a risk premium (equal to AB in Fig. 159) that the business people need to induce them to take the risk. On the other hand, if they thought of themselves as gamblers, they might regard the 50/50 chance of $1 or nothing as the equivalent of, say 75 cents for certain (point C in Fig. 159). By offering business people large numbers of 50/50 chances like the one above, it would be possible to construct complete risk profiles such as those shown in Fig. 159.

Attitudes toward risk do not depend merely on the personality of the person making the decision. They also are influenced by the size of the potential gains and losses involved. When a project risks making a loss so large as to endanger the continuing existence of the sponsoring company, then managers will tend to adopt a cautious view about the risks involved.

Robinson, Joan (1903—1983) English economist from Cambridge University who helped develop the theory of MONOPOLISTIC COMPETITION in her book *The Economics of Imperfect Competition* (1933). Prior to Robinson's work, economists classified markets in two groups: PERFECT COMPETITION, in which firms' products are perfect substitutes; and MONOPOLY, in which a firm's product has no substitutes. Robinson, one of the leaders at Cambridge of post-Keynesian economic theory, argued that in real markets goods are often partial substitutes for other goods, and her theory of monopolistic competition analyzed price and output in such markets. She concluded that firms in monopolistic competition would restrict output in order to maintain price, resulting in a less than optimum level of plant operation. See also CHAMBERLIN.

root-mean-square deviation see STANDARD DEVIATION.

royalty an agreed payment made to the owner of an INDUSTRIAL PROPERTY RIGHT, such as a PATENT or COPYRIGHT, for the grant of an exclusive or nonexclusive LICENSE or FRANCHISE to produce and sell for profit the item concerned.

rule of thumb a rough-and-ready aid in making decisions, providing an acceptably precise solution to a problem. When refined decision processes are expensive in regard to information gathering and information processing, use of a rule of thumb may be justified. For example, COST PLUS PRICING may be used in practice by firms in the absence of sufficient knowledge about future demand and cost conditions to permit marginal weighting of revenues and costs in order to achieve an optimum decision. See RISK AND UNCERTAINTY.

S

salary a payment made to an employee. A salary is similar to a WAGE payment in that it is paid for the use of LABOR as a factor of production. In economic terms, a salary payment differs from a wage payment in two ways. (a) It is not strictly related to the actual number of hours worked by the employee, whereas wage earners are usually paid on an hourly basis. (b) Salaries are often paid monthly or semimonthly, whereas wages are paid weekly.

sale and leaseback see LEASEBACK.

sales forecasts see FORECASTING.

sales promotion and merchandising the measures used by firms to increase the sales of their GOODS and SERVICES. ADVERTISING is the most visible form of sales promotion, but a wide variety of other techniques can be used to create and boost sales: reduced prices, free samples, coupons offering gifts, product competitions offering prizes, trading stamps, demonstrations, point-of-sale displays, etc.

In the economist's models of imperfect competition, these items come under the generic heading of PRODUCT DIFFERENTIATION.

sales revenue the income generated from sale of GOODS and SERVICES. Sales revenue depends on the volume of a product sold and the price of the product.

sales revenue maximization a company objective in the THEORY OF THE FIRM that is used as an alternative to the traditional assumption of PROFIT MAXIMIZATION. The firm is assumed to seek to maximize sales revenue subject to a minimum profit constraint, determined by the need to pay dividends to shareholders and to finance expansion. In Fig. 160, sales revenue is maximized at output level OQ_s. If the firm's minimum profit constraint is at level A, the sales revenue maximizing output level of OQ_s will provide sufficient profit. If the firm's required profit level is B, however, sales revenue maximizing output OQ_s is clearly inadequate. The firm's output would then be lowered to level $OQ_s\star$, which is just compatible with the profit constraint. Clearly, the higher the minimum profit figure required, the more important the constraint becomes, and the closer together the profit maximizing (OQ_m) and sales revenue maximizing output levels become.

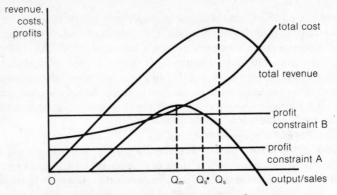

FIG. 160. **Sales revenue maximization.** See entry.

See also MANAGERIAL THEORIES OF THE FIRM, COMPANY OBJECTIVES, DIVORCE OF OWNERSHIP FROM CONTROL.

sales tax a form of INDIRECT TAX that is incorporated into the selling price of a product and borne by the consumer. Sales taxes include VALUE-ADDED TAX and EXCISE DUTY.

sample any part of a total group (see POPULATION) that can be analyzed in order to draw inferences about the group without the difficulty and expense of undertaking a complete census of the entire population. See also RANDOM SAMPLE.

Samuelson, Paul (born 1915) winner of the Nobel Memorial Prize in Economic Sciences, 1970, for actively contributing to the raising of the level of economic analysis. Samuelson was the first American to win the Nobel Prize in economics, and during his long career at MIT he has helped that institution become a center of economic research.

Samuelson has contributed to neoclassical price theory and to stability analysis. A Keynesian, he has held that monetary and fiscal policies must be coordinated to prevent inflation and recession. In his research, he has been able to combine rigorous mathematical analysis with a concern for policy and has published widely in many areas of economic theory, but generations of American business and political leaders know him best for his introductory textbook on economics, long the standard text at the best American colleges.

satisficing theory a THEORY OF THE FIRM postulating that firms typically seek not only to secure satisfactory profits rather than maximum profits, as depicted in the traditional theory of the firm, but that other objectives, such as increasing sales, market share, or the size of the firm, may be accorded equal or greater prominence than profits. Organizational theorists suggest that satisficing behavior is particularly likely to occur in large, hierarchical organizations, in which consensus decision-making, reconciling the diverse aims of the subgroups of the organization, tends to be the norm, as opposed to objectives being set by an individual ENTREPRENEUR.

The problem with this approach to firm behavior is that it is not possible to define unequivocally what is meant by satisfactory and hence to construct a *general* theory of the firm. For example, a profit return considered satisfactory by one firm may be considered too low by another firm. Thus, the predictive powers of satisficing theory are limited.

See also PROFIT MAXIMIZATION, BEHAVIORAL THEORY OF THE FIRM, MANAGERIAL THEORIES OF THE FIRM, ORGANIZATIONAL THEORY.

savings the proportion of INCOME not spent on current CONSUMPTION. Saving is a WITHDRAWAL from the CIRCULAR FLOW OF NATIONAL INCOME MODEL. In the simple circular flow model, all saving is undertaken by households. In the extended model, saving is also undertaken by businesses (*retained profits*) and by governments (*budget surplus*).

In real terms, saving is important in that it may finance physical INVESTMENT. Saving, that is, foregoing current consumption, releases resources that can be devoted to increasing a country's CAPITAL STOCK and hence its capacity to produce a greater quantity of goods over time.See also SAVINGS SCHEDULE, PARADOX OF THRIFT.

savings and loan institution traditionally, a financial institution that accepts deposits from savers and specializes in the long-term lending of money by way of secured mortgages to private individuals for purchases of homes. As a result of changes in state and federal banking laws, savings and loan institutions in recent years have broadened their scope of lending to include business and land investments. See also FINANCIAL SYSTEM.

savings bank a financial institution that accepts deposits from savers and specializes in investments in relatively secure stocks, bonds, and government securities. Some of the larger savings banks also offer depositors limited COMMERCIAL BANKING facilities, for example, checking accounts. See also FINANCIAL SYSTEM.

savings schedule a schedule depicting the relationship between SAVINGS and level of INCOME. In the simple CIRCULAR FLOW OF NATIONAL INCOME MODEL, all consumption and saving are accounted for by households. At low levels of DISPOSABLE PERSONAL INCOME, households consume more than their current income (see DISSAVINGS). At higher levels of disposable income, they consume only a part of their current income and save the rest, as in Fig. 161. Thus, the savings schedule is derived by subtracting the CONSUMPTION SCHEDULE from the 45° line, as shown in the lower part of Fig. 161. The slope of the savings schedule is equal to the MARGINAL PROPENSITY TO SAVE.

See also LIFE-CYCLE HYPOTHESIS, PERMANENT INCOME HYPOTHESIS.

Say, Jean Baptiste (1767—1832) French economist who spread Adam SMITH's theory of the market in his *Traité d'économic politique* (1803). Say argued that since every act of production incurs costs and an equivalent amount of purchasing power, then every product put on the market creates its own demand, and every demand exerted in the market creates its own supply. This statement about interdependence in an exchange economy is often called SAY'S LAW and has been used to deny the possibility of economic crisis associated with general overproduction of goods and services and to suggest that national economies would automatically function at close to full employment.

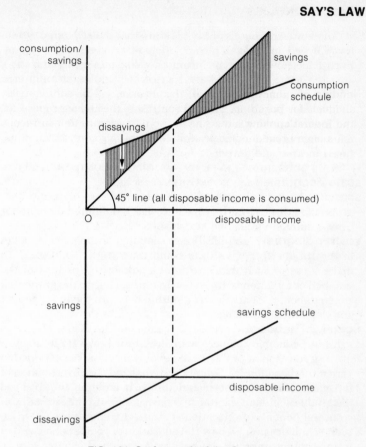

FIG. 161. **Savings schedule.** See entry.

Say's law the proposition that AGGREGATE SUPPLY creates its own AGGREGATE DEMAND. The act of producing a given level of national output generates an amount of income (wages, profits, etc.) exactly equal to the cost of that output. If spent, the income is just sufficient to take up the purchases of the entire output that has been produced. In order to reach the full-employment level of national output, it follows that all that must be done is to increase aggregate supply.

SCALE ECONOMIES

The key assumptions of Say's law are that the economic system is supply-led and that all income, including savings, will be spent. In practice, however, some income is leaked into savings, taxation, etc. (see CIRCULAR FLOW OF NATIONAL INCOME MODEL), and there is no guarantee that all this income will be subsequently reinjected as spending. Thus, in contrast to the above proposition, the Keynesian view is that the economic system is demand-led, a fall in aggregate demand leading to a multiple contraction of national income and output.

See EQUILIBRIUM LEVEL OF NATIONAL INCOME, MULTIPLIER.

scale economies see ECONOMIES OF SCALE.

scarcity the limited availability of economic resources, the FACTORS OF PRODUCTION, relative to society's unlimited demand for GOODS and SERVICES. See ECONOMICS.

scatter diagram a graphical representation of the pairs of values of the INDEPENDENT VARIABLE and DEPENDENT VARIABLE. To make sense of such data, we must examine the pattern of the graphed observations with a view to fitting a line to the graph that adequately represents the relationship between the independent and dependent variables.

Schultz, Theodore (born 1902) winner of the Nobel Memorial Prize in Economic Sciences with Sir Arthur Lewis (1979) for pioneering research in problems of developing countries. Trained in agricultural economics, Schultz systematized the investigation of the effects of investments in agriculture. In addition, he advanced the study of human capital by constructing useful estimates of costs and benefits of education. Toward the end of his active career, Schultz examined how the education of young people and of women might improve the health, welfare, and economic prosperity of the populations of Third World countries.

Schumpeter, Joseph A. (1883—1950) widely respected teacher of economics at Harvard University. He was trained by founders of the Austrian school and did his early work in economic development. In *Business Cycles* (1939), Schumpeter advanced the idea that long-run cycles of economic activity are a result of the clustering of innovations, and downturns come when the spirit of innovation peters out.

Schumpeter's views on the consequences of oligopoly led to

studies of sources and results of technological change, and his books on various aspects of economics always attracted large readership. *Capitalism, Socialism, and Democracy* (1948) proved to be his best-known work. In it, Schumpeter predicted for non-Marxist reasons that capitalism would be succeeded by socialism.

See also MONOPOLY, PRIVATE ENTERPRISE ECONOMY, OLIGOPOLY.

seasonal index see TIME-SERIES ANALYSIS.

seasonal unemployment see FRICTIONAL UNEMPLOYMENT.

seasonal variation see TIME-SERIES ANALYSIS.

second-best (of an economy) departing from an optimal pattern of resource allocation (see PARETO OPTIMALITY), for example, because of MONOPOLY distortions and EXTERNALITIES.

If the production of a product, such as a chemical, leads to environmental POLLUTION, then the marginal SOCIAL COST of producing that output will exceed the marginal PRIVATE COST, and the economy will depart from an optimal pattern of resource allocation. In this second-best situation, the government can improve matters by imposing a pollution tax on offending chemical firms. On the one hand, this will provide an incentive for the firms to adopt less-polluting production processes and, on the other hand, to the extent that the tax is passed on to chemical buyers, will force buyers to pay the full social costs of the products they consume.

sector a part of the economy that has common characteristics enabling it to be separated from other parts of the economy for analytical or policy purposes. A broad division may be made, for example, between economic activities undertaken by a government (the PUBLIC SECTOR) and those undertaken by private individuals and businesses (the PRIVATE SECTOR). The private sector, in turn, may be subdivided into the PERSONAL SECTOR (private individuals and households), the CORPORATE SECTOR (businesses supplying goods and services), and the FINANCIAL SECTOR (businesses providing financial services).

secular trend a long-term movement, either upward or downward, in some economic variable. For example, the US GROSS NATIONAL PRODUCT (GNP) in constant (1982) dollars has risen steadily since 1960. Of course, in some years the increase has been greater than in other years, and there have been a few occasions when GNP has actually fallen, but overall the trend line has been upward. See also TIME-SERIES ANALYSIS, CYCLICAL FLUCTUATION, GROSS NATIONAL PRODUCT.

Securities and Exchange Commission the US governmental body that regulates operations of the New York STOCK EXCHANGE and other US stock exchanges.

seller concentration or **market concentration** an element of MARKET STRUCTURE denoting the number and size distribution of suppliers in a given MARKET. Market theory predicts that MARKET PERFORMANCE will differ according to whether there are many suppliers in the market, with each accounting for only a small fraction of total supply (PERFECT COMPETITION), or only a few suppliers, with each accounting for a substantial proportion of total supply (OLIGOPOLY), or a single supplier (MONOPOLY). See also CONCENTRATION MEASURES.

seller's market a market situation, usually of short duration, in which there is EXCESS DEMAND for goods and services at current prices, which forces prices up to the advantage of the seller. Compare BUYER'S MARKET.

separation of ownership from control see DIVORCE OF OWN-ERSHIP FROM CONTROL.

serial correlation see AUTOCORRELATION.

services any intangible economic activities (counseling, catering, insurance, banking, etc.) that contribute directly (see FINAL PROD-UCTS) or indirectly (see INTERMEDIATE GOODS) to the satisfaction of human wants. Services are an important component of GROSS NATIONAL PRODUCT.

service sector the part of the economy concerned with provision of a wide variety of personal and business services: transportation and retailing, banking and insurance, etc. The service sector, PRI-MARY SECTOR, and INDUSTRIAL SECTOR form an interlocking chain of economic activities that constitute a modern economy. See STRUCTURE OF INDUSTRY.

shadow price the imputed PRICE or VALUE of a good or service where such a price or value cannot be determined accurately due to absence of an ordinary price-determined market, or to gross distortions that may exist in markets. To impute a price or value is to make the best estimate possible of what that price or value would be if a normal market existed.

WELFARE ECONOMICS attempts to equate the price of a product to its marginal social cost. The marginal social cost of a product is the summation of all costs associated with it. For instance, the true cost of electricity comprises not just the capital, labor, and inputs of raw material. It is the additional cost of disposing adequately of waste products plus the decrease in aesthetic appeal of the area in which the power station is situated. No values are given for these externalities, because there are no markets in which to price them. Shadow prices for such items are frequently estimated in COST-BENEFIT ANALYSIS.

Shadow pricing is also encountered in intrafirm trading. The inputs of company division B may be the outputs of company division A. The products in which the two company divisions trade may not have an equivalent market price, because no open market for them exists, for example, intermediate components or managerial services. The transactions are given shadow prices, usually based on estimated costs plus a return on the capital involved. Such an estimate of market prices is used frequently in CENTRALLY PLANNED ECONOMIES.

A particular application of shadow pricing is found in LINEAR PROGRAMMING, when the solution to a problem yields hypothetical prices for scarce factor inputs, showing how much additional profit would result from an extra unit of each fully used resource.

share see COMMON STOCK.

share capital or **capital stock** the money employed in a corporation that has been subscribed by the SHAREHOLDERS of the company in the form of COMMON STOCK (equity) and PREFERRED STOCK and will remain as a permanent source of financing as long as the company remains in existence. See also DEBT CAPITAL, CAPITAL GEARING.

shareholders or **stockholders** the individuals and institutions that contribute funds to finance a corporation in return for SHARES in that company. There are two main types of shareholders: (a) holders of PREFERRED STOCKS, who are entitled to a fixed DIVIDEND from a company's PROFITS (before holders of common stock receive anything), and who have first claim on any remaining assets of the business after all debts have been discharged; (b) holders of COMMON STOCK, who are entitled to a dividend from a company's profits after all other dividends have been paid, and who are entitled to any remaining ASSETS of the business in the event that the business is liquidated.

share price index an index number of the average prices of a sample of company SHARES used as an indicator of general stock price movements. In the United States, stock price movements are monitored by the *Dow Jones Average* and *Standard & Poor's Index.* See PRICE INDEX.

shark repellants see TAKEOVER BID.

shift in tax the redirection of a tax away from its nominal bearer so that it is ultimately paid for by somebody else. For example, suppose the tax authorities impose a PAYROLL TAX on firms as a means of raising revenue. The firms decide to treat the tax as an increase in their costs of production and so raise their prices by an equivalent amount. Then, assuming there is no fall in sales resulting from the price increase, it is the consumers, not the firms, who foot the bill. See also INCIDENCE OF TAXATION.

shift system a method of organizing work that enables a production unit (a plant) to be run on a more intensive basis. For many plants the standard working day of the labor force is eight hours, but by using a two- or three-shift system, the plant can be worked for up to 24 hours.

This enables a firm to make maximum use of its FIXED FACTOR INPUT and lower its unit costs of production accordingly. See RETURNS TO THE VARIABLE FACTOR INPUT.

shop steward a shop-floor employee who is elected by the local members of a LABOR UNION to represent them in day-to-day negotiations with management.

short term or **short run** an abstract time period within the THEORY OF SUPPLY in which some FACTOR INPUTS are fixed (FIXED FACTOR INPUTS, such as plant size), and output can be adjusted only by changing the quantities of VARIABLE FACTOR INPUTS used, for example, raw materials and labor.

In practice, what is defined as the short term can vary greatly from industry to industry. For example, in the petrochemical industry it can take 5 years or more to commission, build, and test a new plant so that any expansion of output within this term can only be achieved by increasing throughput from existing plants. By contrast, in the garment industry it may be possible to buy and install new sewing machines within a few weeks so that in this industry the short term might be a month or less. Compare LONG TERM. See also RETURNS TO THE VARIABLE FACTOR INPUT.

SIC (Standard Industrial Classification) see INDUSTRIAL CLASSIFICATION.

significance (tests of) see HYPOTHESIS TESTING.

Simon, Herbert (born 1916) winner of the Nobel Memorial Prize in Economic Sciences, 1978, for research into how decisions are made within economic organizations. His analysis of this process within business has been referred to as *bounded rationality*. Simon has also investigated so-called artificial intelligence and computer science. He has used computer simulations to explore business psychology and aggregations of microsystems.

simple interest the INTEREST on a LOAN that is based only on the original amount of the loan. This means that interest charges grow over time in linear fashion. For example, a $1000 loan earning simple interest of 10% a year would accumulate to $1100 at the end of the first year and $1200 at the end of the second year, etc. Compare COMPOUND INTEREST.

simulation or **Monte Carlo simulation** a technique for dealing with complex resource allocation problems that cannot be solved exactly by mathematical analysis. The technique involves creating a typical life history of a system that represents the actual problem and its rules of operation. Repeated runs of the simulation, slightly altering the operating rules each time, enables experimentation aimed at discovering methods of improving performance of the system. Such simulation techniques are frequently employed in examining SHAREHOLDING and QUEUEING problems.

sinking fund a fund into which periodic payments are made that, along with earned COMPOUND INTEREST, will ultimately be sufficient to meet a known future capital commitment or discharge a LIABILITY. Such a fund may be used to finance replacement of FIXED ASSETS at the end of their useful life or to repurchase company bonds or debentures on maturity.

skewed distribution a group of numerical observations whose

FREQUENCY DISTRIBUTION takes the form of a HISTOGRAM, or of CONTINUOUS DISTRIBUTION, with two unequally shaped halves with a tail at one end. Compare SYMMETRICAL DISTRIBUTION.

skimming price a pricing policy that involves charging a comparatively high PRICE for a product to secure large profit margins. This policy will be adopted by a firm when consumers are not expected to be price sensitive, that is, demand is price-inelastic (see PRICE ELASTICITY OF DEMAND).

See PRODUCT LIFE CYCLE, PENETRATION PRICE.

slump see DEPRESSION.

Smith, Adam (1723—1790) professor of philosophy at Glasgow University whose writings formed the basis of CLASSICAL ECONOMICS. Smith's most famous book, *An Inquiry into the Nature and Causes of the Wealth of Nations* (1776), stressed the benefits of division of labor, discussed the need for SPECIALIZATION and exchange, and outlined the workings of the market mechanism (PRICE SYSTEM).

Smith argued that if producers were free to seek profits by providing goods and services, the invisible hand of market forces would ensure that the goods and services consumers wanted would be produced at the lowest possible cost. Provided that markets were free of government regulation, in this LAISSEZ FAIRE environment competition would direct production in ways that would increase public well-being.

In competitive markets, producers would compete to sell more goods, forcing prices down to the lowest level that covered production costs and allowed normal profit to be made. Furthermore, if certain goods were scarce, buyers would offer higher prices, drawing more producers into these industries and swelling supply. In this manner production in the market system would be directed by what consumers wanted.

Smith's outline of the market mechanism described the new economic system beginning to emerge in the newly industrializing Western countries.

However, for the system to work Smith acknowledged that two conditions have to be met: (a) markets must be free of government intervention, without the close government regulation of economic activity that prevailed prior to Smith's day; (b) the self-seeking behavior of producers can only be harnessed to the common good when competition prevails, and Smith was deeply suspicious of MONOPOLIES, considering them conspiracies against the consumer. See PERFECT COMPETITION.

social capital see INFRASTRUCTURE

social costs the COSTS borne by society resulting from the actions of FIRMS or people. A firm or a person initiating an action does not necessarily bear all the resulting costs. The costs borne by the firm or person are private costs. The costs not borne by the firm or person are external costs. Social costs are the sum of private and external costs.

Consider a river used both by a chemical firm to dispose of its waste and by a town as a source of drinking water. Assume that continual dumping of waste causes the river to become polluted. The firm incurs *private costs* in producing chemicals but pays out nothing for use of the river or for causing the pollution. The town, by contrast, is forced to install special water treatment plants to counter the pollution. Thus, the *external cost* of cleaning up the river is not borne by the firm but by society.

One way to remedy this divergence of private and social costs is to tax the firm an amount equivalent to the costs of treating the pollution. Making the firm pay the *full* costs of supplying chemicals has the merit of encouraging it to seek the least costly way of disposing of its waste. That is, instead of dumping its waste in the river, it might be cheaper for the firm to invest in a waste disposal plant.

See also EXTERNALITIES, WELFARE ECONOMICS, COST-BENEFIT ANALYSIS.

socialism a political doctrine emphasizing collective ownership of the means of production, ascribing a large role to the government in the running of the economy with widespread public ownership (NATIONALIZATION) of key industries. MARX regarded socialism as a transitional stage between the end of a PRIVATE ENTERPRISE ECONOMY system and the beginnings of COMMUNISM. In the contemporary world, the communist form of socialism involves abolition of most private property and curtailment of civil liberties. In practice, the socialist form of economic system is that of the MIXED ECONOMY, which combines elements of democratic socialism and the private enterprise tradition. See CENTRALLY PLANNED ECONOMY.

social overhead capital see INFRASTRUCTURE.

social products or **merit goods** or **public goods** the GOODS and SERVICES, for example, education, health services, and subsidized housing, provided by a government for the benefit of all or most of the populace. There is no direct link between consumption of a social product and payment for it. Social products are paid for out of general taxation and not by individual consumers buying in the market place. See also COLLECTIVE PRODUCTS.

Social Security Act of 1935 the basic US program, amended subsequently, for providing insurance benefits for old-age survivors, disability and health insurance, and unemployment payments. The Act also provides payments for food, housing, and child support. Portions of these programs are administered by the Federal government, others by state governments, still others by state and local governments, and the rest by all three levels of government.

The social security programs are financed by payroll taxes to which employers and employees contribute. As the US population has aged in recent years, and as new social security programs have been added, the payroll taxes and the benefits paid out have been increased. While the financing of the programs was established on a pay-as-you-go basis, the taxes levied have recently been restructured to produce a surplus as a cushion against the predictable increase in future claims because of the aging population.

social security benefits and **welfare benefits** any benefits provided to the unemployed, retired persons, the disabled, single-parent families, etc. Social security benefits may take the form of money payments, for example, unemployment benefits and pensions, or payments in kind, for example, food stamps. See POVERTY TRAP, NEGATIVE INCOME TAX.

social security tax a tax paid by employees, employers, and the self-employed to finance public insurance plans, such as retirement and disability incomes, health insurance, and unemployment insurance.

social time preference see DISCOUNT RATE.

social welfare function see WELFARE ECONOMICS.

soft currency a foreign CURRENCY that is in weak demand, but in abundant supply on the FOREIGN EXCHANGE MARKET. Soft currency status is usually associated with an economically weak country that is running a large deficit in its BALANCE OF PAYMENTS. The supply of the currency is high enough to finance the purchase of imports, but demand for the currency is relatively weak because the amount of it required for purchase of exports is much lower. However, under a FLOATING EXCHANGE-RATE SYSTEM, in theory the demand for and supply of the currency should be brought into balance by a DEPRECIATION(1) in its EXCHANGE RATE value. Compare HARD CURRENCY.

soft loan a loan carrying a RATE OF INTEREST substantially below that of the interest rate charged normally on a loan for a similar purpose and risk status. Soft loans are often given as a form of ECONOMIC AID to DEVELOPING COUNTRIES by developed countries and international institutions. See also WORLD BANK.

sole proprietor see FIRM.

Solow economic growth model a theoretical construct that focuses on the role of technological change in the ECONOMIC GROWTH process.

In the HARROD ECONOMIC GROWTH MODEL and the DOMAR ECONOMIC GROWTH MODEL, a constant CAPITAL-OUTPUT RATIO is assumed, so there is a linear relationship between increases in the CAPITAL STOCK (through INVESTMENT) and the resulting increase in output. For example, if it requires $3000 of capital to produce $1000 of output, the capital-output ratio is one third, and this is assumed to apply to successive additions to the capital stock. By contrast, the Solow model utilizes a production function in which output is a function of capital *and* labor, with capital being substitutable for labor but with varying degrees of perfection, and which displays DIMINISHING RETURNS. Thus, if capital is increased relative to labor, the resulting increases in output become progressively smaller. On this assumption of a variable capital-output ratio as a country's capital stock increases, diminishing returns set in and produce progressively smaller increments in output. Sustained economic growth thus requires not only CAPITAL WIDENING but also CAPITAL DEEPENING investment. Specifically, TECHNOLOGICAL PROGRESSIVENESS (new production techniques, processes and methods, and new products) plays a necessary role in offsetting diminishing returns to capital as the capital stock increases.

Solow, Robert (born 1914) winner of the Nobel Memorial Prize in Economic Sciences, 1987, for contributions to the theory of economic growth. In addition, Solow has added to the store of knowledge of the sources of increase in income per capita, systematic analysis of markets, and the theory of capital and interest.

sources and uses of funds see FLOW OF FUNDS ANALYSIS.

Special Drawing Right (SDR) a monetary asset held by member countries of the INTERNATIONAL MONETARY FUND (IMF) as part of their INTERNATIONAL RESERVES. Unlike other reserve assets, such as gold, SDRs have no tangible life of their own. They are created by the IMF itself and take the form of bookkeeping entries in a special account managed by the Fund. The SDR is valued in terms of a weighted basket of five currencies: US dollar, West German mark, UK sterling, French franc, and Japanese yen.

specialist a broker's broker, that is, a dealer who acts as a principal in buying and selling securities on the floor of a stock exchange. A specialist usually deals in a small group of securities, which the specialist buys or sells on the specialist's own account or the accounts of others, and holds blocks of these securities. Specialists make their income from the difference between the price at which they are prepared to buy stocks and the higher price at which they usually sell.

Specialists mark their buying and selling prices up or down depending on whether the prices of their blocks of securities are rising or falling. For example, if there is heavy public demand for one of these securities, as the specialist sells some holdings of that security, he or she will mark up the price for it to reflect its increasing scarcity. By being ready always to buy or sell, the specialist's role is that of maintaining a degree of price stability in the market for the securities he or she deals in.

specialization a form of division of labor in which each individual or firm concentrates productive efforts on a single or limited number of activities. If a person specializes in a single task, that person is likely to be much more efficient than by attempting to be a jack-of-all-trades. Specialists can concentrate on the work they are best at doing: familiarity and repetition improve work skills, and time is not lost in moving from one job to another. For these reasons, output is greater as a result of specialization.

Similarly, specialization enables an economy to use its scarce resources more efficiently, thereby producing and consuming a larger volume of goods and services than would otherwise be the case. This fundamental principle can be illustrated assuming, to simplify matters, a two-person, A and B, and two-product, X and Y, economy. Let us suppose that A has the PRODUCTION POSSIBILITY BOUNDARY indicated in Fig. 162a of 12X or 6Y. Thus, A is twice as efficient at producing X as at producing Y—an opportunity cost ratio of 2X/1Y. Let us assume A chooses to produce and consume at point A_{pc} on the A production possibility line (6X and 3Y).

B, by contrast, has the production possibility boundary indicated in Fig. 162b of 12Y or 6X. B is twice as efficient at producing Y as at producing X—an opportunity cost ratio of 2Y/1X. Let us assume B chooses to produce and consume at point B_{pc} on the B production possibility line (6Y and 3X).

Now, assume that A and B specialize in production of the product in which they are most efficient. Thus, A specializes totally in the production of X, and B totally in the production of Y. Transposing Figs. 162a and b onto Fig. 162c, we see the establishment of a new production possibility boundary—and a new opportunity cost ratio of 1X/1Y—for the economy.

Specialization thus results in *production gain*: the economy is now able to produce 12X and 12Y, which is 3 more X and 3 more Y than previously (see Fig. 162d); it also results in *consumption gain*: as a result of specialization *and* exchange, A and B can now consume more of both products. For example, A consumes 8 of the X that A produces and exchanges the remaining 4X for 4Y from B (that is, 1X = 1Y from the opportunity cost ratio 1X/1Y). With specialization and exchange, A is now consuming 2 more X and 1 more Y. By the same token, B consumes 8 of the Y that B produces and exchanges 4Y for 4X from A, thereby increasing B's consumption by 2Y and 1X.

See also PRODUCTIVITY, COMPARATIVE ADVANTAGE, GAINS FROM TRADE.

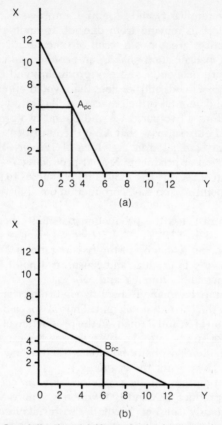

FIG. 162. **Specialization.** (a) A's production/consumption possibility boundary before specialization. (b) B's production/consumption possibility boundary before specialization.

specific tax a tax levied at a fixed rate per physical unit of output. See AD VALOREM TAX, VALUE-ADDED TAX.

speculation the purchase or sale of ASSETS, real or financial, to achieve a CAPITAL GAIN. See ARBITRAGE, SPECULATIVE DEMAND FOR MONEY, SPECULATOR.

speculative demand for money a demand for funds held in

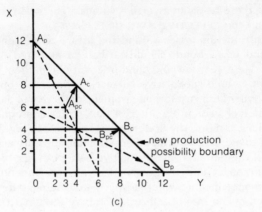

(c)

	Production				Consumption			
	Before		After		Before		After	
	X	Y	X	Y	X	Y	X	Y
A	6	3	12	–	6	3	8(+ 2)	4(+ 1)
B	3	6	–	12	3	6	4(+ 1)	8(+ 2)
Total	9	9	12	12	9	9	12(+ 3)	12(+ 3)

(d)

FIG. 162. (continued)**Specialization.** (c) A and B's combined production/consumption possibility boundary after specialization. (d) The production/consumption limits of A and B before and after specialization.

highly liquid MONEY form in the hope of taking advantage of bargains in the form of low-priced securities or other assets.

Speculative balances are associated with the concept of a normal RATE OF INTEREST. Individual and institutional holders of speculative balances have their own opinions of what this normal rate is. If the current rate of interest is high, it encourages the holding of bonds but discourages money holding because of: (a) the high OPPORTUNITY COST of holding cash in terms of interest foregone; (b) the negligible risks attached to capital losses, because the interest rate is unlikely to rise even further and so reduce the price of bonds, there being an inverse relationship between the price of bonds and the EFFECTIVE RATE OF INTEREST.

The speculation arises around the future movement of bond prices and when bonds should be bought and sold. When the interest rate is very low and bond prices are high, then: (c) people will want to hold speculative balances because the opportunity cost in terms of interest forgone is small; (d) there will be a general expectation of a rise in the interest rate, with a consequent fall in bond prices, and thus the preference is for cash holding. The effect of such forces is to create an inverse relationship between interest rates and the demand for speculative balances.

Precautionary and transaction balances are functions of the level of money income, whereas speculative demand for money is a function of the rate of interest. Compare PRECAUTIONARY DEMAND FOR MONEY, TRANSACTIONS DEMAND FOR MONEY.

speculator a dealer in markets characterized by rapidly changing prices, such as a COMMODITY MARKET or a securities market, who buys and/or sells commodities or securities not because he or she trades in them, but in the hope of making a short-term gain from movements in the prices of these commodities or securities. For example, in the STOCK EXCHANGE, speculators may take a bullish view that a particular stock price will rise, and gamble on this hunch by buying the stock on short-term credit terms at the current price, and reselling it at a higher price after a week or two, using the proceeds from the resale to pay the original seller. On the other hand, speculators may take a bearish view that a share price will fall, and gamble on this hunch by arranging to sell the stocks at the present price, even though they do not own any, using the proceeds from this sale to buy at a lower price the shares they have promised to deliver some time later.

The activities of speculators within a market may be stabilizing or destabilizing, depending on whether or not they take a collective view about future price movements. For example, if some stock exchange speculators feel that the price of a stock is going to rise while other speculators feel that the price of the same stock is going to fall, then the former would seek to buy, adding to demand for it, and the latter would seek to sell, adding to the supply of the stock. Their efforts would cancel out, having little net effect on the stock price. However, if most speculators take the view that a stock price will rise, they will all seek to buy it, and thus add to the demand for it and force up its price. If, on the other hand, most speculators take the view that the stock price will fall, they will all seek to sell it, adding to its supply and forcing the price down.

Whether speculators reduce or accentuate fluctuations in stock prices over time depends on whether their collective view about future prices parallels the underlying price changes or moves in opposition to them. For example, if a stock price is rising, and speculators take a collective view that it will continue to rise, they will seek to buy it in the hope of reselling at a higher price, and this buying will accelerate the upward price movement. On the other hand, if a stock price is rising, and speculators take a collective view that it will begin to fall in the immediate future, they will seek to sell the stock in hope of buying it back later at a lower price, and this selling will slow down the upward price movement.

Speculators operate in both SPOT MARKETS and FUTURES MARKETS and often make considerable use of OPTIONS in their dealings. For example, speculators may purchase stock options that entitle them to buy a certain number of shares of a company's stock at a predetermined price at some future date. They will do this when they think the stock price will increase to more than the predetermined price plus the cost of the option, because they will gain by exercising the option and immediately reselling the shares at the higher price.

See also ARBITRAGE, HOT MONEY.

spot market a market for purchase and sale of COMMODITIES (oil, pork bellies, etc.) and financial instruments (FOREIGN EXCHANGE) for immediate delivery, as opposed to a FUTURES MARKET, which provides for delivery at some future time. Spot prices for commodities and financial instruments transacted at different locations are harmonized by ARBITRAGE.

stabilization policy the application by government and Federal Reserve authorities of available macroeconomic tools to regulate the level of AGGREGATE DEMAND in order to counter CYCLICAL FLUCTUATIONS in economic activity. Left to its own devices, the economy may go through periods of BOOM and DEPRESSION known as BUSINESS CYCLES (the continuous line in Fig. 163). See CIRCULAR FLOW OF NATIONAL INCOME MODEL, DEMAND MANAGEMENT, DEFLATIONARY GAP, INFLATIONARY GAP, POTENTIAL GROSS NATIONAL PRODUCT, MACROECONOMIC POLICY, EMPLOYMENT ACT OF 1946, MONETARY POLICY, FISCAL POLICY.

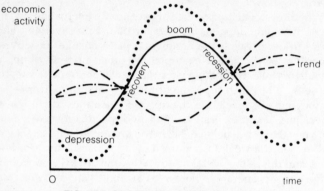

FIG. 163. **Stabilization policy.** See entry.

stagflation a situation of depressed levels of real output combined with increases in prices (INFLATION). Stagflation may be caused by the dual forces of (a) a deficiency in AGGREGATE DEMAND relative to POTENTIAL GROSS NATIONAL PRODUCT (see DEFLATIONARY GAP) and (b) rising FACTOR INPUT costs (see COST-PUSH INFLATION).

Stagflation was a vexing problem in many countries during the 1970s and early 1980s. Some economists believe it was a result of the combined effect of cost-push inflationary pressures emanating from the oil price increases of 1973 and 1979, and the deflationary consequences of reduced real purchasing power in the oil-consuming countries accompanying these increases. This was exacerbated by development of higher inflationary expectations.

Orthodox FISCAL POLICY and MONETARY POLICY, accustomed to an apparent trade-off between inflation and employment/output (see the PHILLIPS CURVE), was found wanting in the new situation, and many countries turned to alternative approaches. In the United States, for example, there was a move toward SUPPLY-SIDE ECONOMICS.

standard deviation or **root-mean-square deviation** a measure of variation within a group of numerical observations, that is, the square root of the average of squared deviations of observations from the group MEAN. Squaring the deviations eliminates negative signs and concentrates attention on the magnitude of the deviations, not on their signs. For example, if five products have prices of $5, $4, $3, $2, and $1, the mean price is:

$$\$\frac{5 + 4 + 3 + 2 + 1}{5} = \$\frac{15}{5} = \$3$$

and the distances by which the various prices depart from the mean price are:

$5−3=	$2	squared deviations:	2×2=4
$4−3=	$1		1×1=1
$3−3=	$0		0×0=0
$2−3=	−$1		−1×−1=1
$1−3=	−$2		−2×−2=4
	$0		$10

The sum of the squared deviations in the example above is $10, and their average is $10/5 = $2. This figure represents the VARIANCE of the group of observations. To compensate for squaring the deviations, the square root of the average is taken, so that in the example above the standard deviation is $\sqrt{2} = \$1.41$.

Compare AVERAGE DEVIATION, COEFFICIENT OF VARIATION.

standard error the error of the MEAN that shows how much means can be expected to vary from sample to sample if repeated random samples are taken from the same POPULATION and the sample means are calculated as an approximation of the true population mean. Standard error can be calculated by using a formula linking the STANDARD DEVIATION of the population and the sample size. The standard error of the mean decreases as the size of sample is increased, so when the sample size is large, the sample mean becomes a more reliable estimate of the true population mean. See also REGRESSION ANALYSIS.

standard industrial classification see INDUSTRIAL CLASSIFICATION.

standard of living a level of monetary income or measure of consumption. INCOME PER CAPITA is also used as a proxy for standard of living. The difficulty lies in assessing the benefits and costs that may improve a person's style of living but that have no immediately attributable economic value. For example, two people may have identical salaries, but one may live in the country and have splendid scenery, peace and quiet, no traffic jams when driving to work, and little pollution. The other person may live in an industrial city that has considerable traffic jams, pollution, noise, and crime but also offers a variety of museums and concert halls. Monetary comparisons would suggest a similar standard of living, but this may not be the case.

stand-by arrangement an arrangement between the INTERNATIONAL MONETARY FUND and a member country under which the member country is entitled to borrow up to an agreed amount of foreign currency from the Fund to cover a possible deficit in its BALANCE OF PAYMENTS.

staple product any product that has an INCOME ELASTICITY OF DEMAND of less than one. This means that as incomes rise, proportionately less income is spent on such products. Examples of staple products include basic food, such as potatoes and bread. By contrast, products with an income elasticity of more than one are referred to as LUXURY PRODUCTS. See also ENGEL'S LAW, NORMAL PRODUCT, INFERIOR PRODUCT, GIFFEN GOOD.

static analysis see COMPARATIVE STATIC EQUILIBRIUM ANALYSIS.

statistical inference a process by which we draw conclusions about a statistical POPULATION from which a SAMPLE has been drawn. For example, if one million New Yorkers vacation in Florida each year, and 200 are asked why they do so, 50% may say because the sun always shines there. From this sample one may infer that 50% of the total population of one million New Yorkers taking a holiday in Florida do so for this reason. However, it is not possible to say with 100% accuracy that this is the case unless the views of all one million are obtained. Nevertheless, it is possible to say with 95% confidence that the estimation of 50% is correct for the whole population.

It is clearly very difficult, expensive, and time-consuming to ask *everybody* the reasons for choosing Florida as a holiday destination. The PROBABILITY that the population, the 1 million on vacation, behaves as the sample, the 200 on vacation, suggests can be statistically determined using HYPOTHESIS TESTING.

statistics 1. a branch of mathematics that studies the theory and methods of collecting, tabulating, and analyzing numerical data. 2. a grouping of data. Economic analysis makes extensive use of economic data that are subjected to statistical analysis in order to test ECONOMIC THEORIES. See HYPOTHESIS TESTING.

stepwise regression a form of multiple regression analysis in which INDEPENDENT VARIABLES are added into the regression equation one at a time, and their impact in terms of adding to the explanatory power of the regression equation is noted.

sterling the name given to the British POUND in international dealings to distinguish it from other countries using the pound as the basis of their currencies. Formerly, most countries extensively involved in international trade kept large sterling balances as part of their INTERNATIONAL RESERVES, but sterling nowadays is little used as a reserve asset except by a number of current and former member countries of the British Commonwealth.

sterling area a group of countries, predominantly former British colonies, whose own national currencies were formerly linked directly to the value of the British POUND, and who hold STERLING as part of their INTERNATIONAL RESERVES.

Stigler, George (born 1911) winner of the Nobel Prize in Economic Sciences, 1982, for seminal studies of industrial structures, functioning of markets, and causes and effects of government regulation. Stigler has also been interested in exploring applied microeconomics. Considered somewhat iconoclastic, Stigler has produced work that has undermined confidence in such ideas as the benefits of rent controls, the usefulness of the theory of monopolistic competition, and the value of pursuit by consumers of the unachievable goal of optimal utility.

Stigler is regarded as a conservative who would restrict government's economic influence, but he has stated that he is not a so-called supply-sider, "whatever that is."

stock a FINANCIAL SECURITY issued by a CORPORATION or by a government as a means of raising long-term capital. In some countries, for example, the United States, stockholders are the owners of the company. In other countries, for example, Britain, stock is a form of repayable, fixed-interest DEBT, and stockholders are creditors of the company not owners. Stocks are traded on the STOCK EXCHANGE. See SHARE CAPITAL.

stockbroker an agent who acts on behalf of individual and company clients, arranging to buy or sell STOCKS and other securities from SPECIALISTS, who make markets in securities. In most countries, individuals and companies can deal directly with specialists, so the roles of stockbroker and specialist are combined. See STOCK EXCHANGE.

stock dividend a DIVIDEND payment whereby a SHAREHOLDER is paid a dividend in the form of additional SHARES in the company rather than in cash. See also STOCK SPLIT.

stock exchange a MARKET that deals in STOCKS and BONDS. Institutions involved in the stock exchange include SPECIALISTSand STOCKBROKERS. The stock exchange performs two principal functions. It provides (a) a primary or new-issue market, in which new capital for investment and other purposes can be raised by issuing financial securities; (b) a secondary market for trading existing securities that facilitates transferability of securities from sellers to buyers. The stock exchange thus occupies an important position in a country's FINANCIAL SYSTEM by providing a mechanism for converting SAVINGS into physical and portfolio INVESTMENT.

In recent years national stock exchanges, such as those based in New York, London, and Tokyo, have become increasingly interdependent as the number of MULTINATIONAL FIRMS has grown and financial institutions and securities firms have become more international in scope.

See also CAPITAL MARKET, SPECULATION, SPECULATOR, FUTURES MARKET, INSTITUTIONAL INVESTORS.

stockpiling the act of accumulating inventories over and above normal requirements. Domestic and foreign trade depend on complex supply lines from the raw material to the finished good. If at any point along the supply chain a shortage or bottleneck can be perceived in advance by firms beyond that point, those firms will attempt to purchase greater stocks than their immediate needs warrant. Stockpiling occurs in many areas of economic life, from a government that stockpiles food or weapons, to the individual consumer who amasses quantities of food in anticipation of a price rise or shortage.

stock split an increase in the number of SHARES in a corporation that does not affect the capitalization of the company. For example, Company X has 10,000 authorized, issued, and fully paid-up shares, each with a par value of $1. Total shareholders' capital is shown in the BALANCE SHEET at $10,000. The STOCK EXCHANGE values the company at $100,000, making each share worth $10. The company wishes to attract a wider shareholder base by reducing the market PRICE of each share, and so undertakes a two-for-one stock split, giving existing shareholders two new 50-cent shares for each share held. The company now has 20,000 authorized, issued, and fully paid-up shares of 50 cents nominal value, and capitalization of the company remains unchanged at $10,000. However, the market price of the shares will be $5, which can be expected to improve the marketability of the shares. See also SHARE CAPITAL.

stock valuation or **inventory valuation** the placing of an appropriate money value on a firm's STOCKS of raw materials, WORK IN PROGRESS, and finished goods. When INFLATION causes the prices of several batches of finished-goods stock bought during a trading period to differ, the firm has the problems of deciding: (a) what money value to place on the period-end physical stock in the BALANCE SHEET and (b) what costs to attach to the sold units in the company accounts. The second decision has a direct bearing on the COST OF GOODS SOLD and so on GROSS PROFIT.

Different formulas used to value stock can lead to variations in the balance-sheet value of stock and in the cost of goods sold. For example, the *first-in, first-out (FIFO)* method assumes that goods are withdrawn from stock in the order in which they are received so that the cost of goods sold is based on the cost of the oldest goods in stock, while the value of closing stock is based on the prices of the most recent purchases. By contrast, the *last-in, first-out (LIFO)* method assumes that the most recently purchased goods are theoretically withdrawn from stock first so that the cost of goods sold is based on the costs of the most recent purchases, while the value of closing stock is based on the oldest goods available. The last-in first-out method gives a higher figure for cost-of-goods sold: one that more closely approximates the replacement cost of goods sold, but it tends to understate the value of period-end stocks.

In the interests of prudence, the firm would tend to value stocks at cost or market value, whichever was lower, to avoid overstating profits.

See also INFLATION ACCOUNTING, DEPRECIATION.

stop-go cycle the application by a government of available macroeconomic tools to stimulate and then damp economic activity. Such tools are used in countercyclical STABILIZATION POLICY to try to offset fluctuations in economic activity associated with the BUSINESS CYCLE. Stop-go policies are often referred to in a negative sense, in that government policies of this type during the 1960s and early 1970s especially were either ill-timed or involved injections or withdrawals of an incorrect magnitude.

Short-term attainment of government economic objectives, such as the level of employment and the exchange rate, is frequently contradictory to the long-term objectives of, for instance, growth. See MACROECONOMIC POLICY.

stop-loss order a mechanism instructing a securities broker to sell the customer's holdings of a stock when it falls to a specified price. See STOP ORDER.

stop order a mechanism instructing a securities broker to buy a specified stock at a price above the current market price, or to sell at a price below the current market price, in order to protect unrealized gains or to limit losses.

store of value an attribute of MONEY enabling people to hold on to money to finance some *future* purchase of a product or asset without loss of PURCHASING POWER in the interim.

straight-line method see DEPRECIATION(2).

strategic decisions any decisions taken by the most senior management that determine the fundamental long-term objectives of an enterprise and the formulation of overall plans to achieve them. Decisions of this nature deal with what may be termed the *entrepreneurial functions* of the enterprise, rather than recurrent operational decisions. Strategic decisions are concerned with identifying the strengths and weaknesses of the enterprise in relation to the opportunities and threats in its environment, and formulating a program of action to exploit opportunities and deal with potential threats. See ENTREPRENEUR.

stratified sample a SAMPLE selected by dividing the total POPULATION into a number of distinct subgroups, then selecting a proportionate number of items from each subgroup. See RANDOM SAMPLE.

strike a concerted stoppage of work by a group of workers as part of an industrial dispute. See INDUSTRIAL RELATIONS, LOCKOUT, PICKET.

structural unemployment the long-term UNEMPLOYMENT caused by decline of certain industries and changes in production processes. It occurs when changing demand patterns in an economy dislocate existing production patterns to the extent that labor is in surplus supply. This is a long-term phenomenon, perhaps requiring the work force to seek other jobs outside the declining industries and possibly in different parts of a country. Countering such unemployment may require extensive occupational retraining programs for the displaced workers, assistance with moving to new areas where jobs are available, and financial inducements to encourage new growth industries to move to regions blighted by concentrations of declining industries. See FRICTIONAL UNEMPLOYMENT, REGIONAL POLICY, DEINDUSTRIALIZATION, ENTERPRISE ZONE.

structure of industry the productive activities undertaken in an economy classified according to broad groupings of activities by sector, or more narrowly on an industry-by-industry basis.

The three basic sectors of an economy are: (a) the primary sector—raw materials and farming; (b) the industrial or secondary sector— manufactured goods, construction, gas and electricity, etc.; and (c) the service sector— data processing, retailing, banking, tourism, etc.

The relative importance of each of these sectors tends to change as an economy expands over time. For example, DEVELOPING COUNTRIES are characterized by very large primary sectors and small industrial and service sectors, whereas DEVELOPED COUNTRIES are characterized by small primary sectors and large industrial and service sectors. Figure 164 shows that in the most advanced countries there has been a relative decline in the industrial sector, and a corresponding increase in the importance of the service sector.

See INDUSTRIALIZATION, DEINDUSTRIALIZATION, INDUSTRIAL CLASSIFICATIONS, ECONOMIC DEVELOPMENT.

subsidiary a company owned by another company. A subsidiary

	Agriculture		Industry		Manufacturing		Services	
	1960	1984	1960	1984	1960	1984	1960	1984
UK	3	2	43	32	32	18	54	66
US	4	2	38	32	29	21	58	66
Japan	13	4	45	42	34	30	42	54
W. Germany	6	2	53	46	40	35	41	52

FIG. 164. **Structure of industry.** The distribution of gross domestic product in percentages from 1960—1984 for the United Kingdom, United States, Japan, and West Germany. (Manufacturing percentages are also included in those for industry.) Source: *World Development Report,* World Bank.

may continue to trade under its own name, but it is subject to complete or partial centralized control by the parent company. See also HOLDING COMPANY.

subsidy a payment made by a government to either: (a) a firm—to enable it to hold or reduce the price of its product to consumers, thus ensuring that people maintain their consumption; (b) declining firms and industries—to enable them to remain in business. In the former cases, subsidies are used as an instrument of income redistribution by reducing the price of products, such as bread and milk, which figure prominently in the budget of lower-income groups, or by directly subsidizing incomes.

Subsidies encourage increased output of favored products, but distort domestic RESOURCE ALLOCATION processes in general, and can adversely affect international trade (EXPORT SUBSIDIES).

See REDISTRIBUTION-OF-INCOME PRINCIPLE OF TAXATION.

subsistence wage rate see WAGES-FUND THEORY, MARX, RICARDO.

substitute products any GOODS or SERVICES considered to be economically interchangeable by buyers. For example, if an increase in the price of coffee causes buyers to switch away from it and buy a greater quantity of tea, these two goods can be regarded as substitutes for one another.

The CROSS ELASTICITY OF DEMAND between two products serves as a measure of the degree of substitutability between them. Products that are close substitutes have a high cross elasticity, while products that are poor substitutes have a low cross elasticity.

See COMPLEMENTARY PRODUCTS.

substitution effect the substitution of one PRODUCT for another resulting from a change in their relative prices. A fall in the price of a product normally results in a greater demand for it. A part of this increase is due to the substitution effect. A lower price for good X, with the prices of other goods remaining unchanged, will increase its relative attractiveness, inducing consumers to substitute good X in place of some of the now relatively more expensive items in their budgets. The substitution effect, together with the INCOME EFFECT, provides an explanation of why DEMAND CURVES are downward sloping. See CONSUMER EQUILIBRIUM, REVEALED PREFERENCE THEORY, PRICE EFFECT.

sufficient condition see NECESSARY CONDITION.

sunk costs any expenditure on durable and specific FACTOR INPUTS, such as plant and machinery, that cannot be used for other purposes or easily be resold. Such sunk costs have no affect on MARGINAL COSTS and do not influence short-term output decisions. See also OPPORTUNITY COST.

super-normal profit see ABOVE-NORMAL PROFIT.

supplier see FIRM.

supply the amount of a PRODUCT made available for sale by FIRMS. In economic analysis, the total supply of a product is reflected in the SUPPLY CURVE, Compare DEMAND.

supply and demand see SUPPLY CURVE, DEMAND CURVE.

supply curve a line showing the relationship between the PRICE of a good and the quantity supplied during a time period. "Supply" means the total quantity of a good or service that firms are prepared to sell at a given price. See Fig. 165. See also SUPPLY CURVE (SHIFT IN), SUPPLY FUNCTION, AVERAGE COST, MARGINAL COST.

supply curve (shift in) a movement of the SUPPLY CURVE from one position to another, either left or right, as a result of some economic change other than PRICE.

A supply curve is always drawn on the CETERIS PARIBUS assumption that all other factors affecting supply, costs in particular, are held constant. If any of these change, however, the change will bring about a *shift* in the supply curve. For example, if costs of production fall, the supply curve will shift to the right (see Fig. 166), so more is supplied at each price than formerly. See also SUPPLY FUNCTION.

supply elasticity see PRICE ELASTICITY OF SUPPLY.

supply function a form of notation linking the DEPENDENT VARI-

SUPPLY FUNCTION

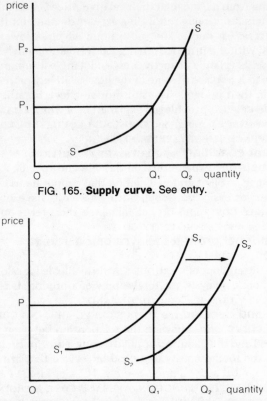

FIG. 165. **Supply curve.** See entry.

FIG. 166. **Supply curve (shift in).** A fall in production costs shifts the supply curve $S_1 S_1$ to $S_2 S_2$, increasing the quantity supplied at price OP from OQ_1 to OQ_2. The magnitude of this shift depends on the sensitivity of product supply to changes in costs.

ABLE, quantity supplied (Q_s), with various INDEPENDENT VARIA-BLES that determine quantity supplied, such as product PRICE (P), prices of factor inputs (P_1 and P_2), state of the technology (T), and business goals (G). The equation states that:

$$Q_s = f(P, P_1, P_2, T, G)$$

Changes in any of these independent variables will affect quantity supplied, and if we wish to investigate the effect of any one of these variables on quantity supplied, we theoretically could hold the influence of the other independent variables constant (CETERIS PARIBUS) while we focus on the effect of that independent variable.

See also SUPPLY CURVE, SUPPLY CURVE (SHIFT IN).

supply schedule a schedule listing the various PRICES of a PRODUCT and the specific quantities supplied at each of these prices. The information provided by a supply schedule can be used to construct a SUPPLY CURVE showing the price/quantity-supplied relationship in graphical form.

supply-side economics the branch of economic analysis concerned with the productive capability of an economy (POTENTIAL GROSS NATIONAL PRODUCT) and with policies designed to improve the flexibility of factor markets and thus generate the largest possible output for a given level of AGGREGATE DEMAND. Supply-side economists have examined institutional rigidities in factor markets and the effect of higher factor prices in pricing people out of jobs. This has led them to condemn the activities of unions in labor markets on the grounds that unions push WAGE RATES up to levels beyond the MARGINAL REVENUE PRODUCTIVITY of the workers concerned, thereby restricting potential employment. Such ideas have also led supply-side economists to condemn certain welfare systems and PROGRESSIVE TAXATION systems on the grounds that they create a so-called POVERTY TRAP, which acts as a disincentive for the unemployed to take low-paying jobs.

Supply-side theorists have argued that reduced income taxes, both individual and corporate, can lead to increased revenues. The reduction in the tax rate would be more than offset by the increased economic activity of firms experiencing greater after-tax profits, by the contributions of individual taxpayers who would be willing to work harder and longer, knowing they would keep more of their increased incomes, and by the entrance into mainstream economic activity of people who now operate in the underground economy in order to escape what they regard as excessive taxation.

See also NEGATIVE INCOME TAX.

surplus value an excess of the receipts of a FACTOR INPUT over its supply PRICE. David RICARDO took the example of rental payments to landlords in possession of superior land. Karl MARX viewed surplus value in terms of labor, whereby workers produce more than their own costs, defined as a subsistence wage. Marx attempted to show that the exchange value of a product was due solely to labor, while others suggest it is the entire production process that produces the exchange value. According to Marx, exploitation of the workers can only be eradicated by paying workers the value of their output rather than a subsistence wage. Alfred MARSHALL noted that all factor receipts in excess of factor costs are in the nature of QUASI-RENT in the short run, so where there are no alternative opportunities for a factor, *all* of its reward is a surplus. See also ECONOMIC RENT, TRANSFER EARNINGS, QUASI-RENT.

swap arrangement the sale of a foreign currency with a simultaneous agreement to repurchase it at some future date, or the purchase of a foreign currency with a simultaneous agreement to resell it at some future date. The purpose of such arrangements is to supply needed liquidity in international finance.

symmetrical distribution a group of numerical observations whose FREQUENCY DISTRIBUTION takes the form of a bell-shaped HISTOGRAM or of a CONTINUOUS DISTRIBUTION with two equally shaped halves. In a perfectly symmetrical distribution, the MEAN will equal the MEDIAN and the MODE. Compare SKEWED DISTRIBUTION.

systematic risk that part of total risk within the CAPITAL-ASSET PRICING MODEL attributable to the holding of a security or portfolio of securities, with a definable relationship in regard to variations of all security yields on the stock market. This definable relationship is termed the BETA COEFFICIENT(2). The beta coefficient (β) estimates the degree of responsiveness of the yield of a particular security to changes in the level of a specified market index, such as the Dow Jones Average. Studies of the measurement of β indicate a linear relationship between movement of a particular security and the market generally. For instance, if $\beta = 1$, a 10% change in security A is associated with a 10% change in the market generally. The security and the market are said to be perfectly correlated. If $\beta = 0$, the security is said to be risk-free because no matter how much the market moves, the security— even if not its market price—remains constant. An asset is considered risky if $\beta > 1$. Unlike NONSYSTEMATIC RISK, it is not possible to diversify the risk away because, however large the portfolio of shares held, they are all influenced by the market generally to a greater or lesser extent. The two components of risk, systematic and nonsystematic, are sometimes referred to as *nondiversifiable* and *diversifiable* for the reasons outlined.

T

table a means of presenting statistical data, often summarized in terms of a FREQUENCY DISTRIBUTION.

Taft-Hartley Act (1947) see NATIONAL LABOR RELATIONS ACT.

takeover the joining together of two or more FIRMS. Unlike a MERGER, which is usually arranged by mutual agreement between the firms involved, takeovers often involve one firm buying out the other without the full agreement of the acquired firm. For publicly traded companies, this involves one company buying controlling interest in the stock of the other, although generally the acquiring company would wish to purchase all the shares of the other company.

Three broad categories of takeovers may be identified: (a) horizontal takeovers involving firms competing directly in the same market, (b) vertical takeovers involving firms that stand in a supplier-customer relationship, and (c) conglomerate takeovers involving firms operating in unrelated markets that are seeking to diversify their activities.

From the firm's point of view, a takeover can be advantageous because it may enable the firm to reduce production and distribution costs, expand its existing activities, move into new areas, or remove troublesome competition and increase its market power. In terms of wider impact on the operation of market processes, takeovers on the one hand may promote greater efficiency in resource use; on the other hand, by reducing competition, takeovers may lead to less efficient allocation of resources. Whether a takeover will be beneficial on balance requires evaluation of the sometimes competing interests of stockholders, managers, employees, creditors, and consumers. In sum, they simultaneously may involve both benefits and damage (see MERGER).

See also ASSET STRIPPER, WILLIAMSON TRADE-OFF MODEL, HO-

RIZONTAL INTEGRATION, VERTICAL INTEGRATION, DIVERSIFICA-
TION.

takeover bid an attempt by a FIRM to take another over by acquiring the majority of shares in a public corporation. A number of
terms are used to describe the tactics available to the bidding and
defending firms, including:

(a) *black knight*: a firm that launches an unwelcome (contested)
takeover bid for some other firm.

(b) *golden parachute*: any generous severance terms written
into the employment contracts of the directors and other officers
of a firm that make it expensive to fire them if the firm is taken
over.

(c) *greenmail*: a situation in which a firm's shares are being
bought up by a potential takeover bidder, who is then headed off
from making an actual bid by that firm's directors, who buy from
the bidder at a premium price the shares already bought.

(d) *leveraged buyout*: a takeover financed primarily by issue of
bonds (often called *junk bonds* because they carry an inordinately
high rate of interest that appears to be unsustainable) rather than
common stock, which increases the CAPITAL GEARING of the en-
larged firm.

(e) *Pac Man defense*: a situation in which the firm being bid for
itself makes a bid for the acquiring firm (see REVERSE TAKEOVER).

(f) *poison pill*: a tactic employed in a takeover bid whereby the
intended victim firm itself takes over or merges (see MERGER) with
some other firm in order to make itself financially or structurally
less attractive to the potential acquirer.

(g) *porcupine*: any complex agreements between a firm and its
suppliers, customers, or creditors that make it difficult for an acquiring company to integrate the firm with its own business.

(h) *shark repellants*: any measures specifically designed to discourage takeover bidders, for example, altering the company's
articles of association to increase the proportion of stockholder
votes needed to approve the bid above the usual 50% mark.

(i) *white knight*: the intervention in a takeover bid of a third
firm, which itself takes over or merges with the intended victim
firm to rescue it from its unwelcome suitor.

tangent a straight line that just touches, but does not intersect, a curve at a particular point. Tangents are usefully applied in economics to determine the slope, or gradient, of a curve at one particular point along its length. For instance, INDIFFERENCE CURVE analysis suggests that a rational consumer would seek to maximize his or her UTILITY by choosing a combination of two products, X and Y, where the consumer's BUDGET LINE is tangential to the highest available indifference curve, for only there do the relative prices of the products match their relative utilities. See Fig. 167.

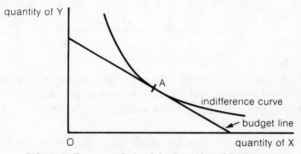

FIG. 167. **Tangent.** Point A is the point of tangency.

tangible assets any physical ASSETS, such as plant, machinery, equipment, vehicles, or inventory, that have a money value.

tariff or **import levy** a duty (a form of tax) that is levied on IMPORTS. There are two main types of tariffs: (a) *ad valorem duty*, which is levied as a fixed percentage of the value of the good; (b) *specific duty*, which is levied as a fixed sum of money per physical unit of the good. See Fig. 168.

Tariffs are used to protect domestic industries from foreign competition and to raise revenue for the government.

See also PROTECTIONISM, NOMINAL RATE OF PROTECTION, EFFECTIVE RATE OF PROTECTION, COMPARATIVE ADVANTAGE.

tax a levy imposed by a government on the income of persons and businesses (DIRECT TAX) and on goods and services (INDIRECT TAX). Taxes are used by a government for a variety of purposes, for example, to: (a) raise revenue for the government, (b) alter the distribution of income and wealth, (c) control the level and distri-

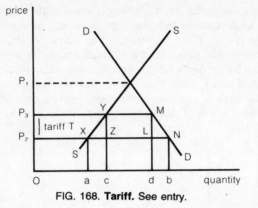

FIG. 168. **Tariff.** See entry.

bution of spending in the economy, (d) control the volume of imports and exports, and (e) alter consumption habits (*sin taxes*). See TAXATION, BUDGET (GOVERNMENT), FISCAL POLICY, PRINCIPLES OF TAXATION.

taxable income the amount of an individual's or corporation's income that is subject to TAXATION once any tax allowances to which the taxpayer is entitled have been deducted.

taxation the government receipts from taxes on household and business income and expenditure. Taxes on income include personal INCOME TAX and CORPORATION TAX, and taxes on expenditure include SALES TAX and EXCISE DUTIES. On the state and local levels, real and personal property taxes as well as sales and income taxes are frequently imposed. Taxation is a WITHDRAWAL from the CIRCULAR FLOW OF NATIONAL INCOME MODEL. Taxes are used to finance GOVERNMENT EXPENDITURE and as instruments of FISCAL POLICY in regulating the level of total spending (AGGREGATE DEMAND) in the economy. See PRINCIPLES OF TAXATION, PROGRESSIVE TAXATION, REGRESSIVE TAXATION, INCIDENCE OF TAXATION.

taxation schedule a schedule that depicts the relationship between TAXATION receipts and the level of NATIONAL INCOME. Under PROGRESSIVE TAXATION, the schedule has a positive slope—tax receipts rise as the level of income rises (see Fig. 169).

Likewise, receipts from expenditure taxes will be greater as the level of spending rises. See also FISCAL DRAG, PROPENSITY TO TAX.

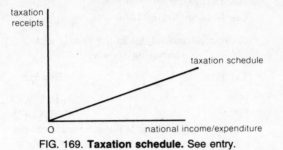

FIG. 169. **Taxation schedule.** See entry.

tax avoidance any efforts by taxpayers to arrange their financial affairs so as to avoid paying taxes by taking maximum advantage of taxation allowances and reliefs. In this way taxpayers can legally minimize their tax burden. Compare TAX EVASION.

tax base the total pool that tax authorities can tap in levying taxes. For example, the tax base for INCOME TAX is total taxable income, and the tax base for CORPORATION TAX is total taxable profits.

tax burden the total amount of taxation on the residents of a country in the form of income tax, corporation tax, sales tax, etc. The total amount of tax as a proportion of GROSS NATIONAL PRODUCT gives some indication of the overall tax burden. See also INCIDENCE OF TAXATION.

tax credit see NEGATIVE INCOME TAX.

tax evasion any efforts by taxpayers to evade taxes by various illegal means, such as not declaring all their income to the tax authorities or falsely claiming deductions to which they are not entitled. Compare TAX AVOIDANCE.

tax haven a country that imposes low rates of personal and corporate taxes and as a consequence tends to attract wealthy individuals and MULTINATIONAL FIRMS seeking to minimize their taxation liabilities. See also TRANSFER PRICE.

Tax Reform Act of 1986 a major revision of federal income taxes in the United States. The Act eliminated most loopholes. It also provided for reductions in the number of tax brackets and in the

average tax rates. In actual practice, this revision proved beneficial for the wealthiest taxpayers, harmful for others. Provisions for
single and married taxpayers follow:

Tax Reform Act of 1986

Married Individuals Filing Jointly and
Surviving Spouses

Tax rate	Brackets
15%	0 to $29,750
28%	Over $29,750

(For married individuals filing separate returns,
the 28-percent bracket begins at $14,875, i.e.,
one half the taxable income amount for joint
returns.)

Heads of Households

Tax rate	Brackets
15%	0 to $23,900
28%	Over $23,900

Single Individuals

Tax rate	Brackets
15%	0 to $17,850
28%	Over $17,850

Beginning in 1989, the taxable income amounts
at which the 28-percent rate starts will be
adjusted for inflation.

From *Internal Revenue Acts, 1985–86,* West
Publications, 1986.

t distribution or **Student's distribution** a theoretical sampling
distribution that closely approximates the NORMAL DISTRIBUTION.
The t distribution is used to establish CONFIDENCE INTERVALS
when using small samples to estimate a true population mean. The
equation used to calculate the t distribution depends on the size
of the sample (n) or, more precisely, on the number of DEGREES
OF FREEDOM (n − 1). When, say, a 95% confidence interval is

calculated from a t distribution for a small sample, it will generate wider confidence intervals than would be the case for a 95% confidence interval for a large sample.

The t distribution is frequently used in formulating levels of significance for HYPOTHESIS TESTING.

technical efficiency an aspect of PRODUCTION that seeks to identify in physical terms the best possible combination of FACTOR INPUTS to produce a given level of OUTPUT. See also EFFICIENCY, PRODUCTION FUNCTION.

technological gap theory a theory that seeks to explain changes in the pattern of INTERNATIONAL TRADE over time and is based on a dynamic sequence of technological and product INNOVATION and diffusion. Technologically advanced countries with a high propensity to innovate, such as the United States and Japan, are able to achieve trade advantages by being able to offer sophisticated new products on world markets, initially unobtainable from other sources. Over time, however, the technology is diffused and adopted by other countries, which then can themselves supply the products. Trade thus increases for the duration of the imitation lag. See also PRODUCT LIFE CYCLE THEORY, THEORY OF INTERNATIONAL TRADE.

technological progressiveness an aspect of MARKET PERFORMANCE that denotes the extent to which firms develop and introduce new and improved products, production, and distribution techniques. Radical INVENTIONS and INNOVATIONS may make it possible to reduce manufacturing and distribution costs, thereby allowing a lowering of the supply price to the consumer. See Fig. 170.

In the theory of costs, firms are assumed to operate within existing technological boundaries in both the short and long terms, but over time technological progressiveness serves to change the underlying cost conditions. Technological progressiveness in aggregate terms affects a country's rate of ECONOMIC GROWTH.

See also MONOPOLY, RESEARCH AND DEVELOPMENT, SOLOW ECONOMIC GROWTH MODEL, PRODUCTIVITY, AUTOMATION.

technological unemployment unemployment resulting from AUTOMATION of production activities. Automation improves labor PRODUCTIVITY, by reducing the labor needed for making and

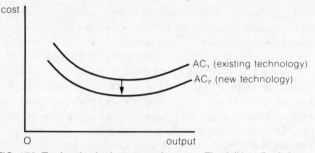

FIG. 170. **Technological progressiveness.** The fall in a firm's long-term average-cost curve from AC$_1$ to AC$_2$ as a result of technological advance.

distributing products so that some labor may become unemployed. If demand rises as a result of reduced costs and prices of products, labor may not be made unemployed, since the same labor force produces a greater output rather than having a reduced labor force produce the same output.

Technological change can be labor displacing or labor attracting. If a new technology reduces costs and prices, demand and employment may increase. Again, technological change may lead to increased employment in production of machinery for the new technology, and this may lead as well to a net gain in overall employment.

Technological unemployment can be particularly problematical at the local level, where industries concentrated in particular regions are affected by dramatic changes in technology. For example, the introduction of numerically controlled machine tools and robot-assembly units has had a specially dramatic effect on employment in some US industries. Government assistance schemes and retraining of labor can alleviate the problem of technological unemployment to some extent, but it is frequently the unskilled workers who first lose their jobs to such progress.

See also STRUCTURAL UNEMPLOYMENT, TECHNOLOGICAL PROGRESSIVENESS.

technology the application of scientific and technical knowledge in order to improve products and production processes. See TECHNOLOGICAL PROGRESSIVENESS, PRODUCTIVITY.

tender a bid for a product, asset, or financial security by a prospective buyer in competition with others. See also CAPITAL MARKET.

term loan a form of BANK LOAN made for a fixed time period at a predetermined RATE OF INTEREST.

terms of trade a PRICE INDEX showing a country's EXPORT prices relative to its IMPORT prices. It is constructed by taking an index of prices received for exports on the one hand, and an index of prices paid for imports on the other, and then dividing the first by the second. An improvement in a country's terms of trade occurs if its export prices rise at a faster rate than import prices over time.

Superficially, an improvement in a country's terms of trade may be considered beneficial. In terms of foreign exchange, a given amount of exports will now finance purchase of a greater amount of imports, or put another way a given amount of imports can now be purchased for a fewer amount of exports. A critical factor in this regard, however, is the PRICE ELASTICITY OF DEMAND for exports and imports. If, for example, export demand is price-elastic, then price rises that make the country's exports less competitive in world markets will result in a more than proportionate fall in export volume, thus lowering foreign-exchange receipts and adversely affecting domestic output and employment.

See also BALANCE-OF-PAYMENTS EQUILIBRIUM, DEVALUATION, REVALUATION.

term structure of interest rates the relationship between the EFFECTIVE RATE OF INTEREST (yield) on a FINANCIAL SECURITY and the unexpired length of time to its maturity. This relationship is known as *yield to maturity* and can be calculated only for securities that have a fixed rate of interest and specified date of maturity, such as TREASURY BILLS and corporate DEBENTURES.

test market a MARKET encompassing a moderately large group of CONSUMERS within a limited geographical area that firms use to market new products as a means of testing consumer response before engaging in full-scale production and national marketing of the products. See also PRODUCT LIFE CYCLE.

test of significance see HYPOTHESIS TESTING.

theory of consumer behavior the body of theory concerned with how individual consumers allocate their income in buying GOODS and SERVICES. A basic assumption made by the theory is that consumers seek to maximize the total UTILITY or satisfaction to be derived from spending a fixed amount of income. The theory provides an explanation of why DEMAND CURVES slope downward. See also CONSUMER EQUILIBRIUM, DIMINISHING MARGINAL UTILITY, PRICE EFFECT, INCOME EFFECT, SUBSTITUTION EFFECT, REVEALED PREFERENCE THEORY.

theory of demand the body of theory concerned with the determinants of the market DEMAND for GOODS and SERVICES and the effects of market demand, together with market supply, on the prices and quantities transacted of particular goods and services. See also DEMAND FUNCTION, DEMAND CURVE, DEMAND CURVE (SHIFT IN), ELASTICITY OF DEMAND.

theory of international trade the body of theory concerned with the determinants of, and the gains to be obtained from, INTERNATIONAL TRADE and SPECIALIZATION. The theory examines the way in which differences between countries in terms of supply costs and demand structures affect the level, product and area composition of international trade, and level and distribution of the GAINS FROM TRADE. See also COMPARATIVE ADVANTAGE, HECKSCHER-OHLIN FACTOR PROPORTIONS THEORY, PREFERENCE SIMILARITY THEORY, PRODUCT LIFE CYCLE THEORY, TECHNOLOGICAL GAP THEORY, EDGEWORTH BOX.

theory of markets the body of theory concerned with how scarce FACTORS OF PRODUCTION are allocated between the multitude of product MARKETS in the economy. More specifically, the theory of markets is concerned with determining the prices and outputs of goods and services and the prices and usage of factors of production.

The theory of markets distinguishes between types of markets by reference to differences in their MARKET STRUCTURE. The main structural distinction is made according to the degree of seller and buyer concentration, that is, the number of suppliers and buyers and their relative size distribution. Other structural features emphasized include the character of the product supplied, that is, whether it is a HOMOGENEOUS PRODUCT or differentiated (see PRODUCT DIFFERENTIATION), and the CONDITION OF ENTRY to the market. Given these structural distinctions, the theory examines the way in which market structure interacts with MARKET CONDUCT to produce particular patterns of MARKET PERFORMANCE.

See also PERFECT COMPETITION, MONOPOLISTIC COMPETI-
TION, OLIGOPOLY, MONOPOLY, RESOURCE ALLOCATION, MARKET
STRUCTURE/CONDUCT-PERFORMANCE SCHEMA.

theory of supply the body of theory concerned with the determinants of the market SUPPLY of GOODS and SERVICES, and the
effects of market supply, together with market demand, on the
prices and quantities transacted of particular goods and services.
See also SUPPLY FUNCTION, SUPPLY CURVE, SUPPLY CURVE (SHIFT
IN).

theory of the firm the body of theory concerned with how individual firms combine quantities of FACTOR INPUTS to produce
OUTPUTS of goods and services and their pricing and output decisions. A basic assumption of the theory is that the objective of the
firm is PROFIT MAXIMIZATION. The theory provides an explanation of why SUPPLY CURVES slope upward.

third world country see DEVELOPING COUNTRY.

tie-in sales a type of RESTRICTIVE TRADE AGREEMENT in which a
supplier requires that the purchaser of product A (the *tying good*)
must also buy one or more other products (the *tied goods*) from
the seller of A. Like an EXCLUSIVE DEALING arrangement, this
may restrict the freedom of the buyer to obtain these goods from
rival suppliers and hence limit effective competition.

tight money or **dear money** the tightness of supply of money
relative to the demand for money. A tight money policy could
result from the Fed's use of its discretionary controls to reduce the
excess reserves of the banks. See also CHEAP MONEY, FEDERAL
RESERVE SYSTEM, MONETARY POLICY.

till money the CURRENCY (notes and coins) held by COMMERCIAL
BANKS to meet the day-to-day cash requirements of their customers. Till money is included as part of the banks' legal reserves.

time lag see LEADS AND LAGS(2).

time-motion study see WORK STUDY.

time preference theory a theory stating that an individual can
allocate his or her expected INCOME stream between two time
periods in such a way that the trade-off between present and
future CONSUMPTION is optimized.

The concept can be illustrated graphically by using INDIFFER-
ENCE CURVES and BUDGET LINES to determine an individual's

preference for present consumption vis-a-vis future consumption. To forgo present consumption, an individual must expect an increased amount of future consumption.

In Fig. 171, indifference curve II exhibits an individual's trade-off between present and future consumption, along which an individual is indifferent between such combinations.

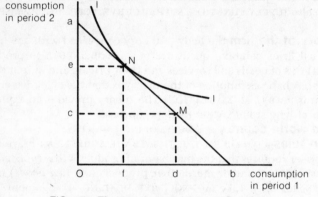

FIG. 171. **Time preference theory.** See entry.

The diagonal line ab is the budget line. The slope of this line determines the ratio between present and future consumption such that $Oa/Ob = 1 + r$, where r is the individual's rate of interest. Clearly, r will differ between individuals according to their willingness to sacrifice future against present consumption.

The point M in Fig. 171 is where an individual spends all present income (Od) and is therefore neither a borrower nor a lender. Point N is where an individual optimizes the trade-off between present and future consumption (indifference curve II) and budget constraint ab. This is optimized where the budget constraint is tangential to the indifference curve.

The amount an individual borrows or lends is therefore proportionate from point M to point N on the budget line where that individual's indifference curve is tangential to it. See also DISCOUNT RATE.

time series any statistical information recorded over successive time periods. See TIME-SERIES ANALYSIS.

time-series analysis the analysis of past statistical data, recorded at successive time intervals, with a view to projecting this experience of the past to predict what will happen in the uncertain future. Thus, time-series information can be used for FORECASTING purposes.

Figure 172 shows a typical time series. The fluctuations in time-series data, which inevitably show up when such series are plotted on a graph, can be classified into four basic types of variations that act simultaneously to influence the time series. These components of a time series are:

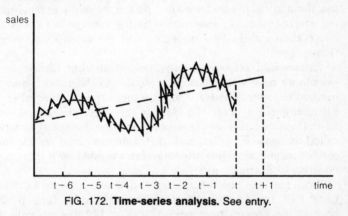

FIG. 172. **Time-series analysis.** See entry.

(a) *secular trend* which shows the relatively smooth, regular movement of the time series over the long term.

(b) *cyclical variation* which consists of medium-term, regular repeating patterns, generally associated with BUSINESS CYCLES. The recurring upswings and downswings in economic activity are superimposed on the secular trend.

(c) *seasonal variation* which consists of short-term, regularly repeating patterns, generally associated with different seasons of the year. These seasonal variations are superimposed on the secular trend and cyclical variations.

(d) *irregular variations* which are erratic fluctuations in the time series caused by unpredictable chance events. These irregular variations are superimposed on the secular trend, cyclical variations, and seasonal variations.

Time-series analysis is concerned with isolating the effect of each of these four influences on a time series with a view to using them to project this past experience into the future. To identify the underlying secular trend in a time series, the statistician may use REGRESSION ANALYSIS, fitting a line to the time-series observations by the method of ordinary least squares. Here time would serve as the INDEPENDENT VARIABLE in the estimated regression equation and the observed variable as the DEPENDENT VARIABLE. Alternatively, the statistician may use a moving average to smooth the time series and help identify the underlying trend. For example, the statistician could use a five-period moving average, replacing each consecutive observation by the average (MEAN) of that observation and the two preceding and two succeeding observations.

Exponential smoothing provides yet another technique for smoothing time-series data. It is similar to the moving-average method but gives greater weight to more recent observations in calculating the average. To identify the effect of seasonal variations, the statistician can construct a measure of seasonal variation, called the *seasonal index*, and use this to deseasonalize the time-series data and show how the time series would look if there were no seasonal fluctuations.

Once the trend has been identified, it is possible to EXTRAPO-LATE that trend and estimate trend values for time periods beyond the present time period. In Fig. 172, for example, the trend for time periods up to and including time t can be extrapolated to time t + 1. Extrapolating thus becomes a method of making predictions or forecasts, although the accuracy of the forecasts will depend on whether underlying forces affecting the time series in the past will continue to operate in the same way in the future.

Tobin, James (born 1918) winner of the Nobel Prize in Economic Sciences, 1981, for analysis of financial markets and their relation to expenditures and employment. A Keynesian economist, Tobin has long had a particular interest in the relation between financial markets and discretionary fiscal and monetary policies. He added to the Keynesian armamentarium by introducing a model of general equilibrium in financial and capital markets, by refining

Keynes's investment theory, and by his searching analysis of Keynesian stabilization policies.

total cost the aggregate sum in the short term of a firm's total FIXED COSTS and total VARIABLE COSTS in producing a particular level of OUTPUT.

The short-term total cost curve in Fig. 173 is the sum of the (constant) total fixed costs and the total variable costs. It has an S shape because at low levels of output total variable costs rise slowly—in light of the influence of increasing RETURNS TO THE VARIABLE FACTOR INPUT—whereas at high levels of output total variable costs rise more rapidly, reflecting the influence of diminishing returns on the variable-factor input.

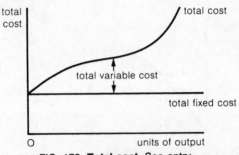

FIG. 173. **Total cost.** See entry.

Total cost interacts with TOTAL REVENUE in determining the level of output at which the firm achieves its objective of PROFIT MAXIMIZATION and LOSS MINIMIZATION.

In the THEORY OF MARKETS, a firm will leave a market if in the short term it cannot earn sufficient total revenue to cover its total variable costs. If it can generate enough total revenue to cover total variable costs and make some contribution toward total fixed costs, it will continue to produce in the short term even though it is still making a LOSS. In the LONG TERM, the firm must earn enough total revenue to cover total variable and total fixed costs— including NORMAL PROFIT—or it will leave the market.

See MARGINAL COST, AVERAGE COST, PROFIT MAXIMIZATION.

total domestic expenditure the total expenditure by residents

TOTAL PHYSICAL PRODUCT

of a country on FINAL PRODUCTS, excluding expenditure on IN-
TERMEDIATE GOODS. When expenditure on IMPORTS is deducted
from this amount and expenditure by nonresidents on domestically produced goods and services is added, the adjusted expenditure provides an estimate of GROSS NATIONAL PRODUCT.

total physical product the total quantity of OUTPUT produced in
the short-term theory of supply by utilizing various amounts of the
VARIABLE FACTOR INPUT in conjunction with a given amount of
FIXED FACTOR INPUT. The total physical product curve as shown
in Fig. 174 rises steeply at first, reflecting increasing RETURNS TO
THE VARIABLE FACTOR INPUT, but then rises more slowly as diminishing returns to the variable input set in.

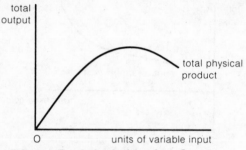

FIG. 174. **Total physical product.** See entry.

total revenue the aggregate revenue obtained by a firm from the
sale of a particular quantity of output, equal to price times quantity. Under conditions of PERFECT COMPETITION, the firm faces a
horizontal DEMAND CURVE at the going market price. Each extra
unit of output sold (MARGINAL REVENUE) adds exactly the same
amount to total revenue as previous units. Hence, total revenue
is a straight upward-sloping line (see Fig. 175a). Under conditions
of imperfect competition, for example, MONOPOLISTIC COMPETI-
TION, the firm faces a downward-sloping demand curve, and price
has to be lowered in order to sell more units. As price is lowered,
each extra unit of output sold (*marginal revenue*) adds successively smaller amounts to total revenue than previous units. Thus,
total revenue rises but at a decreasing rate, and eventually falls
(see Fig. 175b).

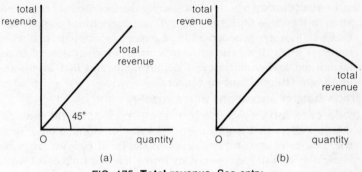

FIG. 175. **Total revenue.** See entry.

Total revenue interacts with TOTAL COST in determining the level of output at which the firm achieves its objective of PROFIT MAXIMIZATION.

total utility the sum total of the satisfaction (UTILITY) an individual derives from use or CONSUMPTION of a given quantity of goods or services. Whereas MARGINAL UTILITY refers only to the utility derived from each additional unit of the good or service used or consumed, total utility refers to the aggregate of the utility so derived. See Fig. 176. See UTILITY FUNCTION, CARDINAL UTILITY, ORDINAL UTILITY.

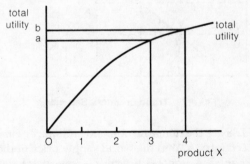

FIG. 176. **Total utility.** The theoretical measurement of total utility derived from three units of product X is the distance Oa. If four units of product X are used, total utility is Ob. Marginal utility, however, is the distance ab, being the increase in satisfaction derived from use or consumption of one additional unit of product X.

TRADE ASSOCIATION

trade association a body representing the interests of firms operating in the same line of business. Trade associations compile statistics on industry production, sales, exports, etc. for circulation to
member firms. They also provide a forum for discussion of trade
affairs and lobby government departments and legislatures regarding matters of mutual concern.

trade barrier see IMPORT RESTRICTIONS.

trade creation an increase in INTERNATIONAL TRADE and economic welfare that results from reduction or elimination of such
trade barriers as TARIFFS and QUOTAS. Tariff cuts etc. may be
instigated by a single country, by formation of a CUSTOMS UNION
or FREE TRADE AREA, or more generally by international negotiation (see GENERAL AGREEMENT ON TARIFFS AND TRADE).

The trade-creating effect of a tariff cut is illustrated in Fig. 177,
which, to simplify matters, is confined to one country (A) and one
product.

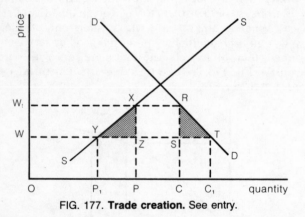

FIG. 177. **Trade creation.** See entry.

DD and SS are the domestic demand and supply curves for the
product in country A. W is the world supply price of the product.
Initially, country A imposes a tariff on imports of the product,
raising its price in the home market to W_t. At price W_t domestic
production is shown by OP, domestic consumption by OC, and
imports by PC.

Removal of the tariff reduces the price of the product in the home market to W. At price W, imports increase to $P_1 C_1$, domestic production falls to OP_1, and domestic consumption increases to OC_1. The home market obtains an increase in economic welfare from this expansion of trade, indicated by the two triangles XYZ and RST. XYZ is the production gain resulting from reallocation of factor inputs to more efficient uses, and RST is the consumption gain resulting from lower prices to consumers.

See also TRADE DIVERSION, GAINS FROM TRADE.

trade credit or **trade debt** a deferred payment arrangement whereby a supplier allows a customer a certain period of time, typically some months, after receiving the products before paying for them. See also CREDIT, CREDITORS, WORKING CAPITAL.

trade deficit an unfavorable balance of trade, that is, a deficit in the BALANCE OF TRADE arising when the value of a country's VISIBLE EXPORTS of goods is less than the value of its VISIBLE IMPORTS of goods. A trade gap as such may be of no particular concern provided it is offset by surpluses generated elsewhere on the BALANCE OF PAYMENTS. See TERMS OF TRADE, BALANCE-OF-PAYMENTS EQUILIBRIUM.

trade discount see DISCOUNT.

trade diversion a redirection of INTERNATIONAL TRADE resulting from formation of a CUSTOMS UNION or FREE TRADE AREA. A customs union/free trade area involves removal of trade obstacles, such as TARIFFS and QUOTAS, on trade between member countries, but the erection or continuance of trade barriers against nonmember countries. This serves to increase trade between member countries (see TRADE CREATION). Part of this increase is at the expense of nonmember countries, however, whose imports are now displaced from the customs union/free trade area. Thus, unlike across-the-board tariff cuts, there may be little net benefit to world economic welfare. See also GENERAL AGREEMENT ON TARIFFS AND TRADE.

trade integration the establishment of FREE TRADE between a number of countries with the aim of securing the benefits of international SPECIALIZATION. There are four main forms of trade integration ranging from a loose association of trade partners to a fully integrated group of nation states:

(a) a FREE TRADE AREA in which members eliminate trade barriers between themselves but continue to operate their own particular barriers against nonmembers.

(b) a CUSTOMS UNION in which members eliminate trade barriers between themselves and establish uniform barriers against nonmembers, in particular a common external tariff.

(c) a COMMON MARKET, that is, a customs union that also provides for free movement of labor and capital across national boundaries.

(d) an ECONOMIC UNION, that is, a common market that also provides for unification of members' general objectives in respect to economic growth, etc., and harmonization of monetary, fiscal, and other policies.

See also GAINS FROM TRADE.

trademark a word (BRAND NAME) or symbol that is used by a supplier to differentiate the supplier's product from products offered by other suppliers. See also INDUSTRIAL PROPERTY RIGHTS, PRODUCT DIFFERENTIATION.

trade war a situation in which countries engaged in INTERNATIONAL TRADE attempt to reduce competing IMPORTS by use of TARIFFS, QUOTAS, or other import restrictions, and expand their EXPORTS through EXPORT INCENTIVES. Such BEGGAR-MY-NEIGHBOR measures, bringing with them an escalation of PROTECTIONISM appear usually to be self-defeating, leading to a fall in total volume of international trade and world income levels.

trading stamps a form of SALES PROMOTION in which a retailer gives customers stamps with a value related to the value of purchases made, which can then be redeemed with a trading-stamp company for goods or cash.

transaction costs the costs incurred in using the MARKET system in buying and selling FACTOR INPUTS and FINAL PRODUCTS. Transaction costs include the costs of locating suppliers or customers and negotiating contracts with them, and the costs associated with imperfect market situations, for example, MONOPOLY surcharges imposed by input suppliers, unreliable sources of supply, and restrictions on sales outlets, TARIFFS and QUOTAS. See also INTERNALIZATION.

transaction demand for money a demand for MONEY held to

facilitate synchronization between receipts and expenditures of individuals and firms. Income, especially wages and salaries, is received at discrete intervals, that is, weekly or monthly, while expenditure occurs on a much more even basis for smaller items, such as lunches or fares. The amount of money an individual desires to hold for such transactions depends on his income.

The size of the money balances that firms hold for transactions depends on the amount of business done by the firm. Transactions and precautionary balances are sometimes considered together, since they both are positive functions of income, the balances held tending to increase as income increases.

Compare PRECAUTIONARY DEMAND FOR MONEY, SPECULATIVE DEMAND FOR MONEY.

transfer earnings the return that a FACTOR OF PRODUCTION must earn to prevent its transfer to an alternative use. The earnings a factor of production receives over and above its transfer earnings is called its ECONOMIC RENT. See also QUASI-RENT.

transfer payments any expenditure by a government for which it receives no GOODS or SERVICES in return. In the main, such payments involve transfer of income from one group of individuals (taxpayers) to other groups of individuals in the form of welfare benefits, for example, UNEMPLOYMENT BENEFIT, SOCIAL SECURITY BENEFIT, and old-age PENSIONS.

Because transfer payments are not made in return for products and services—they do not add to total output—they are not included as factor payments in the NATIONAL INCOME ACCOUNTS, which measure the money value of national output. See also GOVERNMENT (PUBLIC) EXPENDITURE, WELFARE STATE, NATIONAL INCOME ACCOUNTS.

transfer price the internal PRICE at which FACTOR INPUTS and PRODUCTS are transacted between the branches or subsidiaries of an integrated firm (see VERTICAL INTEGRATION, HORIZONTAL INTEGRATION). The transfer price may be set by reference to prices prevailing in outside markets for inputs and products (*arms-length pricing*), or it may be administered (see ADMINISTERED PRICE) according to some internal accounting convention (for example, a FULL-COST PRICE).

Transfer pricing gives a firm added discretion in pricing its products, and the danger is that it could be tempted to employ manipulative transfer pricing to harm competitors, for example, to price squeeze a nonintegrated rival firm. Again, a MULTINATIONAL FIRM to boost its profits might, for example, transfer price across national frontiers so that the greater part of the firm's profits are received in a low-tax economy.

See INTERNALIZATION, TAX HAVEN.

transformation curve see PRODUCTION POSSIBILITY BOUNDARY.

transitional unemployment see FRICTIONAL UNEMPLOYMENT.

transmission mechanism the interlinking causal relationship between exercise of the available tools of FISCAL POLICY and MONETARY POLICY by governments and bank authorities, and the change in the level of economic variables affected by such action. Fiscal policy advocates that a change in government expenditure exerts significant influence on the level of AGGREGATE DEMAND and UNEMPLOYMENT via the RATE OF INTEREST and INVESTMENT. Monetary policy suggests that a change in MONEY SUPPLY via discretionary monetary policies directly affects aggregate demand. See also KEYNESIAN ECONOMICS, MONEY SUPPLY/SPENDING LINKAGES, QUANTITY THEORY OF MONEY, MONETARISM.

Treasury bill a US FINANCIAL SECURITY issued by the Federal Reserve Banks for the Treasury as a means of borrowing money for short periods of time (3 months). Most Treasury bills are purchased by commercial banks and held as part of their secondary reserves.

The monetary authorities use Treasury bills to regulate the liquidity base of the banking system in order to control the MONEY SUPPLY. For example, if the authorities wish to expand the money supply they can buy Treasury bills, which increases the reserves of the banking system and induces a multiple expansion of bank deposits.

See also DEMAND DEPOSIT CREATION, FEDERAL RESERVE SYSTEM.

trust 1. ASSETS held and managed by *trustees* on behalf of an individual or group. While these assets are held in trust, the beneficiaries have no control over the management of them. **2.** (formerly, in the United States) a means of organizing CARTELS, provoking passage of antitrust (antimonopoly) legislation.

trustee see TRUST.

turnkey project a construction project, such as the building of a factory or port, in a country by a FIRM or CONSORTIUM of firms. Turnkey projects involve no further commitment beyond satisfactory completion of the project.

turnover tax see SALES TAX.

type 1 error see HYPOTHESIS TESTING.

type 2 error see HYPOTHESIS TESTING.

U

U-form (unitary form) organization an organizational structure in which a firm is managed centrally as a single unit specialized along functional lines: marketing, production, finance, personnel. Oliver Williamson, who coined the term, argues that firms organized in this fashion are likely to suffer loss of control and end up pursuing nonprofit management goals (see MANAGEMENT-UTILITY MAXIMIZATION), because senior executives responsible for management functions cannot exert sufficient control over their subordinates, who are selling a wide variety of products in many different markets. Williamson predicts that the U-form organization will gradually decline in popularity as companies grow and adopt the M-FORM (MULTIDIVISIONAL FORM) ORGANIZATION. See also MANAGERIAL THEORIES OF THE FIRM, BEHAVIORAL THEORY OF THE FIRM.

uncertainty see RISK AND UNCERTAINTY.

UNCTAD see UNITED NATIONS CONFERENCE ON TRADE AND DEVELOPMENT

underdeveloped country see DEVELOPING COUNTRY.

underwrite see INVESTMENT BANK.

underwriter a person or company that guarantees the sale of a security issue to be offered for sale to the public.

undistributed profits see RETAINED PROFITS.

unearned income see EARNED INCOME.

unemployment the nonutilization of LABOR and CAPITAL resources, as a result of which the actual output of the economy is below its POTENTIAL GROSS NATIONAL PRODUCT. Resources lie idle and output is lost. Elimination of unemployment and achievement of FULL EMPLOYMENT are principal objectives of MACROECONOMIC POLICY. The rate of unemployment is measured as the percentage of the total labor force currently without a job (see Fig. 178a).

UNEMPLOYMENT

	UK	W. Germany	Japan	US
1980	6.6	3.0	2.0	7.0
1981	9.9	4.4	2.2	7.5
1982	11.4	6.1	2.4	9.5
1983	12.6	8.0	2.6	9.5
1984	13.0	8.5	2.7	7.4
1985	13.1	8.6	2.6	7.1
1986	13.3	8.3	2.8	6.8
1987	10.2	6.2	2.8	6.1
1988	8.3	6.1	2.5	5.4

(a)

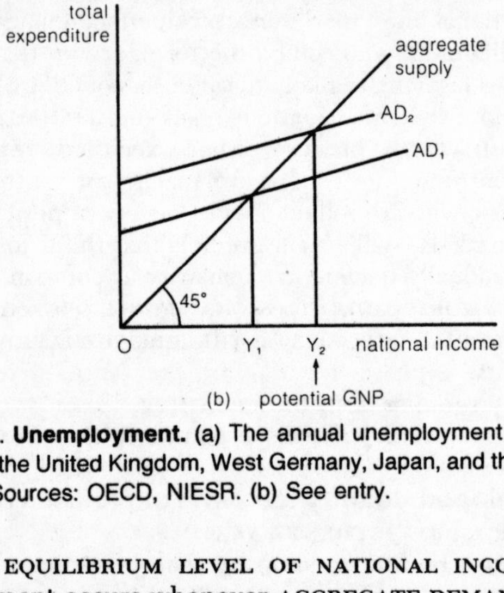

(b)   potential GNP

FIG. 178. **Unemployment.** (a) The annual unemployment percentages for the United Kingdom, West Germany, Japan, and the United States. Sources: OECD, NIESR. (b) See entry.

In the EQUILIBRIUM LEVEL OF NATIONAL INCOME model, unemployment occurs whenever AGGREGATE DEMAND is insufficient to purchase full-employment aggregate supply—potential GNP. Equilibrium national income in Fig. 178b is Y_1, compared with the full employment national income of Y_2. The traditional prescription for this situation is for the authorities to boost spending by reflationary FISCAL POLICY and MONETARY POLICY measures—to shift aggregate demand from AD_1 to AD_2.

Supply-side deficiencies (see SUPPLY-SIDE ECONOMICS) may contribute to generalized unemployment if a country is heavily engaged in international trade. Inefficient use of resources and lack of investment in plant and product modernization may result in progressive displacement of domestic output by more competitive foreign products (see IMPORT PENETRATION) and widespread loss of jobs. Although PROTECTIONISM may be used to contain the situation, this is not a truly effective substitute for industrial efficiency.

The three basic forms of unemployment are FRICTIONAL UNEMPLOYMENT, STRUCTURAL UNEMPLOYMENT and CYCLICAL UNEMPLOYMENT.

See also DEFLATIONARY GAP, DEMAND MANAGEMENT, STABILIZATION POLICY, RESIDUAL UNEMPLOYMENT, DISGUISED UNEMPLOYMENT, HIDDEN UNEMPLOYMENT, POVERTY TRAP, DEINDUSTRIALIZATION, TECHNOLOGICAL UNEMPLOYMENT, EMPLOYMENT ACT OF 1946.

unemployment benefit a type of payment originally provided for in the United States by the Social Security Act as insurance for unemployed workers. The program provides inducements for the individual states to establish unemployment insurance programs, which are financed by payroll taxes.

To be eligible, an employee must have worked in what is termed *covered employment* and be ready, willing, and able to work. The benefits of the program are targeted to provide 6 months at most of income approximating half the worker's average weekly earnings. It must be pointed out that benefits vary from state to state, and most states do not have effective job placement agencies to assist unemployed workers in finding new employment. As a result, the ready-willing-and-able requirement is not assiduously enforced.

unitary elasticity see PRICE ELASTICITY OF DEMAND.

unitary taxation a system of TAXATION operated by a country that taxes a foreign-owned MULTINATIONAL FIRM on a proportion of its world-wide income, rather than on the income the multinational actually earns within that country. This involves use of some rule of thumb to apportion tax liability. For example, if 10% of the total world assets of a multinational are located in that country, then the country may seek to tax 10% of the multinational's world income, making no allowance for any foreign taxes paid. Countries might adopt unitary taxation to increase their taxation revenues and to counter manipulative TRANSFER PRICING by multinationals, but must bear in mind that such a taxation system is likely to discourage domestic investment. Compare DOUBLE TAXATION.

United Nations (UN) an association of countries that have agreed to abide by the principles originally laid down in the UN Charter. Its main objectives are maintenance of international peace and security, upholding of fundamental human rights in all nations, and promotion of social harmony and progress among all nations. The title UN was first used in 1942, when representatives of 26 countries committed their governments to maintain the fight against the Axis powers: Germany, Italy, and Japan. The UN Charter was drawn up by 50 nations and officially created on October 24, 1945. The principal organs of the UN are the General Assembly, Security Council, Economic and Social Council, Trusteeship Council, and Secretariat. There are also many subsidiary organs and affiliated bodies working in accordance with the Charter, such as the INTERNATIONAL MONETARY FUND, the FOOD AND AGRICULTURAL ORGANIZATION, the GENERAL AGREEMENT ON TARIFFS AND TRADE, the WORLD BANK, the UNITED NATIONS CONFERENCE ON TRADE AND DEVELOPMENT, and the INTERNATIONAL LABOR ORGANIZATION.

United Nations Conference on Trade and Development (UNCTAD) a multinational institution established in 1965 to represent the economic interests of DEVELOPING COUNTRIES and to promote the ideals of the NEW INTERNATIONAL ECONOMIC ORDER. UNCTAD's main work is undertaken at a series of conferences, held every 4 years, and has centered on three areas of particular concern to the developing countries:

(a) *exports of manufactures*. UNCTAD has attempted to negotiate TARIFF- and QUOTA-free access to markets of the developed countries. This is in addition to concessions obtained through the GENERAL AGREEMENT ON TARIFFS AND TRADE.

(b) *exports of commodities*. UNCTAD has promoted extension of INTERNATIONAL COMMODITY AGREEMENTS aimed at stabilizing the export prices of primary products as a means of stabilizing developing countries' foreign exchange earnings and producers' incomes.

(c) *economic aid*. UNCTAD has attempted to secure a greater volume of financial assistance and technology transfer from the developed countries.

So far, UNCTAD has achieved little, mainly because developed countries, particularly in the difficult economic conditions prevailing since the oil price increases of 1973, have not been prepared to support UNCTAD initiatives to the fullest extent.

unit of account or **standard of value** an attribute of MONEY that enables people to use money to measure and record the value of GOODS and SERVICES and financial transactions. A unit of account may take a physical form, for example, CURRENCY, or may be an intangible bookkeeping asset, such as the SPECIAL DRAWING RIGHT and the EUROPEAN CURRENCY UNIT.

unit trust a financial institution that sells units to savers at a price based on a proportion of the underlying value of the trust's assets and that specializes in long-term investments in corporate bonds, common stocks, and government securities. See also FINANCIAL SYSTEM, INSTITUTIONAL INVESTORS.

unlimited liability see LIMITED LIABILITY.

unlisted securities market a MARKET for dealing in corporate bonds and common stocks that are not traded on a stock exchange. The unlisted securities market enables smaller companies to raise new capital without the formalities and expense of obtaining a full listing on a principal exchange.

upward-sloping demand curve a DEMAND CURVE that shows a *direct* rather than an *inverse* relationship between the price of a product and the quantity demanded during a period of time, over part or all of its length.

Most demand curves are based on the assumption that consumers are rational in buying products and have full knowledge of price and product characteristics. When either of these assumptions is modified, the DEMAND FUNCTION can result not in a normal product as in Fig. 179a, but in an upward-sloping demand curve as in Fig. 179b.

In Fig. 179a, if price increases from OP_1 to OP_2, quantity demanded *falls* from OQ_1 to OQ_2. In Fig. 179b, if price increases from OP_1 to OP_2, quantity demanded *increases* from OQ_3 to OQ_4. This can be due to: (a) conspicuous consumption (see VEBLEN EFFECT); (b) a real or perceived belief that as price in-

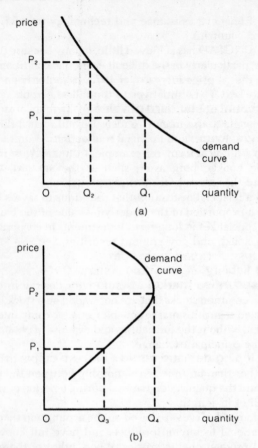

FIG. 179. **Upward-sloping demand curve.** See entry.

creases, quality improves; (c) or because the product is a GIFFEN GOOD.

See also INCOME EFFECT, ENGEL'S LAW, CONSPICUOUS CONSUMPTION.

util a theoretical measure of UTILITY derived from CONSUMPTION of a good or service. Early economists believed that the subjective satisfaction (utility) a person enjoyed from, say, taking a Sunday stroll, could be cardinally measured. The unit of such measurement was termed a "util," and although it was never possible to actually make such a measurement, it conveyed limited theoretical meaning to their analyses. Rarely used in modern economics, the term is occasionally used in a more general sense to establish some degree of utility. See also CARDINAL UTILITY, DIMINISHING MARGINAL UTILITY, ORDINAL UTILITY, TOTAL UTILITY.

utility the satisfaction or pleasure a person derives from the CONSUMPTION of a GOOD or SERVICE. In the context used by economists, utility is not a *property* of a good or service, but the derivation of satisfaction from the *use* of such a good or service. Wheat was an example used in the nineteenth century. It has the same property in glut or famine, but its true utility is to the consumer. The consumer's utility will vary according to the state of body and mind. Utility therefore is a condition unique to each individual.

The concept of utility is not contentious and can be traced back to the attempts of early Greek philosophers to determine economic value. The problem was more one of measurement. The economists of the early eighteenth century believed utility could be expressed as an absolute quantity, one, two, etc., known as CARDINAL UTILITY. Measurement between individuals was therefore possible, as indeed was the measurement between different goods as long as they were independent of each other.

Later economists believed that utility measured on such a scale was neither necessary nor possible. Such economists were termed *ordinalists*, because they believed utility could be measured on an ordinal scale, that is, one in which only rankings of preference were required, not magnitudes on a numerical scale. Such ORDINAL UTILITY rankings could then be represented on an INDIFFERENCE MAP. An abstract unit of measure was devised to help explain an individual's degree of utility (a UTIL), although such measurement is not strictly required for ordinal rankings. See UTILITY FUNCTION.

utility function a mathematical function denoting the quantities of GOODS and SERVICES that constitute an individual's total CONSUMPTION.

Early economists believed that UTILITY depended on the

UTILITY INDEX

amount of a particular good in an individual's possession regardless of other goods in that individual's possession. TOTAL UTILITY was therefore additive and could be written:

$$U_t = U_1(x_1) + U_2(x_2) \ldots U_n(x_n) \qquad (1)$$

where U_t = total utility, $U_1 \ldots U_n$ = utility of each good, $x_1 \ldots x_n$ = number of goods denoted x.

The theoretical notion that the value of a thing lies in the thing itself was rejected in favor of a generalized utility function:

$$U_t = U(x_1, x_2 \ldots x_n). \qquad (2)$$

Equation (2) denotes the fact that the total utility derived (U_t) depends on the amounts and relationship of other commodities. This in turn leads into the law of DIMINISHING MARGINAL UTILITY.

See also CARDINAL UTILITY, MARGINAL UTILITY.

utility index a means of representing attitudes toward RISK AND UNCERTAINTY displayed by decision-makers in terms of the MARGINAL UTILITY they derive from the earnings of risky economic projects. The expected utility index was developed by von Neumann and Morgenstern, who argued that decisions based on expected utility values will differ from those based on expected money values because of changes in the utility a decision-maker derives from money. When each extra dollar a decision-maker acquires increases his or her utility by less than the previous dollar made, this decreasing marginal-utility of money is likely to affect attitudes toward risk. For if each extra dollar received adds less to utility than would be lost if he or she gave up a dollar, the decision-maker would not bet on a project in which the possible money gains equal the possible money losses and each has a probability of 0.5, because the expected utility value of the bet would be negative. Such a decision-maker would be risk-averse. Only when his or her marginal utility of money is constant would the decision-maker display risk-neutral behavior. In all other cases the expected money value and the expected utility-value criteria would rank projects differently. See also RISK PROFILE, DECISION TREE.

utility maximization see CONSUMER EQUILIBRIUM.

V

value the exchange or economic worth of an ASSET or PRODUCT. Early economists, such as Adam SMITH and David RICARDO, stressed that the exchange value of an asset or product could be measured by the amount of LABOR needed to produce it. The classical economists stressed that long-run supply costs—payments to factors of production—established exchange values, while later economists, such as Alfred MARSHALL and William JEVONS, emphasized that the UTILITY of a product to a consumer must be considered. Modern economists, not surprisingly, consider that both supply and demand factors are important in determining the value of a product. See also CONSUMER'S SURPLUS, VALUE ADDED, PARADOX OF VALUE.

value added the difference between a firm's SALES REVENUE and the cost of its purchased materials and services. See VALUE-ADDED TAX, VALUE-ADDED PER EMPLOYEE.

value-added approach to GNP see GROSS NATIONAL PRODUCT.

value-added per employee an accounting measure of a firm's value-added/size relation that expresses the firm's VALUE ADDED as a ratio of its size measured in terms of number of employees.

value-added tax (VAT) an INDIRECT TAX levied by a government on the VALUE ADDED to a good or service. The tax is based on the difference between the value of the output over the value of the inputs used to produce it. The final amount of tax is added on to the selling price of the good and is paid by the buyer. For example, trader B sells output for $10 a unit, the value of B's inputs being $8 a unit. Thus, value added is $2 a unit.

If VAT is set at 10%, the selling price of the good is $11, with $1 being the amount of tax paid by the final buyer. Trader B would then set off against the $1 VAT output tax collected from the final customer the 80-cent VAT input tax B has paid on the $8 of inputs bought, and remit the difference of 20 cents to the government.

VALUE JUDGMENTS

In the same way trader A, who supplied trader B with his or her input for $8 per unit, would have collected 80 cents in VAT-output tax from trader B, against which A will offset any VAT-input tax paid on A's inputs, and remit the difference to the government. The total of all these sums remitted by traders A, B, etc., to the government will equal the $1 charged on the final sale to the customer.

Value-added taxes are much used in Europe and are being considered for use in the United States by some members of Congress.

value judgments see NORMATIVE ECONOMICS.

variable a term that can take a range of numerical values. For example, price, quantity demanded, and quantity supplied are all variables insofar as each can take a number of different values, and these variables form part of an ECONOMIC MODEL of a MARKET. See also DEPENDENT VARIABLE, INDEPENDENT VARIABLE, CONSTANT, CONTINUOUS VARIABLE, DISCRETE VARIABLE, ECONOMETRICS, HYPOTHESIS TESTING.

variable costs any COSTS that tend to vary directly with the level of output. They represent payments made for use of VARIABLE FACTOR INPUTS—raw materials, labor, etc.

A short-term total variable cost curve (TC) is shown in Fig. 180a. It has an S shape because at low levels of output total variable costs rise slowly, reflecting the influence of increasing RETURNS TO THE VARIABLE FACTOR INPUT. At high levels of output, total variable costs rise more rapidly, reflecting the influence of diminishing returns to the variable input. Average variable costs (AVC in Fig. 180b) fall at first, reflecting increasing returns to the variable input, but then rise, reflecting diminishing returns to the variable input.

In the THEORY OF MARKETS, a firm will leave a market if in the short term it cannot earn sufficient TOTAL REVENUE to cover its total variable cost. If it can generate enough total revenue to cover total variable cost and make some CONTRIBUTION toward total FIXED COST, it will continue to produce in the near term even though it is still making a loss.

See also MARKET EXIT, LOSS MINIMIZATION.

variable factor input a FACTOR INPUT to the production process

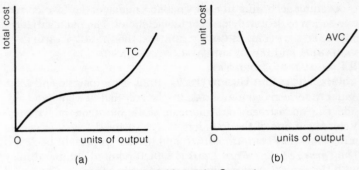

FIG. 180. **Variable costs.** See entry.

that can readily be varied in the near term so as to expand or
reduce output within a plant of fixed size. Variable inputs include
raw materials, heating, and lighting. Variable costs are equal to the
quantities of variable inputs used, multiplied by their prices. See
also FIXED FACTOR INPUT, RETURNS TO THE VARIABLE FACTOR
INPUT.

variable factor proportions (law of) see RETURNS TO THE VARI-
ABLE FACTOR INPUT.

variable overhead any overhead that varies proportionately with
the level of output of a product, so that variable overhead cost per
unit of output is constant. Variable overhead items include fuel
and lubricants, and sales commissions. See also FIXED OVERHEAD.

variance 1. the difference between budgeted and actual results
(see BUDGETING), or between planned costs/revenues and actual
costs/revenues. Variances can be: (a) adverse or negative when
actual revenues fall short of budget, or when actual costs exceed
budget; (b) favorable or positive when actual revenues exceed
budget, or when actual costs are less than budget. **2.** Also called
dispersion. A measure of variation within a group of numerical
observations, that is, the average of the squared deviations of the
observations from the group MEAN. See also STANDARD DEVIA-
TION.

variance analysis the analysis of differences between the
planned cost of a product and its comparable actual cost into their
constituent parts. Variance analysis highlights matters that are not

proceeding according to plan, enabling managers to take corrective action to deal with losses or inefficiencies. The main variances are DIRECT-MATERIALS COST VARIANCE, the DIRECT-LABOR COST VARIANCE, and the OVERHEAD-COST VARIANCE.

VAT see VALUE-ADDED TAX.

Veblen, Thorstein Bunde (1857—1929) a peripatetic and influential American economist despite the fact that he remained outside the mainstream of American academic economic theory. Veblen was one of the founders of a short-lived school of economists known as *institutionalists*, and his first important book was *The Theory of the Leisure Class* (1899). It pointed out that display with the intention of producing an effect in others is a powerful motive for consumers. This insight is still called, in Veblen's classic phrase, *conspicuous consumption*.

Veblen was a severe non-Marxist critic of American capitalism. In a number of his books, he emphasized that there is a deep antagonism in the United States between technocratic and acquisitive instincts. To the detriment of society, he said, the acquisitive frequently triumph.

See VEBLEN EFFECT.

Veblen effect a theory of CONSUMPTION suggesting that consumers may have an UPWARD-SLOPING DEMAND CURVE, as opposed to a downward-sloping demand curve, because they practice CONSPICUOUS CONSUMPTION. A downward-sloping demand curve implies that the quantity demanded of a particular good varies inversely with its price—as price increases, quantity demanded falls. The Veblen effect suggests that quantity demanded of a particular good varies directly with a change in price—as price increases, demand increases. See also VEBLEN, INCOME EFFECT, ENGEL'S LAW, GIFFEN GOOD.

velocity of circulation a measure of the average number of times each MONEY unit is used to purchase the year's output of final goods and services (GROSS DOMESTIC PRODUCT). If, for example, the total value of final output is $100 billion and the total MONEY SUPPLY is $10 billion, then, on average, each $1 unit has changed hands 10 times.

There is controversy between monetarist proponents of the QUANTITY THEORY OF MONEY and Keynesian economists about the stability of the velocity of circulation of money. Monetarists (see MONETARISM) hold that the velocity of circulation is stable or changes only slowly over time, so there is a direct link between the money supply and the price level, and between the rate of growth of money supply and rate of INFLATION. Keynesian economists (see KEYNESIAN ECONOMICS) argue that the velocity of circulation is unstable and that it can change rapidly, offsetting any changes in the money supply.

venture capital any money lent to a company or stock bought in a company by financial specialists, for example, commercial banks and insurance companies, thus enabling investment in processes and products that because of their novelty are rated as especially high-risk projects, and as such would not normally attract conventional finance.

vertical firm see FIRM.

vertical integration an element of MARKET STRUCTURE in which a company undertakes a number of successive stages in the supply of a product, as opposed to operating at only one stage (HORIZONTAL INTEGRATION). *Backward integration* occurs when a company begins producing raw materials that previously were supplied to it by other companies, for example, a camera producer making glass lenses. *Forward integration* occurs when a company undertakes further finishing of a product, final assembly, or distribution, for example, an oil company that sells gasoline through its own gas stations.

From a company's point of view, vertical integration may be advantageous, because it enables the company to reduce its production and distribution costs by linking together successive activities, or because it is vital for the company to secure reliable supplies of inputs or distribution outlets in order to remain competitive.

In terms of its wider impact on the operation of market processes, vertical integration may on the one hand promote greater efficiency in resource use, or on the other hand by limiting competition, lead to less efficient allocation of resources.

Various efficiency gains may accrue through vertical integration. These include technical economies from combining successive production processes, for example, the savings made in reheating costs by combining steel furnace operations. Warehousing economies can also arise from reduction in intermediate contingency and buffer inventories. Vertically integrated firms can eliminate some purchasing and selling expenses in negotiating outside supply and advertising/selling contracts by conducting these transactions within the company (see INTERNALIZATION). Managerial economies may accrue from having a single administrative system to handle several production activities, and financial economies may accrue from bulk-buying discounts, and from lowering the cost of raising capital. When companies achieve such efficiency gains through vertical integration, their average costs will tend to fall, thus facilitating a lowering of market prices and an increase in output.

When a company *already* dominates one or more vertical stages, vertical integration may lead to various anticompetitive effects. Forward integration can secure a market but it can also foreclose it to competitors; similarly, backward integration can guarantee supply sources but it can also be used to prevent rivals from gaining access to those sources. Moreover, if a company acquires the supplier of a scarce raw material used both by itself and its competitors, it may be in a position to operate a PRICE SQUEEZE, that is, squeeze the profit margins of its competitors by charging them a higher price for the raw material than the price charged for its own use, while setting a relatively low final product price. Such tactics serve not only to discipline existing competitors, but also act as a BARRIER TO ENTRY to potential new competitors. Denied access to markets or materials or offered access only on disadvantageous terms, potential competitors would need to acquire the same degree of integration as existing companies, and the large initial capital requirements of such large-scale entry can be prohibitive.

Thus, vertical integration may simultaneously produce both beneficial and detrimental effects.

very long run or **very long term** an abstract time period in the THEORY OF SUPPLY allowing for the technological framework (known production methods) under which firms operate to change as a result of new INVENTIONS and knowledge. See also SHORT TERM, LONG TERM, INNOVATION, TECHNOLOGICAL PROGRESSIVENESS, RESEARCH AND DEVELOPMENT.

visible exports and imports any GOODS such as raw materials and finished manufactures that can be seen and recorded as they cross boundaries between countries. The net exports/imports of these goods constitute the BALANCE OF TRADE. Visible exports and imports, together with INVISIBLE EXPORTS AND IMPORTS, make up the CURRENT ACCOUNT of a country's BALANCE OF PAYMENTS.

voting shares the shares of common stock that enable the SHAREHOLDER to cast a vote for each share held at a company's ANNUAL MEETING.

W

wage differential the payment of different WAGE RATES to different groups of workers. Wage differentials arise from four principal factors: (a) Differences in interoccupational skills, training, and responsibilities—doctors are paid more than nurses; managers are paid more than assembly line workers. (b) Differences in interindustry growth rates and PRODUCTIVITY levels—high-growth, high-productivity industries pay more than declining or low-productivity industries. (c) Differences between regions in income per capita and local employment levels—employers in prosperous areas in general pay more than those in depressed areas. (d) Differences relating to discrimination or other extra-economic factors—men have long been paid more than women for comparable work, and minority workers have generally been denied access to well-paying jobs.

Wage differentials that encourage greater labor MOBILITY between occupations and industries and promote high levels of productivity may play an important part in bringing about effective use of labor resources. On the other hand, some wage differentials may contribute to economic and social distortions, in particular those that reflect racial or sexual discrimination, and the exploitation of workers by powerful employers *sweatshop labor*. By the same token, so-called unjustified wage differentials arising out of the perceived abuse of labor union power work against the best use of labor resources.

wage drift see EARNINGS DRIFT.

wage freeze see PRICES AND INCOMES POLICY.

wage-price spiral see INFLATIONARY SPIRAL.

wage rate the price of labor. In a competitive market the wage rate is determined by the demand for and supply of labor. In the short run, the demand curve for labor as a factor input slopes downward (D in Fig. 181), reflecting a fall in the marginal productivity of labor as more labor is used (see MARGINAL PHYSICAL PRODUCT and MARGINAL REVENUE PRODUCT). The supply curve (S) for labor slopes upward: the higher the wage rate, the greater the number of hours of work offered. The equilibrium wage rate is W_e where the two lines intersect. See MINIMUM WAGE, LABOR MARKET, COLLECTIVE BARGAINING, PRICES AND INCOMES POLICY.

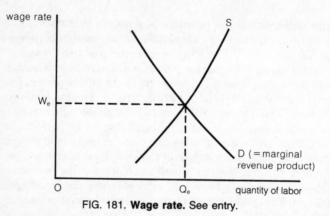

FIG. 181. **Wage rate.** See entry.

wage restraint see PRICES AND INCOMES POLICY.

wages the payments made to workers for use of their efforts as a FACTOR OF PRODUCTION. In aggregate terms, wages are a source of income and are included as a part of NATIONAL INCOME. See also WAGE RATE, NATIONAL INCOME ACCOUNTS.

wages-fund theory a theory developed by John Stuart Mill (see CLASSICAL ECONOMICS) stating that total WAGES in an economy are limited to the extent of available CAPITAL used for paying wages. Notationally this can be written:

$$W = \frac{C}{L}$$

where W = wages per labor unit, C = capital stock for paying wages, L = wage-earning labor force.

The *natural wage rate* is the *subsistence-wage rate*. In the short term it is possible for wage earners to be paid in excess of their natural rate due to short-term fluctuations in demand (the wages fund, C above) and supply (the LABOR FORCE, L above). However, in the longer term, the natural wage rate can only be increased if C increases or L decreases.

The wages-fund theory came under increasing criticism as people argued that it was difficult to attach a specific portion of capital to wage payments, and it came to be accepted that wage rates depended on the forces of demand and supply in the LABOR MARKET. The wages-fund theory thus fell into disfavor and was subsequently replaced by labor market theories in which the MARGINAL REVENUE PRODUCT of labor is the determining employment factor.

See also RICARDO, MARX.

Wagner Act see NATIONAL LABOR RELATIONS ACT.

Wall Street home of the New York Stock Exchange and a symbol for trading in stocks and bonds, for the traders and others who work in the securities business, and generally for US-type capitalism.

Walras's law a law devised by Léon Walras (1834—1910) stating that the total value of goods demanded in an economy—prices times quantities demanded—is always identically equal to the total value of goods supplied—prices times quantities supplied. He innovated a mathematical model of general equilibrium.

This situation can occur only in a barter economy or an economy that uses some form of MONEY for transactions and all money is immediately used for exchange. In an economy that also uses money as a store of value, it is conceivable that the DEMAND for and SUPPLY of money does not equate to the demand for and supply of goods, that is, people may SAVE or overspend.

The study of such interrelations of markets for goods throughout the economy is termed GENERAL EQUILIBRIUM ANALYSIS. Walras used simultaneous equations to show the effect a change in demand and supply of one good would have on all other goods in a situation of general equilibrium. See also SAY'S LAW.

wants the desire for GOODS and SERVICES. The attempt to satisfy wants forms the basis of all economic activity. Wants are expressed in the marketplace not by need or desire but by willingness and ability to purchase the good or service in DEMAND.

wasting asset any NATURAL RESOURCES, such as coal and oil, that have a finite but indeterminate life span depending on the rate of depletion. See ASSET.

wealth the stock of net ASSETS owned by individuals or households. In aggregate terms, one widely used measure of a nation's total stock of wealth is that of marketable wealth, its relatively liquid physical and financial assets (see LIQUIDITY). Marketable wealth is not equally distributed in industrialized countries.

wear and tear the gradual deterioration in the efficiency and value of a productive ASSET through use. See also DEPRECIATION(2), CAPITAL CONSUMPTION.

weighted average a form of arithmetic average, or MEAN, in which each of the items used in a calculation is given a weight, or importance, to reflect the fact that not all items carry the same importance but may vary relative to one another. Weighted averages are frequently used in price indices to reflect the percentage of a CONSUMER's budget spent on various items to enable a more accurate or representative mean price increase to be found. For example, a consumer's STANDARD OF LIVING may be represented hypothetically by three typical purchased goods, A, B, and C. Over the period in question, the three goods have increased in price by 35%, 10%, and 45%, respectively. A consumer, let us assume, spends all his or her INCOME on these goods in the proportion 20%, 50%, and 30%, respectively. An unweighted average would give an average mean price increase of:

$$\frac{35 + 10 + 45}{3} = 30\%$$

A weighted average, on the other hand, would give:

$$\frac{\frac{20}{100} \times 135 + \frac{50}{100} \times 110 + \frac{30}{100} \times 145}{\frac{20 + 50 + 30}{100}} \%$$

i.e., $(20\% \times 35\%) + (50\% \times 10\%) + (30\% \times 45\%)$.

$$= 7 + 5 + 13.5 = \underline{\underline{25.5\%}}.$$

The weighted figure is a more representative average mean-price increase, because not only have the price increases been taken into account but the proportion, or weight, of the price increase has been included. Where the denominator is a real number, not a percentage, the sum of weights is added and becomes the denominator. For example, if the weights attached to three goods are 8, 5, and 2, then the denominator is $8 + 5 + 2$, or 15.

See also INDEX NUMBER, PRICE INDEX.

welfare criteria see WELFARE ECONOMICS.

welfare economics a normative branch of economics concerned with the way economic activity ought to be arranged so as to maximize economic output and social justice. Welfare economics employs value judgments about what *ought* to be produced, how production *should* be organized, and the way income and wealth *ought* to be distributed now and in the future. Unfortunately, every person in a community may have a unique set of value judgments that depend on his attitudes, religion, philosophy, and politics, and the economist has difficulty in aggregating these value judgments in advising policy-makers about decisions affecting the allocation of resources, which involves making *interpersonal comparisons* of UTILITY.

Economists have tried for many years to develop criteria for judging economic efficiency to use as a guide in evaluating actual resource deployments. The classical economists treated utility (see CLASSICAL ECONOMICS) as if it were a measurable scale of consumer satisfaction, and the early welfare economists, such as PIGOU, continued in their vein. Thus, they were able to talk in terms of changes in the pattern of economic activity either increasing or decreasing economic well-being. Once economists rejected the idea that utility was measurable, however, they felt impelled to accept the idea that economic welfare is immeasurable, and any statement about welfare is a value judgment influenced by preferences and priorities of those making the judgment. This led to a search for *welfare criteria* that avoided making interpersonal comparisons of utility by introducing explicit value judgments as to whether or not welfare has increased.

The simplest criterion was developed by Vilfredo PARETO, who argued that any reallocation of resources involving a change in goods produced and/or their distribution among consumers could be considered an improvement if it made some people believe they were better off without making anyone else feel worse off. The Pareto criterion avoids making interpersonal comparisons by dealing only with cases in which no one is harmed. Unfortunately, this makes the criterion inapplicable to most policy proposals, which benefit some and harm others without compensation.

Nicholas Kaldor and John Hicks suggested an alternative criterion, the *compensation principle*, proposing that any economic change or reorganization should be considered beneficial if, after the change, gainers could hypothetically compensate the losers and still be better off than they were before the change. In effect, this criterion divides the effects of any change in two: (a) efficiency gains/losses, and (b) income-distribution consequences. As long as gainers evaluate their gains at a higher figure than the value that losers set on their losses, the efficiency gain justifies the change, even though in the absence of actual compensation payments income redistribution has occurred. When gainers from a change fully compensate losers and still show a net gain, this would rate as an improvement under the Pareto criterion.

In addition to developing welfare criteria, economists such as Paul Samuelson have attempted to construct a *social-welfare function* that can offer guidance as to whether one economic configuration is better or worse than another. The social-welfare function can be regarded as a function of the welfare of each consumer. In order to construct a social-welfare function, however, it is necessary to aggregate preferences of all consumers into a community-preference ordering and some economists, such as Kenneth Arrow, have questioned whether consistent and noncontradictory community orderings are possible. For example, consider a community of three people, 1, 2, and 3, choosing among three alternative policies, A, B, and C. Individual 1 prefers A to B and B to C, hence A to C. Individual 2 prefers B to C and C to A, hence B to A. Individual 3 prefers C to A and A to B, hence C to B.

If we now try to aggregate these individually consistent preferences on the basis of majority rule, we find that 2 out of 3 prefer A to B, and 2 out of 3 prefer B to C. Logically, there should be a social preference for A over C, yet 2 out of 3 prefer C to A.

See also NORMATIVE ECONOMICS, RESOURCE ALLOCATION, UTILITY FUNCTION, CARDINAL UTILITY, ORDINAL UTILITY.

welfare state a country that provides comprehensive social benefits, such as government-sponsored health services, retirement pensions, unemployment and sickness payments, etc. See also TRANSFER PAYMENTS, GOVERNMENT EXPENDITURE.

white knight see TAKEOVER BID.

wholesaling the bulk purchasing of products from manufacturers in order to hold large quantities of stock for physical distribution, and the reselling of these products in smaller consignments to retailers. These functions can be performed either by an independent wholesaler acting as an intermediary between manufacturers and retailers, or the functions may be undertaken directly by the larger retailers themselves. See also INTERNALIZATION, RETAILING.

Williamson trade-off model a model devised by Oliver Williamson (born 1932) for evaluating possible benefits (lower costs) and detriments (higher prices) of a proposed MERGER. The model can be used in the application of a discretionary monopoly policy.

Figure 182 depicts a proposed merger that would introduce market power into a previously competitive market situation. In the premerger market, firms are assumed to produce on identical and constant average-cost curves, which are represented in aggregate by AC_1. The competitive price OP_1 is identical with AC_1, a NORMAL PROFIT equilibrium. The competitive output rate is OQ_1.

By contrast, the postmerger firm is shown to produce on a lower constant average-cost curve, depicted by AC_2, and to establish a price not merely in excess of AC_2 but in excess of AC_1. That is, the price is higher than in the competitive case *despite* the availability of ECONOMIES OF SCALE. In such circumstances, a welfare trade-off is required between loss of CONSUMERS' SURPLUS due to the higher price (shaded area A_1) and the cost savings gain to the producer (shaded area A_2). In simple terms, if A_1 exceeds A_2, the merger should be disallowed. If A_2 exceeds A_1, the merger should be allowed to proceed.

However, even in the latter case there are problems. Any benefits arising from a merger through cost savings accrue initially to

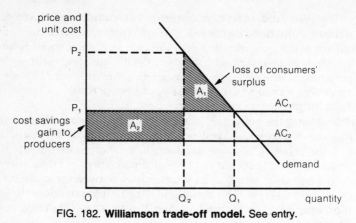

FIG. 182. **Williamson trade-off model.** See entry.

producers. To benefit consumers, these gains must be passed on. Because of the increase in monopoly power, however, there is no guarantee they will be.

withdrawals or **leakages** the part of NATIONAL INCOME not spent by households on CONSUMPTION of domestically produced goods and services. In the basic CIRCULAR FLOW OF NATIONAL INCOME MODEL, all income received by households is spent on current consumption. In the extended circular flow of income model, some of the income received by households, businesses, and government is saved, some of it is taxed, and some of it is spent on imported goods and services. Thus, SAVINGS, TAXATION, and IMPORTS constitute withdrawals, or leakages, from the income-spending flow. Compare INJECTIONS. See also PROPENSITY TO SAVE, PROPENSITY TO TAX, PROPENSITY TO IMPORT.

withholding tax a mechanism for deducting installments of projected income tax from the paychecks of employees. It was first introduced in the United States to require quarterly payment of income taxes instead of once a year. The concept of withholding taxes has recently been extended to pension payments and other types of individual income.

workable competition the specification of standards of MARKET

STRUCTURE and MARKET CONDUCT that are likely to result in acceptable MARKET PERFORMANCE. Figure 183 lists one such classification.

Standards of Structure
1. A large or an appreciable number of suppliers, none of whom dominates the market, or at least as many as scale economies permit.
2. No artificial barriers to entry.
3. Moderate and price-sensitive quality differentials.

Standards of Conduct
1. Active competition between rival suppliers, avoiding collusive agreements to fix prices, market shares, etc.
2. No use of exclusionary or coercive tactics (exclusive dealings, refusal to supply, tie-in contracts) aimed at harming rival suppliers.
3. Sensitivity towards consumers' demands for product variety.

Standards of Performance
1. Minimization of supply costs.
2. Prices consistent with supply costs, including a fair profit return to suppliers in relation to efficiency, risks, investment and innovation.
3. Avoidance of excessive promotional expenses.
4. The introduction of new technology and new products.

FIG. 183. **Workable competition.** The standards of structure, conduct, and performance.

Definitions of workable competition represent an effort to provide more useful guidelines in applying monopoly policy to real world markets than can be drawn from the theoretical ideal state of PERFECT COMPETITION. There are, however, important operational difficulties involved in stipulating acceptable norms. For example, what is meant by an appreciable number of firms? How is it to be established? What levels of profits are fair?

See also MARKET STRUCTURE/CONDUCT-PERFORMANCE SCHEMA, CONTESTABLE MARKET, THEORY OF MARKETS, MONOPOLY.

worker participation the involvement of employees in the decisions made by a FIRM that extends beyond decisions implicit in the specific content of the jobs of employees. Worker participation most commonly refers to processes or activities that occur at the workplace. For example, consider suggestion boxes for workers, job-enrichment programs such as job rotation, and work planning by committees of workers and foremen.

The term INDUSTRIAL DEMOCRACY, often associated with the concept of worker participation, denotes power-sharing by management with workers in corporate decisions decided at higher levels in the organization, even at the board of directors level. In this sense, industrial democracy suggests a system of representation and in keeping with the principle of labor union representation, joint consultation between managers and worker representations, and worker representatives sitting on the board of directors.

Often the more complex systems of worker participation and industrial democracy cannot operate without management willingness to disclose information on profitability, investment, new technology, working conditions, and job prospects to the employee representatives for bargaining purposes.

There is considerable controversy about the effects on economic efficiency of the extension of worker participation.

At the operational level, worker participation can improve output by instilling a greater commitment to, and sense of achievement in, group activities and some hands-on knowledge. At the strategic level, major decisions relating to new investment, introduction of new machinery, and the like may be impaired, it could be argued, by involvement of too many vested interests when what is required is a more detached, longer-term view of the issues involved.

working capital an accounting term denoting a firm's short-term CURRENT ASSETS, which are turned over fairly quickly in the course of business. They include raw materials, work in progress and finished goods inventories, accounts receivable, and cash less CURRENT LIABILITIES. Increases in the volume of company trading generally lead to increases in stocks and amounts owed by debtors, and so to an increase in working capital required. Reductions in delays between paying for materials, converting them to products, selling them, and getting cash in from customers will tend to reduce the working capital needed. See also WORKING CAPITAL RATIO, CASH FLOW, CREDIT CONTROL, FACTORING.

working capital ratio an accounting measure of a firm's ability to pay its short-term liabilities out of CURRENT ASSETS, which expresses the firm's current assets as a ratio of CURRENT LIABILITIES. See also CURRENT RATIO, WORKING CAPITAL, CASH FLOW.

work in progress any goods still in process of being made into final form. Work in progress together with raw materials and STOCKS of finished goods constitute INVENTORY INVESTMENT.

work study or **time-motion study** a discipline concerned with determining how LABOR can be employed most efficiently in relation to other FACTOR INPUTS. Time-motion experts examine the time and effort an employee or a group of employees takes to fulfill a given task, and then analyze the possibility of rearranging the inputs to achieve a reduction in time or effort while maintaining or increasing output. The discipline of work study has two main branches: (a) method study, which is concerned with analyzing the methods employed in doing jobs with a view to improving these methods; (b) time study, which seeks to measure the time required to perform jobs. See also PRODUCTIVITY.

World Bank or **International Bank for Reconstruction and Development** a multinational institution set up in 1947 to be part of the United Nations, after the Bretton Woods Conference of 1944, in order to provide ECONOMIC AID to member countries, mainly DEVELOPING COUNTRIES, in order to strengthen their economies. The Bank has supported a wide range of long-term investments, including infrastructure projects such as building roads, providing telecommunications and electricity supply, assisting agriculture, developing industrial projects including establishment of new industries, and social, training, and educational programs.

The Bank's funds come largely from the developed countries, but it also raises money on international capital markets. The Bank operates according to business principles, lending at commercial rates of interest only to governments considered capable of servicing and repaying their debts. In 1960, however, it established an affiliate agency, the *International Development Association,* to provide low-interest loans to poorer countries.

Another affiliate of the World Bank is the *International Finance Corporation*, which can invest directly in companies by acquiring their stock.

XYZ

X-inefficiency the gap between actual and minimum attainable supply costs. See Fig. 184. The traditional THEORY OF SUPPLY assumes that firms always operate on the outer boundary of their attainable cost curves. In contrast, X-inefficiency postulates that firms typically operate within the outer boundary. This occurs, for example, because of such inefficiencies in work organization as overstaffing and inefficient deployment and management of resources arising from bureaucratic rigidities. X-inefficiency is likely to be present in large organizations, especially monopolies, that lack effective competition to keep them on their toes. See MONOPOLY, PRODUCTIVITY, ORGANIZATIONAL SLACK.

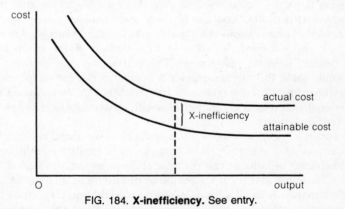

FIG. 184. **X-inefficiency.** See entry.

yield see EFFECTIVE RATE OF INTEREST.
yield curve a line that traces the relationship between the rates of return on BONDS of different maturities. The slope of the line suggests whether RATES OF INTEREST are tending to rise or fall.
zero-based budgeting a management accounting technique

that seeks continually to reexamine and challenge the assumptions underlying a firm's costs. Zero-based budgeting involves preparing a budget from scratch each year for every company department, starting with the premise that each department's budget is zero, then justifying every activity and its associated expenditure before it can be included in the budget. This contrasts with conventional budgeting, in which departmental budgets are often based on the previous year's budget suitably updated. The purpose of zero-based budgeting is to identify and remove inefficient or obsolete activities within the firm. See also X-INEFFICIENCY.

zero-sum game a situation in GAME THEORY in which players compete for the given total payoff, so that gains by one player are at the direct expense of the other player(s). (I win, you lose; you win, I lose.) For example, when two firms compete against each other in a market in which total sales are not expanding, then each firm can only increase its sales and market share at the expense of its competitor.

Z-scale a statistical term for the transformed scale of values applied to observations of a variable with a NORMAL DISTRIBUTION, with the values converted to give them a zero MEAN and unit STANDARD DEVIATION. Use of the Z-scale enables conversion of any set of observations of a variable into standard units with mean = 0 and standard deviation = 1, regardless of the mean and standard deviation of that set. This conversion enables use of a single table for the area under a normal curve for purposes of estimating PROBABILITIES and HYPOTHESIS TESTING, and direct comparison of sets of observations with different means and standard deviations.

Z-score a composite score summarizing the weighted results of a number of accounting ratios that claims to predict a company's likelihood of failure. The concept of Z-scores was developed by applying the statistical technique of discriminant analysis to differentiate values of various performance-and-liquidity ratios for companies that had gone bankrupt and for those that had prospered. The accounting ratios that appeared to discriminate effectively between failed and successful companies were incorporated in a standard formula to calculate an aggregate Z-score.

Analysts can calculate Z-scores for particular companies and use the results to predict whether companies are likely to fail.